English Language Teaching in its Social Context

English Language Teaching in its Social Context offers sociolinguistic, ethnographic, and social-psychological perspectives on TESOL teaching and learning and introduces the relevant literature on second language acquisition. It presents English language teaching in a variety of specific institutional, geographic and cultural contexts.

The articles – which include both classic and specially commissioned pieces – have been carefully chosen and edited to present the main principles of English language teaching. They focus on the roles played by teachers and learners, recognise the individuality of language learners, support teachers in the provision of active guidance for students' learning, and examine both positive and negative patterns of interaction between learners and teachers.

This Reader offers people unfamiliar with research in this field an overall understanding of key issues in contemporary English language teaching while allowing the more experienced reader the opportunity to relate his or her experiences to the theories presented.

Articles by: Michael P. Breen; Anne Burns; A. Suresh Canagarajah; J. Keith Chick; Rod Ellis; Pauline Gibbons; Paul Knight; Patsy M. Lightbown; Angel M.Y. Lin; Michael H. Long; Neil Mercer; Rosamond Mitchell; Florence Myles; David Nunan; Jack C. Richards; Celia Roberts; Peter Skehan; Assia Slimani; Nina Spada; Joan Swann; Leo van Lier

Christopher N. Candlin is Chair Professor of Applied Linguistics and Director of the Centre for English Language Education and Communication Research at the City University of Hong Kong. **Neil Mercer** is Professor of Language and Communications and Director of the Centre for Language and Communications at the Open University, UK.

Companion volumes

The companion volumes in this series are:

Analysing English in a Global Context edited by Anne Burns and Caroline Coffin

Innovation in English Language Teaching edited by David R. Hall and Ann Hewings

These three readers are part of a scheme of study jointly developed by Macquarie University, Sydney, Australia, and the Open University, United Kingdom. At the Open University, the three readers are part of a single course, *Teaching English to Speakers of Other Languages Worldwide* which forms part of the Open University MA in Education (Applied Linguistics) and Advanced Diploma in Teaching English to Speakers of Other Languages. At Macquarie University, the three readers are each attached to single study units, which form part of the Postgraduate Diploma and Master of Applied Linguistics programmes.

The Open University MA in Education is now established as the most popular postgraduate degree for UK education professionals, with over 3,500 students registering each year. From 2001 it will also be available worldwide. The MA in Education is designed particularly for those with experience in teaching, educational administration or allied fields. The MA is a modular degree and students are free to select, from a range of options, the programme that best fits in with their interests and professional goals. The MA in Education programme provides great flexibility. Students study at their own pace and in their own time. They receive specially prepared study materials, and are supported by a personal tutor. (Successful completion of the MA in Education (Applied Linguistics) entitles students to apply for entry to the Open University Doctorate in Education (EdD) programme.)

The Professional Development in Education prospectus contains further information and application forms. To find out more about the Open University and request your copy please write to the Course Reservations and Sales Centre, The Open University, PO Box 724, Walton Hall, Milton Keynes MK7 6ZW, or e-mail ces-gen@open.ac.uk, or telephone +44 (0)1908 653231 or visit the website, *www.open.ac.uk*. For more information on the MA in Education (Applied Linguistics) visit *www.open.ac.uk/applied-linguistics*.

Macquarie University introduced distance versions of its influential on-campus degrees in 1994 and now has students in over thirty countries. Both the Postgraduate Diploma and the Masters are offered in three versions: Applied Linguistics, Applied Linguistics (TESOL) and Applied Linguistics (Literacy). Credits are freely transferable between the Diploma and the Masters and between the three versions, and students may change between distance and on-campus modes or mix modes if desired. Students study at their own pace, with specially developed materials and with support and feedback provided directly from lecturers in the Linguistics Department through e-mail, web, fax, phone and post. A specialised library service provided through the Resources Centre of the National Centre for English Language Teaching and Research (NCELTR). External doctoral programmes are also available.

Information about the Macquarie programmes and application forms are available on *www.ling.mq.edu.au* or by writing to the Linguistics Postgraduate Office, Macquarie University, NSW 2109, Australia (tel: +61 2 9850 9243; fax: +61 2 9850 9352; e-mail: lingdl@ling.mq.edu.au).

English Language Teaching in its Social Context

'Candlin's and Mercer's Reader provides key insights into contemporary knowledge of second language learning, the exploitation of this knowledge in classroom action, and subsequent assessment and analysis. By emphasizing the social context of these three processes, and the relationship between them, the book provides a rewarding introduction to the interaction between theory, research and professional practice which lies at the heart of applied linguistics.' *Guy Cook, University of Reading, UK*

'This volume links the teaching of English to the development of autonomous individuals who prize debate, negotiation and interaction, and who will ultimately be able to build global communications of like-minded English speakers around the world. Readers will find in this collection of excellent papers some of the classic milestones in the field of ELT.' *Claire Kramsch, University of California, Berkeley, California*

Teaching English Language Worldwide

A selection of readers' comments on the series:

'This three-part series offers a map to ELT research and practice . . . it represents the best that ELT, as an Anglo-Saxon institution, has developed over the last thirty years for the teaching of English around the world . . . Readers will find in this series the Who's Who guide to this dynamic and expanding community.' *Claire Kramsch, University of California, Berkeley, California*

'Experienced English language instructors seeking to deepen their knowledge and abilities will find this series forms a coherent basis to develop their understanding of current trends, sociocultural diversity, and topical interests in teaching English as a second or foreign language around the world. All three volumes provide ample flexibility for discussion, interpretation, and adaptation in local settings.' *Alister Cumming, Ontario Institute for Studies in Education, University of Toronto*

'This series provides a collection of essential readings which will not only provide the TEFL/TESOL student and teacher with access to the most up-to-date thinking and approaches to the subject but will give any person interested in the subject an overview of the phenomenon of the use and usage of English in the modern world. Perhaps more importantly, this series will be crucial to those students who do not have available to them articles that provide both a wide spectrum of information and the necessary analytical tools to investigate the language further.' *Joseph A. Foley, Southeast Asia Ministers of Education Organisation, Regional Language Centre, Singapore*

'The strong representation of the seminal Anglo-Australian development of the European functional tradition in the study of language and language education makes this a refreshingly bracing series, which should be widely used in teacher education for English language teaching.' *Euan Reid, Institute of Education, University of London*

'In a principled and accessible manner, these three volumes bring together major writings on essential topics in the study of English language teaching. They provide broad coverage of current thinking and debate on major issues, providing an invaluable resource for the contemporary postgraduate student.' *Guy Cook, University of Reading*

English Language Teaching in its Social Context

A Reader

Edited by

Christopher N. Candlin and Neil Mercer

London and New York
in association with Macquarie University
and The Open University

First published 2001
by Routledge
11 New Fetter Lane, London EC4P 4EE

Simultaneously published in the USA and Canada
by Routledge
29 West 35th Street, New York, NY 10001

Routledge is an imprint of the Taylor & Francis Group

Typeset in Perpetua and Bell Gothic by Keystroke, Jacaranda Lodge, Wolverhampton
Printed and bound in Great Britain by TJ International Ltd, Padstow, Cornwall

British Library Cataloguing in Publication Data
A catalogue record for this book is available from the British Library

Library of Congress Cataloging in Publication Data
English language teaching in its social context / edited by Christopher N. Candlin
and Neil Mercer.
     p.   cm. – (Teaching English language worldwide)
   Includes bibliographical references and index.
   1. English language–Study and teaching–Foreign speakers. 2. English
language–Study and teaching–Social aspects. I. Candlin, Christopher.
II. Mercer, Neil. III. Series
   PE1128.A2 E49 2000
   428'.0071–dc21   00-059195

ISBN 0–415–24121–9 (hbk)
ISBN 0–415–24122–7 (pbk)

Contents

PART TWO
Strategies and goals in the classroom context

PART THREE
Analysing teaching and learning

Illustrations

Figures

Tables

Acknowledgements

The editors and publishers would like to thank the following for permission to use copyright material:

Michael P. Breen and Cambridge University Press for 'The social context of language learning: a neglected situation' in *Studies in Second Language Acquisition*, 7, 1985.

Michael P. Breen and SEAMEO Regional Language Centre for 'Navigating the discourse: on what is learned in the language classroom' in Proceedings of the 1997 RELC Seminar.

Anne Burns for 'Genre-based approaches to writing and beginning adult ESL learners', reprinted from *Prospect* Vol. 5, No. 3, May 1990 with permission from the National Centre for English Language Teaching and Research (NCELTR), Australia. (Macquarie University). Includes material in Fig. 2 adapted from *Learning Styles in Adult Migrant Education* by Willing K., also with permission from the National Centre for English Language Teaching and Research (NCELTR), Australia (Macquarie University).

Cambridge University Press for Assia Slimani 'Evaluation of classroom interaction' in J.C. Alderson and A. Beretta (eds) *Evaluating Second Language Education*, 1992.

A. Suresh Cangaraja and TESOL for 'Critical ethnography of a Sri Lankan classroom: ambiguities in student opposition to reproduction through ESOL' in *TESOL Quarterly*, Vol. 27, No. 4, (TESOL 1993).

J. Keith Chick and Cambridge University Press for 'Safe-talk: collusion in apartheid education' in H. Coleman (ed.) *Society and the Language Classroom*, 1996.

Rod Ellis for 'Second language acquisition research and language pedagogy' in *SLA Research and Language Teaching* by Rod Ellis (Rod Ellis 1997). Reproduced by permission of Oxford University Press.

Patsy M. Lightbown and Nina Spada for 'Factors affecting second language learning' in *How Languages are Learned* (Second Edition) by Patsy M. Lightbown and Nina Spada (Patsy M. Lightbown and Nina Spada 1999.) Reproduced by permission of Oxford University Press.

Angel M.Y. Lin and TESOL for 'Doing-English-lessons in the reproduction or transformation of social worlds?' in *TESOL Quarterly*, Vol. 33, No. 3, (TESOL 1999).

Michael Long and John Benjamin's Publishing Co. for 'Focus on form: a design feature in language teaching methodology' in *Foreign Language Research in a Cross-cultural Perspective*. Edited by K. de Bot, R.B. Ginsberg and C. Krausch. John Benjamin's Publishing Co., 1991.

Rosamond Mitchell and Florence Myles for 'Second language learning: key concepts and issues' in *Second Language Learning Theories*, 1999.

David Nunan and *ELT Journal* for 'Teaching grammar in context' in *ELT Journal*, Vol. 52, No. 2, 1998. Reproduced by permission of *ELT Journal* and Oxford University Press.

Jack Richards and Cambridge University Press for 'Beyond methods' in *The Language Teaching Matrix*, 1990.

Celia Roberts for 'Language through acquisition or language socialisation in and through discourse' in *Working Papers in Applied Linguistics*, Vol. 4, Thames Valley University, 1998.

Peter Skehan for 'Comprehension and production strategies in language learning' in *A Cognitive Approach to Language Learning* by Peter Skehan (Oxford University Press 1998.) Reproduced by permission of Oxford University Press.

Leo van Lier for 'Constraints and resources in classroom talk: issues of equality and symmetry' in *Learning Foreign and Second Languages*. Reprinted by permission of the Modern Language Association of America.

While the publishers and editors have made every effort to contact authors and copyright holders of works reprinted in *English Language Teaching in its Social Context*, this has not been possible in every case. They would welcome correspondence from individuals or companies they have been unable to trace.

We would like to thank the authors who contributed their chapters, as well as colleagues within and outside The Open University and Macquarie University who gave advice on the contents. Special thanks are due to the following people for their assistance in the production of this book.

Helen Boyce (course manager)
Pam Burns and Libby Brill (course secretaries)
Liz Freeman (Copublishing)
Nanette Reynolds, Frances Wilson and the staff of the Resource Centre of the National Centre for English Language Teaching and Research, Macquarie University.

Critical readers

Professor Vijay K. Bhatia (Department of English, City University, Hong Kong)
Geoff Thompson (Applied English Language Studies Unit, Liverpool University, UK)
Professor Leo van Lier (Educational Linguistics, University of Monterey, USA).

External assessor

Professor Ronald Carter (Department of English Studies, Nottingham University, UK).

Developmental testers

Ilona Cziraky (Italy)
Eladyr Maria Norberto da Silva (Brazil)
Chitrita Mukerjee (Australia)
Dorien Gonzales (UK)
Patricia Williams (Denmark).

We have reproduced all original papers and chapters as faithfully as we have been able, given the inevitable restrictions of space and the need to produce a coherent and readable collection for readers worldwide. Where we have had to shorten original material substantially, these chapters are marked as adapted. Ellipses within square brackets mark text that has been omitted from the original. Individual referencing styles have been retained as in the original texts.

Christopher N. Candlin
and Neil Mercer

INTRODUCTION

When Macquarie University, in Sydney, Australia, and The Open University, in Milton Keynes, England, decided to collaborate on the development of new curriculum materials for study at Master's level, the partnership brought together The Open University's experience in open learning in the field of education, and Macquarie's experience in applied linguistics and language education, backed by its own existing distance learning programme. The collection of articles in this book and its two companion volumes are one result of that collaboration. While the edited collections have been designed as one part of an overall study programme, complemented by other learning and study materials comprising study guides and accompanying video and audio recordings, they stand alone as extensive yet focused collections of articles which address key contemporary issues in English language teaching and applied linguistics.

A major concern in editing these three volumes has been the desire to present English language teaching (ELT) in a variety of specific institutional, geographic and cultural contexts. Hence, as far as possible across the three volumes, we have attempted to highlight debate, discussion and illustration of current issues from different parts of the English-speaking and English-using world, including those where English is not learned as a first language. In doing this we recognize that English language teaching comprises a global community of teachers and learners in a range of social contexts.

It is *English Language Teaching in its Social Context* which is the title of this second volume in the series, and it will be useful to decide early on what we mean by this term. We have a number of interpretations and perspectives in mind. One that is central is that of the *classroom context* in which interactions between teachers and learners have an effect on the nature and quality of language learning. No language teaching and learning takes place however, in a classroom which is isolated from the world of experiences and personal engagements and investments of learners outside the classroom itself. In that sense the wider *social context* of life outside the classroom has an important effect on what takes place in these interactions between learners and teachers, and among learners. For many learners, the contexts outside the classroom are not only where they make use of the English they have learned in class, but they can also constitute a powerful incentive (or disincentive) for further learning. Moreover, it is not only the contexts of learning and using English that are important. We need also to understand the *professional context* of teachers' practices themselves within this interactive process of classroom teaching-and-learning. Finally, we need to take account of the *socio-cultural context* by which communicating partners in this process evoke and create shared knowledge and use it for making sense together, in a sense constructing the overarching context for successful language learning.

No collection of papers about English Language Teaching can hope to be comprehensive. The world of ELT in its diversity, of learners, teachers, of schools and institutions, cultures, countries, contents, and pedagogies cannot be captured even in a series of three books. What a structured collection of selected papers like this can do is to map out the territory, and fill in enough of the topographical features so that the beginning reader can obtain an overall impression of its cartography, while the experienced reader can bring her or his own rich experience of travelling and map-making to fill in the details of those territories of which they have special awareness and knowledge. We need to be cautious, however. No map is neutral. The first maps were products of the cartographers of Europe, so their world was a Euro-centric one, and, in their own Sino-centric way, those devised by the Chinese were just as biased. Readers have been alerted, therefore, to a natural tendency towards a particular projection. Our ELT map in this book offers a social and socio-cultural perspective on language learning. At the same time, maps have to be true to their territories, and it would be absurd to ignore a psychological perspective on language learning, one which highlighted the cognitive processes of the individual learner, engaging with the intricacies of a new communicative code. Maps are not only to be followed, however. They have always served as incentives for further and more refined map-making. In the same way, teachers do not just follow a set of presented instructions, they actively create and chart their own progress through the territories of learning in their own classrooms. Accordingly, it is important that such a focused collection as this gives a major place to classroom-based research, in particular, research which examines the processes of teaching-and-learning, using that evidence which is most to hand in classrooms, namely the productive talk of teachers and learners.

What a collection of papers needs to have, is an argument, one which carries the reader towards engagement with particular issues and questions, offering through its structure just that amount of guidance necessary. Ultimately, though, whether we have gauged the right degree of that guidance required, or simply led readers by the nose, only you can say. What we have done as a guiding structure is to take three main perspectives on English language teaching: an explanation of some hypotheses about language learning and its processes; an interpretation of learners' and teachers' strategies and goals in the classroom context, their purposes and their beliefs; and, finally, a description and analysis of teachers' and learners' behaviours and practices, who they are, what they do, what they think about language learning and what their attitudes are.

How is language learning explained?

The argument begins with a focus on the *explanation of language learning* with a paper by Rosamund Mitchell and Florence Myles. The authors outline a model of second language learning and identify its key factors. Three key questions underpin all these factors: What is the nature of language? What is the nature of the language learning process? What are the characteristics of the second language learner? In addressing these questions the paper identifies the complementarity of *nature* and *nurture* in language learning, and relates what research has to say about language learning with what we know about learning more generally. At the same time, the paper highlights one of the abiding questions about teaching and learning, the tension between *systematicity* and *creativity* in learners' performance. Language learning is clearly not just about processes. It involves learners. So, asking questions about who these learners are and what learner characteristics and factors affect language learning, and in which ways, is a central question for teachers of language. Patsy Lightbown and Nina Spada take up this necessary dualism in their account of the cognitive and behavioural characteristics of what some researchers have referred to as the 'good language learner'. As we will see later in the argument of this book, there has to be a third aspect to any such account, namely the influence of the social conditions of language learning on the effectiveness of language learning. Many learners don't learn languages in classrooms. They learn them more or less well or badly, on the street, in the community, and in the workplace. Certainly, Lightbown's and Spada's territory abuts that of Mitchell and Myles. Factors such as motivation, aptitude, personality, intelligence, learner preferences and learner beliefs, will be high on any teacher's list, but so will factors of age, social background, gender and educational attainment.

Researching second language learning, and exploring the relationship between researching and teaching is a key element in what some have referred to as the teacher as 'reflective' practitioner. Rod Ellis' paper on research and pedagogy in the context of second language acquisition squarely addresses this relationship. Questions of decision-driven research emanating from practical classroom problems, or knowledge-driven research starting from theoretical hypotheses, are but two sides of the same coin. At the heart are the practices of the classroom, or encounters with the target language in other contexts. That these worlds of teaching and research have often been at odds is an issue for this paper, and for this book as a whole to explore. What Ellis identifies, however, is the importance of mapping the cultures of teaching and researching and achieving at least mutual understanding, if not active collaboration. What is clear after reading Ellis is that it isn't going to be enough for teachers to write 'Here be dragons' and steer the teaching ship away from the rocky coastline of research. One useful and productive ground for such collaboration is that of researching *learners' styles* and *strategies* in language learning, looking at what learners do as aspects of their personality, or in response to problems and tasks that teaching, or just life itself, confronts them. Peter Skehan's paper has this dual focus and he locates his discussion in the key area of learners' comprehension of foreign language texts, written or spoken, examining the relationship between input to the learner, what the learner confronts, and what the learner produces herself, the output of learning. Important for Skehan, and for our general argument in this book, are the ways in which learners *negotiate meaning*, guided by teachers, in their road towards understanding the foreign language.

If negotiation of meaning smacks of the marketplace, then perhaps that is no bad image for the exchange of language goods which characterizes both classrooms and social interactions more generally. Estimating the values to be placed on these goods is, after all, what a good deal of teaching (and learning) is all about. Leo van Lier's, Celia Roberts' and Michael Breen's papers are all sited in the marketplace of learning and teaching. It is time, then, to begin to look at the *contexts of learning*. Now a new set of questions arise. How learners interact with each other and other speakers, what do they do when they are learning a language, what effect their attitudes, beliefs and feelings have on language learning, what kinds of personal investment they are prepared to make, how far they can draw on the support of others, what effects teaching has on learning, and to what extent the social conditions and priorities of the social world outside the classroom, and the learners' places in that world, affect what learners do in classrooms and how effectively they can learn.

Addressing these questions suggests a need for some redrawing of the dimensions of the second language learning map. In fact, as we will see in the papers which follow in the collection, such questions make us redraw our projection in a number of important ways: to take account of the learning of strategic competence not merely of language competence; of the appraisal of learning sites, contexts and modes as key variables in language acquisition;

of the variably positive and negative effects of learners' social and personal commitment to language learning; of the need to take into account the multiple identities of learners, affected as they are by issues of gender, class, race and power; and, especially, of the need to engage in micro-exploration of the interactions of learners with learners and learners with teachers, or other target language speakers.

In his paper, Leo van Lier draws on exactly this shift of perspective towards the social contextualisation and construction of second language learning. He also takes up in practice many of the issues raised earlier in the Ellis paper, particularly his account of interpretative research. What he adds, however, in his account of the possible types of interaction and types of discourse to be found in the second language classroom, is the importance of the effect of power and control on what kinds of talk are encouraged, discouraged or even forbidden. Such issues are also central to Celia Roberts' paper with its critical evaluation of more traditional and cognitive approaches which see second language learning as essentially a matter of personal endeavour and accomplishment. Her focus on learner identities and the effects of learning contexts on language learning within an overall sociolinguistic and social constructionist model, links learning to living in an original way, and, in so doing, addresses some of the questions we identified earlier as important to the argument of this collection of papers. It is important to note, though, that this shift of emphasis is not one which abandons the necessary inclusion of the personal and cognitive development of the learner's language learning capacity. The point is to forge a connection between both paradigms. This is in large measure achieved in Michael Breen's paper on the social context of language learning. In his anthropological metaphor of the classroom as *coral garden*, teacher-researchers are directed at the importance of the multiple discourses of the classroom, where what is said and how it is expressed among the participants of this cultural world takes on a key significance for the explanation of the processes of language learning, and in particular for our understanding of the essential differences among language learners. His defining characteristics of the classroom as a special socio-cultural world, together with his emphasis on the analysis of the discourses of teaching and learning, offer the teacher-researcher a means by which he or she can stand outside the reality, much like a cartographer, and chart more dispassionately this now newly-imagined and newly-perspectivized setting.

Strategies and goals in the classroom context

As active participants in teaching and learning, teachers and learners do not simply possess and display inherent or socially acquired characteristics in some vacuum; like the inhabitants of Malinowki's *coral garden* (adopted and adapted by Breen), they draw on them to pursue their own strategic goals. Thus, in order to advance the argument of this active participation, all the papers in this second major section of the book target the realization of these strategic goals in classroom action, and the unique role played by teachers in the facilitation and structuring of that action. The way in which teachers carry out this charac-teristic work has traditionally been captured by the metaphors of *method* and *methodology*. We refer to them as *metaphors*, in that they stand for particular, ideologically invested systems of belief, about language, about learning, and about teaching. Like all metaphors they are to be approached warily and treated with caution. Lakoff and Johnson's critical account of the 'metaphors we live by' gives a sense of their powerful influence. We make no apology for being critical in this book of such language learning and language teaching metaphors. In our experience, and that of the authors of some of the papers in this section, methodologies are frequently theorized without a close grounding in teaching experience, and may be insensitive to particular local and cultural conditions. Methods, on the other hand, may shift wildly from one theoretical position about language and learning to another. Whether they are form-focused, function-focused, or learning-focused, methodologies and methods often serve to conceal the rich variety of classroom language learning and teaching work by offering simple labels for what are always complex and contingent processes.

It is important, therefore, to stand back and take a conceptual and historical perspective if we want to understand how such methods and methodologies came to be popular and so widely adopted. Such a perspective is provided by Paul Knight's paper, surveying developments in ELT methodology and illustrating some of their characteristic features. From this paper we come to see that despite their individualizing labels, many methods and methodologies share features in common, that they are rarely except in some extreme cases pursued in some 'pure' form, and that, in the end, they remain profoundly unexplanatory of some of the key factors affecting language learning, both cognitive and social, that we have identified earlier. It is from this starting point that Jack Richards' paper begins. Questioning the dominance of methods and methodologies, Richards' perspective is that we should be less concerned with stipulating what methods to follow and much more concerned with discovering what effective teachers actually do. Resisting the *deprofessionalizing* effect of some slavish adherence to methods frees us and teachers more generally to examine what the practices of reflective and effective language teaching might be. What these practices are is a matter of teachers' strategic choices in relation to some particular content, and taken together with teachers' beliefs and theories about teaching and learning, these constitute a rationale for teaching.

The three papers that follow, by Michael Long, David Nunan, and Anne Burns illustrate these practices in different contexts and with different subject-matter, and involve distinctive genres and modes of communication. Implicitly (or explicitly in the case of Michael Long) they all resist the concept of method, and focus instead on how teachers' varied and contingent *procedures* are the means by which the *processes* and *products* of language learning are made to interact. Long's paper has as its central tenet the important distinction to be drawn between a focus on *form* (i.e. the development of awareness by the learner of the systematic nature of language) and a focus on *forms* (that is, the teaching of isolated and unconnected sentence structures). What is important for the reader of Long's paper is his reliance for his argument on experimentally obtained evidence about learner behaviour. To return, if only briefly, to our map-making metaphor, Long displays the indispensable value of grounding conclusions about the shape of the second language learning territory in carefully observed and recorded data from learner performance.

The issue of form and forms naturally evokes a central area of content in language teaching and learning, the approach that teachers take to the teaching of grammar, itself the topic of David Nunan's paper. With grammar as its focus, what is notable in Nunan's argument is how the way we define grammar is contingent on how we go about teaching it to learners. Many might not easily associate the formal character of grammar with an interactive and participatory, task-based approach to pedagogy, so strong has been the focus in ELT on the didactic instruction of grammatical forms. Yet this paper makes such a connection, and in so doing redefines grammar less as some asocial and technicist form than as a functional resource for making meaning, a means by which speakers and writers can get things done. *How* writers get things done is the topic of Anne Burns' paper; focusing in particular, though, on how teachers can assist learners to get things done in writing. Drawing on work in systemic functional grammar and the concept of genre, she reports on a national project conducted by the National Centre for English Language Teaching and Research (NCELTR) at Macquarie University, Sydney, involving teachers in studying how a genre-based approach to writing could be used by adult second language learners at the beginning stages of learning a second language. Of particular interest in the paper is her exposition of what she and her colleagues refer to as the 'teaching-learning cycle'.

We have emphasized the importance to our understanding of second language learning of exploring the socio-cultural contexts of learning inside and outside the classroom. This has been and is a core theme of many papers in this book. There has, however, been a tacit assumption, though perhaps not so much in the paper by Roberts earlier, that such contexts called up differentiated, but essentially *cooperative* learners. That this may not be so, and often *is* not so, is the theme of the two final papers in this second section of the book, those by Suresh Canagarajah and Keith Chick. Both papers focus on the degree to which external socio-cultural factors, and learners' self-perceptions of their identities as learners of English, affect what they do in class, and what *they are prepared to do* in class, and thus ultimately impinge on their second language learning performance. In particular, the papers identify processes of learners' *resistance*, in the case of Canagarajah, and in the case of Chick, learners' and teachers' *collusion* to frustrate the successful implementation of particular methodologies considered as imported and as culturally alien. Such issues have recently taken on considerable importance in discussions of the cultural appropriateness of some English language teaching. Both these papers have another significance, however, one which relates to Ellis' earlier accounts of researching language learning. The papers are valuable not only for their innovative re-examination of the goals and practices of language teaching, but also for their clear and detailed accounting of a critical ethnographic research methodology intended to be revelatory not only of the goings-on of classrooms but more deeply explanatory of the way in which the learning and teaching of English in particular is deeply embedded in the political, social and educational fabric of post-colonial societies. Once again they reinforce our view that the beliefs and ideologies of teachers about all aspects of their subject-matter and their practice have a profound effect on the planning and the moment-by-moment decisions they take in class. To refer to these latter as intuitive, or personal, downplays both their effect and our capacity to explore their underpinnings. That these are deeply engendered by the social contexualization of learning and teaching, and the educational, social and political contexts of classroom practice can, after reading these latter papers, hardly be in doubt.

Analysing teaching and learning

The importance of the analysis of the interactions among learners and between learners and teachers to an understanding of the processes of language learning has been a central part of the argument of this book. Exploring these relationships has been both the province of researchers as well as of teachers, and several papers in this collection have argued for a closer link between them, given the tendency for both 'cultures' to be separate. Part of this distancing has been due to the difficulty of making the results of research necessarily and directly applicable to changes in classroom practice, or to the design and delivery of innovative teaching and learning materials. Nonetheless, there are studies of classroom behaviour which can help teachers conceptualize those factors which influence life in classrooms, directed at exploring the dual nature of classroom lessons, as pedagogic and as social events. The paper by Michael Breen, cited above, emphasizes this social and interactional nature of language learning.

Influential in this context is the work of the Russian sociocultural psychologist Lev Vygotsky. Central to Vygotsky's theories about learning is the place accorded to language as not only a medium for exchanging and constructing information but also as a tool for thinking. Language is seen by Vygotsky both as a cultural and a cognitive tool, helping us to organize our thoughts but also used for reasoning, planning and reviewing. Of greatest significance for the argument and the map of this book, then, is Vygotsky's insistence that learning is interactive and social. Such a position resonates well with the earlier papers in this collection, notably those by van Lier and Breen, especially with their highlighting of the importance of studying teacher and learner discourses. Neil Mercer's paper provides an example of an in-depth study of these discourses of classroom life, as the data from which inferences may be drawn about the processes of language learning. Mercer's socio-cultural approach to the analysis of classroom behaviour sits well with earlier papers in Part II of this book, and paves the way for a detailed discursive and linguistic analysis of such classroom interaction provided by Pauline Gibbons' exhaustive example in her paper. She draws on Hallidayan systemic functional grammatical analysis to provide her description, incidentally suggesting a link between the work of Michael Halliday and that of Lev Vygotsky, one which many other contemporary researchers of classroom interaction have also made. Gibbons' paper is also noteworthy for her careful analysis of the immediate contexts of that meaning negotiation which we have earlier identified as central to language learning.

It may be useful to recall here our comment at the outset of this Introduction that the papers in this collection are all in different ways intimately concerned with the definition of *context*, in its various interpretations. The relationship between language and context is neither direct nor unitary. We can see in the papers by Gibbons and Mercer two possible interpretations of this relationship. On the one hand, context is a feature of texts, something enduring that belongs to the text-as-entity that linguists seek to describe. In this sense, perhaps that found more in Pauline Gibbons' paper, context may be the texts that learners and teachers produce, or the physical settings within which their texts are produced. On the other hand, perhaps more along the lines suggested by Mercer, context is dynamic, a product of people's thinking, more the configuration of information that people use for making sense of language in particular situations. In this sense, *context* is more of a mental rather than a physical phenomenon, something dynamic and momentary, but dependent for its creation in the classroom on the careful constructing by the teacher of a continuity and a community of shared understanding with learners.

Such a Vygotskian view of context places a premium on the exploration of the emotional and affective engagement of learners in the acts and processes of learning. Such an engagement is not explicable, however, only from an analysis in terms of the activities of the classroom. As in earlier papers in this collection, wider social factors play a role. In her paper, Angel Lin's experience as a teacher-researcher into second language learning in Hong Kong is linked to the work of the French sociologist Bourdieu in an attempt to explain the nature of these factors. Are classrooms replicative of learners' social worlds or do they have the power to challenge and transform them? In reading how Lin addresses this question there is a clear resonance with the papers by Canagarajah and Chick in the second part of this book. One key example of a site for such a transformation is that of the cultural perspectives and ideologies present in typical textbooks and the degree to which classroom practices maintain a conformist, or can exercise a challenging stance in relation to them.

The papers by Mercer, Gibbons and Lin all present analyses of the interactive processes of teaching and learning. Although rather different, the research described in each of them encourages the view that the quality of the interaction between teachers and learners in the language classroom, and between learners if they work together, is a strong determining factor on what, and how much, is learned and understood by learners. The issue of how classroom interaction can be related to assessment of the outcomes of student learning is the key theme in the paper by Assia Slimani which follows. From a teacher-researcher perspective, what is significant about her paper is the way in which she matches learners' own statements about what they believed they had learned, with the evidence offered by analyses of the recorded talk of the lessons concerned. This provided Slimani with a means of evaluating what themes, topics and learning items suggested by learners had actually figured in their classroom interactions. Closely connected with this comparative mode of analysis is Michael Breen's second paper in this collection where he concentrates on what he refers to as the different discourses of the classroom that learners need to 'navigate'. Again, our cartographic metaphor offers perhaps some explanatory value. For Breen, the classroom is full of distinctive discourses, in part pedagogically oriented, in part socially, in part individually. These discourses invoke a range of different meanings and contexts. Learners are faced with the considerable challenge of finding their ways through this obscured terrain, drawing on their natural language instincts and analytical capacity to make sense of a semantically and pragmatically complex environment.

Mapping the territory of second language learning and teaching has been the guiding metaphor for this collection of papers. The cartography of this territory may be left as the province of researchers, or it may be also colonized by reflective teachers eager to explore and understand more of second language learning in action in their own classrooms. Indispensable to such a project, however, is the capacity to describe classroom interaction. This is the theme of the final paper in the collection, by Joan Swann, in which she sets out some procedures that English language teachers can usefully follow if they wish to describe, interpret and explain the interactive processes of their own classrooms or those of colleagues. We think that Swann's paper is an admirable way of closing a theoretical and a practical collection of papers.

What are the general principles that we may derive at the end of this particular journey? From the arguments in the papers here, we would like to identify the following:

- A need to focus on the distinct roles, activities and purposes for teachers and learners that are constructed through classroom practice;
- A need to recognize language learners as individuals, working together in the classroom, but whose learning is shaped by the context of their wider experience of living and learning outside the classroom;
- The requirement on teachers to take an active, guiding role in 'scaffolding' the learning of their students, remembering that this is not to downgrade in any way the need for learners to become actively and increasingly engaged in the processes of classroom language learning and their direction;
- An appreciation that the patterns of interaction between learners and teachers, and the use of certain procedures by teachers, can have both positive and negative effects on language learners.

PART ONE

How is language learning explained?

Chapter 1

Rosamond Mitchell and Florence Myles

SECOND LANGUAGE LEARNING: KEY CONCEPTS AND ISSUES

Introduction

T HIS CHAPTER PROVIDES AN OVERVIEW of key concepts and issues in our discussions of individual perspectives on second language learning. We offer introductory definitions of a range of key terms, and try to equip the reader with the means to compare the goals and claims of particular theories with one another. We also summarize key issues, and indicate where they will be explored in more detail later.

The main themes to be dealt with in following sections are:

1   What makes for a 'good' explanation or theory
2   Views on the nature of language
3   Views of the language learning process
4   Views of the language learner
5   Links between language learning theory and social practice.

First, however, we must offer a preliminary definition of our most basic concept, 'second language learning'. We define this broadly to include the learning of any language to any level, provided only that the learning of the 'second' language takes place sometime later than the acquisition of the first language. (Simultaneous infant bilingualism is a specialist topic, with its own literature. See for example relevant sections in Hamers and Blanc 1989; Romaine 1995.)

For us, therefore, 'second languages' are any languages other than the learner's 'native language' or 'mother tongue'. They encompass both languages of wider communication encountered within the local region or community (e.g. at the workplace, or in the media), and truly foreign languages, which have no immediately local uses or speakers. They may indeed be the second language the learner is working with, in a literal sense, or they may be their third, fourth, fifth language . . . We believe it is sensible to include 'foreign' languages under our more general term of 'second' languages, because we believe that the underlying learning processes are essentially the same for more local and for more remote target languages, despite differing learning purposes and circumstances.

We are also interested in all kinds of learning, whether formal, planned and systematic (as in classroom-based learning), or informal and unstructured (as when a new language is 'picked up' in the community). Some second language researchers have proposed a principled distinction between formal, conscious *learning* and informal, unconscious *acquisition*. This distinction attracted much criticism when argued in a strong form by Stephen Krashen (1981); it still has both its active supporters and its critics (e.g. Zobl 1995; Robinson 1997). We think it is difficult to sustain systematically when surveying SLL research in the broad way proposed here, and unless specially indicated we will be using both terms interchangeably.

What makes for a good theory?

Second language learning is an immensely complex phenomenon. Millions of human beings have experience of second language learning, and may have a good practical understanding of the activities which helped them to learn (or perhaps blocked them from learning). But this practical experience, and the common-sense knowledge which it leads to, are clearly not enough to help us understand fully how the process happens. We know, for a start, that people cannot reliably describe the language rules which they have somehow internalized, nor the inner mechanisms which process, store and retrieve many aspects of that new language.

We need to understand second language learning better than we do, for two basic reasons.

1   Improved knowledge in this particular domain is interesting in itself, and can also contribute to more general understanding about the nature of language, of human learning, and of intercultural communication, and thus about the human mind itself, as well as how all these are interrelated and affect each other.

2   The knowledge will be useful. If we become better at explaining the learning process, and are better able to account for both success and failure in L2 learning, there will be a pay-off for millions of teachers, and tens of millions of students and other learners, who are struggling with the task.

We can only pursue a better understanding of L2 learning in an organized and productive way if our efforts are guided by some form of theory. For our purposes, a *theory* is a more or less abstract set of claims about the units that are significant within the phenomenon under study, the relationships that exist between them, and the processes that bring about change. Thus a theory aims not just at description, but at explanation. Theories may be embryonic and restricted in scope, or more elaborate, explicit and comprehensive. (A theory of L2 learning may deal only with a particular stage or phase of learning, or with the learning of some particular sub-aspect of language; or it may propose learning mechanisms which are much more general in scope.) Worthwhile theories are collaborative affairs, which evolve through a process of *systematic enquiry*, in which the claims of the theory are assessed against some kind of evidence or data. This may take place through a process of *hypothesis testing* through formal experiment, or through more ecological procedures, where naturally occurring data is analysed and interpreted. (See Brumfit and Mitchell 1990 for fuller discussion and exemplification of methods.) Finally, the process of theory building is a reflexive one; new developments in the theory lead to the need to collect new information and explore different phenomena and different patterns in the potentially infinite world of 'facts' and data. Puzzling 'facts', and patterns which fail to fit in, lead to new theoretical insights.

To make these ideas more concrete, an example of a particular theory or 'model' of second language learning is shown in Figure 1.1, taken from Spolsky 1989, p. 28. This represents a 'general model of second language learning', as the proposer describes it (Spolsky 1989, p. 14). The model encapsulates this researcher's theoretical views on the overall relationship between contextual factors, individual learner differences, learning opportunities, and learning outcomes. It is thus an ambitious model, in the breadth of phenomena it is trying to explain. The rectangular boxes show the factors (or variables) which the researcher believes are most significant for learning, i.e. where variation can lead to differences in success or failure. The arrows connecting the various boxes show directions of influence. The contents of the various boxes are defined at great length, as consisting of clusters of interacting 'Conditions' (74 in all: 1989, pp. 16–25), which make language

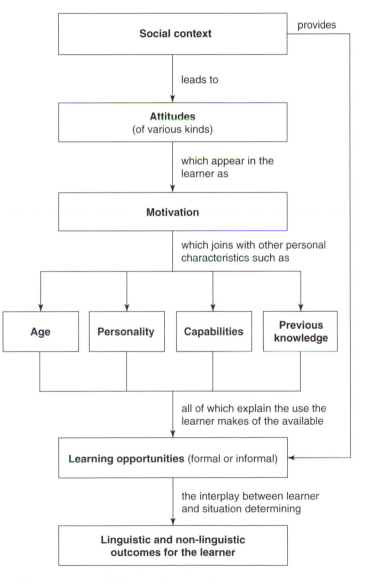

Figure 1.1 Spolsky's general model of second language learning
Source: Spolsky 1989: 28

learning success more or less likely. These summarize the results of a great variety of empirical language learning research, as Spolsky interprets them.

How would we begin to 'evaluate' this or any other model, or even more modestly, to decide that this was a view of the language learning process with which we felt comfortable and within which we wanted to work? This would depend partly on broader philosophical positions: e.g. are we satisfied with an account of human learning which sees individual differences as both relatively fixed, and also highly influential for learning? It would also depend on the particular focus of our own interests, within second language learning; this particular model seems well adapted for the study of the individual learner, but has relatively little to say about the social relationships in which they engage, for example.

But whatever the particular focus of a given theory, we would expect to find the following:

1   clear and explicit statements of the ground the theory is supposed to cover, and the claims which it is making;
2   systematic procedures for confirming/disconfirming the theory, through data gathering and interpretation;
3   not only descriptions of L2 phenomena, but attempts to explain why they are so, and to propose mechanisms for change;
4   last but not least, engagement with other theories in the field, and serious attempts to account for at least some of the phenomena which are 'common ground' in ongoing public discussion (Long 1990a). The remaining sections of this chapter offer a preliminary overview of numbers of these.

Views on the nature of language

Levels of language

Linguists have traditionally viewed language as a complex communication system, which must be analysed on a number of levels: *phonology*, *syntax*, *morphology*, *semantics* and *lexis*, *pragmatics*, *discourse*. They have differed about the degree of separateness/integration of these levels; e.g. while Chomsky argued at one time that 'grammar is autonomous and independent of meaning' (1957, p. 17), another tradition initiated by the British linguist Firth claims that 'there is no boundary between lexis and grammar: lexis and grammar are interdependent' (Stubbs 1996, p. 36). In examining different perspectives on second language learning, we will first of all be looking at the levels of language which they attempt to take into account, and the relative degree of priority they attribute to the different levels. (Does language learning start with words, or with discourse?) We will also examine the degree of integration/separation that they assume, across the various levels. We will find that the control of syntax is commonly seen as somehow 'central' to language learning, and that most general SLL theories try to account for development in this area. Other levels of language receive much more variable attention, and some areas are commonly treated in a semi-autonomous way, as specialist fields; this is often true for SLL-oriented studies of pragmatics and of lexical development (see e.g. Kasper 1996 on pragmatics; Meara 1996a, 1996b on vocabulary).

Competence and performance

Throughout the twentieth century, linguists have also disagreed in other ways over their main focus of interest and of study. Should this be the collection and analysis of actual attested samples of language in use, for example by recording and analysing people's speech? Or should it be to theorize underlying principles and rules which govern language behaviour, in its potentially infinite variety? The linguist Noam Chomsky has famously argued that it is the business of theoretical linguistics to study and model underlying language *competence*, rather than the *performance* data of actual utterances which people have produced (Chomsky 1965). By competence, Chomsky is referring to the abstract and hidden representation of language knowledge held inside our heads, with its potential to create and understand original utterances in a given language. As we shall see, this view has been influential in much second language learning research.

However, for linguists committed to this dualist position, there are difficulties in studying competence. Language performance data are believed to be an imperfect reflection of competence, partly because of the processing complications which are involved in speaking or other forms of language production, and which lead to errors and slips. More importantly, it is believed that, in principle, the infinite creativity of the underlying system can never adequately be reflected in a finite data sample (see e.g. Chomsky 1965, p. 18). Strictly speaking, many students of language competence believe it can be accessed only indirectly, and under controlled conditions, e.g. through *grammaticality judgement tests* (roughly, when people are offered sample sentences, which are in (dis)agreement with the rules proposed for the underlying competence, and invited to say whether they think they are grammatical or not: Sorace 1996).

This split between competence and performance has never been accepted by all linguists, however, with linguists in the British tradition of Firth and Halliday arguing for radically different models in which this distinction between competence and performance does not appear. In a recent review of this tradition, Stubbs quotes Firth as describing such dualisms as 'a quite unnecessary nuisance' (Firth 1957, p. 2n, quoted in Stubbs 1996, p. 44). In the Firthian view, the only option for linguists is to study language in use, and there is no opposition between language as system, and observed instances of language behaviour; the only difference is one of perspective.

Of course, the abstract language system cannot be 'read' directly off small samples of actual text, any more than the underlying climate of some geographical region of the world can be modelled from today's weather (a metaphor of Halliday's: Stubbs 1996, pp. 44–5). The arrival of *corpus linguistics*, in which very large corpora comprising millions of words of running text can be stored electronically and analysed with a growing range of software tools, has revitalized the writing of 'observation-based grammars' (Aarts 1991), of the integrated kind favoured by Firthian linguistics. 'Work with corpora provides new ways of considering the relation between data and theory, by showing how theory can be grounded in publicly accessible corpus data' (Stubbs 1996, p. 46). For example, the English corpus-based work of the COBUILD team directed by John Sinclair has claimed to reveal 'quite unsuspected patterns of language' (Sinclair 1991, p. xvii), offering new insights into the interconnectedness of lexis and grammar.

In making sense of contemporary perspectives on SLL, then, we will also need to take account of the extent to which a competence/performance distinction is assumed. This will have significant consequences for the research methodologies associated with various positions, e.g. the extent to which these pay attention to naturalistic corpora of learner language samples, or rely on more controlled and focused – but more indirect – testing of learners' underlying knowledge. For obvious reasons, theorists' views on the relationship between competence and performance are also closely linked to their view of the language learning process itself, and in particular, to their view of the way in which *language use* (i.e. speaking or writing a language) can contribute to *language learning* (i.e. developing grammatical or lexical competence in the language).

The language learning process

Nature and nurture

Discussions about processes of second language learning have always been coloured by debates on fundamental issues in human learning more generally. One of these is the *nature–nurture* debate. How much of human learning derives from innate predispositions, i.e. some form of genetic pre-programming, and how much of it derives from social and cultural experiences which influence us as we grow up? In the twentieth century, the best-known controversy on this issue as far as first language learning was concerned involved the behaviourist psychologist B. F. Skinner and the linguist Noam Chomsky. Skinner attempted to argue that language in all its essentials could be and was taught to the young child by the same mechanisms which he believed accounted for other types of learning. (In Skinner's case, the mechanisms were those envisaged by general behaviourist learning theory – essentially, copying and memorizing behaviours encountered in the surrounding environment. From this point of view, language could be learned primarily by imitating caretakers' speech.)

Chomsky, on the other hand, has argued consistently for the view that human language is too complex to be learned, in its entirety, from the performance data actually available to the child; we must therefore have some innate predisposition to expect natural languages to be organized in particular ways and not others. For example, all natural languages have word classes such as Noun and Verb, and grammar rules which apply to these word classes. It is this type of information which Chomsky doubts children could discover from scratch, in the speech they hear around them. Instead, he argues that there must be some innate core of abstract knowledge about language form, which pre-specifies a framework for all natural human languages. This core of knowledge is currently known as *Universal Grammar*.

For our purposes, it is enough to note that child language specialists now generally accept the basic notion of an innate predisposition to language, though this cannot account for all aspects of language development, which results from an interaction between innate and environmental factors. That is, complementary mechanisms, including active involvement in language use, are equally essential for the development of communicative competence (see e.g. Foster 1990).

How does the nature–nurture debate impact on theories of second language learning? If humans are endowed with an innate predisposition for language, then perhaps they should be able to learn as many languages as they need or want to, provided (important provisos!) that the time, circumstances, and motivation are available. On the other hand, the environmental circumstances for L2 learning differ systematically from L1 learning, except where infants are reared in multilingual surroundings. Should we be aiming to reproduce the 'natural' circumstances of L1 learning as far as possible for the L2 student? This was a fashionable view in the 1970s, but one which downplayed some very real social and psychological obstacles. In the last twenty years there has been a closer and more critical examination of environmental factors which seem to influence L2 learning; some of these are detailed briefly under 'The relationship between second language use and second language learning', on page 21.

Modularity

A further issue of controversy for students of the human brain has been the extent to which the brain should be viewed as *modular* or unitary. That is, should we see the brain as a single, flexible organism, with one general set of procedures for learning and storing different kinds of knowledge and skills? Or, is it more helpfully understood as a bundle of *modules*, with distinctive mechanisms relevant to different types of knowledge (e.g. Fodor 1983)?

The modular view has consistently found support from within linguistics, most famously in the further debate between Chomsky and the child development psychologist, Jean Piaget. This debate is reported in Piatelli-Palmarini (1980), and has been re-examined many times; a helpful recent summary is offered by Johnson (1996, pp. 6–30). Briefly, Piaget argued that language was simply one manifestation of the more general skill of symbolic representation, acquired as a stage in general cognitive development; no special mechanism was therefore required to account for first language acquisition. Chomsky's general view is that not only is language too complex to be learned from environmental exposure (his criticism of Skinner), it is also too distinctive in its structure to be learnable by general cognitive means. Universal Grammar is thus endowed with its own distinctive mechanisms for learning.

There are many linguists today who support the concept of a distinctive language module in the mind. There are also those who argue that language competence itself is modular, with different aspects of language knowledge being stored and accessed in distinctive ways. However, there is no general agreement on the number and nature of such modules, nor on how they relate to other aspects of cognition.

Modularity and second language learning

The possible role of an innate, specialist language module in second language learning has been much discussed in recent years. If such innate mechanisms indeed exist, there are four logical possibilities:

1   that they continue to operate during second language learning, and make key aspects of second language learning possible, in the same way that they make first language learning possible;
2   that after the acquisition of the first language in early childhood, these mechanisms cease to be operable, and second languages must be learned by other means;
3   that the mechanisms themselves are no longer operable, but that the first language provides a model of a natural language and how it works, which can be 'copied' in some way when learning a second language;
4   that distinctive learning mechanisms for language remain available, but only in part, and must be supplemented by other means.

The first position was popularized in the second language learning field by Stephen Krashen in the 1970s, in a basic form. While Krashen's theoretical views have been criticized, this has by no means led to the disappearance of modular proposals to account for SLL. Instead, this particular perspective has been revitalized by the continuing development of Chomsky's Universal Grammar proposals (Cook and Newson 1996).

On the other hand, thinking about those general learning mechanisms which may be operating at least for adult learners of second languages has also developed further, since e.g. the original proposals of McLaughlin (1987, pp. 133–53). Most obviously, the work of the cognitive psychologist J. R. Anderson on human learning, from an information processing perspective, has been applied to various aspects of second language learning by different researchers (Johnson 1996; O'Malley and Chamot 1990; Towell and Hawkins 1994).

Systematicity and variability in L2 learning

When the utterances produced by L2 learners are examined and compared with target language norms, they are often condemned as full of errors or mistakes. Traditionally, language teachers have often viewed these errors as the result of carelessness or lack of concentration on the part of learners. If only learners would try harder, surely their productions could accurately reflect the TL rules which they had been taught! In the mid-twentieth century, under the influence of behaviourist learning theory, errors were often viewed as the result of 'bad habits', which could be eradicated if only learners did enough rote learning and pattern drilling using target language models.

One of the big lessons which has been learned from the research of recent decades is that though learners' L2 utterances may be deviant by comparison with target language norms, they are by no means lacking in *system*. Errors and mistakes are patterned, and though some regular errors are due to the influence of the first language, this is by no means true of all of them, or even of a majority of them. Instead, there is a good deal of evidence that learners work their way through a number of *developmental stages*, from very primitive and deviant versions of the L2, to progressively more elaborate and target-like versions. Just like fully proficient users of a language, their language productions can be described by a set of underlying rules; these interim rules have their own integrity and are not just inadequately applied versions of the TL rules.

A clear example, which has been studied for a range of target languages, has to do with the formation of negative sentences. It has commonly been found that learners start off by tacking a negative particle of some kind on to the end of an utterance (*no you are playing here*); next, they learn to insert a basic negative particle into the verb phrase (*Mariana not coming today*); and finally, they learn to manipulate modifications to auxiliaries and other details of negation morphology, in line with the full TL rules for negation (*I can't play that one*) (examples from Ellis 1994, p. 100). This kind of data has commonly been interpreted to show that, at least as far as key parts of the L2 grammar are concerned, learners' development follows a common *route*, even if the *rate* at which learners actually travel along this common route may be very different.

This *systematicity* in the language produced by L2 learners is of course paralleled in the early stages through which first language learners also pass in a highly regular manner. Towell and Hawkins identify it as one of the key features which L2 learning theories are required to explain (1994, p. 5).

However, learner language (or *interlanguage*, as it is commonly called) is not only characterized by systematicity. Learner language systems are presumably – indeed, hopefully – unstable and in course of change; certainly, they are characterized also by high degrees of *variability* (Towell and Hawkins 1994, p. 5). Most obviously, learners' utterances seem to vary from moment to moment, in the types of 'errors' which are made, and learners seem liable to switch between a range of correct and incorrect forms over lengthy periods of time. A well-known example offered by Ellis involves a child learner of English as L2 who seemed to produce the utterances *no look my card*, *don't look my card* interchangeably over an extended period (1985). Myles *et al.* (1998) have produced similar data from a classroom learner's French as L2, who variably produced forms such as *non animal*, *je n'ai pas de animal* within the same 20 minutes or so (to say that he did not have a pet; the correct TL form should be *je n'ai pas d'animal*). Here, in contrast to the underlying systematicity earlier claimed for the development of rules of negation, we see performance varying quite substantially from moment to moment.

Like systematicity, variability is also found in child language development. However, the variability found among L2 learners is undoubtedly more 'extreme' than that found for children; again, variability is described by Towell *et al.* (1996) as a central feature of learner interlanguage which L2 theories will have to explain.

Creativity and routines in L2 learning

In the last section, we referred to evidence which shows that learners' interlanguage productions can be described as systematic, at least in part. This systematicity is linked to another key concept, that of *creativity*. Learners' surface utterances can be linked to underlying rule systems, even if these seem primitive and deviant compared with the target language system. It logically follows that learners can produce original utterances, i.e. that their rule system can generate utterances appropriate to a given context, which the learner has never heard before.

There is of course plenty of common-sense evidence that learners can put their L2 knowledge to creative use, even at the very earliest stages of L2 learning. It becomes most obvious that this is happening, when learners produce utterances like the highly deviant *non animal* (no animal = 'I haven't got any pet'), which we cited before. This is not an utterance which any native speaker of French would produce (other than, perhaps, a very young child); much the most likely way that the learner has produced it is through applying an extremely primitive interlanguage rule for negation, in combination with some basic vocabulary.

But how did this same learner manage to produce the near-target *je n'ai pas de animal*, with its negative particles correctly inserted within the verb phrase, and corresponding almost-perfect modification to the morphology of the noun phrase, within a few minutes of the other form? For us, the most likely explanation is that at this point he was reproducing an utterance which he has indeed heard before (and probably rehearsed), which has been memorized as an unanalysed whole, a formula or a *prefabricated chunk*.

Work in corpus linguistics has led us to the increasing recognition that formulas and routines play an important part in everyday language use by native speakers; when we talk, our everyday L1 utterances are a complex mix of creativity and prefabrication (Sinclair 1991). In L1 acquisition research also, the use of unanalysed chunks by young children has been commonly observed. For L1 learners, the contribution of chunks seems limited by processing constraints; for older L2 learners, however, memorization of lengthy, unanalysed language routines is much more possible. (Think of those opera singers who successfully memorize and deliver entire parts, in languages they do not otherwise control!)

Analysis of L2 data produced by classroom learners in particular, seems to show extensive and systematic use of chunks to fulfil communicative needs in the early stages (Myles *et al.* 1998). Studies of informal learners also provide some evidence of chunk use. This phenomenon has attracted relatively little attention in recent times, compared with that given to learner creativity and systematicity (Weinert 1995). However, we believe it is common enough in L2 spontaneous production (and not only in the opera house), to need some more sustained attention from L2 learning theory.

Incomplete success and fossilization

Young children learning their first language embark on the enterprise in widely varying situations around the world, sometimes in conditions of extreme poverty and deprivation, whether physical or social. Yet with remarkable uniformity, at the end of five years or so, they have achieved a very substantial measure of success. Teachers and students know to their cost that this is by no means the case with second languages, embarked on after these critical early years. Few, if any, adult learners ever come to blend indistinguishably with the community of target language 'native speakers'; most remain noticeably deviant in their pronunciation, and many continue to make grammar mistakes and to search for words, even when well motivated to learn, after years of study, residence and/or work in contact with the target language.

Second language learning, then, is typified by *incomplete success*; the claimed systematic evolution of our underlying interlanguage rules towards the target language system seems doomed, most often, never to integrate completely with its goal. Indeed, while some learners go on learning, others seem to cease to make any visible progress, no matter how many language classes they attend, or how actively they continue to use their second language for communicative purposes. The term *fossilization* is commonly used to describe this phenomenon, when a learner's L2 system seems to 'freeze', or become stuck, at some more or less deviant stage.

These phenomena of incomplete success and fossilization are also significant 'facts' about the process of L2 learning, which any serious theory must eventually explain. As we will see, explanations of two basic types have in fact been offered. The first group of explanations are *psycholinguistic*: the language-specific learning mechanisms available to the young child simply cease to work for older learners, at least partly, and no amount of study and effort can recreate them. The second group of explanations are *sociolinguistic*: older L2 learners do not have the social opportunities, or the motivation, to identify completely with the native speaker community, but may instead value their distinctive identity as learners or as foreigners.

Cross-linguistic influences in L2 learning

Everyday observation tells us that learners' performance in a second language is influenced by the language, or languages, that they already know. This is routinely obvious from learners' 'foreign accent', i.e. pronunciation which bears traces of the phonology of their first language. It is also obvious when learners make certain characteristic mistakes, e.g. when a native speaker of English says something in French like *je suis douze*, an utterance parallel to the English 'I am twelve'. (The correct French expression would of course be *j'ai douze ans* = I have twelve years.)

This kind of phenomenon in learner productions is often called by the term *language transfer*. But how important is the phenomenon, and what exactly is being transferred? Second language researchers have been through several 'swings of the pendulum' on this question, as Gass puts it (1996). Behaviourist theorists viewed language transfer as an important source of error and interference in L2 learning, because L1 'habits' were so tenacious and deeply rooted. The interlanguage theorists who followed downplayed the influence of the L1 in L2 learning, however, because of their preoccupation with identifying creative processes at work in L2 development; they pointed out that many L2 errors could not be traced to L1 influence, and were primarily concerned with discovering patterns and developmental sequences on this creative front.

Theorists today, as we shall see, would generally accept once more that cross-linguistic influences play an important role in L2 learning. However, we will still find widely differing views on the extent and nature of these influences. Some researchers have in fact claimed that learners with different L1s progress at somewhat different rates, and even follow different acquisitional routes, at least in some areas of the target grammar (e.g. Keller-Cohen 1979, Zobl 1982, quoted in Gass 1996, pp. 322–3).

The relationship between second language use and second language learning

In an earlier section we considered the distinction between language *competence* and *performance*, which many linguists have found useful. Here, we look more closely at the concept of performance, and in particular, look at the possible relationship between using (i.e. performing in) an L2, and learning (i.e. developing one's competence in) that same language.

We should note first of all, of course, that 'performing' in a language not only involves speaking it. Making sense of the language data that we hear around us is an equally essential aspect of performance. Indeed, it is basic common ground among all theorists of language learning, of whatever description, that it is necessary to interpret and to process incoming language data in some form, for normal language development to take place. There is thus a consensus that language *input* of some kind is essential for normal language learning. In fact, during the late 1970s and early 1980s, the view was argued by Stephen Krashen and others that input (at the right level of difficulty) was all that was necessary for L2 acquisition to take place (Krashen 1982, 1985). This position has been viewed by more recent theorists as inadequate, but a modified and refined version has been developed.

Krashen was unusual in not seeing any central role for language production in his theory of second language acquisition. Most other theoretical viewpoints support in some form the common-sense view that speaking a language is helpful for learning it, though they offer a wide variety of explanations as to why this should be the case. For example, behaviourist learning theory saw regular (oral) practice as helpful in forming correct language 'habits'. This view has become less popular in recent decades, as part of linguists' general loss of interest in behaviourist thinking.

However, various contemporary theorists still lay stress on the 'practice' function of language production, especially in building up fluency and control of an emergent L2 system. For example, information processing theorists commonly argue that language competence consists of both a *knowledge* component ('knowing that') and a *skill* component ('knowing how'). While they may accept a variety of possible sources for the first component, researchers in this perspective agree in seeing a vital role for L2 use/L2 performance in developing the second skill component.

An even more strongly contrasting view to Krashen's is the so-called *comprehensible output* hypothesis, argued for by Merrill Swain and colleagues (e.g. Swain 1985; Swain and Lapkin 1995). Swain points out that much incoming L2 input is comprehensible, without any need for a full grammatical analysis. If we don't need to pay attention to the grammar, in order to understand the message, why should we be compelled to learn it? On the other hand, when we try to say something in our chosen second language, we are forced to make grammatical choices and hypotheses, in order to put our utterances together. The act of speaking forces us to try our ideas about how the target grammar actually works, and of course gives us the chance of getting some feedback from interlocutors who may fail to understand our efforts.

So far in this section, we have seen that theorists can hold different views on the contribution both of language input and language output to language learning. However, another way of distinguishing among current theories of L2 learning from a 'performance' perspective has to do with their view of L2 *interaction* – when the speaking and listening in which the learner is engaged are viewed as an integral and mutually influential whole, e.g. in everyday conversation. Two major perspectives on interaction are apparent, one psycholinguistic, one sociolinguistic.

From a psycholinguistic point of view, L2 interaction is mainly interesting because of the opportunities it offers to individual L2 learners to fine-tune the language input they are receiving. This ensures that the input is well adapted to their own internal needs (i.e. to the present state of development of their L2 knowledge). What this means is that learners need the chance to talk with native speakers in a fairly open-ended way, to ask questions, and to clarify meanings when they do not immediately understand. Under these conditions, it is believed that the utterances that result will be at the right level of difficulty to promote learning; in Krashen's terms, they will provide true 'comprehensible input'. Conversational episodes involving the regular *negotiation of meaning* have been intensively studied by many of the Krashen-influenced researchers.

Interaction is also interesting to linguistic theorists, because of recent controversies over whether the provision of *negative evidence* is necessary or helpful for L2 development. By 'negative evidence' is meant some kind of input which lets the learner know that a particular form is *not* acceptable according to target language norms. In L2 interaction this might take the shape of a formal correction offered by a teacher, say, or a more informal rephrasing of a learner's L2 utterance, offered by a native-speaking conversational partner.

Why is there a controversy about negative evidence in L2 learning? The problem is that correction often seems ineffective – and not only because L2 learners are lazy. It seems that learners often cannot benefit from correction, but continue to make the same mistakes however much feedback is offered. For some current theorists, any natural language must be learnable from *positive* evidence alone, and corrective feedback is largely irrelevant. Others continue to see value in corrections and negative evidence, though it is generally accepted that these will be useful only when they relate to 'hot spots' currently being restructured in the learner's emerging L2 system.

These different (psycho)linguistic views have one thing in common, however; they view the learner as operating and developing a relatively autonomous L2 system, and see interaction as a way of feeding that system with more or less fine-tuned input data, whether positive or negative. *Sociolinguistic* views of interaction are very different. Here, the language learning process is viewed as essentially social; both the identity of the learner, and their language knowledge, are collaboratively constructed and reconstructed in the course of interaction. Some theorists stress a broad view of the second language learning process as an apprenticeship into a range of new discourse practices (e.g. Hall 1995); others are more concerned with analysing the detail of interaction between more expert and less expert speakers, to determine how the learner is *scaffolded* into using (and presumably learning) new L2 forms.

Views of the language learner

Who is the second language learner, and how are they introduced to us, in current SLL research? 'Second language' research generally deals with learners who embark on the learning of an additional language, at least some years after they have started to acquire their first language. This learning may take place formally and systematically, in a classroom setting; or it may take place through informal social contact, through work, through migration, or other social forces which bring speakers of different languages into contact, and make communication a necessity.

So, second language learners may be children, or they may be adults; they may be learning the target language formally in school or college, or 'picking it up' in the playground or the workplace. They may be learning a highly localized language, which will help them to become insiders in a local speech community; or the target language may be a language of wider communication relevant to their region, which gives access to economic development and public life.

Indeed, in the late twentieth century, the target language is highly likely to be English; a recent estimate suggests that while around 300 million people speak English as their first language, another 700 million or so are using it as a second language, or learning to do so (Crystal 1987, p. 358). Certainly it is true that much research on second language learning, whether with children or adults, is concerned with the learning of English, or with a very small number of other languages, mostly European ones (French, German, Spanish). There are many multilingual communities today (e.g. townships around many fast-growing cities) where L2 learning involves a much wider range of languages. However, these have been comparatively little studied.

The learner as language processor

It is possible to distinguish three main points of view, or sets of priorities, among SLL researchers as far as the learner is concerned. Linguists and psycholinguists have typically been concerned primarily with analysing and modelling the *inner mental mechanisms* available to the individual learner, for processing, learning, and storing new language knowledge. As far as language learning in particular is concerned, their aim is to document and explain the developmental route along which learners travel. Researchers for whom this is the prime goal are less concerned with the speed or rate of development, or indeed with the degree of ultimate L2 success. Thus they tend to minimize or disregard social and contextual differences among learners; their aim is to document universal mental processes available to all normal human beings.

As we shall see, however, there is some controversy among researchers in this psycholinguistic tradition on the question of *age*. Do child and adult L2 learners learn in essentially similar ways? Or, is there a *critical age* which divides younger and older learners, a moment when early learning mechanisms atrophy and are replaced or at least supplemented by other compensatory ways of learning? The balance of evidence has been interpreted by Long (1990b) in favour of the existence of such a cut-off point, and many other researchers agree with some version of a view that 'younger = better in the long run' (Singleton 1995, p. 3). However, explanations of why this should be are still provisional.

Differences between individual learners

Real-life observation quickly tells us, however, that even if L2 learners can be shown to be following a common developmental route, they differ greatly in the degree of ultimate success which they achieve. Social psychologists have argued consistently that these differences in learning outcomes must be due to *individual differences* between learners, and many proposals have been made concerning the characteristics which supposedly cause these differences.

In a recent two-part review (1992, 1993), Gardner and MacIntyre divide what they see as the most important learner traits into two groups, the *cognitive* and the *affective* (emotional). Here we follow their account, and summarize very briefly the factors claimed to have the most significant influence on L2 learning success. For fuller treatment of this social psychological perspective on learner difference, we would refer the reader to sources such as Gardner (1985), Skehan (1989), and Ellis (1994, pp. 467– 560).

Cognitive factors

Intelligence: Not very surprisingly perhaps, there is clear evidence that L2 students who are above average on formal measures of intelligence and/or general academic attainment tend to do well in L2 learning, at least in formal classroom settings.

Language aptitude: Is there really such a thing as a 'gift' for language learning, distinct from general intelligence, as folk wisdom often holds? The most famous formal test of language aptitude was designed in the 1950s, by Carroll and Sapon (1959, in Gardner and MacIntyre 1992, p. 214). This 'Modern Language Aptitude Test' assesses a number of subskills believed to be predictive of L2 learning success: (a) phonetic coding ability, (b) grammatical sensitivity, (c) memory abilities, and (d) inductive language learning ability. In general, learners' scores on this and other similar tests do indeed 'correlate with . . . achievement in a second language' (Gardner and MacIntyre 1992, p. 215), and in a range of contexts measures of aptitude have been shown to be one of the strongest available predictors of success (Harley and Hart 1997).

Language learning strategies: Do more successful language learners set about the task in some distinctive way? Do they have at their disposal some special repertoire of ways of learning, or *strategies*? If this were true, could these even be taught to other, hitherto less successful learners? Much research has been done to describe and categorize the strategies used by learners at different levels, and to link strategy use to learning outcomes; it is clear that more proficient learners do indeed employ strategies that are different from those used by the less proficient (Oxford and Crookall 1989, quoted in Gardner and MacIntyre 1992, p. 217). Whether the strategies cause the learning, or the learning itself enables different strategies to be used, has not been fully clarified, however.

Affective factors

Language attitudes: Social psychologists have long been interested in the idea that the attitudes of the learner towards the target language, its speakers, and the learning context, may all play some part in explaining success or lack of it. Research on L2 language attitudes has largely been conducted within the framework of broader research on motivation, of which attitudes form one part.

Motivation: For Gardner and MacIntyre, the motivated individual 'is one who wants to achieve a particular goal, devotes considerable effort to achieve this goal, and experiences satisfaction in the activities associated with achieving this goal' (1993, p. 2). So, motivation is a complex construct, defined by three main components: 'desire to achieve a goal, effort extended in this direction, and satisfaction with the task' (p. 2). Gardner and his Canadian colleagues have carried out a long programme of work on motivation with English Canadian school students learning French as a second language, and have developed a range of formal instruments to measure motivation. Over the years consistent relationships have been demonstrated between language attitudes, motivation, and L2 achievement; Gardner accepts that these relationships are complex, however, as the factors interact, and influence each other (1985, cited in Gardner and MacIntyre 1993, p. 2).

Language anxiety: The final learner characteristic which Gardner and MacIntyre consider has clearly been shown to have a relationship with learning success is language anxiety (and its obverse, self-confidence). For these authors, language anxiety 'is seen as a stable person-ality trait referring to the propensity for an individual to react in a nervous manner when speaking . . . in the second language' (1993, p. 5). It is typified by self-belittling, feelings of apprehension, and even bodily responses such as a faster heartbeat! The anxious learner is also less willing to speak in class, or to engage target language speakers in informal inter-action. Gardner and MacIntyre cite many studies which suggest that language anxiety has a negative relationship with learning success, and some others which suggest the opposite, for learner self-confidence.

The learner as social being

The two perspectives on the learner which we have highlighted so far have concentrated first, on universal characteristics, and second, on individual characteristics. But it is also possible to view the L2 learner as essentially a social being, and such an interest will lead to concern with learners' relationship with the social context, and the structuring of the learning opportunities which it makes available. The learning process itself may be viewed as essentially social, and inextricably entangled in L2 use and L2 interaction. Two major differences appear, which distinguish this view of the learner from the last (for the social psychological view of the learner which we have just dipped into is also clearly concerned with the individual learners' relationship with the 'socio-cultural milieu' in which learning is taking place).

First, interest in the learner as a social being leads to concern with a range of socially constructed elements in the learner's identity, and their relationship with learning – so *class*, *ethnicity*, and *gender* make their appearance as potentially significant for L2 learning research. Second, the relationship between the individual learner and the social context of learning is viewed as *dynamic*, reflexive and constantly changing. The 'individual differences' tradition saw that relationship as being governed by a bundle of learner traits or characteristics (such as aptitude, anxiety, etc.), which were relatively fixed and slow to change. More socially oriented researchers view motivation, learner anxiety, etc. as being constantly reconstructed through ongoing L2 experience and L2 interaction.

Links with social practice

Is second language learning theory 'useful'? Does it have any immediate practical applications in the real world, most obviously in the L2 classroom? In our field, theorists have been and remain divided on this point. Beretta and his colleagues have argued for 'pure' theory-building in SLL, uncluttered by requirements for practical application (1993). Van Lier (1994), Rampton (1995b) and others have argued for a socially engaged perspective, where theoretical development is rooted in, and responsive to, social practice, and language education in particular. Yet others have argued that L2 teaching in particular should be guided systematically by SLL research findings (e.g. Krashen 1985).

This tension has partly been addressed by the emergence of 'instructed language learning' as a distinct sub-area of research (see recent reviews by Ellis 1994, pp. 561–663; Spada 1997). We think that language teachers, who will form an important segment of our readership, will themselves want to take stock of the relations between the theories we survey, and their own beliefs and experiences in the classroom. They will, in other words, want to make some judgement on the 'usefulness' of theorising in making sense of their own experience and their practice, while not necessarily changing it.

References

Aarts, J. (1991) 'Intuition-based and observation-based grammars', in Aijmer, K. and Altenberg, B. (eds), *English corpus linguistics*. Harlow: Longman, 44–62.

Beretta, A. (ed.) (1993) 'Theory construction in SLA'. Special issue of *Applied Linguistics*, **14**, 221–4.

Brumfit, C.J. and Mitchell, R. (1990) 'The language classroom as a focus for research,' in Brumfit, C. J. and Mitchell, R. (eds), *Research in the language classroom*. ELT Documents 133. Modern English Publications/The British Council, 3–15.

Chomsky, N. (1957) *Syntactic structures*. The Hague: Mouton.

—— (1965) *Aspects of the theory of syntax*. Cambridge, MA: MIT Press.

Cook, V. and Newson, M. (1996) *Chomsky's Universal Grammar: an introduction*. Oxford: Blackwell.

Crystal, D. (1987) *The Cambridge encyclopedia of language*. Cambridge: Cambridge University Press.

Ellis, R. (1985) 'Sources of variability in interlanguage' *Applied Linguistics* **6**, 118–31.

—— (1994) *The study of second language acquisition*. Oxford: Oxford University Press.

Fodor, J.A. (1983) *The modularity of mind*. Cambridge, MA: MIT Press.

Foster, S. (1990) *The communicative competence of young children*. Harlow: Longman.

Gardner, R.C. (1985) *Social psychology and second language learning: the role of attitudes and motivation*. London: Edward Arnold.

Gardner, R.C. and Macintyre, P.D. (1992) 'A student's contributions to second language learning. Part I: cognitive variables', *Language Teaching* **25**, 211–20.

—— (1993) 'A student's contributions to second language learning. Part II: affective variables', *Language Teaching* **26**, 1–11.

Gass, S.M. (1996) 'Second language acquisition and linguistic theory: the role of language transfer', in Ritchie, W.C. and Bhatia, T.K. (eds), *Handbook of second language acquisition*. San Diego: Academic Press, 317–45.

Hall, J.K. (1995) '(Re)creating our worlds with words: a sociohistorical perspective of face-to-face interaction', *Applied Linguistics* **16**, 206–32.

Hamers, J. and Blanc, M. (1989) *Bilinguality and bilingualism*. Cambridge: Cambridge University Press.

Harley, B. and Hart, D. (1997) 'Language aptitude and second language proficiency in classroom learners of different starting ages', *Studies in Second Language Acquisition* **19**, 379–400.

Johnson, K. (1996) *Language teaching and skill learning*. Oxford: Blackwell.

Kasper, G. (ed.) (1996) 'The development of pragmatic competence'. Special issue of *Studies in Second Language Acquisition*, **18**, 2.

Krashen, S. (1981) *Second language acquisition and second language learning*. Oxford: Pergamon.

—— (1982) *Principles and practice in second language acquisition*. Oxford: Pergamon.

—— (1985) *The input hypothesis: issues and implications*. Harlow: Longman.

Long, M.H. (1990a) 'The least a second language acquisition theory needs to explain'. *TESOL Quarterly* **24**, 649–66.

—— (1990b) 'Maturational constraints on language development', *Studies in Second Language Acquisition* **12**, 251–85.

—— (1993) 'Assessment strategies for SLA theories'. *Applied Linguistics* **14**, 225–49.

—— (1996) 'The role of the linguistic environment in second language acquisition', in Ritchie, W.C. and Bhatia, T.K. (eds), *Handbook of second language acquisition*. San Diego: Academic Press, 413–68.

McLaughlin, B. (1987) *Theories of second language learning*. London: Edward Arnold.

Meara, P. (1996a) 'The classical research in L2 acquisition', in Anderman, G.M. and Rogers, M.A. (eds), *Words, words, words: the translator and the language learner*. Clevedon: Multilingual Matters, 27–40.

—— (1996b) 'The dimensions of lexical competence', in Brown, G., Malmkjaer, K. and Williams, J. (eds), *Performance and competence in second language acquisition*. Cambridge: Cambridge University Press, 35–53.

Myles, F., Hooper, J. and Mitchell, R. (1998) 'Rote or rule? Exploring the role of formulaic language in classroom foreign language learning', *Language Learning* **48**, 110–135.

O'Malley, J. and Chamot, A. (1990) *Learning strategies in second language acquisition*. Cambridge: Cambridge University Press.

Piatelli-Palmarini, M. (ed.) (1980) *Language and learning: the debate between Jean Piaget and Noam Chomsky*. London: Routledge and Kegan Paul.

Rampton, B. (1995a) *Crossing: language and ethnicity among adolescents*. Harlow: Longman.

—— (1995b) 'Politics and change in research in applied linguistics', *Applied Linguistics* **16**, 233–56.

Robinson, P. (1997) 'Individual differences and the fundamental similarity of implicit and explicit adult second language learning', *Language Learning* **47**, 45–99.

Romaine, S. (1995) *Bilingualism*. 2nd edn, Oxford: Blackwell.

Sinclair, J. (1991) *Corpus, concordance, collocation*. Oxford: Oxford University Press.

Singleton, D. (1995) 'A critical look at the critical period hypothesis in second language acquisition research', in Singleton, D. and Lengyel, Z. (eds), *The age factor in second language acquisition*. Clevedon: Multilingual Matters, 1–29.

Skehan, R (1989) *Individual differences in foreign language learning*. London: Edward Arnold.

Sorace, A. (1996) 'The use of acceptability judgements in second language acquisition research, in Ritchie, W and Bhatia, T. (eds), *Handbook of second language acquisition*. San Diego: Academic Press, 375–409.

Spada, N. (1997) 'Form-focussed instruction and second language acquisition: a review of classroom and laboratory research', *Language Teaching* **30**, 73–87.

Spolsky, B. (1989) *Conditions for second language learning*. Oxford: Oxford University Press.

Stubbs, M. (1996) *Text and corpus analysis*. Oxford: Blackwell.

Swain, M. (1985) 'Communicative competence: some roles of comprehensible input and comprehensible output in its development', in Gass, S.M. and Madden, C.G. (eds), *Input in second language acquisition*. Rowley, MA: Newbury House, 235–53.

Swain, M. and Lapkin, S. (1995) 'Problems in output and the cognitive processes they generate: a step towards second language learning', *Applied Linguistics* **16**, 371–91.

Towell, R. and Hawkins, R. (1994) *Approaches to second language acquisition*. Clevedon: Multilingual Matters.

Towell, R., Hawkins, R. and Bazergui, N. (1996) 'The development of fluency in advanced learners of French', *Applied Linguistics* **17**, 84–115.

Van Lier, L. (1994) 'Forks and hope: pursuing understanding in different ways', *Applied Linguistics* **15**, 328–46.

Weinert, R. (1995) 'The role of formulaic language in second language acquisition: a review', *Applied Linguistics* **16**, 180–205.

Zobl, H. (1995) 'Converging evidence for the 'acquisition-learning' distinction', *Applied Linguistics* **16**, 35–56.

Chapter 2

Patsy M. Lightbown and Nina Spada

FACTORS AFFECTING SECOND LANGUAGE LEARNING

ALL NORMAL CHILDREN, GIVEN a normal upbringing, are successful in the acquisition of their first language. This contrasts with our experience of second language learners, whose success varies greatly.

Many of us believe that learners have certain characteristics which lead to more or less successful language learning. Such beliefs are usually based on anecdotal evidence, often our own experience or that of individual people we have known. For example, many teachers are convinced that extroverted learners who interact without inhibition in their second language and find many opportunities to practise language skills will be the most successful learners. In addition to personality characteristics, other factors generally considered to be relevant to language learning are intelligence, aptitude, motivation, and attitudes. Another important factor is the age at which learning begins.

In this chapter, we will see whether anecdotal evidence is supported by research findings. To what extent can we predict differences in the success of second language acquisition in two individuals if we have information about their personalities, their general and specific intellectual abilities, their motivation, or their age?

Activity

Characteristics of the 'good language learner'

It seems that some people have a much easier time of learning than others. Rate of development varies widely among first language learners. Some children can string together five-, six-, and seven-word sentences at an age when other children are just beginning to label items in their immediate environment. Nevertheless, all normal children eventually master their first language.

In second language learning, it has been observed countless times that, in the same classroom setting, some students progress rapidly through the initial stages of learning a new language while others struggle along making very slow progress. Some learners never achieve *native-like* command of a second language. Are there personal characteristics that make one learner more successful than another, and if so, what are they?

The following is a list of some of the characteristics commonly thought to contribute to successful language learning. In your experience – as a second language learner and as a teacher — which characteristics seem to you most likely to be associated with success in second language acquisition in the classroom? Which ones would you be less inclined to expect in a successful learner?

In each case rate the characteristic as follows:

1 = Very important
2 = Quite important
3 = Important
4 = Not very important
5 = Not at all important

A good language learner:

a	is a willing and accurate guesser	1	2	3	4	5
b	tries to get a message across even if specific language knowledge is lacking	1	2	3	4	5
c	is willing to make mistakes	1	2	3	4	5
d	constantly looks for patterns in the language	1	2	3	4	5
e	practises as often as possible	1	2	3	4	5
f	analyses his or her own speech and the speech of others	1	2	3	4	5
g	attends to whether his or her performance meets the standards he or she has learned	1	2	3	4	5
h	enjoys grammar exercises	1	2	3	4	5
i	begins learning in childhood	1	2	3	4	5
j	has an above-average IQ	1	2	3	4	5
k	has good academic skills	1	2	3	4	5
l	has a good self-image and lots of confidence	1	2	3	4	5

All of the characteristics listed above can be classified into five main categories: motivation, aptitude, personality, intelligence, and learner preferences. However, many of the characteristics cannot be assigned exclusively to one category. For example, the characteristic 'is willing to make mistakes' can be considered a personality and/or a motivational factor if the learner is willing to make mistakes in order to get the message across.

Research on learner characteristics

Perhaps the best way to begin our discussion is to describe how research on the influence of learner characteristics on second language learning has been carried out. When researchers are interested in finding out whether an individual factor such as motivation affects second language learning, they usually select a group of learners and give them a questionnaire to measure the type and degree of their motivation. The learners are then given a test to measure their second language proficiency. The test and the questionnaire are both scored and the researcher performs a *correlation* on the two measures, to see whether learners with high scores on the proficiency test are also more likely to have high scores on the motivation questionnaire. If this is the case, the researcher concludes that high levels of motivation are correlated with success in language learning. A similar procedure can be used to assess the relationship between intelligence and second language acquisition through the use of IQ tests.

Although this procedure seems straightforward, there are several difficulties with it. The first problem is that it is not possible to directly observe and measure qualities such as motivation, extroversion, or even intelligence. These are just labels for an entire range of behaviours and characteristics. Furthermore, because characteristics such as these are not independent, it will come as no surprise that different researchers have often used the same labels to describe different sets of behavioural traits.

For example, in motivation questionnaires, learners are often asked whether they willingly seek out opportunities to use their second language with native speakers and if so, how often they do this. The assumption behind such a question is that learners who report that they often seek out opportunities to interact with speakers of the second language are highly motivated to learn. Although this assumption seems reasonable, it is problematic because if a learner responds by saying 'yes' to this question, we may assume that the learner has more opportunities for language practice in informal contexts. Because it is usually impossible to separate these two factors (i.e. willingness to interact and opportunities to interact), some researchers have been criticized for concluding that it is the motivation rather than the opportunity which makes the greater contribution to success.

Another factor which makes it difficult to reach conclusions about relationships between individual learner characteristics and second language learning is how language proficiency is defined and measured. To illustrate this point let us refer once again to 'motivation'. In the second language learning literature, some studies report that learners with a higher level of motivation are more successful language learners than those with lower motivation, while other studies report that highly motivated learners do not perform any better on a proficiency test than learners with much less motivation to learn the second language. One explanation which has been offered for these conflicting findings is that the language proficiency tests used in different studies do not measure the same kind of knowledge. That is, in informal language learning settings, highly motivated learners may be more successful when the proficiency tests measure oral communication skills. In other studies, however, highly motivated learners may not be more successful because the tests are primarily measures of metalinguistic knowledge. Results such as these imply that motivation to learn a second language may be more related to particular aspects of language proficiency than to others.

Finally, there is the problem of interpreting the correlation of two factors as being due to a causal relationship between them. That is, the fact that two things tend to occur together does not necessarily mean that one caused the other. While it may be that that one factor influences the other, it may also be the case that both are influenced by something else entirely. Research on motivation is perhaps the best context in which to illustrate this. Learners who are successful may indeed be highly motivated. But can we conclude that they became successful because of their motivation? It is also plausible that early success heightened their motivation or that both success and motivation are due to their special aptitude for language learning or the favourable context in which they are learning.

Intelligence

The term 'intelligence' has traditionally been used to refer to performance on certain kinds of tests. These tests are often associated with success in school, and a link between intelligence and second language learning has sometimes been reported. Over the years, many studies using a variety of intelligence ('IQ') tests and different methods of assessing language learning have found that IQ scores were a good means of predicting how successful a learner would be. Some recent studies have shown that these measures of intelligence may be more strongly related to certain kinds of second language abilities than to others. For example, in a study with French *immersion* students in Canada, it was found that, while intelligence was related to the development of French second language reading, grammar, and vocabulary, it was unrelated to oral productive skills (Genesee 1976). Similar findings have been reported in other studies. What this suggests is that, while intelligence, especially as measured by verbal IQ tests, may be a strong factor when it comes to learning which involves language analysis and rule learning, intelligence may play a less important role in classrooms where the instruction focuses more on communication and interaction.

It is important to keep in mind that 'intelligence' is complex and that individuals have many kinds of abilities and strengths, not all of which are measured by traditional IQ tests. In our experience, many students whose academic performance has been weak have experienced considerable success in second language learning.

Aptitude

There is evidence in the research literature that some individuals have an exceptional 'aptitude' for language learning. Lorraine Obler (1989) reports that a man, whom she calls CJ, has such a specialized ability. CJ is a native speaker of English who grew up in an English home. His first true experience with a second language came at the age of 15 when he began learning French in school. CJ also studied German, Spanish, and Latin while in high school. At age 20, he made a brief visit to Germany. CJ reported that just hearing German spoken for a short time was enough for him to 'recover' the German he had learned in school. Later, CJ worked in Morocco where he reported learning Moroccan Arabic through both formal instruction and informal immersion. He also spent some time in Spain and Italy, where he apparently 'picked up' both Spanish and Italian in a 'matter of weeks'. A remarkable talent indeed!

Learning quickly is the distinguishing feature of aptitude. The 'aptitude' factor has been investigated most intensively by researchers interested in developing tests which can be used to predict whether individuals will be efficient learners of a foreign language in a classroom setting. The most widely used aptitude tests are the Modern Language Aptitude Test (MLAT) and the Pimsleur Language Aptitude Battery (PLAB). Both tests are based on the view that aptitude is composed of different types of abilities:

(1) the ability to identify and memorize new sounds;
(2) the ability to understand the function of particular words in sentences;
(3) the ability to figure out grammatical rules from language samples; and
(4) memory for new words.

While earlier research revealed a substantial relationship between performance on the MLAT or PLAB and performance in foreign language learning, these studies were conducted at a time when second language teaching was based on *grammar translation* or *audiolingual* methods. With the adoption of a more communicative approach to teaching, many teachers and researchers came to see aptitude as irrelevant to the process of language acquisition. Unfortunately, this means that relatively little research has actually explored whether having a skill such as the 'ability to identify and memorize new sounds' is advantageous when classroom instruction is meaning-oriented rather than focused on drills or metalinguistic explanations.

Successful language learners may not be strong in all of the components of aptitude. Some individuals may have strong memories but only average abilities in the other components of aptitude. Ideally, one could determine learners' profiles of strengths and weaknesses and use this information to place students in appropriate teaching programs. An example of how this can be done is described by Majorie Wesche (1981). In a Canadian language program for adult learners of French, students were placed in an instructional program which was compatible with their aptitude profile and information about their learning experiences. Students who were high on analytic ability, but average on memory, were assigned to teaching that focused on grammatical structures, while learners strong in memory but average on analytic skills were placed in a class where the teaching was organized around the functional use of the second language in specific situations. Wesche reported a high level of student and teacher satisfaction when students were matched with compatible teaching environments. In addition, some evidence indicated that matched students were able to attain significantly higher levels of achievement than those who were unmatched.

While few second language teaching contexts are able to offer such choices to their students, teachers may find that knowing the aptitude profile of their students will help them in selecting appropriate classroom activities for particular groups of students. Or, if they do not have such information, they may wish to ensure that their teaching activities are sufficiently varied to accommodate learners with different aptitude profiles.

Personality

A number of personality characteristics have been proposed as likely to affect second language learning, but it has not been easy to demonstrate their effects in empirical studies. As with other research investigating the effects of individual characteristics on second language learning, different studies measuring a similar personality trait produce different results. For example, it is often argued that an extroverted person is well suited to language learning. However, research does not always support this conclusion. Although some studies have found that success in language learning is correlated with learners' scores on characteristics often associated with extroversion such as assertiveness and adventurousness, others have found that many successful language learners do not get high scores on measures of extroversion.

Another aspect of personality which has been studied is inhibition. It has been suggested that inhibition discourages risk-taking which is necessary for progress in language learning. This is often considered to be a particular problem for adolescents, who are more self-conscious than younger learners. In a series of studies, Alexander Guiora and his colleagues found support for the claim that inhibition is a negative force, at least for second language pronunciation performance. One study involved an analysis of the effects of small doses of alcohol on pronunciation (Guiora *et al.* 1972). They found that subjects who received small doses of alcohol did better on pronunciation tests than those who did not drink any alcohol. While results such as these are interesting, as well as amusing, they are not completely convincing, since the experiments are far removed from the reality of the classroom situation. Furthermore, they may have more to do with performance than with learning. We may also note, in passing, that when larger doses of alcohol were administered, pronunciation rapidly deteriorated!

Several other personality characteristics such as self-esteem, empathy, dominance, talkativeness, and responsiveness have also been studied. However, in general, the available research does not show a clearly defined relationship between personality and second language acquisition. And, as indicated earlier, the major difficulty in investigating personality characteristics is that of identification and measurement. Another explanation which has been offered for the mixed findings of personality studies is that personality variables may be a major factor only in the acquisition of conversational skills, not in the acquisition of literacy skills. The confused picture of the research on personality factors may be due in part to the fact that comparisons are made between studies that measure communicative ability and studies that measure grammatical accuracy or metalinguistic knowledge. Personality variables seem to be consistently related to the former, but not to the latter.

Despite the contradictory results and the problems involved in carrying out research in the area of personality characteristics, many researchers believe that personality will be shown to have an important influence on success in language learning. This relationship is a complex one, however, in that it is probably not personality alone, but the way in which it combines with other factors, that contributes to second language learning.

Motivation and attitudes

There has been a great deal of research on the role of attitudes and motivation in second language learning. The overall findings show that positive attitudes and motivation are related to success in second language learning (Gardner 1985). Unfortunately, the research cannot indicate precisely *how* motivation is related to learning. As indicated above, we do not know whether it is the motivation that produces successful learning or successful learning that enhances motivation or whether both are affected by other factors. As noted by Peter Skehan (1989), the question is, are learners more highly motivated because they are successful, or are they successful because they are highly motivated?

Motivation in second language learning is a complex phenomenon which can be defined in terms of two factors: learners' communicative needs and their attitudes towards the second language community. If learners need to speak the second language in a wide range of social situations or to fulfil professional ambitions, they will perceive the communicative value of the second language and will therefore be motivated to acquire proficiency in it. Likewise, if learners have favourable attitudes towards the speakers of the language, they will desire more contact with them. Robert Gardner and Wallace Lambert (1972) coined the terms *integrative motivation* to refer to language learning for personal growth and cultural enrichment, and *instrumental motivation* for language learning for more immediate or practical goals. Research has shown that these types of motivation are related to success in second language learning.

On the other hand, we should keep in mind that an individual's identity is closely linked with the way he or she speaks. It follows that when speaking a new language one is adopting some of the identity markers of another cultural group. Depending on the learner's attitudes, learning a second language can be a source of enrichment or a source of resentment. If the speaker's only reason for learning the second language is external pressure, internal motivation may be minimal and general attitudes towards learning may be negative.

One factor which often affects motivation is the social dynamic or power relationship between the languages. That is, members of a minority group learning the language of a majority group may have different attitudes and motivation from those of majority group members learning a minority language. Even though it is impossible to predict the exact effect of such societal factors on second language learning, the fact that languages exist in social contexts cannot be overlooked when we seek to understand the variables which affect success in learning. Children as well as adults are sensitive to social dynamics and power relationships.

Motivation in the classroom setting

In a teacher's mind, motivated students are usually those who participate actively in class, express interest in the subject-matter, and study a great deal. Teachers can easily recognize characteristics such as these. They also have more opportunity to influence these characteristics than students' reasons for studying the second language or their attitudes toward the language and its speakers. If we can make our classrooms places where students enjoy coming because the content is interesting and relevant to their age and level of ability, where the learning goals are challenging yet manageable and clear, and where the atmosphere is supportive and non-threatening, we can make a positive contribution to students' motivation to learn.

Although little research has been done to investigate how pedagogy interacts with motivation in second language classrooms, considerable work has been done within the field of educational psychology. In a review of some of this work, Graham Crookes and Richard Schmidt (1991) point to several areas where educational research has reported increased levels of motivation for students in relation to pedagogical practices. Included among these are:

Motivating students into the lesson At the opening stages of lessons (and within transitions), it has been observed that remarks teachers make about forthcoming activities can lead to higher levels of interest on the part of the students.

Varying the activities, tasks, and materials Students are reassured by the existence of classroom routines which they can depend on. However, lessons which always consist of the same routines, patterns, and formats have been shown to lead to a decrease in attention and an increase in boredom. Varying the activities, tasks, and materials can help to avoid this and increase students' interest levels.

Using co-operative rather than competitive goals Co-operative learning activities are those in which students must work together in order to complete a task or solve a problem. These techniques have been found to increase the self-confidence of students, including weaker ones, because every participant in a co-operative task has an important role to play. Knowing that their team-mates are counting on them can increase students' motivation.

Clearly, cultural and age differences will determine the most appropriate way for teachers to motivate students. In some classrooms, students may thrive on competitive interaction, while in others, co-operative activities will be more successful.

Learner preferences

Learners have clear preferences for how they go about learning new material. The term 'learning style' has been used to describe an individual's natural, habitual, and preferred way of absorbing, processing, and retaining new information and skills (Reid 1995). We have all heard people say that they cannot learn something until they have seen it. Such learners would fall into the group called 'visual' learners. Other people, who may be called 'aural' learners, seem to need only to hear something once or twice before they know it. For others, who are referred to as 'kinaesthetic' learners, there is a need to add a physical action to the learning process. In contrast to these perceptually based learning styles, considerable research has focused on a cognitive learning style distinction between *field independent* and *field dependent* learners. This refers to whether an individual tends to separate details from the general background or to see things more holistically. Another category of learning styles is based on the individual's temperament or personality.

While recent years have seen the development of many learning style assessment instruments, very little research has examined the interaction between different learning styles and success in second language acquisition. At present, the only learning style that has been extensively investigated is the field independence/dependence distinction. The results from this research have shown that while field independence is related to some degree to performance on certain kinds of tasks, it is not a good predictor of performance on others.

Although there is a need for considerably more research on learning styles, when learners express a preference for seeing something written or for memorizing material which we feel should be learned in a less formal way, we should not assume that their ways of working are wrong. Instead, we should encourage them to use all means available to them as they work to learn another language. At a minimum, research on learning styles should make us sceptical of claims that a particular teaching method or textbook will suit the needs of all learners.

Learner beliefs

Second language learners are not always conscious of their individual learning styles, but virtually all learners, particularly older learners, have strong beliefs and opinions about how their instruction should be delivered. These beliefs are usually based on previous learning experiences and the assumption (right or wrong) that a particular type of instruction is the best way for them to learn. This is another area where little work has been done. However, the available research indicates that learner beliefs can be strong mediating factors in their experience in the classroom. For example, in a survey of international students learning ESL in a highly communicative program at an English-speaking university, Carlos Yorio (1986) found high levels of dissatisfaction among the students. The type of communicative instruction they received focused exclusively on meaning and spontaneous communication in group-work interaction. In their responses to a questionnaire, the majority of students expressed concerns about several aspects of their instruction, most notably, the absence of attention to language form, corrective feedback, or teacher-centred instruction. Although this study did not directly examine learners' progress in relation to their opinions about the instruction they received, several of them were convinced that their progress was negatively affected by an instructional approach which was not consistent with their beliefs about the best ways for them to learn.

Learners' preferences for learning, whether due to their learning style or to their beliefs about how languages are learned, will influence the kinds of strategies they choose in order to learn new material. Teachers can use this information to help learners expand their repertoire of learning strategies and thus develop greater flexibility in their way of approaching language learning.

Age of acquisition

We now turn to a learner characteristic of a different type: age. This characteristic is easier to define and measure than personality, aptitude, or motivation. Nevertheless, the relationship between a learner's age and his or her potential for success in second language acquisition is the subject of much lively debate.

It has been widely observed that children from immigrant families eventually speak the language of their new community with native-like fluency, but their parents rarely achieve such high levels of mastery of the spoken language. To be sure, there are cases where adult second language learners have distinguished themselves by their exceptional performance. For example, one often sees reference to Joseph Conrad, a native speaker of Polish who became a major writer in the English language. Many adult second language learners become capable of communicating very successfully in the language but, for most, differences of accent, word choice, or grammatical features distinguish them from native speakers and from second language speakers who began learning the language while they were very young.

One explanation for this difference is that, as in first language acquisition, there is a critical period for second language acquisition. The Critical Period Hypothesis suggests that there is a time in human development when the brain is predisposed for success in language learning. Developmental changes in the brain, it is argued, affect the nature of language acquisition. According to this view, language learning which occurs after the end of the critical period may not be based on the innate biological structures believed to contribute to first language acquisition or second language acquisition in early childhood. Rather, older learners depend on more general learning abilities – the same ones they might use to learn other kinds of skills or information. It is argued that these general learning abilities are not as successful for language learning as the more specific, innate capacities which are available to the young child. It is most often claimed that the critical period ends somewhere around puberty, but some researchers suggest it could be even earlier.

Of course, it is difficult to compare children and adults as second language learners. In addition to the possible biological differences suggested by the Critical Period Hypothesis, the conditions for language learning are often very different. Younger learners in informal language learning environments usually have more time to devote to learning language. They often have more opportunities to hear and use the language in environments where they do not experience strong pressure to speak fluently and accurately from the very beginning. Furthermore, their early imperfect efforts are often praised or, at least, accepted. On the other hand, older learners are often in situations which demand much more complex language and the expression of much more complicated ideas. Adults are often embarrassed by their lack of mastery of the language and they may develop a sense of inadequacy after experiences of frustration in trying to say exactly what they mean.

The Critical Period Hypothesis has been challenged in recent years from several different points of view. Some studies of the second language development of older and younger learners who are learning in similar circumstances have shown that, at least in the early stages of second language development, older learners are more efficient than younger learners. In educational research, it has been reported that learners who began learning a second language at the primary school level did not fare better in the long run than those who began in early adolescence. Furthermore, there are countless anecdotes about older learners (adolescents and adults) who have reached high levels of proficiency in a second language. Does this mean that there is no critical period for second language acquisition?

Critical Period Hypothesis: More than just accent?

Most studies of the relationship between age of acquisition and second language development have focused on learners' phonological (pronunciation) achievement. In general, these studies have concluded that older learners almost inevitably have a noticeable 'foreign accent'. But what of other linguistic features? Is syntax (word order, overall sentence structure) as dependent on age of acquisition as phonological development? What about morphology (for example, grammatical morphemes which mark such things as verb tense or the number and gender of nouns)? One study that attempted to answer these questions was done by Mark Patkowski (1980).

Mastery of the spoken language

Mark Patkowski studied the effect of age on the acquisition of features of a second language other than accent. He hypothesized that, even if accent were ignored, only those who had begun learning their second language before the age of 15 could ever achieve full, native-like mastery of that language. Patkowski examined the spoken English of 67 highly educated immigrants to the United States. They had started to learn English at various ages, but all had lived in the United States for more than five years. The spoken English of 15 native-born American English speakers from a similarly high level of education served as a sort of baseline of what the second language learners might be trying to attain as the target language. Inclusion of the native speakers also provided evidence concerning the validity of the research procedures.

A lengthy interview with each of the subjects in the study was tape recorded. Because Patkowski wanted to remove the possibility that the results would be affected by accent, he did not ask the raters to judge the tape-recorded interviews themselves. Instead, he transcribed five-minute samples from the interviews. These samples (from which any identifying or revealing information about immigration history had been removed) were rated by trained native-speaker judges. The judges were asked to place each speaker on a rating scale from 0, representing no knowledge of the language, to 5, representing a level of English expected from an educated native speaker.

The main question in Patkowski's research was: 'Will there be a difference between learners who began to learn English before puberty and those who began learning English later?' However, in the light of some of the issues discussed above, he also compared learners on the basis of other characteristics and experiences which some people have suggested might be as good as age in predicting or explaining a learner's eventual success in mastering a second language. For example, he looked at the relationship between eventual mastery and the total amount of time a speaker had been in the United States as well as the amount of formal ESL instruction each speaker had had.

The findings were quite dramatic. Thirty-two out of 33 subjects who had begun learning English before the age of 15 scored at the 4+ or the 5 level. The homogeneity of the pre-puberty learners seemed to suggest that, for this group, success in learning a second language was almost inevitable (see Figure 2.1). On the other hand, there was much more variety in the levels achieved by the post-puberty group. The majority of the post-puberty learners centred around the 3+ level, but there was a wide distribution of levels achieved. This variety made the performance of this group look more like the sort of performance range one would expect if one were measuring success in learning almost any kind of skill or knowledge.

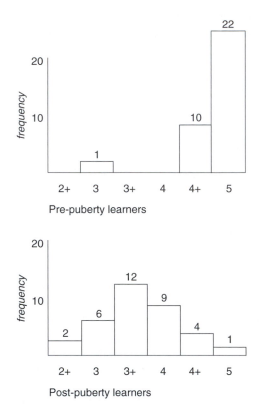

Figure 2.1 Bar charts showing the language levels of pre- and post-puberty learners of English
Source: Patkowski 1980

Patkowski's first question, 'Will there be a difference between learners who began to learn English before puberty and those who began learning English later?', was answered with a very resounding 'yes'. When he examined the other factors which might be thought to affect success in second language acquisition, the picture was much less clear. There was, naturally, some relationship between these other factors and learning success. However, it often turned out that age was so closely related to the other factors that it was not really possible to separate them completely. For example, length of residence in the United States sometimes seemed to be a fairly good predictor. However, while it was true that a person who had lived in the country for 15 years might speak better than one who had been there for only 10 years, it was often the case that the one with longer residence had also arrived at an earlier age. However, a person who had arrived in the United States at the age of 18 and had lived there for 20 years did not score significantly better than someone who had arrived at the age of 18 but had only lived there for 10 years. Similarly, amount of instruction, when separated from age, did not predict success to the extent that age of immigration did.

Thus, Patkowski found that age of acquisition is a very important factor in setting limits on the development of native-like mastery of a second language and that this limitation does not apply only to accent. These results gave added support to the Critical Period Hypothesis for second language acquisition.

Experience and research have shown that native-like mastery of the spoken language is difficult to attain by older learners. Surprisingly, even the ability to distinguish between grammatical and ungrammatical sentences in a second language appears to be affected by the age factor, as we will see in the next study by Johnson and Newport.

Intuitions of grammaticality

Jacqueline Johnson and Elissa Newport conducted a study of 46 Chinese and Korean speakers who had begun to learn English at different ages. All subjects were students or faculty at an American university and all had been in the United States for at least three years. The study also included 23 native speakers of English (Johnson and Newport 1989).

The participants in the study were given a judgement of grammaticality task which tested 12 rules of English morphology and syntax. They heard sentences on a tape and had to indicate whether or not each sentence was correct. Half of the sentences were grammatical, half were not.

When they scored the tests, Johnson and Newport found that age of arrival in the United States was a significant predictor of success on the test. When they grouped the learners in the same way as Patkowski, comparing those who began their intensive exposure to English between the ages of 3 and 15 with those who arrived in the United States between the ages of 17 and 39, once again they found that there was a strong relationship between an early start to language learning and better performance in the second language. Johnson and Newport noted that for those who began before the age of 15, and especially before the age of 10, there were few individual differences in second language ability. Those who began later did not have native-like language abilities and were more likely to differ greatly from one another in ultimate attainment.

This study, then, further supports the hypothesis that there is a critical period for attaining full native-like mastery of a second language. Nevertheless, there is some research which suggests that older learners may have an advantage, at least in the early stages of second language learning.

Is younger really better?

In 1978, Catherine Snow and Marian Hoefnagel-Höhle published an article based on a research project they had carried out in Holland. They had studied the progress of a group of English speakers who were learning Dutch as a second language. What made their research especially valuable was that the learners they were following included children as young as three years old as well as older children, adolescents, and adults. Furthermore, a large number of tasks was used, to measure different types of language use and language knowledge.

Pronunciation was tested by having learners pronounce 80 Dutch words twice: the first time immediately after hearing a native speaker say the word; the second time, a few minutes later, they were asked to say the word represented in a picture, without a model to imitate. Tape recordings of the learners were rated by a native speaker of Dutch on a six-point scale.

In an *auditory discrimination* test, learners saw pictures of four objects. In each group of four there were two whose names formed a minimal pair, that is, alike except for one sound (an example in English would be 'ship' and 'sheep'). Learners heard one of the words and were asked to indicate which picture was named by the word they heard.

Morphology was tested using a procedure like the 'wug test', which required learners to complete sentences by adding the correct grammatical markers to words which were supplied by the researchers. Again, to take an example from English, learners were asked to complete sentences such as 'Here is one boy. Now there are two of them. There are two _____.'

The sentence repetition task required learners to repeat 37 sentences of increasing length and grammatical complexity.

For *sentence translation*, learners were given 60 sentences to translate from English to Dutch. A point was given for each grammatical structure which was rendered into the correct Dutch equivalent.

In the *sentence judgement task*, learners were to judge which of two sentences was better. The same content was expressed in both sentences, but one sentence was grammatically correct while the other contained errors.

In the *Peabody Picture Vocabulary Test*, learners saw four pictures and heard one isolated word. Their task was to indicate which picture matched the word spoken by the tester.

For the *story comprehension task*, learners heard a story in Dutch and were then asked to retell the story in English or Dutch (according to their preference).

Finally, *the storytelling task* required learners to tell a story in Dutch, using a set of pictures they were given. Rate of delivery of speech mattered more than the expression of content or formal accuracy.

The learners were divided into several age groups, but for our discussion we will divide them into just three groups: children (aged 3 to 10), adolescents (12 to 15 years), and adults (18 to 60 years). The children and adolescents all attended Dutch schools. Some of the adults worked in Dutch work environments, but most of their Dutch colleagues spoke English well. Other adults were parents who did not work outside their homes and thus had somewhat less contact with Dutch than most of the other subjects.

The learners were tested three times, at four- to five-month intervals. They were first tested within six months of their arrival in Holland and within six weeks of their starting school or work in a Dutch-language environment.

Activity

Comparing child, adolescent, and adult language learners

Which group do you think did best on the first test (that is, who learned fastest)? Which group do you think was best by the end of the year? Do you think some groups would do better on certain tasks than others? For example, who do you think would do best on the pronunciation tasks, and who would do best on the tasks requiring more metalinguistic awareness? Compare your predictions with the results for the different tasks which are presented in Table 2.1. An 'X' indicates that the group was the best on the test at the beginning of the year (an indication of the rate of learning), and a 'Y' indicates the group that did best at the end of the year (an indication of eventual attainment).

In the Snow and Hoefnagel-Höhle study, the adolescents were by far the most successful learners. They were ahead of everyone on all but one of the tests (pronunciation) on the first test session. That is, within the first few months the adolescents had already made the most progress in learning Dutch. As the table indicates, it was the adults who were better than the children and adolescents on pronunciation in the first test session. Surprisingly, it was also the adults, not the children, whose scores were second best on the other tests at the first test session. In other words, adolescents and adults learned faster than children in the first few months of exposure to Dutch.

By the end of the year, the children were catching up, or had surpassed, the adults on several measures. Nevertheless, it was the adolescents who retained the highest levels of performance overall.

Table 2.1 Comparison of language learning at different ages

Task	Child	Adolescent	Adult
Pronunciation	Y	Y	X
Auditory discrimination		XY	
Morphology	XY		
Sentence repetition		XY	
Sentence translation	*	XY	
Sentence judgement	*	XY	
Peabody picture vocabulary test		XY	
Story comprehension	Y	X	
Storytelling	Y	X	

* These tests are too difficult for child learners.

Snow and Hoefnagel-Höhle concluded that their results provide evidence that there is no critical period for language acquisition. However, their results can be interpreted in some other ways as well:

1 Some of the tasks (for example, sentence judgement or translation) were too hard for young learners. Even in their native language, these tasks would have been unfamiliar and difficult. In fact, young Dutch native speakers to whom the second language learners were compared also had trouble with these tasks.

2 Adults and adolescents may learn faster in the early stages of second language development (especially if they are learning a language which is similar to their first language). Young children eventually catch up and even surpass them if their exposure to the language takes place in contexts where they are surrounded by the language on a daily basis.

3 Adults and adolescents can make considerable and rapid progress towards mastery of a second language in contexts where they can make use of the language on a daily basis in social, personal, professional, or academic interaction.

At what age should second language instruction begin?

Even people who know nothing about the critical period research are certain that, in school programs for second or foreign language teaching, 'younger is better'. However, both experience and research show that older learners can attain high, if not 'native', levels of proficiency in their second language. Furthermore, it is essential to think carefully about the goals of an instructional program and the context in which it occurs before we jump to conclusions about the necessity – or even the desirability – of the earliest possible start.

The role of the critical period in second language acquisition is still much debated. For every researcher who holds that there are maturational constraints on language acquisition, there is another who considers that the age factor cannot be separated from factors such as motivation, social identity, and the conditions for learning. They argue that older learners may well speak with an accent because they want to continue being identified with their first language cultural group, and adults rarely get access to the same quantity and quality of language input that children receive in play settings.

Many people conclude on the basis of studies such as those by Patkowski or Newport and Johnson that it is better to begin second language instruction as early as possible. Yet it is very important to bear in mind the context of these studies. They deal with the highest possible level of second language skills, the level at which a second language speaker is indistinguishable from a native speaker. But achieving a native-like mastery of the second language is not a goal for all second language learning, in all contexts.

When the objective of second language learning is native-like mastery of the target language, it is usually desirable for the learner to be completely surrounded by the language as early as possible. However, early intensive exposure to the second language may entail the loss or incomplete development of the child's first language.

When the goal is basic communicative ability for all students in a school setting, and when it is assumed that the child's native language will remain the primary language, it may be more efficient to begin second or *foreign language* teaching later. When learners receive only a few hours of instruction per week, learners who start later (for example, at age 10, 11, or 12) often catch up with those who began earlier. We have often seen second or foreign language programs which begin with very young learners but offer only minimal contact with the language. Even when students do make progress in these early-start programs, they sometimes find themselves placed in secondary school classes with students who have had no previous instruction. After years of classes, learners feel frustrated by the lack of progress, and their motivation to continue may be diminished. School programs should be based on realistic estimates of how long it takes to learn a second language. One or two hours a week will not produce very advanced second language speakers, no matter how young they were when they began.

Summary

The learner's age is one of the characteristics which determine the way in which an individual approaches second language learning. But the opportunities for learning (both inside and outside the classroom), the motivation to learn, and individual differences in aptitude for language learning are also important determining factors in both rate of learning and eventual success in learning.

In this chapter, we have looked at the ways in which intelligence, aptitude, personality and motivational characteristics, learner preferences, and age have been found to influence second language learning. We have learned that the study of individual learner variables is not easy and that the results of research are not entirely satisfactory. This is partly because of the lack of clear definitions and methods for the individual characteristics. It is also due to the fact that these learner characteristics are not independent of one another: learner variables interact in complex ways. So far, researchers know very little about the nature of these complex interactions. Thus, it remains difficult to make precise predictions about how a particular individual's characteristics influence his or her success as a language learner. Nonetheless, in a classroom, a sensitive teacher, who takes learners' individual personalities and learning styles into account, can create a learning environment in which virtually all learners can be successful in learning a second language.

References

Crookes, G. and Schmidt, R. (1991) 'Motivation: "Reopening the research agenda"', *Language Learning* 41/4: 469–512.

Gardner, R. (1985) *Social Psychology and Second Language Learning: The Role of Attitudes and Motivation*. London: Edward Arnold.

Gardner, R.C. and Lambert, W.E. (1972) *Attitudes and Motivation in Second-Language Learning*. Rowley, Mass.: Newbury House.

Genesee, F. (1976) 'The role of intelligence in second language learning', *Language Learning* 26/2: 267–80.

Guiora, A., Beit-Hallahami, B., Brannon, R., Dull, C. and Scovel, T. (1972) 'The effects of experimentally induced changes in ego states on pronunciation ability in a second language: An exploratory study', *Comprehensive Psychiatry* 13/5: 421–8.

Johnson, J. and Newport, E. (1989) 'Critical period effects in second language learning: The influence of maturational state on the acquisition of English as a second language.' *Cognitive Psychology* 21: 60–99.

Obler, L. (1989) 'Exceptional second language learners', in Gass, S., Madden, C., Preston, D. and Selinker, L. (eds.) *Variation in Second Language Acquisition, Vol. II: Psycholinguistic Issues*. Clevedon, UK/Philadelphia, Pa.: Multilingual Matters, pp. 141–9.

Patkowski, M. (1980) 'The sensitive period for the acquisition of syntax in a second language', *Language Learning* 30/2: 449–72.

Skehan, P. (1989) *Individual Differences in Second Language Learning*. London: Edward Arnold.

Reid, J. (ed.) (1995) Learning Styles in the ESL/EFL Classroom. New York: Heinle & Heinle.

Snow, C. and Hoefnagel-Höhle, M. (1978) 'The critical period for language acquisition: evidence from second language learning', *Child Development* 49/4: 1114–28.

Wesche, M.B. (1981) 'Language aptitude measures in streaming, matching students with methods, and diagnosis of learning problems', in Diller, K. (ed.) *Individual Differences and Universals in Language Learning Aptitude*. Rowley, Mass.: Newbury House. pp. 119–39.

Yorio, C. (1986) 'Consumerism in second language learning and teaching', *Canadian Modern Language Review* 42/3: 668–87.

Chapter 3

Rod Ellis

SECOND LANGUAGE ACQUISITION: RESEARCH AND LANGUAGE PEDAGOGY

Introduction

T HE DOMINANT METHODS FOR TEACHING second languages in the 1960s were the grammar-translation method and the audiolingual method. These methods rested on very different theories of language learning. The grammar-translation method rested on the belief that language learning was largely an intellectual process of studying and memorizing bilingual vocabulary lists and explicit grammar rules. The audiolinguist one drew on behaviourist theories of learning which emphasized habit formation through repeated practice and reinforcement. However, although there had been a number of studies investigating the effects of teaching on learning (Agard and Dunkel 1948) very little was known about how learners actually learnt a second language. L2 learning, at that time, had simply not been rigorously studied.

Starting from the 1960s, two approaches to addressing this lacuna have been evident. The first, a continuation of the approach adopted in earlier research, consists of attempts to investigate the relative effectiveness of different ways of teaching language in terms of the products of learning. Experimental studies by Scherer and Wertheimer (1964) and Smith (1970), for example, compared the learning outcomes of the grammar-translation and audiolingual methods. The results, however, were inconclusive. The studies failed to demonstrate the superiority of one method over the other.

The second approach involved the empirical study of how learners acquired an L2. In the first place, this took the form of studies of learners' errors (e.g. Duskova 1969) and case studies of individual learners learning a second language not in the classroom but through exposure to it in natural settings (e.g. Ravem 1968). These studies involved forms of research to which teachers could easily relate if only because the constructs on which they were based – errors and individual learners – were ones with which they were familiar. Also, these studies proved more rewarding than the global method comparisons, providing clear evidence that L2 learners, like children acquiring their first language (L1), accumulated knowledge of the language they were learning in a gradual and highly systematic fashion. Thus, whereas global method studies soon fell out of fashion,[1] studies of L2 learning took off; SLA was born.

Much of this early work in SLA was pedagogically motivated. That is, researchers conducted studies of L2 learning with the express intention of addressing pedagogic issues.

Many of these researchers were, in fact, originally teachers themselves.[2] The papers they wrote and published about their research typically concluded with a section in which the applications and implications for language pedagogy were spelled out. The studies of learner errors, for example, were used to address issues concerning teachers' attitude to errors, what errors should be corrected and how learner progress could be evaluated. The case studies of individual learners were used to support the radical proposal that teachers should desist from trying to 'intervene' directly in the process of L2 acquisition and, instead, develop approaches that would allow learners to learn 'naturally' (Newmark 1966 and Dulay and Burt 1973).

SLA has grown exponentially since its beginning in the 1960s. One of the outcomes of its growth and diversification is that much of the research is no longer directly concerned with pedagogic issues. According to a theory advanced by Chomsky, children are able to learn their mother tongue because they have innate knowledge of the possible form that the grammar of any language can take. Their task is to establish how the abstract principles that constitute this knowledge are manifest in the particular grammar they are learning. One of the main goals of UG-based SLA is to investigate whether and how these principles operate in L2 acquisition. This research, then, has been motivated by a desire to test a linguistic theory rather than to address the practical problems of teaching; it is oriented towards linguistics rather than language pedagogy (Gass 1989).[3]

Other sub-fields of SLA have continued the tradition of strong links with language pedagogy. Two in particular stand out. The first is the study of the role of input and interaction in L2 acquisition (e.g. Long 1981 and Pica 1992). The question of what constitutes optimal input for language learning is potentially of considerable relevance to teachers. Indeed, one way of characterizing teaching is in terms of providing learners with opportunities to hear and use the L2. The theories and findings which this research has generated have fed into classroom research, as, for example, in studies which have investigated the kinds of input and interaction afforded by different types of language tasks (see Crookes and Gass 1993) and by different modes of classroom participation (e.g. Pica and Doughty 1985). The second sub-field of SLA with clear links to language pedagogy is the study of form-focused instruction. SLA researchers have investigated whether teaching learners particular grammatical structures actually results in their being learnt (e.g. Spada and Lightbown 1993) and, also, what methodological options for teaching grammatical structures are most effective (e.g. VanPatten and Cadierno 1993).

However, irrespective of whether SLA addresses issues of likely relevance to teachers, there is the problem of a gap between SLA and language pedagogy. Ultimately, this gap is not so much a question of what issues SLA addresses, but of the manner in which SLA is conducted. The goal of SLA, like that of all academic disciplines, is to contribute to technical knowledge. This is reflected in the fact that SLA is, by and large, the preserve of university-based researchers, whose primary allegiance is to the conduct of well-designed studies and theory development in their field. This is as true of those researchers who are concerned with areas of potential relevance to language pedagogy (e.g. input/interaction and the study of form-focused instruction) as it is of researchers who see SLA as a means of contributing to other disciplines such as linguistics or cognitive psychology. In contrast, language pedagogy is concerned with practical knowledge. Textbook writers draw on their experience of the kinds of activities that work in classrooms and, of course, on their familiarity with other published materials. Teachers draw on their hands-on knowledge to perform the myriad of tasks that comprise teaching.

Given that a gap exists between SLA and language pedagogy and assuming that SLA is, at least, of some potential relevance, the question arises as to how the gap can be bridged.

My perspective is that of the outsider-insider, for an applied linguist is not a practitioner of language pedagogy (see Corder 1973) but rather someone who looks at language pedagogy from the vantage point of knowledge gleaned from technical sources. In my case, the source is SLA.

Technical and practical knowledge

I have suggested that two types of knowledge can be distinguished: technical knowledge and practical knowledge. This distinction is, in fact, common in the literature on professional knowledge (e.g. Calderhead 1988 and Eraut 1994). Technical knowledge is explicit; that is, it exists in a declarative form that has been codified. For these reasons it can be examined analytically and disputed. Technical knowledge is acquired deliberately either by reflecting deeply about the object of enquiry or by investigating it empirically. The latter involves the use of a well-defined set of procedures designed to ensure the validity and reliability of the knowledge obtained. Technical knowledge is generalized; that is, it takes the form of statements that can be applied to many particular cases. For this reason, it cannot easily be applied 'off the shelf' in the kind of rapid decision-making needed to deal with problems as they occur in day-to-day living.

Over the years, SLA has provided a substantial body of technical knowledge about how people learn a second language. This is reflected in the ever-growing set of technical terms used to label this knowledge: overgeneralization and transfer errors, order and sequence of acquisition, foreigner talk, input and intake, noticing, learning and communication strategies, the teachability hypothesis (see the glossary in Ellis 1994). This technical knowledge and the terms that label it constitute the goods that are carefully guarded by practitioners of SLA.

In contrast, practical knowledge is implicit and intuitive. We are generally not aware of what we practically know. For example, I know how to tie my shoe laces but I have little awareness about the sequence of actions I must perform to do this and could certainly not describe them very well. In contrast to technical knowledge, practical knowledge is acquired through actual experience in the context of performing actions by means of procedures that are only poorly understood. Similarly, practical knowledge is fully expressible only in practice, although it may be possible, through reflection, to codify aspects of it. The great advantage of practical knowledge is that it is proceduralized and thus can be drawn on rapidly and efficiently to handle particular cases.

Practising professionals (lawyers, doctors, and teachers) are primarily concerned with action involving particular cases and for this reason draw on practical rather than technical knowledge in the pursuit of their work. Freidson (1977, cited in Eraut 1994: 53) describes how medical practitioners operate:

> One whose work requires practical application to concrete cases simply cannot maintain the same frame of mind as the scholar or scientist: he cannot suspend action in the absence of incontrovertible evidence or be skeptical of himself, his experience, his work and its fruit. In emergencies he cannot wait for discoveries of the future. Dealing with individual cases, he cannot rely solely on probabilities or on general concepts or principles: he must also rely on his own senses. By the nature of his work the clinician must assume responsibility for practical action, and in so doing he must rely on his concrete, clinical experience.

Teachers, faced with the need to make countless decisions to accomplish a lesson, must also necessarily rely primarily on the practical knowledge they have acquired through teaching or, perhaps, through their experiences of having been taught. However, it may be possible for other practitioners of language pedagogy (e.g. syllabus designers, test constructors, and materials writers) to attempt some integration of technical and practical knowledge, as their activities are more amenable to careful planning and deliberate decision-making.

The crucial issue is the nature of the relationship between technical and practical knowledge. To what extent and in what ways can the technical knowledge derived from deep reflection and research influence actual practice? How can technical knowledge be utilized in the creation of the kind of practical knowledge with which teachers must necessarily work? Weiss (1977) provides a way of addressing these questions. He describes three models of research use.

Decision-driven model According to this model, research is aimed at informing a particular decision. Thus, the starting point for research is not a theory of L2 acquisition or a previous piece of research but rather some practical issue of direct concern to teachers. There is a considerable body of SLA research that appears to fit into this model. However, for this research to be truly decision-driven it needs to be formulated in a manner that teachers will readily understand. This is often not the case, however. Researchers prepare their articles for publication in journals and books that will be read by other researchers even if they address issues of direct concern to teachers. In fact, then, much of the SLA research that apparently belongs to the decision-driven model is more truly representative of Weiss' second model – the knowledge-driven model.

Knowledge-driven model Knowledge-driven research is intended to contribute to a specific discipline. Its primary goal is to advance the knowledge base of the discipline by constructing and testing explicit theories or by developing research methodology. As we have seen, one way of characterizing the development of SLA as a field of study is in terms of a gradual movement towards knowledge-driven research. Much of the earlier research was descriptive in nature (e.g. the studies of learner errors and the case studies of individual learners), motivated quite explicitly by a desire to inform pedagogy and published in a form that was relatively accessible to teachers. Later research, although certainly not all, has been designed to test specific SLA theories, has been increasingly experimental in nature and has been written about with other researchers as the intended audience. Researchers may feel their research is of relevance to language pedagogy but often see little need to consider its applications directly.

Interactive model Here technical knowledge and practical knowledge are inter-related in the performance of some professional activity. The way in which this is achieved is highly complex. Weiss (1977: 87–8) comments:

> the process is not of linear order from research to decision but a disorderly set of interconnections and back-and-forthness that defies neat diagrams. All kinds of people involved in an issue area pool their talents, beliefs, and understandings in an effort to make sense of a problem.

Not surprisingly, then, the interactive model is problematic. As Eraut (1994) points out there are various factors that constrain the professional's ability to make use of the knowledge created through research, particularly in a field such as teaching. Few resources are available for effecting an interaction. Funding for research, for example, is typically awarded to university-based researchers concerned with knowledge-creation rather than to teams of researchers and teachers concerned with solving practical teaching problems through a pooling of expertise. Teachers rarely have the time to familiarize themselves with published research. Also, the very nature of technical and practical knowledge makes it difficult to inter-relate. Considerable effort and probably prolonged interaction are needed to combine the analytical skills of the researcher with the holistic and highly contextualized skills of the teacher.

Similar problems exist regarding the utilization of practical knowledge in the creation of technical knowledge. Practical knowledge is largely tacit and difficult to codify. Conse-quently, its reliability and validity cannot be easily assessed. Given the requirement that technical knowledge is demonstrably reliable and valid, researchers generally avoid refer-ence to practical knowledge. However, as Eraut (1994) notes, researchers' own practical experiences may often influence their work in subtle and unstated ways. To a certain extent, then, the interaction model may work implicitly.

This discussion of technical and practical knowledge helps us to understand why SLA, as it has evolved since its inception, cannot automatically be assumed to be of use in language pedagogy and, particularly, to classroom teachers. The gap between SLA and language pedagogy is a product of both the types of knowledge these two fields typically employ and the lack of opportunity to bridge the gap.

The SLA researchers' perspective

The nature of the relationship between SLA and language pedagogy has attracted the attention of a number of researchers over the years. A useful starting point in our exploration of how SLA might inform pedagogy is to take a look at what these SLA researchers have had to say.

The application of SLA can take place in two rather different ways. As Corder (1977) has pointed out, the starting point can be the research itself with the applied linguist cast in the role of innovator or initiator, advancing pedagogical proposals on the basis of his/her knowledge of SLA. This corresponds to Weiss's knowledge-driven model of research use. Alternatively, the starting point can be unsolved practical problems in language pedagogy, in which case the SLA researcher takes on the role of a consultant who is approached by practitioners for possible solutions. This corresponds to Weiss's decision-driven model of research use. We find both types of application discussed in the literature but it is probably the first that is paramount, reflecting, perhaps, the dominance of the researcher's perspective over that of the teacher's.

In general, SLA researchers with a strong interest in pedagogy have been cautious about applying SLA. Early articles by Tarone et al. (1976) and Hatch (1978) emphasized the need to be careful. Hatch lamented that researchers have often been over-ready to make applications to pedagogy, pointing out '. . . our field must be known for the incredible leaps of logic we make in applying our research findings to classroom teaching'. Tarone et al. (1976) advanced a number of reasons why SLA could not serve as an adequate basis for advising teachers. Among other points, they argued that the research to date was too limited in scope, that the methodology for collecting and analysing data was unproven and that too few studies had been replicated. They also noted that the practices of research and teaching were very different in nature. Whereas researchers adopted a slow, bit-by-bit approach, teachers had immediate needs to meet. In the previous section, we considered this important difference in terms of the distinction between technical and practical knowledge.

The concerns voiced by Tarone *et al.* (1976) and Hatch (1978) are very real ones. They reflect the understandable reticence of researchers to plunge in before they are certain of their results. This uncertainty about the quality of the research being produced may have been one of the reasons why some researchers stopped adding sections on the applications of their research to their published articles.[4] In retrospect, however, I am not so sure that researchers need to be so cautious. As Corder (1980) noted, teachers cannot wait until researchers are completely satisfied that their results are robust and generalizable. Should teachers not be permitted to base their pedagogical decisions on the best information available even if this is still inadequate in the eyes of researchers? More importantly, the apply-with-caution approach makes certain assumptions about the relationship between research/theory and practice which are themselves challengeable. It appears to view the practitioner as a consumer of research. From such a stance, of course, it is essential to make sure that the product being marketed is a sound one. But, as we will see later, this rather positivist view of the relationship between research and practice[5] is not acceptable to many educators and may not serve as the most appropriate model for discussing how SLA can aid teaching.

There are alternatives to the instrumental view of SLA implicit in the early articles by Tarone *et al.* (1976) and Hatch (1978). One is that SLA should not so much be used to tell practitioners what to do, as to inform their understanding of how L2 acquisition takes place so that they will know better what it is possible to achieve in a classroom. This is the position adopted by Lightbown (1985). She argues that SLA has nothing to tell teachers about what to teach but serves as a guide about how to teach. Lightbown recognizes that teachers will need to rely primarily on their own practical experience of which approaches work and which do not but she suggests that familiarity with the results of SLA research will help teachers make up their minds. For Lightbown, then, the value of SLA lies not in identifying innovative techniques or new teaching approaches but rather in shaping expectancies and in lending support to particular approaches, such as communicative language teaching. From this perspective, however, SLA is of limited relevance to language pedagogy, for as Lightbown (*ibid.*: 182) comments:

> Second-language acquisition research does not tell teachers *what* to teach, and what it says about *how* to teach they have already figured out.

If this is all SLA can do for teachers, one might well ask whether it is worth their while making the effort to become familiar with it.

Not all researchers/theorists have felt the need to play down the contribution that SLA can make to language pedagogy. Some have looked for ways of bridging the gap between research and classroom practice. One way is to construct a theory of L2 acquisition that is compatible with the available research but which also is tuned to the needs of teachers. This is what Krashen has tried to do. Krashen (1983) argues that it is not the research itself that should be used to address pedagogical issues but rather the theory derived from the research. Even applied SLA research should be related to practice via theory. Theory is important because it provides teachers with 'an underlying rationale for methodology in general' (Krashen 1983: 261) and thus helps them to adapt to different situations and constitutes a basis for evaluating new pedagogical ideas. Krashen argues that the theory must be a theory of L2 acquisition as opposed to a linguistic theory or a theory of general learning. Indeed, he claims that teachers have grown suspicious of 'theory' because of the failure of linguistic and psychological theories to solve pedagogic problems. He believes that SLA theory, because it explains how learners actually learn a second language, is of more direct relevance. Krashen also argues that theory must be empirically grounded (i.e. based on actual L2 research) rather than on armchair speculation.

Much of Krashen's published work has been concerned with the applications of his own forcefully promoted theory (i.e. the Monitor Model and, more recently, the Input Hypothesis), as in Krashen and Terrell (1983). It should be noted, however, that contrary to some criticisms levelled at him (see Widdowson 1990: 34) Krashen has *never* sought to preclude teachers exploring pragmatic options derived from ideas outside his theoretical framework. Krashen argues in favour of the utilization of theory in general, not just *his* theory. Also, he explicitly recognizes that teachers will and should bring ideas and intuitions based on their own practical experience to decision making. As Krashen (1983: 261) says 'teaching remains an art as well as a science'.

There are obvious attractions of theory-based as opposed to research-based applications. A theory affords a composite view of L2 acquisition. Proposals based on it cannot be dismissed by pointing out the limitations of specific research studies. A theory is general in nature and, thus, any proposals derived from it are potentially valid in a variety of teaching contexts. In contrast, individual research studies are necessarily located in specific contexts, making it difficult to advance proposals of general applicability. Also, proposals based on a theory are likely to possess a coherence lacking in the piecemeal application of individual studies. One of the attractions of Krashen's theory is that it offers teachers an overarching view of what and how to teach.

However, there are obvious dangers of theory-based applications. As Beretta (1991) and Long (1993) have pointed out, SLA theories do not tend to go away, even when they are in obvious opposition to each other. In a thoughtful discussion of why this is so, Schumann (1993) points out that it is extremely difficult to falsify a theory. One reason is that whereas hypotheses are typically tested in isolation they exist in 'a network of auxiliary assumptions' (*ibid.*: 259) with the result that even if a particular hypothesis is not supported it cannot be dismissed because it is impossible to tell exactly where the problem lies. Thus, theorists usually experience little difficulty in immunizing their theories against counter findings; they simply adjust an underlying assumption or reconceive the construct on which the hypothesis is based. Krashen has proven adept at maintaining his own theory despite concerted criticism from prominent researchers and applied linguists. But if theories cannot be falsified and, therefore, are able to survive more or less indefinitely how, then, can teachers evaluate the legitimacy of proposals based on them? In the case of Krashen, for example, how can teachers evaluate his principal proposal, namely that teachers should be primarily concerned with providing plentiful comprehensible input so that acquisition (i.e. subconscious language learning) can take place? In short, applications based on an SLA theory are risky because they have to be taken on faith. This might not matter so much if theory were used to advance suggestions for teachers to test out in their own practice but, more often than not, theory-derived applications are vested with an authority that works against such pedagogic experimentation. For example, Krashen's claim that learning (i.e. the conscious study of linguistic forms) has a relatively minor role to play in L2 acquisition works against teachers' investigating, in the context of their own teaching, how form-focused instruction can complement and perhaps enhance acquisition.

There is a more serious objection to Krashen's proposal that SLA theory should guide language pedagogy – one that has already been hinted at in the discussion of technical knowledge and practical knowledge. SLA theories, such as Krashen's, are typically the product of the contemplative approach to enquiry that characterizes much modern scientific thinking (see Lantolf 1995). Such theories have been developed through formulating and systematically testing hypotheses based on them. The result is 'technical knowledge'. However, such knowledge, because of the very form in which it is couched, is not readily accessible to practitioners in their day-to-day work, although Krashen has done as good a job as any to make it so. For a theory to be of maximum use to teachers it has to take the form of praxis – a theory of action. This is a point that will be taken up later in this chapter.

Another way of bridging the gap between SLA and language pedagogy is through what Johnston (1987) has called 'a technology of teaching'. Johnston draws an analogy between engineering and teaching. He argues that whereas engineering has successfully defined its own problem space as independent from that of supporting disciplines, such as physics, language teaching has not yet done so. This is because it lacks a sound body of practical knowledge developed through experimentation in the classroom itself. Johnston distinguishes pure research (i.e. the research carried out by SLA researchers such as himself) and classroom research. He recognizes that pure research can only provide guidelines and suggestions, which have to be put to the test. For Johnston, then, the gap between SLA and language pedagogy needs to be filled by conducting experimental studies in actual classrooms. He is optimistic that such research will ensure that 'the language teaching of 10 to 15 years hence will be rather different from the hit and miss methods of today' (ibid.: 38).

There is a logical objection to Johnston's position. If the kind of classroom research Johnston has in mind is controlled experimentation (where the realities of the classroom have to be manipulated to control for unwanted variables that may influence the effect of a given treatment), there may not, in fact, be any difference between pure and classroom research. In this respect, Wright's (1992) distinction between research in classrooms and research on classrooms is relevant. To develop the technology of teaching that Johnston considers necessary it is the latter that is required, for as Wright (ibid.: 192) argues 'an understanding of the L2 classroom might best proceed . . . from its investigation as a culture in its own right'. However, controlled experimentation may not be the best way to carry out research on classrooms.

The case for basing pedagogical decisions on L2 classroom research has been advanced by a number of other researchers and language educators. Jarvis (1983: 238), for example, argues that 'Our knowledge must come from our own research' and laments the fact that it has typically not done so. Long (1983b) reports the results of a survey of methods courses in Masters programmes in TESOL in the United States and Canada. Only 18% included reference to classroom-centred research (CCR). Long (ibid.: 284) suggests that this may reflect the practical orientation of methods courses but he argues that classroom-centred research is 'eminently practical' because it is 'concerned with what actually goes on in the classrooms, as opposed to what is supposed to go on', a point that is only true, of course, if the researcher accepts the realities of classroom behaviour and makes no attempt to manipu-late it for research purposes. Long gives three reasons why classroom-centred research should be included in methods courses: it has already produced some practical information; teachers can use the research tools that have been employed to investigate their own classrooms; classroom-centred research will help teachers become sceptical about relying on single teaching methods. In a subsequent paper, Long (1990) argues the need for a common body of knowledge which can be transmitted to teachers in much the same way as a common body of knowledge about medicine is conveyed to doctors. He suggests that although L2 classroom research is limited in a number of respects it constitutes 'a growing body of tangible evidence about language teaching' (ibid.: 116). For Long, this constitutes hard evidence which is better than the prejudices and suppositions which he believes characterize most pedagogical decision-making. Like Johnston, then, Long envisages class-room research as the means by which researchers can most effectively influence language pedagogy.

There are serious reasons for disputing the optimism that both Johnston, Long, and others share regarding the effect such research will have on language pedagogy. As Stenhouse

(1979: 71–7) has so amusingly demonstrated in his fictional account of how a teacher grapples with the attempt to apply the results of research concerning strategies for teaching about race relations, classroom research is unlikely to produce clear answers to teachers' questions because it only demonstrates what works by and large or for the most part whereas teachers are concerned with what will work in their own particular teaching contexts. Stenhouse (1975: 25) has stated the essential problem more formally elsewhere:

> The crucial point is that the proposal (from research) is not to be regarded as an unqualified recommendation but rather as a provisional specification claiming no more than to be worth putting to the test of practice. Such proposals claim to be intelligent rather than correct.

In other words, classroom research, although potentially closer to the realities teachers have to grapple with than non-classroom research, is still remote from actual practice. The gap between SLA and practice may be narrowed somewhat but it cannot be filled by classroom research, even when this is research on, rather than just in, classrooms.

So far we have considered what various SLA researchers have had to say regarding the application of research/theory to language pedagogy. The view of change implicit in all of the positions we have examined is a top-down one. Applied linguists draw on information from SLA to initiate – tentatively or confidently – various pedagogic proposals. The proposals may be based on pure research, on a theory of L2 acquisition, or on classroom-centred research but in each case the presumed originator of the proposal is the SLA researcher/theorist. It is time now to briefly consider an alternative way in which SLA can be used to inform language pedagogy.

When the researcher functions as a consultant he or she functions as a resource helping teachers solve the practical problems they have identified. A good example of this approach can be found in Pica (1994). Pica's starting point is not SLA itself but rather the questions that teachers have asked her 'both in the privacy of their classrooms and in the more public domain of professional meetings' (ibid.: 50). Pica offers a list of ten questions dealing with such matters the relative importance of comprehension and production, the role of explicit grammar instruction, and the utility of drill and practice.[6] Pica provides answers to these questions based on her understanding of the SLA research literature.

The obvious advantage of such an approach to applying SLA is that the information provided is more likely to be heeded by teachers because it addresses issues they have identified as important. Bahns (1990: 115) goes so far as to claim:

> The initiative for applying research results of any kind to any field of practice whatsoever should come from the practitioners themselves.

Such a statement ignores, however, some obvious limitations in this insider approach. Teachers can only ask questions based on their own experience. They cannot ask questions about issues they have no knowledge of. If Bahns's dictum were to be religiously adhered to many of the developments in language pedagogy over the last twenty years would probably not have taken place. For example, teachers would have been unlikely to ask 'What is the best way to organize a syllabus – in terms of structures, notions, or tasks?' because they would not have known what 'notions' or 'tasks' (in its technical sense) were. These concepts have been derived from the work of linguists or applied linguists, but have not arisen spontaneously through the practice of teaching. Thus, although much can be said in favour of an insider approach, there is also a case for the outsider application of SLA.

A number of more recent discussions of the relationship between SLA and language pedagogy have grappled with this issue. Gass (1995: 16), for example, suggests that one way round the insider/outsider problem is for researchers and teachers to work 'in tandem to determine how SLA findings can be evaluated and be made applicable to a classroom situation, and to determine which SLA findings to use'. The kind of collaborative endeavour Gass has in mind is one where researchers and teachers seek to understand each other's goals and needs and she suggests a number of areas where the concerns of the two groups coincide (e.g. the issue of correction). However, true collaboration involves not just agreement about what to investigate but also how. Gass partly addresses this by quoting from Schachter (1993: 181):

> We need to create a mindset in which both teachers and researchers view classrooms as laboratories where theory and practice can interact to make both better practice and better theory.

The problem here is that whereas researchers may feel comfortable in viewing classrooms as laboratories, teachers may not. It is also mistaken to imply – as Schachter seems to do – that researchers engage in theory and teachers in practice. SLA and language pedagogy are both characterized by theory and practice, albeit of different kinds. The issue of how researchers and teachers can effectively collaborate is complex. It is one that has been addressed in some depth in the education literature. As Gass acknowledges, however, SLA researchers have paid scant attention to this literature.

From this initial exploration of what it means to apply SLA research it is clear that there is no easy answer. For some, the immaturity of SLA as a field of enquiry precludes applications. For others, SLA can only hope to shape teachers' expectations of what is possible in the classroom. Others have developed specific proposals on the basis of general theories of L2 acquisition. Others have suggested that the gap between SLA and teaching can be filled by conducting research in and on L2 classrooms. Finally, some researchers have argued for an approach where they act as consultants addressing issues raised by teachers or where they participate in collaborative research with teachers.[7] As we have seen, each of these approaches has something in its favour but none of them is entirely successful in closing the gap between SLA research and language pedagogy. In the next section we consider the views of a number of educators on how research can be made relevant to teachers.

Educational perspectives

Earlier we noted that the once close connection which SLA researchers initially envisaged between SLA and language pedagogy has not continued. To understand the gulf that frequently divides the theory and practice of research on the one hand, and the theory and practice of teaching on the other, we need to examine the guiding principles and assumptions of each. We need to consider the culture of research and the culture of teaching.

Let us begin with research. It is customary to distinguish two broad traditions in empirical enquiry – the confirmatory and the interpretative. The confirmatory tradition is interventionist. It is manifest in carefully designed experiments, such as the agricultural experiments of R. A. Fischer (1935) in the United States, which were designed to discover which treatment produced the best crop yields. The key characteristics of the confirmatory tradition are the use of random sampling (i.e. subjects are randomly distributed into an experimental and a control group) and the careful control of extraneous variables (i.e. those variables that might confound the study of the particular variable under investigation). The interpretative tradition is reflected in Weber's (1961) famous definition of sociology: 'Sociology . . . is a science which attempts the interpretative understanding of social action.' It is manifest in non-interventionist studies that seek to develop an understanding of the social rules that underlie a particular activity by examining the meaning that the social actors involved in the activity themselves put on it. As Van Lier (1990) points out, where confirmatory research seeks causes, interpretative research looks for reasons.

Both of these traditions can be found in SLA. As we have already noted, SLA began with case studies of learners (e.g. Ravem 1968). These studies focused on individual learners, collecting samples of spoken language by observing the learners in naturally occurring environments.[8] These case studies investigated naturalistic learning by examining the language produced by learners, the processes and strategies they used and how individual and social factors affected their progress. One of the outcomes of this tradition of research in SLA was descriptive information about the order in which learners acquired different grammatical structures and the sequence of stages they followed in mastering particular structures such as negatives, interrogatives, and relative clauses. Another branch of the interpretative tradition of research in SLA can be found in ethnographic studies of L2 classrooms (e.g. Van Lier 1988, Markee 1994a). These studies have sought to describe the kinds of discourse in which classroom learners engage and how these influence their L2 development.

The confirmatory tradition is evident in much of the work based on Universal Grammar (e.g. Flynn and Martohardjono 1995), where data elicited by means of such instruments as grammaticality judgement tests have been used to examine whether learners with different first languages manifest access to particular principles of language. It is also evident in studies of form-focused instruction (e.g. Spada and Lightbown 1993, VanPatten and Cadierno 1993).

Where applications to teaching are concerned, the confirmatory tradition frequently entails a particular view of what it means for a teacher to be professionally competent. According to this view, education is an applied science. Researchers do research, discovering the best ways to achieve predetermined educational goals. These are then passed on to teachers, who function as technicians carrying out the researchers' prescriptions. This presupposes a means-to-end view of education (Tyler 1949), where the curriculum is viewed as a delivery system, with research providing information about the most effective means for delivering the curriculum. Research, therefore, is concerned with means rather than ends, which are taken as given. This view of the relationship between research and education is evident in the opinions of Johnston (1987) and, in part, of Long (1983a, 1990) discussed in the previous section.

There are many problems with the applied science view of the relationship between research and practice. As we have already noted, the information provided by even the best designed experimental study may not be applicable to other teaching contexts. Also, it is doubtful whether the information obtained from experimental research has the objective status often claimed for it, as subjective and social factors play a crucial role in the production of any kind of knowledge, including that obtained experimentally (see Kuhn 1970). As Carr and Kemmis (1986) point out, the separation of ends (or values) and means is not really possible. Also, ends should not be taken as given but should themselves be the subject of critical scrutiny, as protagonists of critical pedagogy have argued (see Pennycook 1989). A good example of the need to consider ends as well as means can be found in investigations of teachers' questions. A number of L2 studies have investigated the effect of display and referential questions on learner output (e.g. Brock 1986). In these studies it is assumed that teachers will and should ask questions and the only issue is what kind of questions work best for language learning. One might legitimately challenge this assumption however. It has been suggested that classroom L2 acquisition is likely to proceed most smoothly if learners enjoy the same participant rights as their teacher (Pica 1987). However, teachers' questions, in any form, imply an asymmetrical power structure in the classroom and, therefore, may not be the most effective way of creating conditions conducive to language learning. A more serious problem is that the applied science view of teaching allocates particular roles to researchers and to teachers, which are necessarily social and value laden in nature. Researchers are the producers of knowledge while teachers are consumers; researchers are experts whereas teachers are mere technicians. The applied science view, therefore, implies a hierarchical relationship between researchers and teachers (hence the term 'top-down'), mirroring the kind of division which exists between teachers and students in traditional classrooms and, arguably, reinforcing it.

At first glance, the interpretative tradition of research avoids many of these problems. By adhering to what van Lier (1990) calls the emic principle (i.e. try to understand how a social context works through the perspectives of the participants) and the holistic principle (i.e. try to understand something in terms of its natural surroundings), it may make application to different contexts less problematic, if only because teachers will be able to see clearly whether their own teaching contexts are the same as, or different from, the contexts studied in the research. Also interpretative research does not claim to provide objective knowledge. Indeed, it makes a virtue of seeking out subjective knowledge.[9] Thus, even though interpretative research may have theory construction as its ultimate goal, it can be considered practical in nature. Carr and Kemmis (1986) explain how interpretative accounts facilitate dialogue between interested parties (i.e. researchers and teachers). They can lead to changes in the way actors comprehend themselves and their situations; 'practices are understood by changing the ways in which they are understood' (ibid.: 91). In fact, interpretative research achieves validity when it passes the test of participant confirmation. Thus, the beliefs, values, and perceptions of teachers are not ignored (or controlled) as in educational research in the confirmatory tradition, but are given a constitutive place in the research. The traffic of ideas between researcher and teacher is, potentially at least, two way.

Again, though, there are problems. One is that because interpretative research insists on explanations that are consistent with the participants' own perceptions it runs the risk of accepting accounts that are illusory. Obviously, actors can be mistaken, so their interpretations of events need to be examined critically. In other words, adherence to the emic principle can lead to faulty understandings. The holistic principle is also problematic. It can result in information that is too rich, so detailed that the wood cannot be seen for the trees. The major problem, however, as with confirmatory research, lies in the relationship between the researcher and the teacher. For, although the gap has been narrowed, they still inhabit different worlds. Carr and Kemmis (1986: 99) put it this way:

> Despite their differences . . . both the 'interpretative' and the positivist [i.e. confirmatory] approach convey a similar understanding of educational researchers and of the relationship to the research act. In both approaches, the researcher stands outside the researched situation adopting a disinterested stance in which any explicit concern with critically evaluating and changing the educational realities being analysed is rejected.

The truth of this is evident in what is perhaps the best piece of interpretative research in SLA to date – van Lier's (1988) study of aspects of classroom discourse (i.e. turn-taking, topic and activity, and repair work). Although van Lier offers a few comments on how teachers might profitably engage in interpretative research themselves (*ibid.*: 230 onwards), the bulk of his book is written from the standpoint of the researcher functioning as a gatherer of knowledge and concerned with truth rather than from the standpoint of the practitioner concerned with action.

Researchers, then, follow agendas that are set by the requirements of the research traditions to which they adhere. They also have their own social agendas. As members of university departments, researchers are expected to be producers of research and are rewarded according to the quantity and quality of the research they produce. To publish they must satisfy their peers (i.e. other researchers), who function as reviewers for the journals in which they seek to be published. Their research must demonstrate that it meets established criteria of reliability and validity (i.e. that it is well designed and that the results warrant the conclusions made). Researchers are not obliged to make their research accessible to teachers or to demonstrate that it is relevant to them. Still less are they required to work with teachers to find ways in which research can be converted into action. Indeed, it may well be that in the departments where the researchers work practical research receives less recognition than pure research.

As we have seen, teachers have very different agendas and operate from a different knowledge base. Whereas researchers are concerned in establishing the truth, teachers are interested in finding out what works. Teachers select tasks that they believe will contribute to their students' learning but they are rarely able to investigate whether their predictions are borne out. They determine the success of the tasks in other ways (e.g. by impressionistically evaluating whether the task stimulates active participation by the learners). Teachers work from practical knowledge. They use their experience of teaching (and of learning) in classrooms to develop a body of knowledge as habit and custom, as skill knowledge (e.g. how to deal with a student who dominates classroom discussion), as common-sense knowledge about practice, as contextual knowledge (i.e. regarding the particular class they are teaching) and, over time, as a set of beliefs about how learners learn an L2. Polanyi (1958) refers to this kind of knowledge as personal knowledge. As Schön (1983) has observed, and as we noted earlier, much of this knowledge is only evident in use (i.e. it is revealed in actual teaching but the teacher cannot articulate it) although some of it may become espoused through reflection (i.e. the teacher can provide an explicit account of it).

Given these differences in goals and in what counts as knowledge, the gap between research and pedagogy and the gulf between researchers and teachers is not surprising. Zahorik (1986), cited in Freeman and Richards (1993), has identified a number of different ways in which teaching can be conceptualized. Scientifically based conceptions emphasize the development of models of effective classroom practice based on the results of empirical research. This is the kind of conception we are likely to find in researchers. Alternative conceptions are values-based (i.e. effective practice is that which takes into account the identity and individuality of learners) and art–craft (i.e. effective practice is built up gradually through experience and reflection). It is these conceptions that we are more likely to find in teachers. As a consequence, some teachers may feel that research is of little value to them, not just because it is difficult to access (a familiar complaint), but because it does not conform with their own ideas of what teaching is and, therefore, does not address their concerns. Other teachers, however, may feel that their own conceptions of teaching lack value and status in comparison to the scientifically-based conceptions of researchers. As Bolitho (1991: 25) notes, 'teachers often take up extreme positions, often deferring blindly to theory or rejecting it out of hand as irrelevant to classroom issues'. In either case, the outcome is unsatisfactory'.

What then can be done about all this? Clearly, something is needed to bring the worlds of the researcher/theorist and the teacher closer together. One way might be to find ways of familiarizing teachers with the technical knowledge obtained from research and, also, of making it meaningful to them. Another way is by encouraging teachers to become researchers in their own right. We will briefly examine both of these.

An assumption of many educators, is that both pre-service and in-service teacher education courses should provide students with an understanding of a range of academic issues considered relevant to their work as teachers. Teacher preparation and further education programmes, therefore, typically offer courses designed to familiarize teachers with these basic elements. In the case of programmes for L2 teaching there is a broad consensus regarding what these elements consist of: what language is; how it is used in speech and writing; how language reflects the workings of different social groups; how language curricula can be developed, taught, and evaluated and how language is learnt.[10] One of the grounds for offering this kind of education is to develop an awareness in teachers that there is no one 'best' way to teach a language, but rather options from which teachers must select in accordance with the particular contexts in which they work.

The need for a foundation in these basic elements has been strongly argued by Stern (1983). In the introduction to his book *Fundamental Concepts in Language Teaching*, Stern argues the need for guides to help the student teacher 'pick his way through the mass of accumulated information, opinion, and conflicting advice; to make sense of the vast literature, and to distinguish between solid truth and ephemeral fads or plain misinformation' (*ibid.*: 1–2). He sees such guides as not telling teachers what to think but rather helping them to sharpen their own judgements. He works on the common-sense premise that judgements that are informed, based on sound theoretical foundations, will produce better results than those that are not. Stern's own guide is comprehensive, involving sections dealing with historical perspectives, concepts of language, concepts of society, concepts of language learning and concepts of language teaching. Other guides have focused on specific areas, including SLA (e.g. Larsen-Freeman and Long 1991, Lightbown and Spada 1993, Ellis 1994).

The aim of these guides is to make technical knowledge available to teachers in a digestible form. There is still the question of how teachers are to integrate this knowledge into their own practice. As Hirst (1966: 40) has pointed out:

> To try to understand the nature and pattern of some practical discourse in terms of the nature and patterns of some purely theoretical discourse can only result in its being radically misconceived.

Often enough, teachers in training, particularly pre-service, complain about the lack of relevance of the foundation courses they have taken to the actual task of teaching (see for example Schuyler and Sitterley 1995). This has led to the suggestion that teachers should become more than consumers of theories and research; they should become researchers and theorists in their own right.

The case for teachers conducting research in their own classrooms is now well established in education, largely as a product of the pioneering work of such educators as Stenhouse (1975), Elliott and Ebutt (1985) and Kemmis and McTaggert (1981) among others. More recently, educators of language teachers (e.g. Nunan 1990 and Crookes 1993) have also argued the need for teachers to research their own classrooms. One form of teacher research that is commonly advocated is action research.

Action research originates in the work of Kurt Lewin in the United States (see Adelman 1993 for a review of Lewin's work and its contribution). Lewin was concerned with decision-making centred around changes in practice in the work place. He was interested in what effect involving workers in the decision-making process (the research) had on factory production (the action). His approach is exemplified in his experiment in the Harwood factory in Virginia. Lewin was able to show that when change was imposed on workers by management, production dropped substantially, that when representatives of the workers were involved in researching the change, production initially dropped but later recovered and that when all the workers participated in the decision-making, production rose markedly after only two days. The study demonstrated the practical benefits of involving actors in decision-making.[11] More importantly for Lewin, it demonstrated the need for and the advantages of democracy in the workplace. Lewin's work is of interest because it reflects the twin goals of action research, as it has been applied subsequently to education: action research is intended both to improve classroom practice and also to serve as a means for emancipating teachers. It has both an instrumental function and a social or ideological function. In the case of the latter, it may be politically charged and, for that reason, potentially risky.

It is customary to identify three kinds of action research. First, there is technical action research, where outside researchers co-opt practitioners into working on questions derived from theory or previous research. Crookes (1993) characterizes this kind of action research as a relatively conservative line, noting that it is likely to result in work published by scholars for academic audiences. Such research, he suggests, is approved because it fosters connections between universities and schools while maintaining the values and standards of traditional research.

Second, there is research undertaken by teachers in their own classrooms with a view to improving local practices. Carr and Kemmis refer to this kind of research as practical action research but Hopkins (1985) prefers the term teacher research. As Long (1983a: 268) points out, the aim of teacher research is not to turn teachers into classroom researchers, but to provide a means by which they can monitor their own practice. It involves a cycle of activities as shown in Figure 3.1, taken from Carr and Kemmis (1986). The starting point is planning (i.e. the identification of some problem that needs solving). This results in action (i.e. the teaching of a lesson in which the problematic behaviour will arise). Observation of the action provides material for reflection, which may then lead to further planning. Each step or moment in the cycle looks back to the previous step and forward to the next step. The cycle serves to link the past with the future through the processes of reconstruction and construction. Furthermore, it links discourse (i.e. talking about the action) with actual practice (i.e. the action in context). The starting point of the cycle, planning, is generally seen as the most problematic. Ideally, teachers should form plans for action based on an analysis of their own experience, but in reality they are likely to pick out issues from the educational or applied linguistics literature (see, for example, McDonough and McDonough's (1990) study of language teachers' views about research). Carr and Kemmis acknowledge a role for an outside facilitator in helping teachers formulate appropriate plans of action.

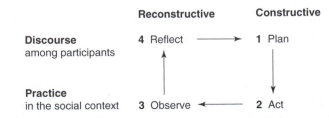

Figure 3.1 'Moments' of action research
Source: Carr and Kemmis 1986: 186

The third type of action research is critical action research – research that is not only directed at improving practice but at emancipating those that participate in it. It is this kind that most closely reflects Lewin's original formulation. Crookes considers it more progressive. Teachers are required not only to understand local problems and identify solutions but to examine the underlying social causes of problems and what needs to be done about them. Teachers need to become aware that their capacities for reflection (an essential part of the action research cycle) are influenced by social factors. They need to recognize that their understandings of classrooms may be distorted. The mechanism for achieving this is discourse in the sense intended by Habermas (1979) – free communication among participants who share equal discourse rights. In critical action research teachers need to take responsibility for carrying out research and for discoursing on it. The presence of an outside researcher, while not outlawed, is seen as dangerous because it is likely to undermine the social symmetry needed to ensure collaborative discourse.

Action research, then, bridges the gulf between the researcher and the teacher. Crookes (1993) suggests that it overcomes the limitations of traditional research by ensuring that its results are relevant to the needs of teachers; by encouraging and supporting teacher reflection and through this professional development; by encouraging teachers to engage in other kinds of research and use the results of such research; and, in the case of critical action research, by prompting teachers to address the unquestioned values embodied in educational institutions. According to Carr and Kemmis (1986) action research provides a basis for developing truly educational theories through theorizing about practice.

Action research is not without its critics, however. Hopkins (1985) argues that the action research practised in education has departed from Lewin's original concept of externally initiated intervention for assisting a client system. He also suggests that the models of action research such as that shown in Figure 3.1 may strait-jacket teachers making them reluctant to engage in independent action. These criticisms, however, do not seem to be especially damaging as there is no reason why educationalists should adhere to Lewin's initial conception of action research nor is there any reason why teachers should not depart from the proposed cycle whenever they feel the need to do so. More serious are criticisms concerning the impracticality of asking teachers to engage in research and the quality of the research they produce.

Teachers do not always find it easy to undertake research. Nunan (1990), drawing on his experience of working with teachers in Australia, lists a number of difficulties they experienced. Because the teachers were not used to observing each other teach, they found collaboration difficult. They tended towards excessive self-criticism when they first engaged in analysing their own classrooms. Their proposals tended to be rather grand and unmanageable in nature because they did not find it easy to identify specific research questions, a problem often commented on in the literature (see, for example, Hopkins 1985, McDonough and McDonough 1990). It proved extremely time-consuming to design properly formulated projects. The teachers were unclear as to how the research should be reported because they were uncertain who their audience was. Finally, there was a host of problems to do with the range and scope of the research. Over time, of course, such problems can be overcome as teachers accumulate experience of how to do research, but initially the task they face can appear daunting.

Another objection to action research concerns doubts about the quality of research carried out by teachers. Brumfit and Mitchell (1990a: 9) argue that 'there is no good argument for action research producing less care and rigour (than other modes of research) unless it is less concerned with clear understanding, which it is not'. Implicit in this statement is a belief that many teachers will not be able to achieve the standards professional researchers deem necessary. Crookes (1993), however, argues that when research is entirely local and no attempt to generalize is made it is less necessary to conform to the requirements of reliability, validity, and trustworthiness. He also suggests that action research reports do not need to be academic in style. They can take the form of 'teacher-oriented reports' and thus be more discursive, subjective, and anecdotal. The difference between the positions of Brumfit and Mitchell and Crookes are indicative of the lack of clear criteria for determining what constitutes good quality action research.

From the educational perspective described above, the gap between the researcher/ theorist on the one hand and the practitioner on the other is seen as the inevitable product of the social (and, one might add, political) worlds which they inhabit. As Kramsch (1995) has pointed out the behaviours that these two social groups typically manifest are symbolic of the value systems to which they adhere. The move to involve teachers in research can be seen, in part, as a move to reshape the symbolic capital of teachers' behaviour by inves- tigating it with the authority to be derived from research. This is one reason why the rationale for action research so frequently makes reference to its contribution to professionalism in the teaching fraternity.

One way of viewing action research is as a means by which teachers can test 'provisional specifications' (Stenhouse 1975) in the context of their own classrooms. These specifications can be drawn from the teacher's own practical knowledge, in which case action research can help to make explicit the principles, assumptions, and procedures for action that comprise this kind of knowledge. Alternatively, the specifications can be drawn from the technical knowledge provided by research. Action research serves as an empirical test of whether the generalizations provided by confirmatory research or the understandings provided by inter- pretative research are applicable to specific classroom settings. When teachers consistently find the results of their own research do not support the findings of confirmatory or interpretative research they need to be prepared to reject these as inapplicable to their own contexts. Action research, then, functions as a way of implementing the third of Weiss' models of research use – the interactive model – by bridging the gap between technical knowledge and practical knowledge.

The question arises as to whether the applicability of proposals based on research must necessarily be submitted to an empirical test by requiring teachers to take on the role of researcher (as Stenhouse advocates) or whether it might be possible to predict which proposals are likely to be acted on through an examination of the proposals themselves. It seems reasonable to suppose that some proposals are inherently more practical than others. What makes them so? To address this question we turn to the study of the uptake of innovations.

Innovationist perspective

A number of applied linguists have recently turned to work on innovation to help them understand the variable success they have observed in both large-scale language projects in the developing world and the variable response to new ideas among teachers in the developed world. Kennedy (1988), White (1988 and 1993) and Markee (1993) have all drawn on innovation research in a variety of disciplines (e.g. Rogers (1983) in sociology, Lambright and Flynn (1980) in urban planning, Cooper (1989) in language planning and Fullan (1982) and (1993) in education). Henrichsen (1989), Beretta (1990), Stoller (1994) and Markee (1994b) have reported actual studies of innovation in language teaching. It should be noted, however, that to date there has been no study of innovations stemming from proposals based on SLA.[12]

Innovation can be conceived of in two different ways – a distinction that is important where SLA is concerned. First, we can talk about absolute innovation in the sense that a proposal represents a completely new idea, not previously evident in practice anywhere. There are probably very few instances of absolute innovation in language teaching, although, arguably Wilkins' (1976) proposal for constructing syllabuses around notions constituted such an innovation. Second, there are perceived innovations. That is, the change is perceived as innovatory by the practitioners who adopt it. Most innovations are probably of this kind and, indeed, most definitions of innovation make particular reference to adopters' perceptions.

As Lightbown (1985) has observed, SLA has not produced much in the way of new pedagogic proposals. Thus, proposals derived from SLA typically lead to perceived rather than absolute innovations. For example, Krashen and Terrell (1983) view their Natural Approach as a reinstitution of the principles and techniques of earlier methods rather than as original. However, they clearly believe that their proposals will be new to many practitioners. SLA may also serve to provide a rationale for innovations that have originated elsewhere. For example, the idea of the information-gap task (Johnson 1982) originated from a theory of communicative language teaching, but it has undoubtedly received support and, arguably, been refined through SLA research (see, for example, Long 1981 and Skehan 1996).

Innovation is inherently threatening, as Prabhu (1987: 105) has pointed out in the context of discussing his proposal for a procedural syllabus in India:

> A new perception in pedagogy, implying a different pattern of classroom activity, is an intruder into teachers' mental frames – an unsettling one, because there is a conflict of mismatch between old and new perceptions and, more seriously, a threat to prevailing routines and to the sense of security dependent on them.

What then determines whether and to what extent teachers cope with these threats? The answer to this question involves a consideration of four sets of factors:

* the sociocultural context of the innovation
* the personality and skills of individual teachers
* the method of implementation
* attributes of the proposals themselves.

First, as Kennedy (1988) notes, there is a hierarchy of interrelating sub-systems in which any innovation has to operate. Thus, the success of any proposal emanating from SLA (or any other source) regarding classroom practices may be determined by institutional, educational, administrative, political, or cultural factors. Kennedy comments: 'the cultural system is assumed to be the most powerful as it will influence both political and administrative structures and behaviour' (*ibid.*: 332). This is a point that Widdowson (1993) also emphasizes. He cites an unpublished paper by Scollon and Scollon to the effect that 'conversational methods' may fail to take root in China because they may appear incompatible with the Confucian emphasis on benevolence and respect between teacher and students.

Second, the success of an innovation will also depend on the personality and qualities of individual teachers. Some teachers (e.g. those who are well-educated and upwardly mobile) may be more inclined to adopt new practices than others. Rogers (1983) distinguishes five categories of adopters: innovators, early adopters, early majority adopters, late majority adopters, and laggards. Personal factors are likely to play a major part in determining which category a teacher belongs to.

Third, the method of implementation is likely to influence to what extent an innovation takes root. Havelock (1971) distinguishes three basic models of innovation. The research, development and diffusion model views the researcher as the originator of proposals and the teachers as consumers and implementors of them. It is likely to be used in conjunction with a power-coercive strategy, where some authority takes a decision to adopt an innovation (e.g. a new syllabus) and then devises ways of providing teachers with the knowledge and skills they need to implement it. Innovation in this model, then, takes place top-down. The problem-solving model involves engaging teachers in identifying problems, researching possible solutions and then trying them out in their teaching. Innovation in this model, then, originates with the teachers. A social interaction model emphasizes the importance of social relationships in determining adoption and emphasizes the role of communication in determining uptake of an innovatory idea. To a large extent, these three models parallel the three approaches to relating research and pedagogy discussed in the previous section. That is, the research development and diffusion model reflects the positivist, technical view; the problem-solving model reflects the call for teacher research, while the importance placed on communication in the social interaction model mirrors that placed on discourse in critical action research.

The fourth set of factors governing the uptake of innovatory proposals concerns the attributes of the proposals themselves. These are of particular interest to us because they may provide the applied linguist with a basis for evaluating proposals emanating from SLA. The principal attributes discussed in the literature (see Kelly 1980, Rogers 1983, and Stoller 1994) are listed in Table 3.1, together with brief definitions. Some of these attributes are

Table 3.1 Attributes of innovation

Attribute	Definition
Initial dissatisfaction	The level of dissatisfaction that teachers experience with some aspect of their existing teaching.
Feasibility	The extent to which the innovation is seen as implementable given the conditions in which teachers work.
Acceptability	The extent to which the innovation is seen as compatible with teachers' existing teaching style and ideology.
Relevance	The extent to which the innovation is viewed as matching the needs of the teachers' students.
Complexity	The extent to which the innovation is difficult or easy to grasp.
Explicitness	The extent to which the rationale for the innovation is clear and convincing.
Triability	The extent to which the innovation can be easily tried out in stages.
Observability	The extent to which the results of innovation are visible to others.
Originality	The extent to which the teachers are required to demonstrate a high level of originality in order to implement the innovation (e.g. by preparing special materials).
Ownership	The extent to which teachers come to feel that they 'possess' the innovation.

seen as increasing the likelihood of an innovation becoming adopted (e.g. feasibility, relevance and explicitness). That is why they are to be viewed positively. Other attributes are likely to inhibit innovation (e.g. complexity). Still others may promote or inhibit innovation depending upon the particular adopters. For example, in the case of originality, some teachers may be more likely to implement an innovation if it calls for their own original contribution (e.g. in developing new teaching materials) whereas others may be less likely to do so. The attributes also vary in another way. Some (e.g. initial dissatisfaction and relevance) seem to be more relative than absolute in the sense that their application depends on the particular context in which teachers are working, whereas others (i.e. complexity, explicitness, triability, and observability) seem more concerned with the inherent characteristics of the innovation. Applied linguists interested in evaluating proposals drawn from SLA are likely to benefit from paying close attention to the inherent rather than the relative attributes of proposals.

In addition to these sets of factors that influence the uptake of innovatory ideas, there is also the question of what aspects of language pedagogy are involved in the change. This, too, can influence the likelihood of the innovation being successful. Markee (1994b), drawing in particular on the work of Fullan (1982 and 1993) in education, suggests that innovations in the form of the development and use of new teaching materials constitute the easiest kind of change. Innovations requiring change in methodological practices and, even more so in the teachers' underlying pedagogical values, are less likely to prove successful.

There have been relatively few attempts to apply an innovationist perspective to language pedagogy. Beretta (1990) sought to evaluate the extent to which the methodological innovations proposed by Prabhu as part of the Communicational Teaching Project (CTP) in India (Prabhu 1987) were actually implemented by the teachers involved. This project is based on the assumption that learners acquire grammar subconsciously when their attention is focused on communicating in meaning-focused tasks. Although Prabhu did not draw directly on SLA research/theory, his proposal is very similar to that advanced by Krashen and for this reason is of considerable interest here. Beretta collected historical narratives from 15 teachers involved in the project and then rated these according to three levels of implementation:

1   orientation (i.e. the teacher demonstrates he/she does not really understand the innovation and is unable to implement it)
2   routine (i.e. the teacher understands the rationale of the CTP and is able to implement it in a relatively stable fashion), and
3   renewal (i.e. the teacher has adopted a critical perspective on the innovation, demonstrating awareness of its strengths and weaknesses).

Forty per cent of the teachers were rated at Level 1, 47 per cent of teachers at Level 2 and 13 per cent at Level 3. Beretta considered Levels 2 and 3 demonstrated an adequate level of adoption. However, when he distinguished between regular and non-regular classroom teachers involved in the project, he found that three out of four of the regular teachers were at Level 1. He concluded that:

> . . . it seems reasonable to infer that CTP would not be readily assimilable by typical teachers in South Indian schools (or, by extension, in other schools elsewhere where similar antecedent conditions pertain) (ibid.: 333).

He points out that the failure of the regular teachers to reach an acceptable level of implementation reflects their lack of ownership of the innovation and problems regarding the innovation's feasibility because, for example, the teachers lacked the command of English required for fluency-based teaching. There are problems with Beretta's study – for example, we cannot be sure whether the regular teachers really failed to adopt the innovation or whether they simply lacked the English needed to produce narrative accounts of their experience – but, nevertheless, it demonstrates the potential of an innovationist perspective for evaluating pedagogic proposals derived from SLA theory and research.

Probably the most comprehensive study of innovation in language pedagogy is to be found in Stoller's (1994) study of innovation in intensive English language programmes in the United States. Stoller obtained completed questionnaires from 43 such programmes and also conducted in-depth interviews with five programme administrators. She found that the most frequently cited innovations related to the development of new curricula or the restructuring of the old. Some attributes were perceived as more important than others for successful innovation. Attributes rated as particularly important were usefulness (relevance), feasibility, improvement over past practices (which would seem to relate to initial dissatisfaction) and practicality (which relates to acceptability). Stoller was able to identify three major factors in the questionnaire responses. One factor was what she termed a 'balanced divergent factor'. The attributes involved here were explicitness, complexity, compatibility with past experiences, visibility, flexibility, and originality. In the case of this factor, however, the attributes operated in a zone of innovation in the sense that they facilitated innovation when they were present to a moderate degree but not when they were strongly or weakly present. The second factor was dissatisfaction and the third factor viability. Stoller also demonstrates that there appear to be different paths to innovation depending on the nature of the innovation. Thus, in the case of curricular innovation, viability was seen as the most important followed by dissatisfaction and finally the balanced divergent factor. The emphasis that Stoller places on viability in this type of innovation reflects the importance that Beretta attaches to feasibility in the communicational teaching project.

An innovationist perspective, then, would seem to afford applied linguists a way of evaluating the extent to which their proposals are likely to succeed. It will not be possible, of course, to make very precise predictions about which proposals will be taken up and which ones will not, but, arguably, the very act of evaluating their potential will help researchers to make them more practical. One might also add that an innovationist analysis, using the kinds of categories discussed in this section, may provide teachers with an explicit and relatively systematic way of determining whether specific proposals derived from SLA are of use to them. The study of innovations, therefore, offers another possible way of bridging the gap between SLA and language pedagogy.

Applied linguist's perspective

I have defined an applied linguist as a person who seeks to apply ideas derived from linguistics, psycholinguistics, sociolinguistics, education, and any other area of potentially relevant enquiry to language pedagogy. It is important to make a clear distinction between 'applied linguistics' and 'linguistics applied'. One obvious reason is that applied linguistics utilizes information sources other than linguistics, as the above definition makes clear. There is, however, a deeper reason. Widdowson (1984) argues that 'it is the responsibility of applied linguists to consider the criteria for an educationally relevant approach to language' (*ibid.*: 17) and that this cannot be achieved by simply applying linguistic theory. This is because the way linguists conceive of their task is inherently different from the way teachers conceive of theirs. Linguists are concerned with the precise description of language and with its explanation. Teachers are concerned with the effective use of language and with its propagation.

Just as we can distinguish between applied linguistics and linguistics applied so we can also distinguish applied SLA and SLA applied. In the case of the latter, an attempt is made to apply SLA research and theory to language pedagogy. This is what many SLA researchers have expressed doubt about doing, advising caution. In the case of applied SLA, however, an attempt is made to examine the relevance of SLA in educational terms; it requires the SLA researcher to have knowledge of the theory and practice of both SLA and language pedagogy. Only when SLA researchers engage in applied SLA do they function as applied linguists.[13]

A good example of applied SLA is to be found in Brindley's (1990) account of a course he taught as part of a postgraduate diploma in adult TESOL. Brindley dismisses what he sees as the traditional approach of SLA courses which he characterizes as 'we give you the theory – you apply it' (the approach implicit in Stern's 1983 advocacy of foundation studies) in favour of an approach that provides opportunities for the participants to analyse data. This encourages them to reformulate broad SLA research questions in terms of classroom implications and includes a strong problem-posing/problem-solving element by inviting the participants to address specific classroom situations in the light of insights drawn from their study of SLA and to discuss options for classroom applications. Brindley did include a knowledge component of the course (i.e. he provided an introduction to key topics and terminology) but in accordance with his applied SLA stance, he invited the participants to identify those SLA topics they found most relevant to their concerns. Interestingly, he found that psycholinguistic studies of developmental sequences (generally considered of central importance by SLA researchers) came bottom of the list, possibly because the teachers' primary concern was with teaching rather than learning.

Applied SLA, then, as a branch of applied linguistics, must necessarily concern itself with relevance. SLA is concerned with developing models of how L2 learners acquire knowledge of a second language but it cannot be assumed that these models are of any value to teachers. Indeed, in many cases they probably are not. It is no more correct to assume that a theory of language learning is of relevance to teachers than it is to assume that a theory of language is. Relevance must necessarily be determined not from within SLA but from without – by demonstrating how the findings of SLA address the needs and concerns of practitioners.

How then can SLA be made relevant to pedagogy? An answer to this question can be found in Widdowson's (1990) discussion of the roles of the applied linguist (see Figure 3.2).

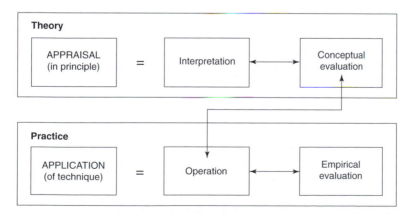

Figure 3.2 Relating disciplinary theory and language pedagogy
Source: Widdowson 1990: 32

For Widdowson, the applied linguist's task is to mediate between disciplinary theory/ research and language pedagogy. He suggests that this mediation involves two interdependent processes. The first is *appraisal*, which involves interpretation (i.e. the explication of ideas within their own terms of reference), followed by conceptual evaluation (i.e. 'the process of specifying what might be called the transfer value of ideas' (*ibid.*: 31)). The second process is *application*, which also involves two phases. In the case of *operation*, specific techniques are proposed based on the conclusions of the conceptual evaluation. Alternatively, specific techniques taken from teachers' customary practices can be subjected to scrutiny, a process that both draws on the results of prior conceptual evaluation and potentially contributes to it. The result of this process is a rationale for proposed action. The second phase of application is what Widdowson calls 'empirical evaluation'. This is undertaken by teachers, possibly with the assistance of applied linguists, and involves monitoring the effects of their actions by examining the relationship between teaching and learning. It calls for teacher research.

Widdowson's framework provides a basis for applying SLA in the following ways:

1 Making SLA accessible

This function involves interpretation. Because the bulk of SLA publications were written for researchers and not practitioners, there is an obvious need for summaries of the main findings. Such summaries will have four major purposes: to make a principled selection of those findings that are likely to be of interest to teachers; to provide surveys of the findings of a wide range of research which has addressed these issues; to evaluate the findings in their own terms (i.e. to establish which ones are valid, reliable and trustworthy); to present the surveys in a language that makes them accessible to practitioners and which provide the means by which teachers can receive a foundation in SLA.

The organization of these summaries bears some thought. One possibility is to structure them around the issues identified in the research. This would lead to surveys of such issues as learner errors, input and interaction, fossilization, the role of formal instruction, etc. An alternative, however, is to base the surveys on pedagogical concepts. This would lead to surveys of research findings that are relevant to such issues as error treatment, the use of the learner's L1 in the classroom, and options in grammar teaching. This latter approach is clearly more demanding but is likely to increase the perceived relevance. It provides a bridge between interpretation and conceptual evaluation.

2 Theory development and its application

One way of conducting conceptual evaluation is through theory construction. As Krashen (1983) has noted there are dangers in trying to apply the results of individual research studies and a more principled approach is to use research to construct a theory which can then be applied. One advantage of such an approach to conceptualization is that it provides an opportunity for developing a pedagogically relevant theory. As Brumfit (1983) has noted, teachers necessarily operate with category systems. A theory of instructed language acquisition can assist them in creating appropriate categories. We noted earlier, however, that there are also dangers in such an approach. In particular, so much investment may be made in a theory that it becomes petrified, resistant to modification in the light of counter arguments and new research findings. If this happens, of course conceptual evaluation gives way to persuasion.

The application of the hypotheses that comprise a theory is one way of operationalizing SLA for pedagogy. This operationalization takes the form of specific proposals for the practice of teaching. The proposals may concern overall approaches, the aims of the language curriculum, the content and organization of a syllabus, teaching activities, methodological procedures, and methods of testing learners and evaluating curricula – in other words any aspect of language pedagogy. These proposals, may take the form of original ideas, but as I have already pointed out, it is more likely that they will identify options already to be found within pedagogy. Irrespective of their form, these proposals cannot have the status of prescriptions. Rather they serve as illuminative ideas. They are suggestions which practitioners, if they see fit, may or may not choose to experiment with. The provisional nature of proposals is determined not by doubts about the validity of the theory/research upon which they are based (even though such doubts may well exist) but by the recognition that no theory and no research can claim to be applicable to the myriad contexts in which practitioners operate. The applied SLA researcher, however, has a duty to ensure that any proposal has potential for application and, in this respect, the attributes of different proposals can be examined from the innovationist perspective described in the previous section. In this way, it may be possible to identify which proposals have a good chance of being adopted by teachers.

3 Researching the L2 classroom

As we have seen, another way of operationalizing constructs, whether these have been derived from pure research or from teachers' personal knowledge, is to carry out investigations of classroom learners. However, this should involve research on classrooms, not just research in classrooms (Wright 1992). Such research provides a means of empirically testing pedagogic proposals (Long 1990). It provides some assurance that the proposals are sound. It helps to ward off attacks that proposals derived from teachers' own experience or from methodologists' writings are nothing more than hunches or unproven prescriptions. Furthermore, practitioners are likely to attend to classroom research more seriously than to pure research because it directly addresses issues that they are concerned with.

Classroom-centred research conducted by researchers, however, does not supply a body of information about effective pedagogy which can be transmitted to teachers as solutions to their problems any more than does pure research. The most that can be said is that proposals that are tested through classroom research may become more fully illuminated. In accordance with the views of Stenhouse, Verma, Wild, and Nixon (1982), the external validity of any research, including classroom research, can only be established by individual teachers in the contexts of their own classrooms. It follows, then, that what Widdowson (1990) refers to as 'outsider research' needs to be complemented by insider research, which is research conducted by teachers themselves.

4 The teacher as researcher

We saw earlier in our discussion of the educational perspective that there is a compelling case for involving teachers in researching their own classroom. Teacher research focuses on problems identified by teachers. It provides means of enabling teachers to reflect on their own practice and, thereby, of developing theories of language learning and teaching that are relevant to their own classroom contexts. The advocacy of teacher research (e.g. Nunan 1990) in recent years reflects the increasing awareness that language teaching is an educational enterprise and, thus, needs to be informed by mainstream educational thinking. Widdowson (1990) sees the need for teachers to be engaged in the active process of experimenting in their classrooms as a way of determining the practical effect of ideas in action.

There is still a role for SLA in teacher-led research, however. As Widdowson (1993) has pointed out, action research, like any other kind of research, cannot take place without theorizing. Teachers need to engage in the process of conceptual evaluation in order to identify research problems. A familiarity with SLA, then, can help teachers shape problems in a way that makes them researchable. In so doing, however, it must not impose issues on teachers but rather act as a resource by which teachers can refine questions derived from their own experience. As Widdowson (1993) puts it, theorizing must be client-centred.

SLA can help in another way. It can provide teachers with information about the kinds of instruments and procedures they will need to use in order to collect and analyse data. Some thirty years of researching L2 acquisition have led to the development of a number of research tools (see Larsen-Freeman and Long 1991, Allwright and Bailey 1991), many of which can be used by teachers in their own classrooms.

As we noted earlier, the idea of the teacher as researcher will not always be welcomed by teachers. For some teachers, at least, however, SLA can be made real through the discoveries they make about how their own learners learn a second language.

From an applied linguist's perspective, then, SLA is relevant to language pedagogy in a number of ways. It can contribute to the appraisal of pedagogic issues. To this end, the applied SLA worker can assist by making research accessible to teachers, by developing theories of instructed L2 acquisition and by advancing pedagogic proposals based on these theories. SLA also has a role in application. The applied SLA researcher can seek to illuminate pedagogic problems and their possible solutions through conducting experimental and interpretative studies in and, particularly on L2 classrooms. Finally, the SLA worker can act as a facilitator of teachers' own research by helping them formulate research questions and choose appropriate research methods. These functions can be seen as strung out on a continuum with 'outsider activity' at one pole and 'insider-activity' at the other. While it can be argued that the relevance of SLA increases as one moves along the continuum, outsider activity should not be disparaged, as has become fashionable in some quarters. Teachers can and do benefit from an understanding of the issues discussed in SLA. However, the determination of relevance is ultimately the duty of the teacher, not the applied SLA worker, although the latter can aid the process and, doubtlessly, should try to do so.

Finally, it must be clearly acknowledged that SLA does not constitute a body of knowledge that is necessary for the development of effective teaching skills. As Brumfit (1983: 61) has observed, 'learning to perform competently is never the same as learning how to understand the process of performance and to explain it'. SLA can contribute to teachers' understanding; it cannot ensure competent practice and, to quote Brumfit again, 'there is always the possibility that practice will run ahead of theory, as well as the reverse' (*ibid.*: 68).

Notes

1   The failure of the comparative method studies to demonstrate the superiority of one method over another did not lead to the abandonment of classroom research based on pedagogical constructs, however. Rather it led to a focus on particular aspects of teaching, such as error treatment or learner participation. Allwright (1988) describes how the global method studies gave way to the detailed study of classroom processes.

2   SLA researchers who began their careers as teachers include Vivian Cook, Pit Corder, Mike Long, John Schumann, Elaine Tarone and myself.

3   Precisely what counts as a relevant field of enquiry in SLA where language pedagogy is concerned is, of course, debatable. In Ellis (1995), I argue the case for the irrelevance of UG-based research and theory. Another area in which I have personally been able to find little relevance is language transfer. The competition model (Bates and MacWhinney 1982) has proved productive in promoting research but to date has had little to say to teachers. However, this failure to find relevance should not be perceived as a criticism of these areas

of enquiry. The study of language transfer, for example, is obviously of central importance for understanding L2 acquisition, the goal of SLA.

4   Other factors to do with the relative status of pure research (i.e. research directed exclusively at the creation of technical knowledge) as opposed to applied research (i.e. research directed at addressing practical issues) in the university settings in which researchers typically work may also have contributed to the diminishing interest in adding application sections to published papers.

5   According to the positivist view of the relationship between research and language pedagogy, research provides technical knowledge which teachers use in making decisions about what and how to teach. Research prescribes and proscribes what teachers should do.

6   Pica (1994) does not indicate how her teachers arrived at the questions they asked. One possibility is that their questions were influenced, in part at least, by their knowledge of the SLA literature and their perception of what this literature claims is important and relevant. It would be interesting to know what kinds of questions are asked by teachers who are not familiar with SLA. I am grateful for Jim Lantolf for raising this point.

7   It should be noted that some researchers see a positive disadvantage in trying to establish links with language pedagogy. Newmeyer and Steinberg (1988), for example, consider that one of the reasons for the immaturity of SLA is precisely the felt need to make applications.

8   Sometimes, however, these natural samples of spoken language were supplemented with samples of elicited language. For example, Cazden, Cancino, Rosansky, and Schumann (1975) used experimental elicitations by asking their subjects to imitate or transform a model utterance.

9   The interpretative tradition of research, wedded to ideas borrowed from critical sociology, has more recently been used to examine a third type of knowledge – socially constructed knowledge. This post-modern approach has, until recently, not been strongly reflected in SLA.

10 Richards (1991), in a survey of 50 MA TESOL programmes listed in the TESOL directory, found that 29 of them included required courses on SLA.

11 There is, of course, a dual application of Lewin's model of action research to teaching. One is that researchers interested in changing classroom practices need to work with teachers with a similar interest in researching change. The other is that teachers need to work with learners in negotiating the activities they will engage in. The latter application is reflected in the idea of a process syllabus (Breen 1984), according to which the content, method-ology, and methods of evaluation for a language course are established jointly by teacher and students as the course takes place. To the best of my knowledge, however, proponents of the process syllabus have not made direct links between their ideas and those of Lewin.

12 Markee's (1994b) study examined task-based language teaching, which, as Markee points out, has been influenced by psycholinguistic theories of L2 learning.

13 It should be clear from this that the SLA researcher and the applied linguist can be one and the same person. Indeed, many SLA researchers (myself included) would consider themselves applied linguists. It should be equally clear that the two roles need not be related; there are many SLA researchers who are not applied linguists. There are also some SLA researchers with no foundation in language pedagogy who engage in 'SLA applied'.

References

Adelman, C. (1993) 'Kurt Lewin and the origins of actions research', *Educational Action Research* 1: 7–24.

Agard, P. and Dunkel, H. (1948) *An Investigation of Second Language Teaching*. Boston, Mass.: Ginn.

Agnew, J. (ed.) (1980) *Innovation, Research and Public Policy*. Syracuse, N.Y.: Syracuse University.

Alatis, J. (ed.) (1991) *University of Georgetown Round Table on Language and Linguistics*. Washington D.C.: Georgetown University Press.

Alatis, J., Stern, H. and Stevens, P. (eds) (1983) *Applied Linguistics and the Preparation of Teachers: Toward a Rationale*. Washington D.C.: Georgetown University Press.

Allwright, R. (1988) *Observation in the Language Classroom*. London: Longman.

Allwright, D. and Bailey, K. (1991) *Focus on the Language Classroom: An Introduction to Classroom Research for Teachers*. Cambridge: Cambridge University Press.

Bahns, J. (1990) 'Consultant not initiator: the role of the applied SLA researcher'. *ELT Journal* 44: 110–16.

Bates, E. and MacWhinney, B. (1982) 'Functionalist approaches to grammar', in Wanner and Gleitman (eds) (1982).

Beebe, L. (ed.) (1988) *Issues in Second Language Acquisition: Multiple Perspectives*. New York: Newbury House.

Beretta, A. (1990) 'Implementation of the Bangalore Project', *Applied Linguistics* 11: 321–40.

—— (1991) 'Theory construction in SLA: complementarity and opposition', *Studies in Second Language Acquisition* 13: 493–511.

Bolitho, R. (1991) 'A place for second language acquisitions in teacher development and in teacher education programmes', in Sadtono (ed.) (1991).

Breen, M. (1984) 'Process syllabuses for the language classroom' in Brumfit (ed.) (1984b).

Breen, M. (1985) 'Authenticity in the language classroom', *Applied Linguistics* 6: 60–70.

Breen, M. and Candlin, C. (1987) 'Which materials? a consumer's and designer's guide' in Sheldon (ed.) (1987).

Bright, J. and McGregor, G. (1970). *Teaching English as a Second Language*. London: Longman.

Brindley, G. (1990) 'Inquiry-based teacher education: a case study'. Paper presented at 24th Annual TESOL Convention, San Francisco March 6–10, 1990.

Brock, C. (1986) 'The effects of referential questions on ESL classroom discourse'. *TESOL Quarterly* 20: 47–48.

Brooks, N. (1960) *Language and Language Learning*. New York: Harcourt Brace and World.

Brown, H. (ed.) (1975) *Papers in Second Language Acquisition*. Ann Arbor, Mich.: Language Learning, University of Michigan.

Brown, H., Yorio, C. and Crymes, R. (eds) (1977) *On TESOL '77*. Washington D.C.: TESOL.

Brumfit, C. (1983) 'The integration of theory and practice', in Alatis *et al.* (eds) (1983).

—— (ed.) (1984) *General English Syllabus Design*. ELT Documents 118. Oxford: Pergamon.

Brumfit, C. and Mitchell, R. (1990a) 'The language classroom as a focus for research', in Brumfit and Mitchell (eds) (1990b).

Brumfit, C. and Mitchell, R. (eds) (1990b) 'Research in the Language Classroom'. *ELT Documents* 133. London: Modern English Publications.

Calderhead, J. (ed.) (1988) *Teachers' Professional Learning*. London: Falmer.

Carr, W. and Kemmis, S. (1986) *Becoming Critical: Education, Knowledge and Action Research*. London: Falmer.

Cazden, C., Cancino, E., Rosansky, E. and Schumann, J. (1975) *Second Language Acquisition in Children, Adolescents and Adults*. Final Report. Washington D.C.: National Institute of Education.

Clarke, M. and Handscombe, J. (eds) (1983) *On TESOL '82: Pacific Perspectives on Language and Teaching*. Washington, D.C.: TESOL.

Cook. G. and Seidlhofer, B. (eds) (1995) *Principle and Practice in Applied Linguistics: Studies in Honour of H. G.Widdowson*. Oxford: Oxford University Press.

Cooper, R. (1989) *Language Planning and Social Change*. Cambridge: Cambridge University Press.

Corder, S. P. (1973) *Introducing Applied Linguistics*. Harmondsworth: Penguin.

—— (1977) 'Language teaching and learning: a social encounter', in Brown *et al.* (eds) (1977).

—— (1980) 'Second language acquisition research and the teaching of grammar', *BAAL Newsletter* 10: 1–12.

Crookes, G. (1993) 'Action research and second language teachers: going beyond teacher research'. *Applied Linguistics* 14: 130–44.

Crookes, G. and Gass, S. (eds) (1993) *Tasks and Language Learning: integrating Theory and Practice*. Clevedon, North Somerset: Multilingual Matters.

Dahl, H. (ed.) (1979) *Spotlight on Educational Research*. Oslo: Oslo University Press.

Dulay, H. and Burt, M. (1973) 'Should we teach children syntax?' *Language Learning* 23: 245–58.

Duskova, L. (1969) 'On sources of errors in foreign language learning', *IRAL* 7: 11–36.

Eckman, F., Highland, D., Lee, P., Mileham, J. and Weber, J. (eds) (1995) *Second Language Acquisition Theory and Pedagogy*. Mahwa, N.J.: Lawrence Erlbaum.

Elliott, J. and Ebutt, D. (1985) *Facilitating Educational Action Research in Schools*. New York: Longman.

Ellis, R. (1994) *The Study of Second Language Acquisition*. Oxford: Oxford University Press.

—— (1995) 'Appraising second language acquisition theory in relation to pedagogy', in Cook and Seidlhofer (eds) (1995).

Eraut, M. (1994) *Developing Professional Knowledge and Competence*. London: Falmer.

Fischer, R. (1935) *The Design of Experiments*. Edinburgh: Oliver and Boyd.

Flowerdew, J., Brooks, M. and Hsia, S. (eds) (1992) *Perspectives on Second Language Teacher Education*. Hong Kong: Hong Kong City Polytechnic.

Flynn, S. and Martohardjono, G. (1995) 'Towards theory-driven language pedagogy', in Eckman *et al.* (eds) (1995).

Freeman, D. and Richards, J. (1993) 'Conceptions of teaching and the education of second language teachers'. *TESOL Quarterly* 27: 193–217.

Freidson, E. (1977) *Profession of Medicine: A Study of Sociology of Applied Knowledge*. New York: Dodd, Mead and Co.

Fullan, M. (1982) *The Meaning of Educational Change*. New York: Teachers College Press.

Fullan, M. (1993) *Change Forces: Probing the Depths of Educational Reform*. London: Falmer.

Galton, M. (ed.) (1980) *Curriculum Change*. Leicester: Leicester University Press.

Gass, S. (1989) 'Language universals and second language acquisition'. *Language Learning* 39: 497–534.

Gass. S. (1995) 'Learning and teaching: the necessary intersection', in Eckman *et al.* (eds) (1995).

Gass, S. and Schachter, J. (eds) (1994) *Issues in Constructing Second Language Classroom Research*. Hillsdale, N.J.: Lawrence Erlbaum.

Habermas, J. (1979) *Communication and the Evolution of Society* (tr. T. McCarthy). Boston: Beacon Press.

Harley, B, Allen, P., Cummins, J. and Swain, M. (eds) (1990) *The Development of Second Language Proficiency*. Cambridge: Cambridge University Press.

Hatch, E. (1978) 'Apply with caution'. *Studies in Second Language Acquisition* 2: 123–43.

Havelock, R. (1971) 'The utilization of educational research and development'. *British Journal of Educational Technology* 2: 84–97.

Henrichsen, L. (1989) *Diffusion of Innovations in English Teaching: The ELEC Effort in Japan*. New York: Greenwood Press.

Hirst, P. (1966) 'Educational theory' in Tibbles (ed.) (1966).

Hopkins, D. (1985) *A Teacher's Guide to Classroom Research*. Milton Keynes: Open University Press.

Jarvis, G. (1983) 'Pedagogical knowledge for the second language teacher', in Alatis *et al.* (eds) (1983).

Johnson, K. (1982) 'Five principles in a "communicative" exercise type', in Johnson, K. (1982). *Communicative Syllabus Design and Methodology*, Oxford: Pergamon.

Johnston, M. (1987) 'Understanding learner language' in Numan (ed.) (1987).

Kelly, P. (1980) 'From innovation to adaptability', in Galton (ed.) (1980).

Kemmis, S. and McTaggert, R. (1981) *The Action Research Planner*. Victoria, Australia: Deakin University Press.

Kennedy, G. (1988) 'Evaluation and the management of change in ELT projects'. *Applied Linguistics* 9: 329–42.

Kramsch, C. (1995) 'The politics of applied linguistics'. Plenary lecture, Annual Conference of the American Association for Applied Linguistics, Long Beach, California.

Kramsch, C. and McConnell-Ginet, S. (eds) (1992) *Text and Context: Cross-Disciplinary Perspectives on Language Study*. Lexington, Mass.: D.C. Heath and Company.

Krashen, S. (1983) 'Second language acquisition theory and the preparation of teachers', in Alatis *et al.* (eds) (1983).

Krashen, S. and Terrell, T. (1983) *The Natural Approach: Language Acquisition in the Classroom*. Oxford: Pergamon.

Kuhn, T. (1970) *The Structure of Scientific Revolutions* (2nd edn.). Chicago: Chicago University Press.

Lambright, W. and Flynn, P. (1980) 'The role of local bureaucracy-centered coalitions in technology transfer to the city' in Agnew (ed.) (1980).

Lantolf, J. (1995) 'Second language acquisition theory'. Plenary address, 1995 Annual BAAL Conference, Southampton, UK.

Larsen-Freeman, D. and Long, M. (1991) *An Introduction to Second Language Acquisition Research*. London: Longman.

Lightbown, P. (1985) 'Great expectation: second language acquisition research and classroom teaching'. *Applied Linguistics* 6: 173–89.

Lightbown, P. and Spada, N. (1993) *How Languages are Learned*. Oxford: Oxford University Press.

Long, M. (1981) 'Input, interaction and second language acquisition' in Winitz (ed.) (1981b)

—— (1983a) 'Training the second language teacher as classroom researcher' in Alatis *et al.* (eds) (1983).

—— (1983b) 'Native speaker/non-native speaker conversation in the second language classroom', in Clarke and Handscombe (eds) (1983).

—— (1990) 'Second language classroom research and teacher education', in Brumfit and Mitchell (eds) (1990b).

—— (1993) 'Assessment strategies for SLA theories'. *Applied Linguistics* 14: 225–49.

Markee, N. (1993) 'The difference of innovation in language teaching'. *Annual Review of Applied Linguistics* 13: 229–43.

Markee, N. (1994a) 'Towards an ethnomethodological respectification of second-language acquisition studies', in Gass and Schachter (eds) (1994).

—— (1994b) 'Curricular innovation: issues and problems'. *Applied Language Learning* 5: 1–30.

McDonough, J. and McDonough, S. (1990) 'What's the use of research?' *ELT Journal* 44: 102–9.

Newmark, L. (1966) 'How not to interfere in language learning'. *International Journal of American Linguistics* 32: 77–87.

Newmeyer, F. and Steinberg (1988) 'The ontogenesis of the field of second language learning research' in Flynn and O'Neill (eds) (1988).

Noffke, S. and Stevenson, R. (eds) (1995) *Educational Action Research: Becoming Practically Critical*. New York: Teachers' College Press.

Nunan, D. (ed.) (1987) *Applying Second Language Acquisition Research*. National Curriculum Research Centre, Adelaide, Australia: Adult Migrant Education Program.

Nunan, D. (1990) 'The teacher as researcher', in Brumfit and Mitchell (eds) (1990b).

Pennycook, A. (1989) 'The concept of method, interested knowledge, and the politics of language teaching'. *TESOL Quarterly* 25: 589–618.

Pica, T. (1987) 'Second language acquisition: social interaction in the classroom'. *Applied Linguistics* 7: 1–25.

—— (1992) 'The textual outcomes of native speaker-non-native speaker negotiation: what do they reveal about second language learning' in Kramsch and McConnell-Ginet (eds) (1992).

—— (1994) 'Questions from the language classroom: research perspectives'. *TESOL Quarterly* 28: 49–79.

Pica, T. and Doughty, C. (1985) 'The role of group work in classroom second language acquisition'. *Studies in Second Language Acquisition* 7: 233–48.

Polanyi, M. (1958) *Personal Knowledge: Towards a Post-Critical Philosophy*. London: Routledge.

Prabhu, N. S. (1987) *Second Language Pedagogy*. Oxford: Oxford University Press.

Ravem, R. (1968) 'Language acquisition in a second language environment'. *IRAL* 6: 165–85.

Richards, J. (1991) 'Content knowledge and instructional practice in second language teacher education', in Alatis (ed.) (1991).

Rogers, R. (1983) *The Diffusion of Innovations* (3rd ed.). London and New York: Macmillan and Free Press.

Sadtono, E. (ed.) (1991) *Language Acquisition and the Second/Foreign Language Classroom*. Singapore: SEAMFO Regional English Language Centre.

Schachter, J. (1993) 'Second language acquisition: perception and possibilities'. *Second Language Research* 9: 173–87.

Scherer, A. and Wertheimer, M. (1964) *A Psycholinguistic Experiment in Foreign Language Teaching*. New York: McGraw Hill.

Schön, D. (1983) *The Reflective Practitioner*. New York: Basic Books.

Schumann, J. (1993) 'Some problems with falsification: an illustration from SLA research'. *Applied Linguistics* 14: 295–306.

Schuyler, P. and Sitterley, D. (1995) 'Pre-service teacher supervision and reflective practice', in Nolfke and Stevenson (eds) (1995).

Skehan, P. (1996) 'Second language acquisition research and task-based instruction', in Willis and Willis (eds) (1996).

Smith, P. (1970) 'A comparison of the Audiolingual and Cognitive Approaches to Foreign Language Instruction: The Pennsylvania Foreign Language Project.' Philadelphia: Center for Curriculum Development.

Spada, N. and Lightbown, P. (1993) 'Instruction and the development of questions in L2 classrooms'. *Studies in Second Language Acquisition* 15: 205–24.

Stenhouse, L. (1975) *An Introduction to Curriculum Research and Development*. London: Heinemann.

—— (1979) 'Using research means doing research', in Dahl (ed.) (1979).

Stenhouse, L., Verma, G., Wild, R. and Nixon, J. (1982) *Teaching about Race Relations*. London: Routledge.

Stern, H. (1983) *Fundamental Concepts of Language Teaching*. Oxford: Oxford University Press.

Stoller, F. (1994) 'The diffusion of innovations in intensive ESL programs'. *Applied Linguistics* 15: 300–27.

Tarone, E., Swain, M. and Fathman, A. (1976) 'Some limitations to the classroom applications of current second language acquisition research'. *TESOL Quarterly* 10: 19–31.

Tibbles, J. (ed.) (1966) *The Study of Education*. London: Routledge and Kegan Paul.

Tyler, R. (1949) *Basic Principles of Curriculum and Instruction*. Chicago: Chicago University Press.

Van Lier, L. (1988) *The Classroom and the Language Learner*. London: Longman.

—— (1990) 'Ethnography: bandaid, handwagon, or contraband' in Brumfit and Mitchell (eds) (1990b).

VanPatten, B. and Cadierno, T. (1993) 'Explicit instruction and input processing'. *Studies in Second Language Acquisition* 15: 225–41.

Wanner, E. and Gleitman, L. (eds) (1982) *Language Acquisition: The State of the Art*. New York: Cambridge University Press.

Weber, M. (1961) *The Theory of Social and Economic Organization*. New York: The Free Press.

Weiss, C. (ed.) (1977) *Using Social Research in Public Policy-making*. Lexington: D.C. Heath.

White, R. (1988) *The ELT Curriculum: Design, Innovation and Management*. Oxford: Basil Blackwell.

—— (1993) 'Innovation in program development'. *Annual Review of Applied Linguistics* 13: 244–59.

Widdowson, H. (1984) 'Applied linguistics: the pursuit of relevance' in Widdowson (1984) *Explorations in Applied Linguistics* 2. Oxford: Oxford University Press.

—— (1990) *Aspects of Language Teaching*. Oxford: Oxford University Press.

—— (1993) 'Innovation in teacher development'. *Annual Review of Applied Linguistics* 13: 260–75.

Wilkins, D. (1976) *Notional Syllabuses*. Oxford: Oxford University Press.

Willis, J. and Willis, D. (eds) (1996) *Challenge and Change in Language Teaching*. Oxford: Heinemann.

Winitz, H. (ed.) (1981) 'Native Language and Foreign Language Acquisition'. *Annals of the New York Academy of Sciences* 379.

Wright, T. (1992) 'Classroom research and teacher education: towards a collaborative approach', in Flowerdew *et al*. (eds) (1992).

Zahorik, J. (1986) 'Acquiring teaching skills', *Journal of Teacher Education* 27: 21–25.

Chapter 4

Peter Skehan

COMPREHENSION AND PRODUCTION STRATEGIES IN LANGUAGE LEARNING

IN AN INFLUENTIAL PAPER WHICH discusses differences between first and second language learning, Bley-Vroman (1989) draws attention to the extent to which second language (L2) learning often does not lead to success while first language learning, except in unusual cases, does. Faced with such an unsettling vote of no confidence, it is hardly surprising that the language teaching profession has explored many alternatives in the search to find more effective methods (Larsen-Freeman 1986). And it is equally unsurprising that one of the responses the profession has made is to see whether approaches to second language teaching which connect with *first* language acquisition hold out any promise.

This chapter will review two such instructional approaches. The first is broadly concerned with comprehension-driven learning, regarding second language development as likely to proceed, under the right conditions, simply as a result of exposure to meaningful input. The second, which in some ways arose out of dissatisfaction with the first, proposes that engaging in interaction and producing output will be sufficient to drive second language development forward. In each case, clearly, interlanguage development is seen to be the by-product of engaging in meaning-processing – in the first case through comprehension, and in the second through production. As a broader aim, the chapter develops the claim that instructional activities that emphasize meaning, whether comprehension or production-based, may induce learners to rely on strategies for communication which result in a bypassing of the form of language.

The place of comprehension in language learning

The clearest example of a comprehension-based account of second language development derives from Krashen (1985). He proposed that comprehensible input is the driving force for interlanguage development and change, and that the effects of such change carry over to influence production – that is, one learns to speak by listening, a claim which is interesting because of its counter-intuitive nature. Krashen argues that the predictability of the context makes what is said function as a commentary on what is already understood. The result is that it is more likely that the interlanguage system will be extended by the context-to-language mapping involved.

Krashen articulates a rationale for comprehension-based instruction. He draws attention to the success that various listening-based methodologies can claim, such as Total Physical Response (Asher 1977), as well as more experimental research in its support (Winitz 1978; Postovsky 1977). Most of all, though, he is enthusiastic about the achievements of immersion education, in which content-based learning 'drags' language learning with it parasitically. The features of immersion education, such as learning environment which is supportive, and where bilingual teachers provide ample content-based input while allowing learners to produce language at their pace, are seen as consistent with Krashen's position. Many evaluations of such an approach to foreign language education (Swain and Lapkin 1982) have shown that immersion-educated children reach much higher levels of achievement than do children educated by traditional 'core' methods, and in some areas perform at levels comparable to those of native-speaker children. And this is achieved without compromising content-based learning in areas such as geography, mathematics, science, and so on.

Krashen's views have been influential within second language education and have had considerable impact on the nature of pedagogic provision. Not surprisingly, therefore, they have been subjected to searching criticism, and it would now seem that the claims that were made cannot be substantiated. General criticisms of the theoretical status of Krashen's Monitor Model can be found in McLaughlin (1987), Gregg (1984), Spolsky (1985) and Skehan (1984). The present discussion will be confined to analyses of the functioning of comprehension, and the ways that comprehension-driven learning may (or may not) occur.

Perhaps, first of all, however, it is worth returning to the Canadian immersion pro-grammes. Earlier evaluations were generally favourable, and suggested that such an approach to language provision might be worth adapting in other contexts. However, more recently the limitations of immersion approaches have also become apparent. In particular, attention is now increasingly drawn to the contrast in achievement between receptive and productive skills. Although the children concerned perform at levels of comprehension close to native speakers, the same cannot be said of their production abilities. Harley and Swain (1984) and Swain (1985) report that immersion-educated children, after many years of instruction, still make persistent errors when speaking and writing, suggesting that the automatic transfer between comprehension and production that Krashen argues for does not occur with any certainty.

This sort of evaluation demonstrates that an unqualified interpretation of the benefits of comprehension-based methodologies is not justified. In retrospect, it is difficult to see how comprehension-based approaches could have been so readily accepted, since they offered only rudimentary accounts of the mechanisms and processes by which comprehension was supposed to influence underlying interlanguage and generalize to production. Consequently, the next section will examine comprehension processes in more detail to try to account for the immersion evaluation findings.

Comprehension strategies

The findings become much more understandable if one examines the relevance of native-speaker comprehension models for the process of second language learning. Looking at comprehension in more 'micro' terms, Clark and Clark (1977) have argued that native-speaker listeners typically draw upon a range of comprehension strategies when they are listening. They focus on how syntactic and semantic strategies may be used to recover the meaning of what is heard in a rather improvisatory manner (*ibid.*: 57–85). Examples of syntactic strategies that they discuss are:

1   Whenever you find a determiner (a, an, the) or quantifier (some, all, many, two, six, etc.) begin a new noun phrase.
2   Whenever you find a co-ordinating conjunction (and, or, but, nor) begin a new constituent similar to the one you just completed.
3   Try to attach each new word to the constituent that came just before.

(ibid.: 66)

They illustrate this last strategy through an advertising campaign run by a London evening paper with posters such as 'Zoo keeper finds Jaguar queuing for underground ticket', and 'Butler finds new station between Piccadilly and Oxford Street'. The paper wanted more people to realize how useful its small advertisements section was and to attract their attention to posters they would normally glance at only briefly while passing. So they exploited the 'double-take' that readers were led into by using the third of the above micro-strategies. Readers then had to recognize the improbability of their first interpretation of 'queuing' being attached to 'Jaguar' and 'new station' to 'between Piccadilly and Oxford Street', and move the link to the first noun in each sentence.

Clark arid Clark (*ibid.*: 72–79) also discuss semantic strategies, such as:

4   Using content words alone, build propositions that make sense and parse the sentence into constituents accordingly.

Fillenbaum (1971) illustrates the operation of this strategy by showing that when people were asked to paraphrase 'perverse' sentences like 'John dressed and had a bath', they normalized them, with more than half of his subjects even asserting there was 'not a shred of difference' between the paraphrase and the original.

Clark and Clark are, in effect, arguing that native-speaker comprehension is probabilistic in nature, and does not follow any sort of deterministic model which would rely on an exhaustive parsing of the utterance concerned. Instead, listeners use a variety of means to maximize the chances that they will be able to recover the intended meaning of what is being said to them. They are not, in other words, using some linguistic model to retrieve meaning comprehensively and unambiguously. Instead, they cope with the problem of having to process language in real time by employing a variety of strategies which will probably combine to be effective, even though there is no guarantee that this will be the case. Presumably if a comprehension difficulty arises during ongoing processing, the listener can shift to a different mode of meaning extraction, as perhaps in the case of the zoo keeper and the Jaguar (as was intended by the authors of the poster). But this is not done routinely: the primary strategy is to achieve effectiveness in very fast language processing. Most listeners, in their native language, prefer to make a best-guess and keep up, rather than be accused of being slow-witted but accurate pedants (although we can all bring to mind some members of this species).

These 'micro' issues discussed by Clark and Clark (1977) can be located within a wider model of comprehension, which has a more macro perspective. The following table is adapted from Anderson and Lynch (1988: 13), who suggest that comprehension (again, for the moment, native-speaker comprehension) is dependent on three main sources of knowledge:

Schematic knowledge
    background knowledge
      – factual
      – sociocultural

procedural knowledge
    – how knowledge is used in discourse

Contextual knowledge
    knowledge of situation
       – physical setting, participants, etc.
    knowledge of co text
       – what has been, will be said

Systematic knowledge
    syntactic
    semantic
    morphological

These knowledge sources are drawn on, interactively, to achieve comprehension. Micro approaches (compare Clark and Clark 1977) are largely concerned with the operation of systematic knowledge which allows effective guesses to be made as to the meaning of what is being said. But Anderson and Lynch are proposing that listeners build meanings by drawing on a wider range of resources, including both schematic and contextual knowledge. This implies that we are not exclusively dependent on the nature of the sounds addressed to us to achieve meaning. If we can relate what is being said to previous knowledge that we have, then we may be able to make very effective inferences about the messages concerned. Similarly, if we relate the message to the probable things that are likely to be said given the nature of the situational context, for example the bus queue, or what has been said previously, we are cutting down the range of possible meanings that we encounter, and making our guesses about meaning more likely to work. In this respect, listeners are behaving in exactly the same way as skilled readers do when they sample the printed material in front of them, rather than poring over every letter. Comprehension, in other words, is a mixture of bottom-up and top-down processes (Eskey 1988), with the more effective use of top-down processes reducing the extent of the dependence on the acoustic or visual stimulus involved.

What all this implies is that the comprehension process can be partly detached from the underlying syntactic system and from production. If comprehension draws on effective strategy use and on a capacity to relate input to context, then it may partly be an autonomous skill, whose development does not transfer automatically to other areas. A good comprehender may be an effective and appropriate strategy user, rather than someone who necessarily extracts useful syntactic inferences from the language which is being processed (Swain 1985). Effective comprehension may leave the underlying interlanguage system untouched and unscathed.

These arguments apply particularly forcefully to the second or foreign language learner. In such cases, we are dealing with people who do not lack schematic knowledge, but who do have limited systemic knowledge. Such learners, when confronted by comprehension problems, are likely to exploit what they are best at – mobilizing relevant schematic and contextual knowledge to overcome their systemic limitations. As a result, the need for the interlanguage system to be engaged, and to have the chance to change and grow, is reduced. To put this as directly as possible, it would seem that, after all, learning to speak a second language, at least for most people, is not accomplished simply by listening to it.

From comprehension to production

Krashen's proposal (1985), that comprehensible input drives forward language development and generalizes to speaking was attractive. Claiming that we learn through exposure to meaningful material may not be very startling – we are unlikely to learn from material we do not understand, after all. But claiming that interlanguage change arises in a receptive modality and later becomes available to production was by no means self-evident – hence the attraction of the argument.

We have seen, though, that the evidence reported from evaluations of immersion was supportive of the original claim and so we have to accept that speaking does not come 'for free' simply through listening to comprehensible input. In this respect, Long (1985) makes a three-level distinction between conditions for second language learning. He suggests that it is valuable to consider whether factors such as input are:

1   necessary
2   sufficient
3   efficient

Logically, an influence might operate at a level 1, 2, or 3, with 3 efficiency constituting the most searching criterion, that an influence is not just causative (necessary and sufficient), but is likely to produce successful language learning most quickly. At the other extreme, level 1, necessary, an influence would have to be present, but would not be enough, in itself to produce successful learning (let alone accomplish this rapidly) since it would act simply as a precondition. Krashen's proposal was that input is necessary, sufficient, and efficient, while the preceding pages have argued against this.

Roles for output

Swain (1985; Swain and Lapkin 1982), an important contributor of immersion-based evidence, was led to consider whether other factors besides input might take us further in meeting the three levels of condition proposed by Long, and account for how language development might be driven forward. In particular, she proposed the Comprehensible Output Hypothesis, that to learn to speak we have to actually speak! Drawing on her specific suggestions (Swain 1985), as well as on other sources, several roles for output can be identified that are relevant to language learning. The first two of the proposed roles still have a connection with input, but rework this relationship in some way. The remaining roles for output are more specifically targeted on the productive modality itself.

To generate better input

Paradoxically, one needs to start by drawing attention to the way in which one could only get good quality input by using output (speaking) to give one's interlocutor feedback, so that the input directed to the listener is more finely tuned to the listener's current competence (Long 1985). In this view, output is important as a signalling device to negotiate better input: input would still be the major explanatory construct, but output would be necessary to generate it most effectively. Simply listening would not ensure that good quality input would be received, since one would have to rely on good luck or the sensitivity of one's interlocutor, neither of which is very dependable. The strongest form of this account concerns the 'negotiation for meaning' literature (Pica 1994). This proposes that engaging in meaning negotiation, as indexed by the use of, for example, clarification requests, confirmation checks, and comprehension checks, evidences efficient signalling of miscomprehension and the clear engagement of a malleable interlanguage system which is more likely, as a result, to develop productively. In such cases, better input should be received, but in addition the attempt to engage in conversation will trigger support at very important points for interlanguage development.

To force syntactic processing

Swain (1985) argues that knowing that one will need to speak makes one more likely to attend to syntax when one is listening. She suggests that if listeners are aware that it is not enough simply to extract meaning from input, but that they may also need to pay attention to the means by which meanings are expressed in order to use such knowledge as the basis for their own production later, they will be more likely to pay attention to the syntax underlying speech. It is similar to watching a top-class tennis player, say, and making a distinction between simply observing and admiring a stroke, on the one hand, and observing and analysing the stroke so that it can be emulated later, on the other. So once again, we are dealing here with output having an indirect effect in that it causes input and listening to be used more effectively for interlanguage development.

To test hypotheses

To accept the input hypothesis is to be dependent on what is said by others. If this is enlightening, given the learner's current state of interlanguage grammar, then progress may result. But one is extremely unlikely to be so fortunate as to receive relevant information for specific points of interlanguage development relevant to the areas where one is framing hypotheses at exactly the right time. Speaking, in contrast, allows the speaker to control the agenda and to take risks and look for feedback on the points of uncertainty in a developing grammar (Swain 1985; 1995). This is unlikely to make learning more efficient, since the speaker can control what is going on and engineer feedback that is likely to be most revealing.

To develop automaticity

To be effective in the use of a language, one needs to be able to use the language with some ease and speed. Earlier, in the section on comprehension, the 'real time' problem was mentioned, according to which it is important to posit mechanisms of comprehension which have some chance of explaining listening in real time. The same basically applies to speaking, the only way in which learners can go beyond carefully constructed utterances and achieve some level of natural speed and rhythm. To obtain the automaticity that this involves requires frequent opportunity to link together the components of utterances so that they can be produced without undue effort, so that what will be important will be the meanings underlying the speech rather than the speech itself. In this respect, there is an aspect of speaking which makes it an example of skilled behaviour, like driving a car, or, probably more relevantly, like playing a musical instrument. Only by frequent use is the fluency side of speech likely to be improved.

This applies to all speech, but it is likely to apply even more forcefully to some aspects than others. It may affect morphology vitally, but hardly affects word order. Hence the opportunity to practise speech in languages where morphology plays a more prominent role may be all the more important.

To develop discourse skills

The previous arguments for the importance of output have not challenged the view that language learning is essentially the development of a sentence-based interlanguage system. But it has been claimed (Brown and Yule 1983) that much ELT work focuses excessively on 'short turns', and that as a result learners' capacities to take part in extended discourse are not stretched. Certainly, current developments in discourse analysis suggest that there is a lot to be learned if one is to become an effective communicator. Discourse management (Bygate 1987), turn-taking skills, and a range of similar capacities which underlie the negotiation of meaning in ongoing discourse (Cook 1989), can only be achieved by actually participating in discourse. If meaning-making is a jointly collaborative activity, then we cannot read about these skills, or even acquire them passively, but instead have to take part in discourse and realize how our resources are put to work to build conversations and negotiate meaning. Extensive speaking practice is therefore unavoidable.

To develop a personal voice

A learner who is completely dependent on what others say, is unlikely to be able to develop a personal manner of speaking. Such a learner will be dependent on the sorts of meanings that he or she has been exposed to, and will not be able to exert an influence on conversational topics. This implies a strange, passive view of what language is used for, and how personal concerns are manifested by it. It seems inevitable that if one wants to say things that are important, one must have, during language learning, the opportunity to steer conversations along routes of interest to the speaker, and to find ways of expressing individual meanings. A role for output here seems unavoidable.

The importance of output

These six reasons for the importance of output provide yet another argument against the sufficiency of a comprehension-based approach. They detail the inadequacy of simply listening, and show that output too is a necessary condition for successful language learning. But the next question is to consider whether output, in turn, is sufficient and efficient as a condition for language.

The six roles for output listed above might suggest that it is. The first such use, obtaining better input (see p. 79), will not be pursued here since it is only a more sensitive form of Krashen's views. The last two roles, acquiring discourse skills and developing a personal voice (see above), are more concerned with the construct of communicative competence. The central roles for output in promoting interlanguage development are forcing syntactic processing, testing hypotheses, and developing automaticity. The first two of these central roles focus on form while the third is more concerned with performance and fluency.

The contrast implied here between attention to form and attention to performance, suggests a question which is susceptible to empirical investigation. We need to devise studies which can establish whether actual output favours form or emphasizes fluency at the expense of form. Although output may generally be a good thing, the roles it serves in specific situations may not be so beneficial. It then becomes important to establish, through research, the conditions and constraints under which output promotes a focus on form.

In the literature, two general accounts of the role of communication in language development have been proposed: language development through the negotiation of meaning (Pica 1994, for example); and development through the operation of strategic competence (such as Bialystok 1990). We will examine each of them in turn to assess whether they can clarify whether output and interaction have a positive influence, and if so, what that influence might be.

Negotiation of meaning

Advocates of the negotiation of meaning approach (Gass and Varonis 1994 and Pica 1994, for example) suggest that the ongoing identification of difficulties in interactive encounters stimulates learners to overcome such difficulties. In so doing, it is hypothesized that modifications which are made to speech in the service of repairing conversational breakdown have beneficial spin-off effects on underlying interlanguage. Conversation is then seen as the ideal supportive mechanism to:

1   identify areas where interlanguage is limited and needs extension;
2   provide scaffolding and feedback at precisely the point when it will be most useful since the learner will be particularly sensitive to the cues provided to enable new meanings to be encoded.

Conversational moves such as comprehension checks, clarification requests, and the like will reflect how conversation leads to engagement with an underlying interlanguage system when it is made unusually malleable. To link back with the roles for output discussed above, such negotiation of meaning provides ideal opportunities for hypotheses to be tested and a syntactic mode of processing to be highlighted.

There are, however, problems here. Aston (1986), for example, has questioned the desirability of contriving interactions intended to generate extensive negotiation of meaning, and whose value is judged according to how well this is achieved. He proposes, in fact, that such interactions can be irritating for students, and unrepresentative as far as natural discourse is concerned. The wider issue, essentially, is that it is one thing for successful negotiation to take place, but quite another for this to have beneficial consequences for interlanguage development. Far from scaffolding interlanguage development, negotiation sequences may distract the learners and overload the processing systems they are using, with the result that even when successful scaffolded negotiations occur which produce more complex language, these may not have an impact upon underlying change because there is no time to consolidate them.

In any case, there is also the possibility that such studies may have over-estimated the empirical importance of negotiation for meaning. Foster (1998) demonstrates that although one can, indeed, point to differences between interaction types and participation patterns as far as negotiation of meaning indices are concerned, global figures disguise the true state of affairs. In fact, unusually active students, whatever the task or participation pattern, engage in the same amount of negotiation of meaning – nil. As a result, we have to conclude that for most students this aspect of output does not have a definite impact on interlanguage change and development.

Strategic competence

The situation is not particularly different with respect to the operation of strategic competence and communication strategies, the other more general framework which might provide a rationale for output-led interlanguage development. This literature (Tarone 1981; Færch and Kasper 1983; Bialystok 1990) has examined the ways in which the strategies that learners adopt when faced by communication problems can be described clearly and classified. Many categorization systems have been proposed, such as Færch and Kasper's (1983) distinction between achievement and avoidance strategies, and Bialystok's (1990) contrast between linguistic and cognitive factors. One attraction of such systems is that they account for the range of strategies which are used as parsimoniously and yet as comprehensively as possible. In addition, it is useful if they can be grounded in related fields, as is the case with Færch and Kasper's (1983) appeal to general psycholinguistic models.

However, a central issue is whether the operation of such strategies of communication at a particular time to solve particular problems has any implications for interlanguage change and development over time.[1] One could ask, for example, whether achievement strategies (that is, retain the original intention of meaning, and use resources creatively to solve a communication problem) are more likely to lead to development than avoidance strategies (that is, do not extend one's linguistic repertoire, but instead change the message to be communicated so that it comes within available resources). Similarly, one could ask whether there are different implications from the use of linguistic strategies compared with cognitive ones.

A different way of examining essentially the same point is to consider the relationship between communication strategies and the Canale and Swain (1980) model of communicative competence. This contains three (Canale and Swain 1980) or four (Canale 1983) competences: linguistic, sociolinguistic, discourse, and strategic (discourse being the added fourth competence: see the discussion in McNamara 1995). Linguistic, sociolinguistic, and discourse competences are, in a sense, more basic, since they represent areas of coherent competence in relation to different aspects of communication. Strategic competence, in this formulation, has a less integrated quality in that it is meant to function in an improvisatory manner when problems are encountered because other competences are lacking (see Bachman 1990). Presumably the capacity to negotiate meaning would be part of a more general strategic competence.

A weak interpretation of what is happening would be that such strategies have no other function than to solve some sort of communicative breakdown in order that conversation can proceed. With this interpretation, all that happens when a problem is encountered is that some degree of resourcefulness is drawn on, and the problem in question may or may not be solved. In this view, it is not assumed that there is much *trace* from the activity of solving the problem in question. Although the 'solution' may enable further interaction to take place (which is, of course, not a bad thing), its details are regarded as transitory and unimportant.

However, a stronger interpretation is that when communication strategies are used, they have implications for longer-term language development. There are three requirements for this to happen. First, it is necessary that solving current communicative problems leaves some sort of trace. In other words, what is initially an improvisation to convey one's meaning when resources are limited is noticed and becomes more than a transitory but evanescent success; there must be something about the interaction which is sufficiently salient, and/or the processing capacity available allows such attention. Second, the improvisation which has become a solution must be useful to future problems – it must have some transfer or generalizing power. Such an outcome would reflect the way the interaction itself has led to useful hypothesis generation or to syntactic processing (Swain 1985; 1995). Third, the communicative solution needs to become proceduralized, either because it is so striking during *one* occurrence (Logan 1998), or because its strength is built up more gradually through repeated related solutions to essentially the same communicative problem

(Anderson 1992). In any case, it becomes available as part of one's communicative repertoire on subsequent occasions when problems similar to the original one are encountered. If all these conditions are met, and interlanguage development occurs, then we do indeed have a case of learning to talk by talking. In this case solving communicative problems engages a language learning capacity directly, since solving problems is what puts pressure on the communicative system to change.

Problems with communication strategies

There are a number of problems with such an interpretation of how communication strategies function beneficially over time. Of course, what would be ideal, in this regard, would be longitudinal studies of the impact of different patterns of communication strategy use on interlanguage development, since such studies would chart the nature of interlanguage change, for relevant learners, relating interaction patterns and strategic language use to the underlying systems change which occurs. Unfortunately, such studies are in short supply and isolated case studies have to be relied upon to an excessive degree. (The thrust of most such research has been to establish classification schemes or analytic frameworks which have little to say about longer-term change.) Even so, there is some information available.

Empirically-motivated concerns

Schmidt (1983) reports the case of Wes, a Japanese learner of English in Hawaii. Schmidt studied Wes over an extended period, gathering data on his language performance in informal settings over two years. Schmidt used as a guiding theoretical framework the Canale and Swain (1980) model of communicative competence mentioned earlier. He also drew attention to Wes's attitude to learning and using English, since Wes was quite clear that he was uninterested in instruction or correctness, and was more concerned with achieving effective communication with those people he wanted to talk to. In this he was successful, since in the period of the study he went from being regarded as a minimal English speaker to being taken as a worthwhile interlocutor by native speakers who clearly reacted to him, at the end of the period of study, as a conversational equal.

The most interesting aspect of the study, however, is that when Wes's improvement over the period was charted in terms of the Canale and Swain framework, it was apparent that while his strategic and discourse competence changed markedly for the better, his improvement in terms of linguistic competence was minimal (and his syntax was as fractured at the end of the period as it was at the beginning), while in the sociolinguistic area the change was not very great. In this case, then, Wes's reliance on strategic capabilities to achieve communication was spectacularly successful when judged in terms of conveying meanings and being acceptable as a conversational partner, but very unsuccessful when judged in terms of development in his underlying interlanguage system. Reliance on communication strategies, that is, seemed to be harmful to his linguistic health, a point that evidently did not disturb Wes, since he had achieved the goals he had set for himself as far as communication was concerned.

A similar conclusion arises from work done at the Foreign Service Institute (Higgs and Clifford 1982), which is also of a longitudinal nature. The Foreign Service Institute (FSI) training programme emphasizes the acquisition of oral skills, and is accompanied by the administration of the FSI-ILR (Interagency Language Roundtable) oral interview test (Lowe 1982). This test enables both a global and an analytic view of the competence of the personnel being trained to be obtained. The former is based on a five-step scale on which global proficiency can be estimated (supplemented by plus scores for each numerical category). The latter gives separate ratings for syntax, vocabulary, fluency, and other skill areas. In this way, the longitudinal development of the learners can be monitored through an examination of the profiles generated by the analytic markings scheme over several points in time.

Higgs and Clifford (1982) report that profiles of students at earlier points of instruction can be used predictively to estimate the likely later gain of the candidates in question. Given the basic five-step scale, candidates whose grammar ratings were above or equal to their ratings in vocabulary or fluency tended to continue to progress and reach higher performance levels as they received more instruction. In other words, balanced analytic ratings or higher grammar predicted continued gain and capacity to profit from instruction. In contrast, students whose earlier profiles showed strong fluency and vocabulary skills did not manifest the same degree of sustained improvement. Higgs and Clifford (1982) called these learners 'terminal 2's' (from the five-step scale), suggesting that the earlier profile was associated with a probable plateauing in achievement at around Level 2. It seemed as though the earlier fluency and vocabulary gains comprised continued development, and may have been associated with fossilization. These learners corresponded, in some ways, to Schmidt's Wes, since earlier communicative effectiveness (and the higher fluency and vocabulary scores earlier in instruction might be connected with a communicative orientation on the part of such learners) represented a short-term advantage which proved expensive in the longer run since it was associated with an interlanguage system which became less permeable. Once again, the suggestion is that unless there is direct involvement of the underlying language system in communication, it need not develop, even though communicative effectiveness does change.

Theoretically-based concerns

In addition to these empirically motivated concerns over the usefulness of communication strategies, there are some more theoretically-based worries. First of all, there are what might be termed logical criticisms of the viewpoint. For example, it is difficult to imagine exactly how such strategies can leave a trace. It is likely that interesting operations will occur when achievement strategies are used to cope with communicative problems whose solution will require some adaptation of the underlying system. But in such cases the need to solve unforeseen problems will ensure that the lion's share of cognitive resources will be directed to conveying meanings. As a result, it is not easy to see how memory of what exactly has worked can be effectively retained for the next occasion when the strategy may be useful, since this outcome would require the spare capacity to fumble towards such a solution *and* simultaneously to monitor its nature and its effect. It seems unlikely that the conflicting calls on limited resources will allow this with any dependability. VanPatten (1990) makes a similar point in relation to comprehension, where he demonstrates that syntactic and semantic processing seem to conflict as far as attentional resources are concerned, and that attention span is too limited to allow both to be emphasized simultaneously. One can only assume that speaking, as part of the interaction, will pose significantly greater problems for learning.

More generally, for the use of communication strategies to work to foster progress systematically, it would be necessary to show not simply that they leave a trace, but also that the use of such strategies has some cumulative building potential. For if SLA research has demonstrated anything, it is that developmental sequences have considerable importance. It would be necessary, therefore, to show that the progressive improvisations which solve communication problems build upon one another, and are not isolated chance manipulations of language elements in one restricted area, but have system-developing potential, and push the interlanguage system in some consistent direction. Unfortunately, this argument seems hard to envisage. Communication strategies seem much easier to imagine as unplanned resourceful solutions rather than as cumulative building blocks. It would seem that researchers in this area have devoted much more effort to debating the relative merits of different classification systems for strategies than to examining the developmental potential of the different strategy types that have been classified. When one examines the literature on types of strategy used, things are distinctly unpromising. First of all, a research bias in this area often leads investigators to provoke the need for strategy use by requiring subjects to focus on vocabulary problems. As a result, the area we know most about is probably the least relevant for interlanguage development. Further, when one looks at examples of strategies (for example, approximation, word coinage, circumlocution, literal translation, avoidance, and so on (Bialystok 1990)), one can hardly see how they can help make a sustained contribution to language development. Similarly, negotiation of meaning sequences (Pica 1994; Lyster and Ranta 1997) show little evidence of useful modifications to interlanguage being made, or of the incorporation of scaffolded supports for more complex language. So, once again, a *potential* way in which interaction could drive forward interlanguage development reveals itself to be implausible.

Even more generally there is the point that much of communication is elliptical, a joint creation by the participants in conversation who each spend their time working out what the other knows. In other words, if Grice's maxims are being followed, speakers will judge their contributions to conversation so that they are relevant and brief. Such people, native speakers or learners, are going to place great emphasis on communicating meanings, but may not necessarily worry about the exact form that they use (Kess 1992). In this respect, Grice (1975) has made it clear that maxims for conversation make for a considerable processing burden because of what is *not* said. To spell everything out in complete and well-formed sentences would soon empty rooms, and get one classified as a boring pedant. Much adult conversation is elliptical and incomplete in surface form, heavy in the assumptions that it makes about background knowledge which enables inferences about intended meaning, speaker attitudes, and so on (Widdowson 1989). It goes against the grain, in other words, to do more than use form as one element or pressure in native-speaker communication, where the major emphasis will be on the satisfactoriness of the flow of the conversation, not the correctness, or completeness (or the usefulness for interlanguage development amongst learners) of what is said.

So speakers will generally, or at least often, say only what needs to be said, confident that their interlocutors will engage in whatever conversational implicature is necessary to recover the intended meaning (or will say something that will enable the first speaker to correct any misinterpretation that will occur). Learning to participate in such conversations will therefore not be learning to use complete and well-formed sentences, but instead learning how to make well-judged interventions which one's conversational partners will judge as furthering the conversation. And just as with comprehension, the problem from a language learner's point of view is that mature language users are just *too good* at grasping the full meaning of utterances which are elliptical. The knowledge sources covered earlier from Anderson and Lynch (1988) in relation to comprehension (schematic, contextual, and systemic) are just as relevant in the case of production, since the speaker is framing what is said with the comprehension abilities of the listener in mind. In this respect we have a clear difference between the mature and the child language learner. The mature language learner is able to draw on vastly greater stores of schematic and contextual knowledge, and is not (particularly) egocentric in orientation (although we can all quickly think of exceptions amongst our acquaintances). Consequently he or she is able to bypass syntax for a great deal of the time. Since it is meanings which are primary, as long as the speaker feels that communication is proceeding satisfactorily, the need for precise syntax is diminished. This contrasts very clearly with the younger language learner who has much less schematic and contextual knowledge available personally, and who is also much less able to imagine what his or her interlocutor has by way of knowledge in each of these areas. As a result, the child has much less scope to take syntactic liberties and short cuts.

We are now facing quite a changed picture regarding the usefulness (or lack of it) of conversation for language development. There is less need, for the older learner, to produce complete and well-formed utterances, because most interactions require collaborative construction of meaning rather than solipsistic party pieces. Further, when communicative problems occur, the strategies second language learners adopt are not likely to push forward underlying system change in any cumulative way. Finally, there is the issue that, even if conversation were by means of complete, well-formed utterances, *and* attempts to cope with communicative problems were useful, there is still the likelihood that attempts to cope with ongoing processing demands would not allow the learner to capitalize upon such a temporary breakthrough, establish a memory trace of it, and use it in the future.

Conclusion

The central theme of this chapter has been that syntax has fragile properties. Normal communication is pervaded by the pressures of processing language in real time. We comprehend and produce language not by exhaustively analysing and computing (although we can do these things if we have to, for reasons of creativity or precision) but instead by drawing shamelessly on probabilistic strategies which work effectively enough (given the support and potential for retrieval of miscommunication that discourse provides) at considerable speed of processing. We rely on time-creating devices, context, prediction skills, elliptical language, and a range of similar performance factors to reduce the processing load that we have to deal with during conversation. And the older we become (up to a point) the more adept we can be at exploiting these resources.

The central point is that language use, in itself, does not lead to the development of an analytic knowledge system since meaning distracts attention from form. But clearly communication does proceed, so one can infer that speakers draw upon other non-analytic knowledge systems which, one assumes, have qualities relevant to real-time communication.

Note

1   In one sense, of course, this point is addressed through the distinction between communication and learning strategies. The former emphasizes solutions to immediate communication problems, while the latter are concerned with activities which are intended by the learner to lead to longer-term development. In some cases this distinction is clear, as when, for example, a communication strategy deals with (say) how to express an idea when a lexical item is missing (and has no lasting effect) or when a learner deliberately organizes a list of words for memorization, not attempting to use these words immediately, but instead working towards the extension of an underlying vocabulary. But the central issue is that one can also regard the operation of many communication strategies as containing learning potential, for example when a useful communication strategy becomes proceduralized and so reusable. It is precisely this type of communication strategy that is relevant in this section.

References

Anderson, A. and Lynch, T. (1988) *Listening*. Oxford: Oxford University Press.

Anderson, J.R. (1992) 'Automaticity and the ACT theory'. *American Journal of Psychology* 105: 165–80.

Asher, J.J. (1977) *Learning Another Language Through Actions: The Complete Teacher's Guidebook*. Los Gatos, Calif.: Sky Oaks Publications.

Aston, G. (1986) 'Trouble-shooting in interaction with learners: the more the merrier?' *Applied Linguistics* 7: 128–43.

Bachman, L. (1990) *Fundamental Considerations in Language Testing*. Oxford: Oxford University Press.

Bialystok, E. (1990) *Communication Strategies: A Psychological Analysis of Second Language Use*. Oxford: Blackwell.

Bley-Vroman, R. (1989) 'The logical problem of second language acquisition', in Grass, S. and Schachter, J. (eds) *Linguistic Perspectives on Second Language Acquisition*. Cambridge: Cambridge University Press.

Brown, G. and Yule, G. (1983) *Teaching the Spoken Language*. Cambridge: Cambridge University Press.

Bygate, M (1987) *Speaking*. Oxford: Oxford University Press.

Canale, M. (1983) 'On some dimensions of language proficiency' in Oller (ed.).

Canale, M. and Swain, M. (1980) 'Theoretical bases of communicative approaches to second language teaching and testing'. *Applied Linguistics* 1: 1–47.

Clark, H.H. and Clark, E. (1977) *Psychology and Language*. New York: Harcourt, Brace, Jovanovitch.

Cook, G. (1989) *Discourse*. Oxford: Oxford University Press.

Eskey, D. (1988) 'Holding in the bottom', in Carrell, P., Devine, J. and Eskey, D. (eds) *Interactive Approaches in Second Language Reading*. Cambridge: Cambridge University Press.

Færch, C. and Kasper, G. (1983) *Strategies in Interlanguage Communication*. London: Longman.

Fillenbaum, J. (1971) 'On coping with ordered and unordered conjunctive sentences'. *Journal of Experimental Psychology* 87: 93–8.

Foster, P. (1998) 'A classroom perspective on the negotiation of meaning'. *Applied Linguistics* 19/1.

Gass, S. and Varonis, E.M. (1994) 'Input, interaction, and second language production'. *Studies in Second Language Acquisition* 16: 283–302.

Gregg, K. (1984) 'Krashen's Monitor and Occam's Razor'. *Applied Linguistics* 5: 79–100.

Grice, H.P. (1975) 'Logic and conversation', in P. Cole and Morgan, J. (eds) *Syntax and Semantics 3: Speech Acts*. New York: Academic Press.

Harley, B. and Swain, M. (1984) 'The interlanguage of immersion students and its implications for second language teaching', in Davies, A., Criper, C. and Howatt, A. (eds) *Interlanguage*. Edinburgh: Edinburgh University Press.

Higgs, T. and Clifford, R. (1982) 'The push toward communication', in Higgs, T. (ed.) *Curriculum, Competence, and the Foreign Language Teacher*. Skokie, Ill.: National Textbook Company.

Kess, J.E. (1992) *Psycholinguistics*. Amsterdam: John Benjamins.

Krashen, S. (1985) *The Input Hypothesis*. London: Longman.

Larsen-Freeman, D. (1986) *Techniques and Principles in Language Teaching*. New York: Oxford.

Logan, G.D. (1988) 'Towards an instance theory of automatisation'. *Psychological Review* 95: 492–527.

Long, M. (1985) 'Input and second language acquisition theory', in Gass, S. and Madden, C. (eds) *Input and Second Language Acquisition*. Rowley, Mass.: Newbury House.

Lowe, P. Jr. (1982) *TLR Handbook on Oral Interview Testing*. Washington, D.C.: Defense Language Institute.

Lyster, R. and Ranta, L. (1997) 'Corrective feedback and learner uptake: negotiation of form in communicative classrooms'. *Studies in Second Language Acquisition* 19: 37–66.

McLaughlin, B. (1987) *Theories of Second Language Acquisition*. London: Edward Arnold.

McNamara, T. (1995) 'Modelling performance: opening Pandora's box'. *Applied Linguistics* 16: 159–79.

Oller, J.W. (1983) (ed.). *Issues in Language Testing Research*. Rowley, Mass.: Newbury House.

Pica, T. (1994) 'Research on negotiation: what does it reveal about second language learning, conditions, processes, outcomes?'. *Language Learning* 44: 493–527.

Postovsky, V. (1977) 'Why not start speaking later?', in Burt, M., Dulay, H. and Finocchiaro, M. (eds) *Viewpoints on English as a Second Language*. New York: Regents.

Schmidt, R. (1983) 'Interaction, acculturation, and the acquisition of communicative competence', in Wolfson, N. and Judd, E. (eds) *Sociolinguistics and Second Language Acquisition*. Rowley, Mass.: Newbury House.

Skehan, P. (1984) 'On the non-magical nature of foreign language learning'. *Polygot* 5: *Fiche 1*.

Spolsky, B. (1985) 'Formulating a theory of second language learning'. *Studies in Second Language Acquisition* 7: 269–88.

Swain, M. (1985) 'Communicative competence: some roles of comprehensible input and comprehensible output in its development', in Gass, S. and Madden, C. (eds) *Input in Second Language Acquisition*. Rowley, Mass.: Newbury House.

Swain, M. (1995) 'Three functions of output in second language learning', in G. Cook and B. Seidlhofer (eds) *Principles and Practice in Applied Linguistics*. Oxford: Oxford University Press.

Swain, M. and Lapkin, S. (1982) *Evaluating Bilingual Education: A Canadian Case Study*. Clevedon, Avon: Multilingual Matters.

Tarone, E. (1981) 'Some thoughts on the notion of communication strategy'. *TESOL Quarterly* 15: 2845–95.

VanPatten, B. (1990) 'Attending to content and form in the input: an experiment in consciousness'. *Studies in Second Language Acquisition* 12: 287–301.

Widdowson, H.G. (1989) 'Knowledge of language and ability for use'. *Applied Linguistics* 10: 128–37.

Winitz, H. (1978) 'A reconsideration of comprehension and production in language training'. *Applied Health and Behavioural Sciences* 1: 272–315.

Chapter 5

Leo van Lier

CONSTRAINTS AND RESOURCES IN CLASSROOM TALK: ISSUES OF EQUALITY AND SYMMETRY

MOST CURRENT VIEWS OF LANGUAGE education are based on the assumption that social interaction plays a central role in learning processes, as a quick glance at the dominant terminology shows. "Communication," "negotiation of meaning," "co-construction," "cooperative learning," "responsive teaching," and many other terms like them testify to a fundamental shift from conditioning, association, and other laboratory-based notions of learning to human learning as it is situated in the everyday social world of the learner.

This shift to the social context (and construction) of language learning does not make the investigation of learning processes any easier. On the contrary. The security of isolating variables and defining them operationally, a security obtained by laboratory-like experiments and statistical inferences, is largely lost, as the researcher is forced to look for determinants of learning in the fluid dynamics of real-time learning contexts.

Traditionally we have thought of scientific research as a matter of looking into causes and effects, and the benefits have been cast in the shape of generalizations from a sample to a population and of accurate predictions of future occurrences. This research scenario, while adequate for simple physical processes and laboratory-controlled behaviors, will no longer work once we venture forth into the real world of complexity, in which many people and circumstances act and interact. Here there are no simple causes, and predictability must yield to contingency. Research must be aimed at increasing our understanding, both holistically and in the smallest details, of the social setting as a complex adaptive system. Increased understanding allows us not to generalize but to particularize, that is, to adapt our skills, ideas, and strategies to the changing circumstances and the multifarious influences of the contexts in which the investigated processes occur.

It is of the utmost importance to realize how different the job of researching language learning becomes once we decide that the social context is central. To continue looking for operationally defined, discretely measured, statistically manipulated, and causally predictive variables would be to approach one job with tools that belong to another. It would be like going to an archaeological site with a combine harvester or like shining shoes with a nail file.

In this essay I examine social interaction in language-learning settings from the point of view that such settings are complex systems in which both attention to detail and global understanding are necessary. There are many different kinds of interaction that may occur in these settings, but I group them into two broad types: teacher–learner interaction and learner–learner interaction. Both have been the subject of considerable research, and their potential to facilitate (or hinder) language learning has been much debated. I look at transcribed examples of learning talk to try to understand how social interaction facilitates learning.

The first example is an extract from a teacher–learner interaction; the second, an extract from a learner–learner interaction. (In the transcriptions that follow; *x*'s in parentheses indicate an unintelligible, brief exclamation or word; a left square bracket indicates overlap; colons indicate lengthening of the previous sound; the equals sign indicates that the turn continues below at the next equals sign; and three ellipsis dots indicate a pause of about one second.

Teacher: *Put the umbrella . . .*
Student: *Put the umbrella on the floor . . .*
Teacher: *On the floor . . .*
Student: *. . . between . . .*
Teacher: *. . . between . . .*
Student: *. . . the bookshelf and the TV.*
Teacher: *Very good.*

In this example of interaction in an ESL classroom, it is easy to distinguish teacher from student. The teacher prompts and gives feedback, while the student produces language as part of a task (here, placing objects in a picture as a way of practicing prepositions).

That such classroom interaction is easily recognizable is often taken as evidence of its artificiality. The characteristic pattern has the teacher doing most of the talking while the students act as rather passive responders and followers of directions. As Anthony Edwards and David Westgate (1987) put it, classroom talk seems to run along "deep grooves," even in settings that aim to break new ground. Students "have only very restricted opportunities to participate in the language of the classroom," as John Sinclair and David Brazil (1982) note.

What makes classroom talk the way it is? How does it differ from interaction in other settings, and how can it be brought in line with present-day critical and constructivist goals for education?

Learner 1: *Here I — sometimes go to the beach (xxxxxx)*
Learner 2: *Pebble Beach?*
Learner 1: *Not Pebble Beach. My (xxxxxx)*
Learner 2:   *[They near — Oh, yeah.*
Learner 1:   *[Uhuh*
Learner 2: *Wow. Is it good?*
Learner 1: *Yeah, I think so.*
Learner 2: *But I think here the beach not beautiful*
Learner 1: *O:h, re::ally?*
Learner 2: *Yes. It's not white. The sand is not white.*
Learner 1:   *[Uhuh*
Learner 2: *And the water — you cannot swim.*
Learner 1: *I see because yeah! We can swim but=*
Learner 2: *[This water is —*
Learner 1: *[=the water is cold.*

In this conversation between two ESL learners, in contrast to the teacher–student interaction above, no one dominates or is in control: both learners contribute fairly equally to the talk. The learners understand each other perfectly and are able to express viewpoints and advance arguments. They do not, at least not in this extract, infect each other with linguistic errors or create some form of interlingual pidgin, as teachers sometimes fear learners might do when left to their own devices.

But what kinds of opportunities do learners have to learn new language when they talk to each other in this way? Are the blind leading the blind here, or can such learner–learner conversation become a sort of interactional bootstrapping, where participants assemble learning material or contribute learning material to each other in the natural course of their talk?

The effectiveness of teacher talk and of learner talk as input for learning has been extensively discussed and researched (Chaudron 1988; Pica 1987; Ellis 1994). Teacher talk has been lauded for being comprehensible and criticized for being inauthentic and not attuned to student needs. Learner talk has been lauded for providing opportunities for negotiating meaning and criticized for being a defective model, riddled with inaccuracies. On the whole, research has been supportive of learner–learner interaction more than of teacher talk, but the learner–learner talk studied has usually been interactional (e.g., as group work; see Long and Porter 1985), and the teacher talk has tended to be monologic (e.g., in the form of lectures or instructions; see Parker and Chaudron 1987). We therefore do not know if it is the nature of the talk or the nature of the interlocutor or a combination of both that makes the difference.

Constraints and resources

The British sociologist Anthony Giddens describes the structure of social systems in terms of rules that both enable and constrain characteristics. Just as in a game, and I include the special sense that Ludwig Wittgenstein attaches to "language game," the social world is governed by rules that allow certain moves to be made while disallowing (or disfavoring) others.[1] In a game like chess, these rules and moves are clear and circumscribed, but in social settings the rules are often tacit and ambiguous, and their precise interpretation or definition may have to be negotiated in interaction.

In the social setting of the classroom, interaction among participants takes place against a backdrop of constraints and resources that are in some ways different, in some ways similar, to those that characterize other settings. The classroom thus can be seen to constitute a speech exchange system (Sacks, Schegloff, and Jefferson 1974) that has its own rules for turn taking and gives its participants certain rights and duties. The classroom is the primary setting in which talk-for-language-learning (learning talk) is carried out, and as such the classroom demonstrates the norms for proper behavior (what is called "fixity" by Giddens (1984) or "habitus" by Bourdieu (1990)) that underlie the institutional task of language teaching.

People in language classrooms, engaged in the official business of language learning, tend to behave and talk in ways that ratify that business, in other words, they behave and talk "appropriately" (see Fairclough (1992) for an incisive discussion of this problematic term). Elements of appropriateness, most prominent inside the classroom, may remain visible also outside the classroom, whenever learning talk is carried out in nondesignated places and at nonscheduled times (in cafeterias, around picnic tables, and so on), as when two students in the extract of learner–learner interaction given above agree to engage in a conversation at the request of a researcher. But time and place may make a difference in the way talk is conducted, and learning talk inside lessons may differ structurally from learning talk outside lessons. This possibility needs to be taken into account when learners' and teachers' interactions are analyzed.

There are practical consequences of this constraints–resources view of language learning contexts. In an article entitled "No Talking in Class," J. H. Lii (1994) depicts the traditional role of teacher as one of lecturing and that of students as "mostly listening passively in class." Indeed, a student is quoted as saying that he used to have "trouble concentrating because he was so bored by lectures." These comments fit the known stereotypes of teaching well enough. The interesting twist here is that in the innovative class described (which has twenty-five students), the problem is solved not by the teacher's changing his way of speaking and interacting with the students but by the placing of a computer between the teacher and the taught. Thanks to the insertion of the computer, students "now have the opportunity to interact with teachers and receive instant feedback." A skeptical person might ask, Why do interaction and feedback require an artificial interface? Why can't professors interact with their students without a computer?

Pierre Bourdieu and Jean-Claude Passeron, in their work on cultural reproduction, suggest that the institution equips the teacher with certain distancing techniques; the most efficient technique is "magisterial discourse," which condemns the teacher to "theatrical monologue." So powerful is this institutional control over the teacher's language use, according to Bourdieu and Passeron (1977) that "efforts to set up dialogue immediately turn into fiction or farce". The possibility that computer use may be able to circumvent these institutional constraints is intriguing.[2]

This characterization of teacher–student interaction may seem overdrawn and unrepresentative of today's classrooms, many of which are more dynamic and democratic. But there is no doubt that in various subtle or overt ways the institutional setting constrains the types of talk that can occur within its domain; and it is an open question whether a teacher is free to ignore such constraints in the interests of pedagogical action. Bourdieu and Passeron are clearly skeptical about the possibility of that freedom, though perhaps transformation-minded educators may want to see how far they can go, and to what effect.

The institutional setting, of course, offers resources and facilitates their deployment in the tangible form of budgets, materials, equipment, and the like, but also in the form, less palpable though perhaps more important, of authority and power: the authority to set the agenda, the power to judge (and grade, test, pass, fail); the authority to speak, the power to control and evaluate the speech of others. This authority and this power have traditionally defined the teacher and the work of teaching, but they are increasingly viewed as no longer appropriate in today's learning environments. John Merrow reports the story of a teacher's not knowing how to continue with a multimedia project after a specialized instructor was laid off. It had not occurred to this teacher that she could ask the students to teach her; asking them did not fit her concept of the teacher's role. As Merrow (1995) suggests, "teachers won't survive, and school will become increasingly irrelevant, if teachers don't change their style of teaching," a style he refers to as "the bank deposit approach".

It is within the structure of institutional constraints and resources that the teacher's interaction with learners must take place. When teacher talk and teacher–learner interaction are examined, particularly when recommendations for changes are made, these structuring forces must be kept in mind. If interaction is as important for language learning as current theories claim it is, then the kinds of interaction the classroom permits and the changes the teacher can realistically make to those kinds of interaction are of great importance to research.

Taking a closer look at teacher–learner interaction in the language classroom, I ignore such common types of teacher talk as the lecture, the story, and various forms of explanation and instruction, since my focus is on social interaction. But I do not deny the importance and potential value for learning of these more monologic forms.

The initiation-response-feedback exchange

Teacher: *What is this called?*
Learner: *Plastic.*
Teacher: *You called it plastic. Good! It's plastic. But it's got another name too . . . . . . a transparency.*

This exchange between a teacher and a learner is unmistakably classroom talk. It contains the following steps:

1   The teacher, holding up an overhead transparency, asks a question to which the teacher already knows the answer.
2   The teacher wishes to see if the learner has some particular piece of knowledge and can display this knowledge.
3   The learner responds effectively and efficiently, but also elliptically, using just one word.
4   The teacher evaluates the learner's response, approving of it, but then suggests that there might be another, more felicitous, answer.

This particular form of classroom interaction, the teaching exchange, is considered among the most frequently occurring types of teacher–student talk in the classroom (Sinclair and Coulthard 1975; Mehan 1979; van Lier 1988; Wells 1993) and is usually called an IRF exchange, since it consists of these three parts (or moves): initiation, response, feedback.

In the IRF format, a number of different things can be accomplished. At the most mechanical, rote-learning end of IRF, the teacher's questions require the students merely to recite previously learned items. IRF may also be used by the teacher to see if students know a certain word or linguistic item. IRF can demand more, challenging students to think, reason, and make connections. At the most demanding end of IRF, students must be articulate and precise; they are pushed by successive probing questions, to clarify, substantiate, or illustrate some point that they made previously.

Teacher–learner interaction in the three-turn format of IRF therefore occupies a continuum between mechanical and demanding, as shown in the figure below.

Given the variety of pedagogical work that the IRF format permits, it would be a mistake to dismiss it altogether as bad practice. Every case must be examined on its merits. As a rule of thumb, the precise nature of the IRF being employed in a particular instance is revealed in the third turn,[3] since this is where the teacher typically reveals the purpose of the question or sequence of questions. After the following question-answer pair

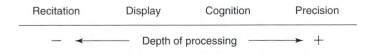

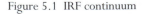

Figure 5.1 IRF continuum

Teacher: *What's the difference between "water is heating" and "water is heated"?*
Learner: *Water is heating, it — it's the one who's heating.*

a variety of third turns are possible. In each case, a different type of task is revealed to be in progress:

Teacher: *Good. Say the whole sentence: Water is heating the radiators.*
   (recitation)

Teacher: *Good. What do we call that construction?*
   (display)

Teacher: *And can you think of some things that it might be heating?*
   (cognition)

Teacher: *Aha, can you explain that in a little more detail?*
   (precision)

Adapted from van Lier (1996a)

This example shows that the IRF structure cannot be regarded as a single type of pedagogical activity. All four IRF types of teacher–learner interaction given above can be used to evaluate or control or to invite participation. Knowing the purpose of a particular IRF exercise, though this may not always be easy, is crucial in determining its pedagogical value. But there are some things that all IRF sequences have in common, and these common features must be examined before IRF can be assessed as a pedagogical tool.

Learning as co-construction: the limits of IRF

The central feature of IRF is that the teacher is unequivocally in charge. This being in charge manifests itself in a number of ways.

Every IRF exchange is a step in an overall plan designed by the teacher. The plan may be to check what the students know (as in recitation or display), to construct knowledge or an argument, perhaps along Socratic lines, or to push the students toward clarity of expression. It is important to note that the plan is not coconstructed. To varying degrees, students may be aware of the nature of the plan and aware of the direction in which the discourse is moving, but usually these matters are revealed only gradually and incidentally.

The teacher does all the initiating and closing (in other words, takes all the first and third turns), and the students' work is done exclusively in the response slot. The IRF format therefore discourages student initiation and student repair work. As Denis Newman, Peg Griffin, and Michael Cole (1989) note, "the three-part unit has a built-in repair procedure in the teacher's last turn so that incorrect information can be replaced with the right answers". It is extremely hard, if not impossible, in the IRF format, for the student to ask questions, to disagree, to self-correct, and so on. Indeed, I found that such student utterances overwhelmingly occur as private turns, side sequences, or in other ways outside the IRF format. Often they are whispered comments to a fellow learner or questions written down in a notebook. The IRF format discourages interruption (or disruption) and can therefore be called a closed rather than open discourse format, in that it structurally and functionally controls what takes place. It is like a discursive guided bus tour, but the itinerary is often unknown to the students.

Students' opportunities to exercise initiative (see van Lier 1988; Kinginger 1994) or to develop a sense of control and self-regulation (a sense of ownership of the discourse, a sense of being empowered) are extremely restricted in the IRF format. Not only are student utterances often highly elliptical and syntactically reduced, occurring only in the response slot, sandwiched between two teacher turns (van Lier 1996a), they also prevent the student from doing turn taking, topic development, and activity structuring work. They do not allow, to any significant extent, negotiation of the direction of instruction.

Given these basic features, how does IRF relate to current recommendations of co-construction, responsive teaching (Bowers and Flinders 1990; Shuy 1991), or the instructional conversation (Tharp and Gallimore 1988), especially if such recommendations are discussed from the perspective of critical pedagogy (Darder 1991; Shor 1992)? I explore this question from three different though related angles.

Vygotsky's zone of proximal development and the notion of pedagogical scaffolding

Lev Vygotsky discusses the range of activities a learner can accomplish with the assistance of a more capable person, such as a teacher. At any point in a learner's development, some activities (skills, operations, etc.) are within the learner's competence (this might be called the area of self-regulation), others can be accomplished only with special guidance, and yet others lie entirely outside the learner's scope. The middle band of activity, which is naturally the focus of pedagogical action, is referred to by Vygotsky as the zone of proximal development (1978). Working within this zone (the "construction zone" in Newman, Griffin, and Cole), a teacher develops strategies for assisting the learner. The various kinds of assistance, which guide a learner into an activity that initially is too complex, are often called scaffolding (Bruner 1983).

The initiation-response-feedback exchange, at least when it moves beyond mere recitation and display, can be regarded as a way of scaffolding instruction, a way of developing cognitive structures in the zone of proximal development, or a way of assisting learners to express themselves with maximum clarity. IRF is frequently used to draw on students' prior experiences and current background knowledge to activate mental schemata and to establish a platform of shared knowledge that will facilitate the introduction and integration of new knowledge. IRF used in several steps in a lesson or during one activity among other activities (see Wells 1993), contributes to the attainment of a larger goal. Once it has served its purpose, it yields to other ways of structuring participation.

Scaffolding, to be of true pedagogical benefit, must be temporary. The scaffold must be gradually dismantled as the learner shows signs of being capable of handling more of the task in question. This process is called handover (Bruner 1983), and without it scaffolding would simply breed dependence and helplessness. It is unclear whether IRF has in its structure the flexibility to effect handover. I suspect that, for handover to be possible, IRF must be abandoned at some point to make place for autonomous learner discourse. This switch from IRF to more open discourse structures may be a crucial pedagogical decision point, and research should focus on it closely.

Intrinsic motivation and learner autonomy

Intrinsic motivation can be defined as the human response to innate needs for competence, relatedness, and autonomy (Deci and Ryan 1992; Deci, Vallerand, Pelletier, and Ryan 1991). It expresses itself as a here-and-now interest in conducting an activity for its own sake, for the pleasure, stimulation, or challenge the activity provides. Intrinsic motivation is closely related to the perception of being able to choose and of being somehow in control of one's actions. Actions that are perceived as being externally controlled have a tendency to reduce intrinsic motivation, as do extrinsic rewards and praise or criticism (see Deci and Ryan 1985, 1992 for examples and summaries of research into intrinsic motivation; see van Lier 1996a).

Since IRF is clearly other-controlled (from the learner's perspective) and since the rewards (in the form of teacher approval or praise in the third turn) are extrinsic, prolonged use of the IRF format may have a negative effect on intrinsic motivation and cause a decrease in levels of attention and involvement. IRF exchanges are like discoursal training wheels. In bicycle riding the training wheels must eventually come off, and likewise in interaction IRF must be replaced by free social interaction.

According to proponents of intrinsic motivation (see van Lier 1996a), pedagogical action must be oriented toward increasing levels of intrinsic motivation and hence toward increasing self-regulation and autonomy. IRF must break its lockstep and yield to other participation patterns, ones that allow student initiative and choice to develop.

Transformation; or, changing educational reality through interaction

Critical pedagogy seeks to transform existing structures of control and inequality (Young 1992; Darder 1991) and to allow students to find voices of their own and become critical and autonomous learners (Wertsch 1991). This emancipatory process requires true dialogue, which, according to Paulo Freire (1972), can flourish only in a climate of equality among participants. Freire maintains that dialogue is indispensable for education: "Without dialogue there is no communication, and without communication there can be no true education".

Characterized by one-sided control, IRF is only minimally dialogic, and the students' participation in its construction (and in the progression toward the overall goal) is largely passive. Therefore IRF cannot not be regarded as fostering equality or contributing to a transformation of educational reality; it embodies the status quo. Yet, as indicated above, it may be used as a preparatory step toward more emancipatory forms of discourse; it may be valuable not for what it is but, rather, for what it potentially leads to. For that potential to be realized, discourse must move from the patterns Robert Young (1992) aptly calls WDPK (What do pupils know?) and GWTT (Guess what teacher thinks) to more discursive patterns marked by shared inquiry. It thus becomes important to investigate how IRF itself can be transformed and how transitions from IRF to other discourse forms can be effected.

Equality and symmetry

The IRF structure is clearly a significant advance over the ritual magisterial performances Bourdieu and Passeron referred to as "theatrical monologue" (see above), since at least it involves students and asks them to contribute, albeit within someone else's agenda. However, in terms of communication, control, initiative, meaning creation and negotiation, message elaboration, and a number of other features characteristic of social interaction, the learner's side of the IRF interaction is seriously curtailed.

It is therefore useful to consider other forms of interaction, including conversational (such as learner–learner interactions) and see what characteristics they have that might be relevant to language learning. For a general examination of interaction, I suggest that there are two main groups of issues:

Issues of equality and inequality, including control and power. In this context, one thinks primarily of teacher talk, but more generally the question of equality may play a role in any interaction between native and nonnative speakers or between a more proficient and a less proficient nonnative speaker (van Lier and Matsuo 1995).

Issues of negotiation and the joint construction of talk. This relates to shared rights and duties of participation, that is, interactional symmetry. Such symmetry, most clearly visible in conversation among equals, may be more difficult to achieve for less proficient speakers. But, as the conversation between two ESL students quoted above demonstrates, it is by no means impossible.

The phenomena relating to, on the one hand, control, power, and equality and, on the other, conversational symmetry and negotiation of meaning are connected: unequal participants tend to have asymmetrical interactions. But a distinction must be made between interactions that are oriented toward achieving symmetry and those that are not (IRF, lectures, instructions, and other common teacher talk belong to the second category).

An orientation toward symmetry does not necessarily involve an assumption of equality or some sort of abdication of authority. A separation between symmetry and equality is crucial for the possibility of fruitful communication between teachers and learners and, indeed, between native speakers and nonnative speakers. If true communication were possible only between equals, then teachers and learners (and even parents and their children) would be forever condemned to pseudo-communication. This is obviously not so.

Having postulated that communication, whether between equals or unequals, requires an orientation toward interactional symmetry, I now show, first, how such an orientation may be visible and, second, what benefits it might have for language learning.

In what ways can utterances be oriented toward symmetry? Basically, the orientation expresses itself in relations of contingency between an utterance and other entities – primarily other utterances (preceding, concurrent, and following), shared knowledge, and relevant features in the world (Gibson (1979) calls them affordances; see further below).

Contingency

The term *contingency* refers to two distinct characteristics of interaction: first, the signaling of relations between a current utterance and previous utterances, either directly (utterance to utterance) or through shared knowledge or shared affordances in the environment; second, the raising of expectations and the crafting of deliberate ambiguities so that future utterances can find a conversational home (see van Lier 1992, 1994 and 1996a). The first characteristic has been well studied under the heading of contextualization by John Gumperz (1992). The ways in which utterances are linked to one another have also been studied extensively by ethnomethodologists,j who have used related concepts such as conditional relevance and reflexive tying (Garfinkel 1967; Sacks, Schegloff, and Jefferson 1974).

My preoccupation with contingency originates in the belief that speakers, by using language contingently, unite structure and function in the most fundamental way possible (unite the given and the new, the topic and the comment, the foregrounded and the back-grounded). Contingent language use encourages, justifies, and motivates grammatical-ization. Noncontingent language use – or, rather, less contingent, since the quality of contingency exists on a continuum – proceeds more statically and encourages a treatment of language as either form or function instead of as an organic whole.

Contingent features are most visible in the kind of talk usually referred to as conversational. Of all forms of talk, conversation is perhaps the hardest to define. It is, in a sense, a catchall concept that can contain other kinds of talk – such as instructions, requests, stories, business deals. A complication is that other kinds of talk can have conversation embedded in them. Interviews, lessons, or sales transactions may suddenly become chatty, then after a while switch back to business. So neat boundaries cannot be drawn around the phenomenon of conversation. Yet we usually know when a conversation is taking place.

In conversation, every utterance is connected by many links – some of them overt, many more of them covert – to previous utterances and through them to the shared (or to-be-shared) world of the participants. Every utterance sets up expectations for what will be said next. Utterances in conversation are thus, at the same time, predicted and predicting; in this way the interactants' mutual engagement (what Rommetveit (1974) calls intersubjectivity) is achieved and maintained.

When talk is contingent, utterances are constructed on the spot rather than planned in advance. In addition, there is symmetry, that is, equal rights and duties of participation, at least ideally.[4] I say "ideally" since it often happens that one person monopolizes the conversation and does not let the others get a word in edgewise. But the orientation toward symmetry still holds, since the participants will note that the conversation was one-sided, that so-and-so monopolized it, and that it was therefore not a "good" conversation.

To illustrate what makes an interaction conversational, I quote two extracts from nonnative speaker interactions. In the first there is a high level of contingency; in the second, a much lower level:

Speaker 1:   *From my room I can see the ocean view*
Speaker 2:   *Wow*
Speaker 1:   *And –*
Speaker 2:   *[And how many room do you have?*
Speaker 1:   *Two bedroom two full bathroom*
Speaker 2:   *What what what*
Speaker 1:   *Two bedroom=*
Speaker 2:   *[Two bedroom*
Speaker 1:   *=and two full bathroom*

Speaker 1:   *I never asked you, what did you do in Japan before you came here?*
Speaker 2:   *Uhm – after finish high school*
Speaker 1:   *Uhuh*
Speaker 2:   *I work – for . . .   . three years*
Speaker 1:   *Hmm*
Speaker 2:   *And –*
Speaker 1:   *[Where did you work?*
Speaker 2:   *It – this is very – difficult for explain*
Speaker 1:   *Try*
Speaker 2:   *I use . . .the computer*
Speaker 1:   *Uhuh*

Speaker 2, an ESL learner, is the same person in both interactions, but in the first her interlocutor is of roughly equal proficiency and in the second her interlocutor is a nativelike bilingual speaker. The first extract illustrates symmetry, and all utterances exhibit a high degree of contingency. The second extract is more like an interview in which speaker 1 encourages speaker 2 to speak. Relations of contingency are weaker, and symmetry is reduced. If contingency could be visualized as bundles of strings connecting utterances, then the strings would be thicker and more numerous in the first conversation and more sparse and spindly in the second.

Many sorts of devices can be used to create contingency: empathy markers ("*Wow!*"), repetitions of parts of each other's utterances ("*two bedroom – two bedroom*"), intonation patterns, gestures, and so on. The devices come from a stock of resources similar to Gumperz's (1992) "contextualization cues" (indeed, as I suggested above, the creation of contingencies overlaps significantly with the process of contextualization), though any interactional marker that can be used to make a contingent link can also be used for other purposes, and this makes tabulating and quantifying contingency impossible.

Contingency, negotiation, and language learning

The dynamics of interaction have been studied in most detail by Teresa Pica and her colleagues (Pica 1987, 1992; Pica and Doughty 1985; Pica, Young, and Doughty 1987). This research, which focuses on opportunities for learners to carry out repair strategies following communicative problems, has revealed various conditions that favor or disfavor such interactional modification and has shown how it benefits comprehension. According to Pica (1987), "What enables learners to move beyond their current interlanguage receptive and expressive capacities when they need to understand unfamiliar linguistic input or when required to produce a comprehensible message are opportunities to modify and restructure their interaction with their interlocutor until mutual comprehension is reached".

By resolving communicative problems through the use of interactional modifications (requests for clarification or confirmation, comprehension checks, recasts, and other such repairing moves), the learner obtains comprehensible input or makes new input available for learning. Research has shown how learners actively work on the language to increase their knowledge and proficiency.

The following observations, based on these analyses of repair in inter-language talk, might help to place repairing in the overall context of interactional language use.

First, as Guy Aston has pointed out, repair work and adjustments of various kinds can be used to express convergence of perspectives among participants or to "seek closure on a problem" (Rudduck 1991), not necessarily to make something comprehensible. George Yule (1990) found that more-proficient interlocutors sometimes simply decide to give up on certain problematic items in a task and move on. Therefore repair may have results other than increased comprehension, though increased comprehension can reasonably be regarded as its chief aim.

Second, the preponderance of repair (in the highly visible form of interactional modifications) may be the result of the type of discourse investigated. In much of the work of Pica and associates (Pica, Young, and Doughty 1987; Pica 1992), the activity types in question are communication tasks in which participants (often a native speaker and a nonnative speaker) need to exchange information. This need leads to interaction that is usually both asymmetrical and unequal, an environment in which explicit repair, with imbalances of the kind illustrated by Yule, tends to be salient. A similar focus on repair can be seen in the analysis by Michael Moerman (1988) of interaction among native speakers of Thai. He concludes that "repair is of central importance to the organization of conversation". Moerman's discussion of repair, however, is based on transcripts of testimony in Thai court cases, where the status of overt repair is probably different from that in general conversation. Indeed, ethnomethodological analyses of repair and related matters in conversation (Schegloff, Jefferson, and Sacks 1977; Heritage 1984; Pomerantz 1984) indicate a strong preference for self-repair and an avoidance of overt reactive repair, that is, repair that follows communication problems.

Third, and related to the second observation, the interactional activity of repairing must be placed in its social context. Repairing, an attempt to achieve mutual understanding in the face of problems, is one set of actions among many that manifest orientation toward mutual engagement (inter-subjectivity) and symmetry. Repairing occurs in response to the perception of those troubles. But since troubles should be avoided in the first place, it makes sense to focus attention also on other mechanisms for achieving mutual understanding and intersubjectivity. It makes no sense, from a discourse-analytical or a pedagogical perspective, to assign special status to an activity that is undertaken only when other, more-preferred activities have been unsuccessful. To use an analogy, ice skaters are judged more on how they skate than on how they pick themselves up after falling on the ice.

Success in interaction – that is, the achievement of mutual understanding, contingency, and intersubjectivity – is dependent on the skillful use of all relevant social and linguistic resources, including those described by Gumperz as contextualization cues and those that create contingency. These resources can be divided into three categories, as follows (see Atkinson and Heritage 1984; Duncan 1972; Kasper 1989; van Lier and Matsuo 1995 for additional examples):

Proactive (planning, predicting)

Opening sequences	(By the way; Do you know what?)
Cataphora	(Now; Listen to this)
Grounders and preparers	(OK, three points I wanna make)
Strategic moves	(Let me give you an example)

Concurrent (making signals during one's own or another person's turn)

Back channels	(Uhuh; Hm)
Gaze	(eye contact, looking away)
Turnover signals	(Let me finish; What do you think?)
Empathy markers	(Oh; Wow; Really?)

Reactive (summarizing, rephrasing, wrapping up)

Repair and correction	(Do you mean x?; Actually it's y)
Demonstrations of understanding	(Oh; I see)
Gists and upshots	(So; In a nutshell; What you're saying is)

The relations between interaction and learning are not explained by this list or, indeed, by any other that might be devised. But at the very least the analysis shows that the concept of negotiation may need to be expanded from Pica's definition: "When a listener signals to a speaker that the speaker's message is not clear, and listener and speaker work interactively to resolve this impasse" (1992). Negotiation includes the proactive and concurrent resources for utterance design, as well as reactive resources other than repair. Repair is thus only one among many forms of negotiation of meaning.

A fourth and final consideration goes to the very foundations of learning and its relation to the environment. Almost all the work in applied linguistics that addresses the role of input and interaction (see Ellis (1994) for an overview) assumes an input–output model of communication and learning. This model is based on a view of language use as the transfer of linguistic matter from one person to another and largely ignores issues of reciprocity and contingency. Being basically a transmission model (as words like *input* and *output* indicate), it does not address learning as transformation and language learning as grammaticalization (the development of grammatical complexity in the organic sense, outlined, e.g., by Rutherford (1987)). It is likely that the true role of interaction in learning and the true sense of what Vygotsky meant by the zone of proximal development can be revealed only through an organic or ecological approach (see Gibson 1979; Bowers and Flinders 1990). In such an approach, notions like contingency and symmetry will be central, and overt acts of repairing will be epiphenomenal (Marcus and Zajonc 1985; Graumann 1990; Platt and Brooks 1994). Linguistic matter in the environment, to the extent that the learner has access to it (see van Lier (1996) for a detailed discussion of access), provides affordances to the active and perceptive learner (Gibson 1979; Deci and Ryan 1992).[5] Whether or not such affordances are packaged as repair sequences is likely to be a minor issue.

A theoretical conclusion

I have discussed two different types of interaction in language learning, teacher–learner interaction in the IRF mode and learner–learner interaction, to illustrate equality and symmetry. I have suggested that interaction is particularly beneficial for learning when it is contingent. Symmetrical interaction is naturally contingent in a variety of ways, but asymmetrical interaction is deficient in contingency. Unequal discourse partners tend to find it more difficult to orient their interaction toward symmetry; as a result their interactions often look like IRF sequences or interviews where one of the partners takes a controlling role.

Two questions remain: What are some ways in which unequal discourse partners – such as teachers and learners or native speakers and nonnative speakers – can engage in symmetrical and contingent interaction, and how would that engagement benefit learning? What are the pedagogical benefits of various forms of asymmetrical discourse, such as lectures and IRF exchanges?

Language learning depends on the access learners have to relevant language material (affordances) in the environment and on internal conditions like motivation. Social inter-action is the prime external condition to ensure access and learners' active engagement. Contingent interaction provides an "intrinsic motivation for listening" (Sacks, Schegloff, and Jefferson 1974). Learners' natural learning processes, through the desire to understand and be understood, synchronize with efficient perception and focusing. Learners will be vigilant toward linguistic features and will make an effort to be pragmatically precise yet ambiguous where ambiguity is needed. Grammaticalization is thus a natural by-product of contingent interaction. To put this idea in the strongest possible (though of course hypothetical) terms: the organic, self-regulating process of contingent interaction is a necessary and sufficient condition for language development to occur. In the absence of appropriate research, this is of course a speculative hypothesis.

But that is only one side of the coin. To the extent that the target of language learning is a standardized, official code (a set of cultural habits) to which the learner has to or wants to conform, linguistic affordances marked as appropriate and desirable must be presented in the environment, and access to these affordances must be facilitated. Here organic language development and external language demands (socioculturally and institutionally mandated) meet each other halfway, and Vygotsky's zone of proximal development is the space wherein internal and external realms (inner resources and outer constraints) of language are mediated.

This mediation takes place under the guidance of parents, teachers, and other competent persons, and the different ways they do this can be captured by terms such as Bruner's *scaffolding*. (*Teaching*, *didactics*, *instruction*, *training*, *drilling*, and so on are of course also terms that have traditionally been used for such expert-novice activities.)

If this view of the relations between language learning and social interaction has merit, then the dynamic connections between more didactic (asymmetrical, less contingent) and more conversational (symmetrical, more contingent) forms of interaction are of central importance in the language learning enterprise.

A practical conclusion

In a book on talented teenagers, Mihaly Csikszentmihalyi, Kevin Rathunde, and Samuel Whalen (1993) compare current teaching with the traditional role of the master in an apprentice system. They observe that the teacher, instead of being a practitioner in a domain, is now a transmitter of information and thus discourages the development of extended and transforming relationships such as those between master and apprentice. Relationships between teachers and students are depersonalized and "kept highly specialized, programmatic, and brief". Technical terms such as "instructional delivery systems" and detailed specifications of instructional objectives corroborate this tendency. Things can only get worse when, as is currently happening in many parts of the Western world, class sizes and school sizes keep increasing, as do teachers' workloads.

There are thus physical and institutional constraints that tend to minimize the possibilities for meaningful interaction between teachers and students. In Giddens's structuration theory, constraints ideally direct and guide, facilitating the deployment of resources. But in a defective institution (definable as one in which constraints and resources are out of balance), constraints may obstruct the very purposes for which they were brought into being. Against constraints of this second type, the teacher must marshal all the resources, meager though they often appear to be, that are available to provide learning opportunities to students. As the history of educational reform movements shows, large-scale reforms tend to achieve little transformation of the status quo. But grassroots, bottom-up innovations, usually based on individual initiative, can produce dramatic results, albeit at the local level only.

Marshaling available resources to promote rich and varied interaction with and among students must be the individual responsibility of every teacher. For teacher development this responsibility means the promotion of what Max van Manen (1991) calls "pedagogical thoughtfulness" or "tact," a mindful, understanding orientation in dealings with students and an ability to act wisely. Many teachers have responded to calls for more interactive and responsive ways of teaching by reducing their teacher-fronted activities and increasing learner–learner interaction through cooperative learning and task-based learning. In current jargon, they have become a "guide on the side" instead of a "sage on the stage".

However, before we swing the pendulum from teacher-centered entirely to teacher-peripheral, it may be worth reflecting on what the optimal roles of a teacher should be.

Learners need, in addition to peer interaction, direct interaction with the teacher, provided it is quality interaction. If we ask learners, many will say that they want lectures, explanations and other forms of explicit teacher guidance. And we should never neglect the universal power of stories (Egan 1986).

The answer to a disproportionate amount of highly controlling and depersonalized teacher talk is not to minimize all teacher talk per se but to find ways to modify it in more-contingent directions. In addition, teacher–learner interaction, such as the IRF, that is designed for scaffolding learners' language use (cognitively or socially) must contain within it the seeds of handover (Bruner 1983), that is, the teacher must continually be on the lookout for signs that learners are ready to be more autonomous language users.

The classroom must regularly provide learners with opportunities to engage in symmetrical interactions, since such interactions immerse learners in contextualized and contingent talk, and since these interactions are intrinsically motivating and attention focusing. Symmetrical interactions are most easily achieved when interlocutors are equal in status and proficiency, but equality is not always essential. Research by Yule suggests that inequality in proficiency can be counterbalanced by having the less proficient speaker carry the main burden of information transfer.

Teachers can also experiment with ways of counterbalancing the inherent inequality of their talk with learners (though in most institutional and cultural settings it would be absurd for them to pretend that status differences between them and their learners do not exist). In a documentary video, classes in various British schools set up links with classes in far-flung places like Finland, Greece, and Portugal (Twitchin 1993). At one point, a fax came in from a class in Greece; it contained drawings and descriptions of weaving techniques, with labels and expressions in Greek. The teacher and learners were naturally at the same level with respect to this text, and interaction among them became symmetrical and exploratory. When a parent who knew Greek was found and invited to class to explain the text, the teacher and his students were all learners.

Taking guidance from these and other examples, the thoughtful teacher-researcher looks for ways to make classroom interaction varied and multidimensional. In the world of language, we all embody different voices on different occasions (Bakhtin 1981; Wertsch 1991; Maybin 1994). It is useful for learners to find that their teachers have various voices and that the learners themselves can experiment with multiple voices in the target language. Such experimentation is crucial if they are to find their own voice, and this is the true purpose of language education.

NOTES

I thank Kathi Bailey for insightful comments on an earlier draft.

1   I realize I gloss over the problems that are inherent in the concept of rule and that have been highlighted in much of the work of Wittgenstein, for example, *Philosophical Investigations*.

2   While the problem of poor teacher–student communication cannot be solved by just any computer work, there is certainly evidence that innovative use of computers can enhance interaction, for example, through interactive writing programs and collaborative project work (for extensive discussion, see Crook 1994; van Lier 1996).

3   Wells distinguishes between third turns that evaluate or provide follow-up (29–30). See also Barnes (1976).

4   Symmetry and contingency are closely related but not synonymous. Symmetry is a

structural discourse term, the result of interactional work by participants. Contingency is a cognitive quality. They usually occur together, but this does not mean that they are identical. As an analogy, light and heat often occur together, for example, in flames, sunlight, and light bulbs, but they are not the same.

5   Gibson describes *affordance* as follows: "The affordances of the environment are what it offers the animal, what it provides or furnishes, either for good or ill . . . something that refers both to the environment and the animal. . . . It implies the complementarity of the animal and the environment" (127). The term *affordance* specifically refers to those aspects of the linguistic environment that become perceivable by the learner as a result of meaningful activity. Affordance is neither the external language nor the learner's internalization of it. It refers to the relations among the engaged learner, meaningful signs, and relevant properties of the real world.

References

Aston, G. (1986) "Trouble-shooting in Interaction with Learners: The More the Merrier?" *Applied Linguistics* 7: 123–43.

Atkinson, J.M. and Heritage, J. (eds) (1984) *Structures of Social Action: Studies in Conversation Analysis*. Cambridge: Cambridge University Press.

Bakhtin, M.M. (1981) *The Dialogic Imagination*. Austin: University of Texas Press.

Barnes, D. (1976) *From Communication to Curriculum*. Harmondsworth: Penguin.

Bourdieu, P. (1990) *The Logic of Practice*. Stanford: Stanford University Press.

Bourdieu, P. and Passeron, J.C. (1977) *Reproduction in Education, Society and Culture*. London: Sage.

Bowers, C.A., and Flinders, D.J. (1990) *Responsive Teaching: An Ecological Approach to Classroom Patterns of Language, Culture, and Thought*. New York: Teachers Coll. Press.

Bruner, J. (1983) *Child's Talk: Learning to Use Language*. New York: Norton.

Chaudron, C. (1988) *Second Language Classrooms: Research on Teaching and Learning*. Cambridge: Cambridge University Press.

Crook, C. (1994) *Computers and the Collaborative Experience of Learning*. London: Routledge.

Csikszentmihalyi, M., Rathunde, K. and Whalen, S. (1993) *Talented Teenagers: The Roots of Success and Failure*. Cambridge: Cambridge University Press.

Darder, A. (1991) *Culture and Power in the Classroom: A Critical Foundation for Bicultural Education*. New York: Bergin.

Deci, E.L., and Ryan, R.M. (1992) "The Initiation and Regulation of Intrinsically Motivated Learning and Achievement" in *Achievement and Motivation: A Social-Development Perspective*, Ann K. Boggiano and Thane S. Pittman (eds) Cambridge: Cambridge University Press.

——— (1985) *Intrinsic Motivation and Self-Determination in Human Behavior*. New York: Plenum.

Deci, E.L., Vallerand, R.J., Pelletier, L.G. and Ryan, R.M. (1991) "Motivation and Education: The Self-Determination Perspective." *Educational Psychologist* 26: 325–46.

Duncan, S. (1972) "Some Signals and Rules for Taking Speaking Turns in Conversation." *Journal of Personality and Social Psychology* 23: 283–92.

Edwards, A.D., and Westgate, D.P.G. (1987) *Investigating Classroom Talk*. London: Palmer.

Egan, K. (1986) *Teaching as Storytelling*. Chicago: University of Chicago Press.

Ellis, R. (1994) *The Study of Second Language Acquisition*. Oxford: Oxford University Press.

Fairclough, N. (1992) 'The Appropriacy of "Appropriateness"', in *Critical Language Awareness*, Norman Fairclough (ed.). London: Longman: 33–56.

Freire, P. (1972) *Pedagogy of the Oppressed*. New York: Herder.

Garfinkel, H. (1967) *Studies in Ethnomethodology*. Englewood Cliffs: Prentice.

Gass, S.M., and Madden, C.G. (1985) *Input in Second Language Acquisition*. Rowley: Newbury.

Gibson, J.J. (1979) *The Ecological Approach to Visual Perception*. Boston: Houghton.

Giddens, A. (1984) *The Constitution of Society*. Berkeley: University of California Press.

Graumann, C.F. (1990) "Perspectival Structure and Dynamics in Dialogue", in *The Dynamics of Dialogue*, Marková, I. and Foppa, K. (eds). New York: Harvester.

Gumperz, J.J. (1992) "Contextualization and Understanding", in *Rethinking Context: Language as an Interactive Phenomenon*, Duranti, A. and Goodwin, C. (eds). Cambridge: Cambridge University Press.

Heritage, J. (1984) "A Change-of-state Token and Aspects of Its Sequential Placement", in Atkinson and Heritage: 299–345

Kasper, G. (1984) "Variation in Speech Act Realization", in *Variation in Second Language Acquisition*, Gass, S., Madden, C., Preston, D. and Selinker, L. (eds) Clevedon, Eng.: Multilingual Matters.

Kinginger, C. (1994) "Learner Initiative in Conversation Management: An Application of Van Lier's Pilot Coding Scheme." *Modern Language Journal* 78: 29–40.

Lii, J.H. "No Talking in Class." *New York Times* 10 Apr. 1994, educ. supp 7.

Long, M. and Porter, P; (1985) "Group Work, Interlanguage Talk, and Second Language Acquisition." *TESOL Quarterly 19*: 207–28.

Marcus, H. and Zajonc, R.B. (1985) "The Cognitive Perspective in Social Psychology", in *Theory and Method*, Lindzey, G. and Aronson, E. (eds). New York: Random. 137–230. Vol. 1 of *Handbook of Social Psychology*. 3rd ed.

Maybin, J. (1994) "Children's Voices: Talk, Knowledge, and Identity", in *Researching Language and Literacy in Social Context*, Graddol, D., Maybin, J. and Stierer, B. (eds). Clevedon, Eng: Multilingual Matters: 131–50.

Mehan, H. (1979) *Learning Lessons: Social Organization in the Classroom*. Cambridge: Harvard University Press.

Merrow, J. (1995) "Four Million Computers Can Be Wrong!" *Education Week* 29 Mar. 1995: 52+.

Moerman, M. (1988) *Talking Culture: Ethnography and Conversation Analysis*. Philadelphia: University of Pennsylvania Press.

Newman, D., Griffin, P. and Cole, M. (1989) *The Construction Zone: Working for Cognitive Change in School*. Cambridge: Cambridge University Press.

Parker, K. and Chaudron, C. (1987) "The Effect of Linguistic Simplifications and Elaborative Modifications on L2 Comprehension." *University of Hawaii Working Papers in English as a Second Language* 6.2: 107–33.

Pica, T. (1987) "Second Language Acquisition, Social Interaction, and the Classroom" *Applied Linguistics* 7: 125.

—— (1992) "The Textual Outcomes of Native Speaker-Non-native Speaker Negotiation: What Do They Reveal about Second Language Learning?", in *Text and Context: Cross-Disciplinary Perspectives on Language Study*, Kramsch, C. and McConnell-Ginet, S. (eds). Lexington: Heath: 198–237.

Pica, T., and Doughty, C. (1985) "Non-native Speaker Interaction in the ESL Classroom", in *Input in Second Language Acquisition*, Gass, S. and Madden, C. (eds). Rowley: Newbury: 115–32.

Pica, T., Young, R. and Doughty, C. (1987) "The Impact of Interaction on Comprehension." *TESOL Quarterly* 21: 737–58.

Platt, E., and Brooks, F.B. (1994) "The 'Acquisition-Rich Environment' Revisited." *Modern Language Journal* 78: 497–511.

Pomerantz, A. (1984) "Pursuing a Response" in Atkinson and Heritage: 152–63.

Rommetveit, R. (1974) *On Message Structure*. New York: Wiley.

Rudduck, J. (1997) *Innovation and Change: Developing Involvement and Understanding*. Milton Keynes: Open University Press.

Rutherford, W. (1987) *Second Language Grammar: Learning and Teaching*. London: Longman.

Sacks, H., Schegloff, E. and Jefferson, G. (1974) "A Simplest Systematics for the Organization of Turn Taking in Conversation." *Language* 50: 696–735.

Schegloff, E.A., Jefferson, G. and Sacks, H. (1977) "The Preference for Self-Correction in the Organization of Repair in Conversation." *Language* 53: 361–82.

Shor, I. (1992) *Empowering Education: Critical Teaching for Social Change*. Chicago: University of Chicago Press.

Shuy, R. (1991) "Secretary Bennett's Teaching: An Argument for Responsive Teaching", in *The Enlightened Eye: Qualitative Inquiry and the Enhancement of Educational Practice*, Elliott Eisner (ed.). New York: Macmillan.

Sinclair, J.M., and Brazil, D. (1982) *Teacher Talk*. Oxford: Oxford University Press.

Sinclair, J.M., and Coulthard, M. (1975) *Towards an Analysis of Discourse*. Oxford: Oxford University Press.

Tharp, R. and Gallimore, R. (1988) *Rousing Minds to Life*. Cambridge: Cambridge University Press.

Twitchin, J. (1993) *European Awareness in Primary Schools*. Mosaic Films. Central Bureau for Educ. Visits and Exchanges.

van Lier, L. (1988) *The Classroom and the Language Learner: Ethnography and Second-Language Classroom Research*. London: Longman.

—— (1992) "Not the Nine O'clock Linguistics Class: Investigating Contingency Grammar." *Language Awareness* 1.2: 91–108.

—— (1994) "Language Awareness, Contingency, and Interaction", in *Consciousness in Second Language Learning*, Hulstijn, J. and Schmidt, R. (eds) *AILA Review* 11: 69–82.

—— (1996a) *Interaction in the Language Curriculum: Awareness, Autonomy and Authenticity*. London: Longman.

—— (1996b) "Social Interaction and Cooperative Learning at, around, with, and through Computers." Eleventh World Congress of Applied Linguistics (AILA 96). University of Jyväskylä, Finland. 5 Aug. 1996.

van Lier, L., and Matsuo, N. (1995) "Varieties of Conversational Experience." Unpublished essay. Monterey Institute of International Studies.

van Manen, M. (1997) *The Tact of Teaching: The Meaning of Pedagogical Thoughtfulness*. Albany: State University of New York Press.

Vygotsky, Lev, S. (1978) *Mind in Society*. Cambridge: Harvard University Press.

Wells, G. (1993) "Reevaluating the IRF Sequence: A Proposal for the Articulation of Theories of Activity and Discourse for the Analysis of Teaching and Learning in the Classroom." *Linguistics and Education* 5: 1-37.

Wertsch, J.V. (1991) *Voices of the Mind: A Sociocultural Approach to Mediated Action*. Cambridge: Harvard University Press.

Wittgenstein, L. (1958) *Philosophical Investigations*. Oxford: Blackwell.

Young, R. (1992) *Critical Theory and Classroom Talk*. Clevedon, Eng: Multilingual Matters.

Yule, G. (1990) "Interactive Conflict Resolution in English." *World Englishes* 9: 53–62.

Chapter 6

Celia Roberts

LANGUAGE ACQUISITION OR LANGUAGE SOCIALISATION IN AND THROUGH DISCOURSE?

Towards a Redefinition of the Domain of SLA

Introduction

OVER THE LAST TWENTY YEARS SLA studies have not ignored issues of discourse and the social context. But often the references to social or socio-cultural context give it only a marginal role in the processes of language development. Equally, there is relatively little concern with the social import of second language development. By 'social import' I mean the effect on social identities, groups and relationships of the multitude of intercultural interactions which take place every day. I also include the effect of these intercultural encounters on individuals – who are, themselves, part of these wider social forces.

So, this paper is concerned with second language development and the immediate social context in which individuals succeed, or fail, to construct local meaning together; with how they connect it to wider knowledge sets and experiences and the social outcomes of this. It is also concerned with the wider social context. In particular, how social processes are constituted in such interactions and how these processes in turn feed back into intercultural encounters and so provide the conditions (or not) for discourse production and interpretation.

Language socialisation rather than language acquisition better describes how learners come to produce and interpret discourse and how such learning is supported (or not) by the assumptions of society at large about multilingualism and second language learners. These issues are particularly salient when researching SLA with minority group workers. And here, Gumperz's notion of contextualisation illuminates the ways in which local understandings and misunderstandings have an effect both on the immediate context for learning and on the wider assumptions and ideologies about linguistic minority groups which also enter into and have an effect on local interactions and conditions for discourse development.

The transformation of many cities in Western and Northern Europe from monolingual to multilingual environments creates crucial sites for the study of second language development. Adult minority workers who are struggling to make a new life for themselves represent a particularly significant group when researchers are considering what constitutes the domain for second language acquisition studies. For many of them, contact with the majority group is in institutional settings – at work or in bureaucratic encounters – and these become the sites where their competence in the new language is put to the test. These settings provide far from ideal conditions for language learning and yet they may be the only ones where the new language is used at all. Charting the interactions and relative progress of this group in an indifferent and often hostile world drives the researcher to conceptualise individuals not simply as language learners but as social beings struggling to manage often conflicting goals. After all, the researcher may be interested in their language development, but the minority workers are concerned with getting things done. As Bourdieu asserts: "What speaks is not utterance, the language, but the whole social person" (Bourdieu, 1977, p. 653). Looking at the 'whole social person' argues for a more holistic approach to second language development than orthodox SLA studies offers, both theoretically and methodologically.

Limits to a social perspective on SLA

Interaction and pragmatics in SLA

There is of course an extensive literature on interaction studies in SLA which examines the conversational devices which foster certain linguistic features. In a more dialogic vein, recent Vygotskian approaches focus on the negotiation of 'comprehensible input' in social interaction. But despite the concentration on collaborative dialogue, language is still conceived of as a product to be acquired rather than as a discourse – a social process – into which members of a community are socialised. Learners are now characterised as 'socially constituted', as "responsible agents with dispositions to think and act in certain ways rooted in their discursive histories" (Lantolf and Pavlenko, 1995, p. 116) but the goal of dialogic learning is still the ability to deploy linguistic phenomena. Methodologically, the analysis tends to focus on a particular feature of language rather than examine in depth local interpretations and reactions. Unsurprisingly, therefore, there is little or no ethnographic evidence to support conclusions drawn. The relatively new field of interlanguage pragmatics would seem to be a more promising area for looking at the whole social person. But despite its concern with contextual factors, it is the narrow concept of the learner and her capacity to realise specific speech acts which generate the key research questions. The endeavour remains an essentially cognitive one as the authors' recognition of the *potential* significance of sociocultural issues implies:

> It would be a mistake to view developmental issues in ILP (interlanguage pragmatics) in purely cognitive terms because the strategies for linguistic action are so closely tied to self-identity and social identity. (Kasper and Schmidt, 1996, p. 159)

To date, however, these issues of social identity and, indeed, other social issues outside the immediate context of utterance, have not figured to any significant extent in interlanguage pragmatics.

Finally, the interaction and pragmatics studies in SLA literature continue the tendency in SLA more generally to reify language so that French, English and so on are treated unproblematically as homogenised 'target languages'. This essentialising of a language assumes that there is only one variety to be learned and that the language and communicative style of the broker's yard or the baker's is similar to that of the standard variety.

A sociolinguistic perspective on SLA

From a sociolinguistic point of view mainstream SLA studies remain asocial – the social import of learning to interact through language remains hidden. A sociolinguistic perspective shifts away from the linguistic system and from a concern with specific items of prag-matic and discourse development to looking at language as a set of norms, at language diversity and ideologies. Specifically, this more holistic view is concerned with interaction as communicative practice and how such practice helps us to understand larger social forces and, in turn, their impact on interactions. This connecting up the macro and the micro in sociolinguistic theory gives due recognition to interactions as sites where minority workers are not simply exposed to and able to negotiate comprehensible input but are social actors struggling to get things done with their emergent competence in a second language.

Reconstituting learners as social actors brings into focus issues of social identity. There is a developing literature on language and social identity and its relation to SLA in which applied and sociolinguistics meet. Within this literature, the learner is understood as a person with multiple identities, many of them contradictory. Identity is dynamic across time and place and language use, social identity and ethnicity are inextricably linked and understood within larger social processes. For example, Pierce (1995) discusses the personal and social investments in learning English as a second language among adult ethnic minority women, how these are observable in their interactions and the ways in which certain social identities are foregrounded or backgrounded. Once notions of social identity are called up, the dominant tradition of SLA as an asocial phenomenon is put into question.

Language socialisation

One response to the critique of the relatively asocial character of SLA is to suggest language socialisation as an alternative perspective. The concept was originally developed within anthropology to describe the process whereby a child becomes an emergent member of the community in which they are growing up. More recently it has been extended to include second language socialisation (SLS) (Duff, 1996). It includes both the socialisation required to use language in specific interactional sequences and the process of socialisation through language – the indirect means of developing socio-cultural knowledge. Where SLA has used modelling and experimentation as the dominant paradigm to research how linguistic features are attended to, stored and accessed, language socialisation studies have used participant observation. Studies of adult minority workers based on naturally occurring language use provide data that more nearly resembles child language socialisation studies. Such data can offer insights into the SLS process provided that it is also supplemented by ethnographic data on speech events and local histories and identities of participants.

In the following example (from Bremer et al., 1996, pp. 60–61) Marcello, an Italian worker in Germany, is being interviewed by T, a counsellor in the Job Centre. Marcello was one of the informants on the European Science Foundation project on natural second language acquisition. He had been in Heidelberg for about a year when this interview was taped, having come to Germany as a real beginner. He was still seeking work and the interview with the counsellor was both an opportunity to find out about work possibilities and to use his developing German. As an example of language socialisation, Marcello needed to be socialised into the specific genre of counselling interviews and use this interaction as an opportunity to develop his socio-cultural knowledge of how bureaucracies work, how work is categorised, what the goals of such an interview are likely to be and so on:

Data Example 1

1   M: wir muss vergessen <laughs>
           we have to forget

2   T: ja + gut + dann hatten wir die saache fur heut
           ok good so we're through for today

3   und wenn sie also in zukunft noch fragen haben kommen sie bei mir vorbei ja
           and if you have any questions in future you'll look in ok

4   M: ja
           yes

5   T: <rufen sie an > ok <leans, back, speaks quietly, looks at door, stands up>
           give me a call ok

6   M: so und jetzt muss ich gehen
           so and now I must go

7   T: <ja>

8   M: < > <both laugh>

9   T: wiedersehen
           bye

10   M: wiedersehen danke
           bye thank you

Transcription Conventions

+	short pause
< >	additional comments on way of speaking etc.
[ ]	overlap
(xxx)	inaudible or omitted word

At one level, this could be construed as a simple case of pragmatic failure. Marcello fails to understand the pre-closing signals of T including "ja", "gut" and "dann hatten wir die sache für heut" and advice for the future. It is only with the non-verbal cues that Marcello realises that they are in the middle of leave taking. His interpretive difficulty is not surprising since as Scarcella (1982) has argued conversational features such as greetings are acquired before pre-closings. But this sequence is also an unusually explicit moment of language socialisation when at line 6 Marcello topicalises the act of departure. This is more than just a matter of picking up on some pre-closing signals, and it is worth mentioning here that the crucial nonverbal signals which are part of the interactive environment are rarely considered in linguistic pragmatics.

In order for Marcello to manage this type of institutional discourse and understand when, how, and why the encounter closes at a particular point, he needs to be socialised into the norms, role relationships and goals of 'gatekeeping' encounters. Ethnographic evidence from minority workers' experience of counselling interviews (Bremer *et al.*, 1996; Gumperz, 1982a, 1982b; Roberts *et al.*, 1992) suggests that issues of speaker rights and responsibilities, expectations about specific goals and the boundaries of what constitutes the personal may differ markedly from that of the majority gatekeepers. In this instance, one of the difficulties for Marcello is the relatively inconclusive way in which the interview appears to end. Whereas counsellors see such interviews as an opportunity to discuss work preferences, minority workers are more likely to expect to be given specific information about particular jobs. Once this information has been given, they expect the interview to be terminated. But in this instance, the counsellor ends the encounter once some information has been elicited from the client and some advice given.

Another frequently occurring example of difference surrounds the issue of the categorisation of work experience around skills and responsibilities and often, therefore, around social status. In the next example (from Bremer *et al.*, 1996, p. 63), Ilhami, a Turkish worker from Germany, is interviewed for an apprenticeship in a garage and is asked what job his father does:

Data Example 2

1   T: e was arbeit' denn dein vater was macht der von beruf
          what work does your father do what is his job

2   I: metallberuf [und]
          metal job

3   T.   [ja] und
          ok and

4   I: (wxxx) schnellpresse <names the town>
          (wxxx) stamping press

5   T: in der schnellpresse in w.
          in the stamping press in w.

6   I: [ja] mhm
          yes

7   T: [ja] und dort tut er metall
          and he does metal there

8   I: metall [und]
          metal and

9   T: [aha]

10   I: die machen auch das macht auch papier
          they also make it makes paper too

11   T: mhm ah so ist das
          mhm ah its like that

(For transcription conventions see Data Example 1.)

This question and answer sequence is unsatisfactory because Ilhami is unaware of the underlying question which is about the social status of his father's job and so of his father's class position. The garage owner interrupts on several occasions to elicit a more specific reply but never makes explicit what he wants to know. These are examples of 'socio-pragmatic failure' in Thomas' terms (Thomas, 1983). But this term tends to emphasise the pragmatic difficulties rather than highlight the process of language socialisation which in this instance concerns the discourse around class position in a gatekeeping interview.

Some problems with the model of SLS

SLS as an apprenticeship model

SLS can be seen as an apprenticeship model. The learner over time participates in the interactional life of the new community and is gradually inducted into what are taken to be its pre-existing discourses. Such a model implies a 'learning by doing' approach in which, for example, the adult minority worker learns from her interactions with her supervisor how to evaluate her role in dealing with complaints about quality (Clyne, 1995). This learning is part of what Rogoff (1984) calls "the social orchestration of thinking through cultural institutions and normative techniques of problem solving" (p. 5). But socialisation is more than cognitive learning in social contexts. It assumes a process of 'belonging', of being part of the 'new community'. And this is where the notion of SLS runs into difficulties since it "assumes that groups are sociocultural totalities and that people eventually arrive at an endpoint of expert belonging" (Rampton, 1995b, p. 487).

The apprenticeship model of SLS is, therefore, only part of the story. It does not fully take account of the relationship between the discourses to which learners are exposed and the learners themselves. In other words it is an overly functionalist model. It underplays the total role and self identity involved in learning and using a new discourse and the constructed nature of intercultural contact in plural and fragmented societies.

So, it is not possible to talk unproblematically of socialisation through language as the means of developing sociocultural knowledge as if there is a stable body of such knowledge. The idea of gradually being inducted into a community's pre-existing discourses suggests a simple, functional model which does not accord with our data of naturally occurring intercultural encounters. In other words, such events are not simply opportunities for the transmission, however indirectly, of the necessary socio-cultural knowledge, but they are sites where social identities are constructed, where the interactants are positioned and position themselves. People speak from within a particular discursive formation. In the case of minority workers, this includes the discourses of ethnic and class position, the wider discourses of racism, their communicative competence and perceived competence and the local positioning which emerges from each interaction.

Positioning in and through discourse

The detailed ways in which interactants position themselves and are positioned illuminates some of the problems with an orthodox view of language socialisation. Different minority workers invest in interactions and in the process of language socialisation in different ways and are themselves defined relatively differently.

There are numerous examples of this positioning in the *Second Language by Adult Immigrants* project (Bremer *et al.*, 1996; Perdue, 1993). A contrastive study of two Italian informants in Britain who are enquiring about buying property in an estate agents (Roberts and Simonot, 1987) shows how they are positioned differently. One of Santo's strategies which helps to maintain conversational involvement is to make general, evaluative comments:

Data Example 3

1   N: then you might get one for about fifty or sixty + or say forty eight sixty something
            like that

2   S: very expensive area anyway
3   N: well this/ this is expensive this is less expensive

By contrast Andrea's strategies are reactive and he tends to develop only those themes which the estate agent has implicitly sanctioned:

1   N: blackstock road er thats a one bedroom flat
2   A: yeah
3   ON: its not two bedrooms
4   A: mhm

(Roberts and Simonot, 1987)

Santo's socialisation into maintaining conversational involvement in service encounters means that he elicits more helpful and extended comments from the clerk. Andrea's encounters are less successful, do not produce opportunities for learning how to do this type of conversational involvement and, as ethnographic evidence shows, cumulatively, position Andrea as marginalised discursively and socially (Roberts and Simonot, 1987).

For other informants in this project, the learning of socio-cultural knowledge is refracted through their experience of living in a racist society. For example, Abdelmalek, a Moroccan worker in France, talks of his politeness strategies and how he has learnt ways of being particularly polite in order to get a favourable response from the most racist of his interlocutors (Bremer *et al.*, 1996).

Data from multilingual British factories also shows how minority workers position themselves strategically in order to attempt to co-construct an argument in their favour. In this example (Roberts *et al.*, 1992, p. 39), the minority worker, IA, is trying to negotiate a job for his son in the same factory as he works in. The problem is that his son is only sixteen years old and is not allowed to work the regulation 55 hour week:

Data Example 4

1   Mrs B: Can't help him.
2   IA: What for?
3   Mrs B: All the men in this mill are on 55 hours
4   IA: 55 hours?
5   Mrs B: All the men
6   IA: Old men?
7   Mrs B: All men
8   IA: Young men and just 8 hours every day
9   Mrs S: But Mrs B says not the OLD men. All the men – everybody – must work 55 hours
10   Mrs B: Ladies work 40 hours
11   IA: This is young boy, the same like lady (laughter)
12   They are too young. If not wanted then too long time . . . just 40 hours per week

Despite the misunderstanding at line 6, IA, at lines 8 and 11–12, begins to negotiate his way around the company rule. He does this by capping Mrs B's assertion with his own assertions about young men and prevents this from becoming a distancing strategy by claiming solidarity through the joke that young men are similar to ladies. The conditions for furthering his sociocultural competence are in place since his assertions are responded to by Mrs B and the encounter ends with her agreeing to talk to the overlooker about her son.

The contingent nature of such interactional positioning means that conditions for the production and interpretation of discourse vary from interaction to interaction. But these conditions are also constrained by wider socio-political formations – such as the inequalities that exist in a stratified multi-lingual society. So a model of second language socialisation needs to include an understanding of the ideologies which feed into and are constructed out of interactions.

Language practice and ideology

The notion of language as 'social practice' helps us to see the ideological in interactions. There has been a lot of discussion around the term 'practice' in what has been called the New Literacy Studies in Britain and the USA. 'Practice' or more usefully 'practices' are more than action and events. In the case of literacy practices for example, they include both the literacy event and the knowledge and assumptions about what this event is and what gives it meaning. For example, what counts as literacy in a subgroup is determined by those in dominant positions in a society. Literacy practices, therefore, are profoundly associated with identity and social position.

The notion of 'practice' has also been used and debated in critical and anthropological linguistics as both action and the ideologies which surround it. Fairclough (1992) makes the point that language practices are constructed not only out of sociocultural knowledge but out of the discourses which were produced earlier, are produced in the interaction and in subsequent discourses. So, for example, within this critical perspective, questions have been raised about taken for granted notions of what constitutes a speaker of a particular language. what is a non-native speaker, what certain groups count as 'target language' and so on. However, this problematising work, although it has influenced applied linguistics, has had little influence within mainstream SLA. For example, the minority worker will be positioned, by the linguistic ideologies that circulate, as a 'non-native', 'second language speaker', 'poor communicator' and so on. These feed into the interaction itself and feed off it to recirculate in the wider discourses around language and ethnicity.

Within the British tradition there are two competing sets of discourses around ethnicity. The first has been widely reflected in government policy and popular discourse. This tends to essentialise ethnic groups, equate land, language and ethnicity and cast minority ethnic groups as incompetent in English. (See Gilroy, 1987, for a discussion). In the Netherlands, van Dijk and his associates have traced similar processes in the discourses of elite groups which show

> how ethnic beliefs are strategically expressed, acquired and distributed throughout the dominant group, that is as part of managing ethnic affairs and reproducing elite power and white group dominance. (Van Dijk et al., 1997, p. 165)

An extreme example of this first set of discourses is from data gathered in multiethnic British workplaces during the late 1970s (Roberts et al., 1992). A supervisor was running through a routine list of questions in English as part of a simple recruitment procedure. The South Asian applicant had answered several questions about himself and his previous work experience when he was asked "Do you speak English?" to which he replied, "What do you think I'm talking to you in now!" The current discourse that was circulating at the time assumed that someone of South Asian background was unlikely to speak English and the evidence to the contrary did not appear to dent the supervisor's certainty that here was another non-English speaker. We could speculate on the outcomes of such an encounter and the possible tensions set up for the individual minority worker who both needs to become a participating member of a new community but who is insultingly positioned by a member of that community as a non-English speaker.

The second set of discourses stem from the British-based Cultural Studies and, in particular, Hall's (1988) notion of 'new ethnicities' and what Hewitt (1986) has called 'local multiracial vernaculars'. Recent research has shown the destabilisation of inherited ethnicities and the emergence of new ethnolinguistic identities which challenge the orthodox essentialist ideas of language and race (Gilroy, 1987; Hewitt, 1986; Rampton, 1995a). This second set of discourses suggest that the process of second language socialisation is not a straightforward case of becoming communicatively competent within a fixed sociocultural group. It is rather a hybrid process of both learning to belong and yet remaining apart – of having several social identities and affiliations to several languages (Pierce, 1995). And this in turn has an impact on the wider social formations which themselves determine what socialisation means.

Contextualisation and wider social processes

The link between SLS and these wider social processes is well illustrated in Gumperz's studies and their recent formulation in Eermans *et al.* (1997). As Levinson (1997) in the same volume asserts:

> it is the large-scale sociological effects of multitudes of small-scale interactions that still partially fuels his (Gumperz's) preoccupations with conversations, most evident perhaps in his concern with the plight of the individual caught up in these large-scale forces. (p. 24)

Levinson captures here many of the elements central to a redefinition of second language acquisition as a social phenomenon. The focus on the micro – the fine-grained detail of conversations – is linked to the macro – the wider social processes where social networks, identities and relationships are structured and restructured. What is significant for a redefinition of SLA as part of this is the fact, as Gumperz asserts, that individuals are 'caught up in these large-scale forces'. So every encounter where there are language differences is both an opportunity for language socialisation but also a site where identities and relationships are played out through the dominant discourses of language and ethnicity, albeit within a conventionally respectful interpersonal framework. And this may be why Levinson talks of the 'plight' of individuals since the kind of intercultural interactions that routinely occur in institutional settings are unequal encounters.

Gumperz's concern with the linguistic dimension of social action shows how aspects of linguistic signalling and cultural and social background knowledge work together to produce communicative involvement (or not) and outcomes at both individual and societal levels. His focus, therefore, in line with the discussion above is on communicative *practice*. In order to analyse these practices, Gumperz draws on an eclectic bag of tools and, as Levinson (1997) suggests, there is none of the theoretical cleanliness in his approach which can be found in Conversation Analysis. Gumperz draws on pragmatic notions in his interpretive procedures but as part of a wider sociological interest. Similarly, he has been much influenced by Conversation Analysis. Like CA his analysis focuses on members' procedures, elucidating how participants use their interactional resources to maintain the interaction and create a level of mutual interpretation. But Gumperz suggests CA is limited in as far as the participants' interpretations are seen as depending on sequential ordering rather than on active involvement. And this involvement rests on two key terms for Gumperz: 'conversational inference' and 'contextualisation'.

The capacity to understand interactions and be socialised into new communities of practice depends absolutely on some level of shared inferential processes. This does not mean that interlocutors share interpretive conclusions about the meaning of things but that ways of processing are sufficiently shared for them to engage with each other and be able to undertake some level of 'repair'. This is in no sense an absolute sharing since any conclusions over meaning have to be accomplished, not taken for granted. And, as I have suggested above, being competent is not a simple process of learning to manage institutional discourse since it is just these institutional discourses which may position the minority worker as resistant or at least ambiguous about the majority community.

Nevertheless, the process of socialisation, however ambiguous, must rely on negotiating local meanings through conversational inference. The question is: What is the relationship between the linguistic signs that participants must process and conversational inference? Gumperz has proposed the notion of 'contextualisation cues' to account for how these signs are taken up by interactants. Contextualisation consists of:

> all activities by participants which make relevant, maintain, revise, cancel, any aspect of context which in turn is responsible for the interpretation of an utterance in its particular locus of occurrence. (Auer, 1992, p. 4)

Contextualisation cues are defined as:

> constellations of surface features of message form . . . The means by which speakers signal and listeners interpret what the activity is, how semantic content is to be understood and how each sentence relates to what precedes or follows. (Gumperz, 1982a, p. 131)

These cues serve to foreground or make salient a particular linguistic feature in relation to others and so call up situated interpretations. So, for example, the job counsellor in Data Example 1 signals a preclosing sequence with the words 'ok' and 'good' both spoken with falling intonation. These contextualisation cues routinely mark the closing of a particular topic or 'activity' (Gumperz, 1982a) in an interaction.

Contextualisation cues call up background knowledge which not only relates to traditional linguistic and pragmatic knowledge but to social relations, rights and obligations, linguistic ideologies and so on. In Ilhami's case, mentioned above, the question about his father's job within the speech event of an interview and occurring at that point in the sequence is expected to cue in information about social status. (See also Tyler, 1995, on the interactive negotiation of participant status.)

Not only are contextualisation cues heavily charged with social and cultural freight, the ways in which they invoke context mark them as problematic for the minority speaker. Levinson, in providing an analytic framework for contextualisation cues, makes the important point that message and context are not in opposition – the message can carry with it or project the context (Levinson, 1997). This makes the process of coming to a level of shared understanding, and learning from this experience, an extremely complex one. Levinson argues that contextualisation cues invoke context in particular ways. The cue is:

a conventional reminder, like a knot in a handkerchief, where the content of the memo is inferentially determined. Thus the 'cue' cannot be said to encode or directly invoke the interpretive background, it's simply a nudge to the inferential process . . . The interpretive process may be guided by general pragmatic principles of a Gricean sort, and thus be in many ways universal in character: but the 'cues' are anything but universal, indeed tending towards sub-cultural differentiation. (p. 29).

There are several problems here for minority language speakers. Firstly, they have to identify that there is a cue (for example a particular prosodic feature may have conventional significance in one language or variety and not in another). Secondly, as Levinson (1997) suggests, the socio-cultural background is not directly invoked by a particular cue. It sets off the inferential process but unless interactants share interpretative procedures, there is no knowing what particular aspects of background knowledge may be called up. Thirdly, there is the fact that contextualisation cues are reflexive. Language shapes context as much as context shapes language. So the majority and minority interlocutors may make differing situated judgements both linguistically and contextually moment by moment in the interaction: a misread prosodic cue can index a set of pre-suppositions about speaker perspective, for example, which creates a new interpretative context and sets the interaction on a different footing.

These issues are central to an understanding of what it might mean to be socialised into a second language. The meaning of contextualisation cues can only be learnt by the linguistic minority speaker if there is extended exposure to the communicative practices of the group or network from which the majority language speaker comes.

> It is long-term exposure to . . . communicative experience in institutionalised networks of relationship and not language or community membership as such that lies at the root of shared culture and shared inferential practices. (Gumperz, 1997, p. 15)

The need for this long exposure or immersion is that, as I have said, the relationship between cue and context is indirect. Cues function relationally, that is in contrast to what has not been said, just been said and so on (Gumperz, 1992). Also many of the formal properties of contextualisation cues are difficult to process, for example aspects of prosody. Finally, they are about invoking context more than message and yet the learner is orientated towards processing the message. In sum, contextualisation cues are slippery features.

Equally important is the fact that contextual cues are indexical markers of membership of a particular group. Knowing how to use and interpret a particular cue means at least for that interactional moment that you are a 'belonger'. And in contrast, the failure to pick up on a cue not only creates misunderstanding but sets the minority linguistic speaker apart. She is not in that interactional moment an emergent member of the same communicative community. As a result, small interactive differences can contribute to large social consequences both for the individual, for example, in failing to be allocated a house or get a job and, in terms of the social order, feeding into the structuring of ethnic relations in a multilingual society.

Contextualisation, therefore, functions at the micro level, both guiding (or not) minute by minute interpretative processes and also indexes "those implicit values of relational identity and power that . . . go by the name of culture" (Silverstein, 1992, p. 57) at the macro level. Local situated meaning and wider ideological concerns are caught up together. It is not simply a case of pragmatic failure or even of socialisation into some stable body of socio-cultural knowledge. Rather, it is a question of the struggle over meaning at many levels. Any item produced by either side may lack stability and create new and confusing contexts. But there is also the struggle over meaning at a more macro socio-political level. Here it is a question of what counts as meaning. What does the gatekeeper have the right to know? What counts as adequate and relevant evidence? On what basis will the applicant be judged? What does 'understanding' the other's intent mean in these contexts? The uncertainty that inhabits these interactions is rapidly converted into the certainty of fixed judgements and positions after the event since it is the gatekeeper who, as representative of a major social institution, controls the way in which reality is represented and contributes to the dominant discourses about minority identities. And despite the respectful inter-personal conduct of the gatekeeper, minority workers, as I indicated above in the case of Abdelmalek, are aware of the racism of the dominant group and this is likely to affect any orthodox process of socialisation. Abdelmalek may be developing a competence in interpreting change of topic cues and even in understanding the goals of such counselling interviews. But the developing competence that results from such socio-cultural knowledge may be matched by ambiguity, anomaly or resistance. Socialisation assumes a sense of 'belonging' in a new community and yet the institutions where language socialisation can take place represent what is different, 'other', even hostile and discriminatory.

The instability of meaning and the contestation over meaning create a complex set of social conditions within which there is the potential for communicative and material success or not and the potential for language socialisation and the readiness for it – or not. Given the wider discourses that circulate about ethnic minorities, each intercultural interaction can both produce relatively adverse conditions for language learning and can feed into these wider discourses each time a misunderstanding remains unresolved.

Some methodological implications

The connection between micro and macro in redefining the domain of SLA has method-ological as well as theoretical implications. As several examples in this paper have shown, analysis of text, using a CA and interactional sociolinguistic approach, is essential in understanding the sequential ordering of interaction but it needs to be complemented by ethnographic methods. Whereas CA is concerned with the general procedures employed by members in accomplishing interaction, a method that will help analysts draw conclusions about online inferencing is also needed. In intercultural communication, the analyst needs to participate in the everyday routines of a particular group in order to understand conventionalised ways of interpreting meaning.

Ethnographic methods are also needed to understand interactants' subjectivity (Bremer et al., 1996; Gumperz, 1982b; Pierce, 1995). Ethnographic interviews and regular par-ticipation in the lives of a particular sub-group contribute to the analysts' understanding of how minority workers are positioned in encounters with the majority and the long-term effect of this on individual motivation, personal and social investment and the construction of social identities within the relations of domination that characterise a multilingual society.

Conclusion

By looking at the environment within which a particular group of people are expected to develop communicative competence – minority workers in a stratified multilingual society

– a number of questions have been raised about SLA and its relatively asocial perspective. Language socialisation better describes the process of being a social actor in a new language but in its orthodox form it does not fully account for the connection between micro interactional processes and the macro social issues. Wider discourses of racism, indifference and stratification feed into and off local interactional differences, misunderstandings and covert or explicit opposition. The environments created by these social forces, at micro and macro levels, produce complex and often hostile conditions for the understanding and production of discourse in a second language. By examining these conditions, it is possible to begin to redefine the process of second language acquisition as second language socialisation but in so doing, questions are also raised about any orthodox SLS. Learning to belong to a new community may also mean learning to resist, or at the least take up an ambiguous position in relation to the socio-cultural knowledge and discourses which constitute it. As in many other theoretical and practical areas, the transformation of Western Europe into a multilingual society illuminates the process of second language development and redefines its domain as centrally concerned with the social.

Acknowledgements

My thanks are due to Mike Baynham, Ben Rampton, Jo Arditty and Marie Thérèse Vasseur for comments on earlier drafts of this paper.

References

Auer, P. (1992) 'Introduction: John Gumperz's approach to contextualisation', in Auer, P. & di Luzio, A. (eds) *The contextualisation of language* (pp. 1–37). Amsterdam: Benjamins.

Bourdieu, P. (1977) *Outline of a theory of practice*. Cambridge: Cambridge University Press.

Bremer, K., Roberts, C., Vasseur, M., Simonet, M. and Breeder, P. (1996) *Achieving understanding: Discourse in intercultural encounters*. London: Longman.

Clyne, M. (1994) *Intercultural communication at work*. Cambridge: Cambridge University Press.

Duff, P. (1996) 'Different languages, different practices: Socialization of discourse competence in dual-anguage school classrooms in Hungary', in Bailey, K. and Nunan, D. (eds) *Voices from the language classroom: Qualitative research in second language education research* (pp. 407–433). New York: Cambridge University Press.

Eermans, S., Prevignano, C. and Thibault, P. (eds) (1997) *Discussing Communication Analysis 1: John J. Gumperz* (pp. 6–23). Lausanne: Beta Press.

Fairclough, N. (1992) *Discourse and social change*. Cambridge: Polity Press.

Gilroy, P. (1987) *There ain't no black in the Union Jack*. London: Hutchinson.

Gumperz, J. (1982a) *Discourse strategies*. Cambridge: Cambridge University Press.

——— (ed.) (1982b) *Language and social identity*. Cambridge: Cambridge University Press.

——— (1992) 'Contextualisation and understanding', in Duranti, A. and Goodwin, C. (eds) *Rethinking Context: Language as an interactive phenomenon* (pp. 229–252). Cambridge: Cambridge University Press.

——— (1997) 'A discussion with John J. Gumperz' (discussants: C. Prevignano and A. di Luzio), in Eerdmans, S., Prevignano, C. and Thibault, P. (eds), pp. 6–23.

Hall, S. (1988) 'New ethnicities', *ICA Documents*, 7, 27–31.

Hewitt, R. (1986) *White talk black talk*. Cambridge: Cambridge University Press.

Kasper, G. and Schmidt, R. (1996) 'Developing issues in interlanguage pragmatics'. *Studies in Second Language Acquisition*, *18*, 149–163.

Lantolf, J. and Pavlenko, A. (1995) 'Sociocultural theory and second language acquisition'. *Annual Review of Applied Linguistics*, *15*, 108–124.

Levinson, S., (1997) 'Contextualising "contextualisation cues"', in Eermans, S., Prevignano, C. and Thibault, P. (eds), pp. 24–30.

Perdue, C. (ed.) (1993) *Adult language acquisition. Cross-linguistic perspectives* (Vols. 1 and 2). Cambridge: Cambridge University Press.

Pierce, B. (1995) 'Social identity, investment and language learning'. *TESOL Quarterly*, *29*, 9–31.

Rampton, B. (1995a) *Crossing: Language and ethnicity among adolescents*. Harlow: Longman.

—— (1995b) 'Language crossing and the problematisation of ethnicity and socialisation'. *Pragmatics*, *5*, 485–515.

Roberts, C., Davies, E. and Jupp, T. (1992) *Language and discrimination. A study of communication in multiethnic workplaces*. Harlow: Longman.

Roberts, C. and Simonot, M. (1987) '"This is my life": How language acquisition is interactionally accomplished', in Ellis, R. (ed.) *Second language acquisition in context* (pp. 133–148). Hemel Hempstead: Prentice-Hall.

Rogoff, B. (1984) 'Introduction: Thinking and learning in social context', in Rogoff, B. and Lave, J. (eds) *Everyday Cognition: The development in social context* (pp. 1–8). Cambridge, MA: Harvard University Press.

Scarcella, R. (1982) 'Discourse accent in second language production', in Selinker, L. and Gass, S. (eds) *Language transfer in language learning* (pp. 306–326). Rowley, MA: Newbury House.

Silverstein, M. (1992) 'The indeterminacy of contextualisation: When is enough enough?', in Auer, P., and di Luzio, A. (eds) *The contextualisation of language* (pp. 55–76). Amsterdam: Benjamins.

Thomas, J. (1983) 'Cross-cultural pragmatic failure'. *Applied Linguistics*, *4*, 91–112.

Tyler, A. (1995) 'The co-construction of cross-cultural miscommunication'. *Studies in Second Language Acquisition*, *17*, 129–152.

van Dijk, T., Ting-Toomey, S., Smitherman, G. and Troutman, D. (1997) 'Discourse, ethnicity, culture and racism', in van Dijk, T. (ed.) *Discourse as social interaction: Discourse studies 2* (pp. 144–180). London: Sage.

Chapter 7

Michael P. Breen

THE SOCIAL CONTEXT FOR LANGUAGE LEARNING: A NEGLECTED SITUATION?

Introduction

I WISH TO EXPLORE THE BELIEF that the classroom will have certain effects upon language learning. The assumption resting within what I have to say is that relationships can be discovered between the social processes of the classroom group and the individual psychological process of second language development. Given the present state of our knowledge about the learning of foreign languages, this assumption is supported upon tenuous foundations. As most people at least begin to learn new languages in classrooms, the researcher can hardly fail to locate some variable of classroom life that will have a systematic effect upon language learning, or some variable of learning behaviour which has correlational potential with instructional treatment. The researcher may ask: "What are the *specific* contributions of the classroom to the process of language development?" The assumption being that we may be able to explain how classroom-based instruction influences and interacts with learning if we come to understand the special workings of the classroom context. The teacher's priorities – perhaps more urgent and direct – are to build upon those inherent features of the classroom situation which may facilitate the learning of a new language. The teacher's question may be: "In what ways might I exploit the social reality of the classroom as a *resource* for the teaching of language?"

This paper offers particular answers to both the researcher's and the teacher's questions. It begins with an examination of the approaches of current research towards the language class. I offer a particular evaluation of recent developments in investigations devoted to second language acquisition and to language learning in the classroom situation. This evaluation, though necessarily brief, has three purposes. First, to identify the possible contributions of the language classroom which are perceived and revealed by current research. Second, to identify what seem to be significant contributions of the classroom which current research appears to neglect. And third, to deduce certain implications for future research and for language teaching.

The researcher and the teacher are confronted by a crucial common problem: how to relate social activity, to psychological change and how to relate psychological processing to the social dynamics of a group. The researcher must explain these relationships if he is to understand adequately language learning as it is experienced by most people – in a gathering made up of other learners and a teacher. The teacher is a direct participant in this social event with the aim of influencing psychological development. The teacher is obliged continually to integrate the learning experiences of individuals with the collective and communal activities of a group of which, unlike the researcher, he is not an outsider. The researcher enters the classroom when a genuine sociocognitive experiment is already well under way. In evaluating the findings of research, because of abstraction from the daily life of the class, we need to discover and make clear for ourselves the particular *perceptions* of a classroom which we, as researchers, hold either before we enter it or subsequent to the collection of our data. It is a truism of social anthropology that no human social institutions or relationships can be adequately understood unless account is taken of the expectations, values, and beliefs that they engage. This is no less true of the institution of research. The definition of the classroom situation that we hold will influence how we perceive the classroom group and how we might act within it, and this is as unavoidable for the researcher as it is for a teacher or a learner. One of the paradoxes of research is to challenge taken-for-granted beliefs whilst, at the same time, clinging to beliefs which sustain the research endeavour. Belief allows the researcher (and many teachers and learners) to take for granted the capacity of a classroom to metamorphose instructional inputs into learning outcomes. Is there psychological proof for this relationship between teaching and learning, or is it a belief sustained primarily by the social purpose *that we invest* in a gathering of teacher and taught?

Can we detect particular definitions of the classroom situation within current language learning research? What metaphors for a classroom are available to us as researchers at present? I wish to explore two metaphors for the classroom that emerge from two recent and influential research traditions. I am conscious that there may be as many metaphors for the classroom as there are researchers in language learning. But I have to be brief and I am encouraged to generalise here by the tendency of researchers to seek security around particular dominant paradigms or ways of seeing.[1] One prevailing metaphor is the classroom as experimental laboratory, and another, more recently emergent, is the classroom as discourse. I will briefly explore both.

The classroom as experimental laboratory

We are encouraged to regard the classroom as experimental laboratory by the area of theory and research known as Second Language Acquisition (SLA). Its tradition can be traced back to studies in first language acquisition, through investigation of the natural order of acquisition of certain grammatical morphemes, through the comprehensive theories of Krashen, and up to the recent flowering in the identification of learner strategies from retrospective accounts offered by individual learners – either verbally or within learning diaries. The primary function of the language classroom as implied or sometimes directly recommended by SLA research is that the learner, by being placed in a classroom, can be exposed to a certain kind of linguistic input which may be shown to correlate with certain desirable learning outcomes. Here, the value and purpose of the classroom is its potential to provide linguistic data that are finely tuned for the efficient processing of new knowledge; classrooms can wash learners with optimal input. Researchers' more recent inferences from learners' accounts of their own strategies encourage us to deduce further that the classroom is a place in which we might reinforce good language-learning strategies so that the input becomes unavoidably optimal. As the mainstream of SLA research rests on the assumption that the comprehension of input is the catalyst of language development, it implies a role for the teacher that is delimited yet complex. In essence, either the teacher must facilitate comprehension through the provision of linguistic input sensitive to individual learner inclinations, or the teacher should endeavour to shape individual learning behaviours so that each learner may attain a repertoire of efficient processing strategies. The SLA metaphor for the classroom implies teacher as surrogate experimental psychologist and learners as subject to particular input treatments or behavioural reinforcement.

However, this view of the language classroom leaves us with a number of unresolved problems that warrant more attention if we seek to understand the relationship between a language class and language learning. First, the interesting variables of linguistic input and the strategic behaviour of learners *are not special to classrooms*. They were not uncovered as prevailing features of classroom life at all.[2] The second and perhaps more significant problem is that two crucial intervening variables seem to have been bypassed by SLA research. Both of these variables are centrally related to the processing of input. Both will determine what a learner might actually *intake*. SLA research which emphasises linguistic input (provided by instruction or exposure) as the independent variable and some later learner output (in a test or in spontaneous speech) as the dependent variable leaps blindly over any active cognition on the part of the learner. With its heavy reliance on linguistic performance criteria for psychological change there is a resultant superficiality in its attention to learners' internal perceptual processes. The research takes for granted what the *learner* may define as optimal for him. More fundamentally, it does not address the question of *how* a learner selectively perceives parts of linguistic data as meaningful and worth acting upon in the first place. Therefore, the intervening variable of what the learner actually does to input or with input is neglected. Given the importance attached to comprehension by SLA research it seems paradoxical that the active reinterpretation and reconstruction of any input by the learner is not accounted for. The search for correlations between, for example, the frequency of a grammatical form in input and the frequent occurrence of that form in some later learner performance seems motivated by a rather narrow view of human learning. The research leads us to a causal conditioning as opposed to a cognitive and interactive explanation of language development. We are left unsure *how and why* learners do what they do in order to intake selectively.

On the face of it, learning strategy research seems to offer some help here. However, these investigations primarily confirm that learners are unpredictable, inconsistent, and sometimes seemingly inefficient processors. Thus, the same learning outcome can be achieved by different strategies while different learning outcomes can be achieved by the same strategy. Investigations into learner strategies have not yet helped us to understand how or why it is that one thing can be interpreted or learned by any two learners with seemingly different profiles of strategies. Until we understand these things, the capacity of instruction to encourage or shape desirable or efficient strategic behaviour of learners remains unfounded.[3] This problem emerging from the data we derive from learners concerning their strategies leads to the second crucial intervening variable which seems to be neglected in SLA research. Learners certainly are strategic in how they go about learning, but if we ask them what they think they do, or if they keep a diary of what they do, such retrospections, inevitably *post hoc* rationalisations, will exhibit a coherence that bears only metaphorical resemblance to the actual moment of learning. Something intervenes between a learner's introspections to a researcher or to a diary reader, just as something intervenes between input to a learner and between what a learner has intaken and some later test performance. I suggest that one thing which crucially intervenes is the learner's definition of situation: the definition of being an informant to someone investigating strategies, the definition of being a language learner in a classroom, and the definition of doing a test. If we hope to explain fully the relationship between classroom input and learning outcomes, or to explain possible relationships between strategic behaviour and language learning, then we need to locate these relationships *socially*. How and why learners do what they do will be strongly influenced by their situation, who they are with, and by their perceptions of both.[4]

Given that we wish to understand how the external social situation of a classroom relates to the internal psychological states of the learner, the metaphor of the classroom as provider of optimal input or reinforcer of good strategies is inadequate. It *reduces* the act or experience of learning a language to linguistic or behavioural conditioning somehow independent of the learner's social reality. Not only is SLA research currently offering us a delimited account of language learning, reducing active cognition to passive internalisation and reducing language to very specific grammatical performance, the mainstream of SLA research is also asocial. It neglects the social significance of even those variables which the investigators regard as central. The priority given to linguistic and mentalistic variables in terms of the efficient processing of knowledge as input leads inevitably to a partial account of the language learning process. The social context of learning and the social forces within it will always shape what is made available to be learned *and* the interaction of individual mind with external linguistic or communicative knowledge. Even Wundt, the first experimental psychologist, believed that he could not study higher mental processes such as reasoning, belief, thought, and language in a *laboratory* precisely because such processes were rooted within authentic social activity.[5] A more recent research tradition – an offspring of work in SLA – does address intervening social variables. This tradition provides my second metaphor.

The classroom as discourse

Recent classroom-based or classroom-oriented research explicitly seeks to describe what actually happens in a rather special social situation. This research relies upon methods of conversational and sociolinguistic data collection and analysis, thereby seeking to offer a richer and less prescriptive account of classroom language learning than earlier investigations of the comparative effects of different teaching methodologies.[6] Classroom-oriented research focuses primarily upon the discourse of classroom communication. It sees teacher and learners as active participants in the generation of the discourse of lessons. Here, the researcher explores the classroom as a text which reveals such phenomena as variable participation by learners, various error treatments by teachers, and specific features of classroom talk such as teacher evaluation, teacher–learner negotiation, and prevalent instructional speech acts including display questions, formulation or explanation, and message adjustment. Although much of this research seems to avoid being intentionally explanatory in terms of the possible effects of classroom discourse upon language learning, some investigators seek to correlate selected features of classroom talk with certain learning behaviours or learned outcomes. Classroom-oriented research rests on the assumption that the discourse of a language class will reveal what is special and important about that language learning situation. It intends no practical implications for the teacher, although some of the more overtly correlational studies may encourage the teacher to assume that he must endeavour to orchestrate his own and the learners' contributions to the discourse according to conversational moves or speech acts which exemplify "good" instruction and "good" learner participation.

Clearly, this focus upon the actual discourse of classroom communication provides a valid location if we wish to begin to understand the experience of learning a language in a classroom. However, even with such an ecologically valid point of departure, current classroom-oriented research leaves us with two important areas of uncertainty. We have to question the extent to which the surface text of classroom discourse can adequately reveal the underlying social psychological forces which generate it (the expectations, beliefs and attitudes of the participants) and also reveal the sociocognitive effects it may have (the specific interpretations and learning it provokes). This central issue leads us back into the long-established debate on the possible relationships between communicating and learning, between language and cognition. A number of the correlational studies within classroom-oriented research avoid the complexities of this debate by appearing to assume that certain phenomena in classroom discourse *cause* learning to occur. Any correlation between observable features of discourse and testable learning outcomes – a teacher's formulation of a rule, for example, and a learner's later use or reformulation of that rule – does not explain how or why a learner actually achieved such things. This dependency on the superficial features of classroom talk can force us to deduce that if other learners in the class failed to use the rule correctly or were unable to reformulate it then the teacher's original formulation was inadequate. But what of the internal dimensions of classroom communication: the learners' variable perception, reinterpretation, and accommodation of whatever may be provided through classroom discourse? In these matters, classroom-oriented research seems to share a psychological naivety with SLA research.

The second area of uncertainty is perhaps more fundamental. Most current classroom-oriented research paradoxically reduces the external dimensions of classroom communication, the actual social event, to observable features of the talk between teacher and learners. Sixty years ago, Edward Sapir pointed out that we cannot use observable data alone from social events even if we merely aim to describe them adequately. Nor can we interpret the observable data through our eyes only if we ever seek to explain what those data actually *mean*. Even Del Hymes, who was foremost in proposing the ethnography of speaking which now underlies much sociolinguistic research, also insisted that if we wish adequately to explain any speech event we need to discover its existential and experiential significance for those taking part.[7] These proposals imply that the meanings and values of classroom discourse reside behind and beneath what is said and unsaid. A researcher's interpretation of the "text" of classroom discourse has to be derived through the participants' interpretations of that discourse. Is the teacher's treatment of an error taken as error treatment by a learner? Is a learner's request for information – even if responded to as such by the teacher – actually a piece of time-wasting or even expressing something else entirely? Is superficial negotiation of meaning or a learner's generation of further input evidence of the wish to learn more?

To begin to understand language learning experience in a classroom the researcher must discover what teacher and taught themselves perceive as inherent within the discourse of lessons. More importantly, recent classroom research clearly shows the researcher as someone who *invests* into his text of classroom discourse certain patternedness or meaningfulness. Classroom communication, like any text, realizes and carries meaning potential. Because of this, if we wish to discover what the teaching and learning of a language in a classroom is for the people undertaking it, we need to know what orderliness and sense *they invest* in the overt communication of the class. Put simply, the discourse of the classroom does not itself reveal what the teacher and the learners experience from that discourse. Such experience is two-dimensional: individual-subjective experience and collective-intersubjective experience. The subjective experience of teacher and learners in a classroom is woven with personal purposes, attitudes, and preferred ways of doing things. The intersubjective experience derives from and maintains teacher and learner shared definitions, conventions, and procedures which enable a working together in a crowd. Of course, the discourse of a classroom may provide a window onto the surface expression of the intersubjective experience and even onto momentary expressions of subjective experiences, for these two dimensions of experience must interrelate and influence one another. However, classroom discourse alone allows us a partial view from which we are obliged to describe others' experiences as if "through a glass darkly."

Classroom-oriented research shares with SLA studies the tendency to reduce or avoid consideration of certain intervening variables which inevitably influence how and why learners may internalise input and how and why learners interact with a teacher in the ways they do. This reductionism is characterised by an emphatic focus upon linguistic performance – upon observable features of language and discourse. To be fair, neither research tradition may intend to understand or even explain language learning *in* the classroom situation. However, any researcher who tries to correlate features of linguistic performance data in terms of classroom input with some learning outcome is, at least implicitly, seeking a possible explanation of that learning outcome. And such an explanation can only be causal. Classroom research is not asocial like SLA research, but it does share a non-cognitive view of learner comprehension and reconstruction of input despite its potentially richer view of input as discourse rather than merely grammatical data. Classroom-oriented research perceives the learner as actively contributing to the discourse. But how can we relate such contributions or even non-contributions to language learning? Learners and teachers are not dualities of social being and mental being – an idea apparently unfortunately supported by the very separateness of SLA and classroom-oriented research priorities. It is incumbent upon classroom-based investigations of language learning to account for those social psychological forces which generate classroom discourse and for those socio-cognitive effects of the discourse *even if* its objective is primarily to describe social phenomena. If the subjective and intersubjective experiences of and from classroom discourse are reduced to what we can find in the discourse alone, then we are allowed to deduce that classroom language learning results from discoursal conditioning – no more nor less than social determinism!

It appears that the two metaphors for the classroom which we have available to us at present offer definitions of the classroom situation which seem to neglect the social reality of language learning *as it is experienced and created* by teachers and learners. Both metaphors unfortunately constrain our understanding of language learning because each takes for granted crucial intervening psychological and social variables which are the fulcra upon which language learning is balanced. The reconstructive cognition of learners and the social and psychological forces which permeate the processes of teaching and learning must reside within any explanation concerning how and why people do what they do when they work together on a new language. More seriously, perhaps, both contemporary metaphors implicitly reduce human action and interaction to classical conditioning, wherein learners though superficially participating are essentially passive respondents to observable linguistic and discoursal stimuli. It therefore appears necessary that research has still to adopt a definition of the classroom which will encompass *both cognitive and social variables* so that their mutual influence can be better understood. More precisely, we need a metaphor for the classroom through which teacher and earners can be viewed as thinking social actors and not reduced to generators of input-output nor analyzed as dualities of either conceptual or social beings. Perhaps the metaphor we require can provide a basis for the synthesis of SLA and classroom-oriented research endeavours whilst necessarily being more comprehensive than both. These deductions lead me to propose a third metaphor for the classroom in the hope that it might further facilitate our understanding of classroom language learning. One of the characteristics of my third metaphor is that it is likely to be more *experientially* familiar to most language teachers and learners than it may be to some researchers.

The classroom as coral gardens

A proposal that the classroom situation could be perceived as coral gardens may be initially reacted to as rather odd. The metaphor derives from Malinowski's classical studies of Trobriand island cultures, in particular those investigations he described in *Coral Gardens and Their Magic*. I offer the metaphor because it entails three requirements for research devoted to classroom language learning. First, in order to understand the process of learning within a human group, our investigations are necessarily an anthropological endeavour. Second, the researcher should approach the classroom with a kind of anthropological humility. We should explore classroom life initially as if we knew nothing about it. And, third, it is more important to discover what people invest in a social situation than it is to rely on what might be observed as inherent in that social situation. Just as gardens of coral were granted magical realities by the Trobriand islanders, a language class – outwardly a gathering of people with an assumed common purpose – is an arena of subjective and intersubjective realities which are worked out, changed, and maintained. *And these realities are not trivial background to the tasks of teaching and learning a language.* They locate and define the new language itself as if it never existed before, and they continually specify and mould the activities of teaching and learning. In essence, the metaphor of classroom as coral gardens insists that we perceive the language class as a genuine culture and worth investigating as such.[8]

If we can adopt this definition of the classroom situation, then research may get closer to the daily lives of teachers and learners. We can approach the raison d'être of a language class – the working upon and rediscovering of language knowledge – as involving socio-cognitive construction and reinterpretation. A particular culture, by definition, entails particular relationships between social activities and psychological processes and changes. SLA research asserts comprehension as central, whilst the classroom as culture locates comprehension within the intersubjective construction of meaningfulness and the subjective reinterpretation of whatever may be rendered comprehensible. In other words, input is never inherently optimal, for any new knowledge is socio-cognitively rendered familiar or unfamiliar by those who participate in its exploration. The culture of the class *generates knowledges* and a focus upon any internalised linguistic outcomes will tell us little about classroom language learning in action. Classroom-oriented research explores the discourse of lessons, whilst the classroom as culture extends across islands of intersubjective meaning and depths of subjective intentions and interpretations which only rarely touch the surface of talk and which the discourse itself often deliberately hides. The discourse of lessons will mainly *symbolise* what participants contribute to those lessons and it will not signify what they actually invest in them or derive from them.

It is, of course, incumbent upon me to justify my own belief in the classroom as genuine culture. In order to meet the charge that such a metaphor may be too idealised or abstract, I need to identify some of the essential features of the culture of the language classroom. I will briefly describe eight essential features:

The culture of the classroom is interactive

The language class involves all its participants in verbal and non-verbal interaction of certain kinds. This interaction exists on a continuum from ritualised, predictable, phatic communication to dynamic, unpredictable, diversely interpreted communication. Of course, human interaction will be relatively located on this kind of continuum in all social situations. One special characteristic of classroom interaction, however, is that it is motivated by the assumption that people can learn together in a group. This means that a high premium is placed upon consensus whilst misunderstandings, alternative interpretations, and negotiable meaning will paradoxically be the norm, and from which participants will seek to make their own sense and upon which participants will impose their own purposes. This is not to say that the observable interaction will not be patterned or constrained, but that it is very likely to be patterned differently in the interpretations invested in it by each person in the class. Therefore the researcher needs to be wary of assuming that the patterns of interaction which we perceive as significant have the same salience for both teacher and taught. A special characteristic of the language class is that interaction is further motivated by the assumption that people can objectify a language and talk about it and analyse it in ways they may not naturally do if left alone. The language class implies metalinguistic interaction. However, it is often further assumed that the language class can provide opportunities for genuine interaction through the new language code. A language class entails interaction about language and interaction through *languages* in continual juxtaposition.

All these and other characteristics of the interactive process of the language class may or may not be efficient or optimal for language learning. However, all represent the *inherent authenticity* of the interaction within a language class given the external constraints of space, time, participation, etc., which typify any classroom devoted to any subject matter. A significant paradox for the language teacher – a paradox of which teachers are well aware – is that the established interaction which is evolved and maintained by the culture of the classroom group often conflicts with efforts towards communication through the new language. Communication in the new language requires the temporary suspension of those cultural conventions governing the everyday interaction of the particular classroom group. It requires communication which is, in fact, *inauthentic* to the interactive context in which it has to occur. This implies that one of the conventions assumed to be honoured by participants in the culture of a language class is the willingness and capacity to suspend disbelief, to participate in simulated communication *within* classroom-specific interaction.[9]

The culture of the classroom is differentiated

Although the language class may be one social situation, it is a different social *context* for all those who participate within it. The culture of the classroom is an amalgam and permutation of different social realities. This means that the content of lessons (the language being taught) and the procedures of teaching and learning (the things being done) are both continually interpreted differently as the life of that language class unfolds. The classroom is the meeting point of various subjective views of language, diverse learning purposes, and different preferences concerning how learning should be done. Such differentiation brings with it potential for disagreement, frustrated expectations, and conflict. The culture of the classroom does not erase these differences; it contains them. A major challenge for teacher and learners is the maintenance of a fine balance between conflicting internal social realities (a kind of subjective anarchy!) and an external reality which has to be *continually negotiated*.

The outside observer has access to the compromise which results, but we would be naive to deduce that such a compromise represents what is actually intended or perceived as the social reality for any one person in the class.

The culture of the classroom is collective

The culture of the classroom represents a tension between the internal world of the individual and the social world of the group, a recurrent juxtaposition of personal learning experiences and communal teaching-learning activities and conventions. The culture of the class has a psychological reality, a mind of its own, which emerges from this juxtaposition. The psyche of the group – the group's values, meanings, and volitions – is a distinct entity other than the sum of the individual psychological orientations of teacher and learners. Socially, the sometimes ritualised and sometimes overtly dynamic behaviour of the group will both contain and influence the behaviour of the individual just as the overt contributions of a teacher or a learner will fit, or divert the workings of the class. But this social framework builds upon and constructs a particular world which has to be accommodated as a point of departure for psychological change. A teacher and a learner have to discover *that* definition of situation which seems to maintain the group and its activities – *that* definition of situation which will be relatively distinct from their personal definitions. This involves all members of the group in empathising with the roles and views of others and continually checking such external frames of reference. The individual has to adapt his learning process to the social-psychological resources of the group. So also the group's psychic and social process will unfold from the individual contributions of a learner. This interplay between individual and collective consciousness (and the values, beliefs, and attitudes it generates) implies that the researcher should be wary of crediting the classroom with powers separable from what individual learners actually *make* classrooms do for them, and similarly wary of crediting individual learners with powers separable from what the classroom group provides. An individual learner in a classroom is engaged in both an individual learning process *and* a group teaching-learning process. Therefore individual psychological change will continually relate to group psychological forces. The researcher is obliged to discover these two worlds because they are distinctive. To *infer* individual learning process from classroom process or vice versa will lead to a partial understanding of classroom language learning. We need to explore both and how they relate one to the other.

The culture of the classroom is highly normative

Our membership in any culture implies that our behaviour will be evaluated against certain norms and conventions – membership entails *showing* we belong. However, in all our lives, classrooms are very special in this regard. Schools and classrooms are among the main agencies for secondary socialisation and, as the first public institution most of us enter during our lives, our views of classrooms will be significantly coloured by this initial experience. More importantly, our personal identities as learners within a group derive much from such experience. This is due to the fact that our public learning selves have been moulded by a continual and explicit evaluation of *our worth as learners*. When a language learner enters a classroom, he anticipates that the evaluation of him as a learner is going to be a crucial part of that experience. This implies that the search for external criteria for success in coping with language learning and, less optimistically perhaps, the day-to-day search for ways of reducing the potential threat of negative judgements of one's capabilities will impinge upon whatever internal criteria a learner may evolve regarding his own learning progress.

Learners in a class will obviously vary with regard to their relative dependence upon external and internal criteria. However, one of the prevalent features of the culture of the classroom is the establishment of overt and covert criteria against which its members are continually judged. In other words, the culture of the classroom *reifies* the persons who participate within it into "good" learners and "bad" learners, "good" teachers and "bad" teachers, "beginners," "advanced," "high" participators and "low" participators, etc., etc. Put bluntly, the language class is a highly normative and evaluative environment which engages teacher and taught in continual judgement of each other, less as persons, but as members who are supposed to learn and a member who is supposed to teach. This highly normative characteristic of classroom life implies for the researcher that we need to discover the overt and covert group criteria (*and* members' individual interpretations of these criteria) against which learning behaviour and progress are judged. To infer, for example, that a teacher's error corrections are consistently based upon objective linguistic criteria or are otherwise apparently random would lead to a superficial analysis of phenomena which, though opaque, are deeply significant for a teacher and learners in the particular classroom.

The culture of the classroom is asymmetrical

Because teachers are expected to know what learners are expected not to know, certain social and psychological consequences inevitably obtain for the human relationships in the class. The culture of the classroom insists upon asymmetrical relationships. The duties and rights of teacher and taught are different. More significantly, both teacher and taught may be *equally reluctant* to upset the asymmetry of roles and identities to which these duties and rights are assigned. In most societies – perhaps all, despite some relative variation – an egalitarian relationship between teacher and taught is a contradiction of what a classroom should be. Teachers and learners are very familiar with the experience of gradually establishing the precise degree of asymmetry which enables them to maintain a relatively harmonious working group. As teachers, we are also familiar with a class which erodes what they perceive as being too democratic or too authoritarian an approach on our part, even though we ourselves may perceive our teaching style as consistently something else entirely! Here is a paradox. Learners *give* a teacher the right to adopt a role and identity of teacher. And a teacher has to *earn* particular rights and duties in the eyes of the learning group. However, the history of the tribe marches behind the teacher, and a teacher *through* the unfolding culture of the particular classroom group will similarly allocate rights and duties to learners. Indeed, one of the rights and duties of a teacher is to do precisely that! However, asymmetrical relationships do not only exist between teacher and taught. Sub-groupings which are asymmetrical with the dominant classroom culture also emerge and prosper, such as anti-academic peer groupings or certain learners who identify themselves as more successful or less successful and even groups who share a common identity (such as friendship groups) outside the classroom. Thus, not only is the culture of the classroom individually differentiated yet collective, it is also made up of sub-groups which develop for themselves mainly covert, though sometimes overtly expressed, roles and identities which are potentially asymmetrical with both the dominant culture and with other sub-groupings in the class.

Asymmetry of roles and identities, and of the rights and duties they bear, derives from and further generates conceptual and affective dissonances. Asymmetrical relationships very often entail disagreement in beliefs, in attitudes, and in values held. The collective nature of the classroom culture and the negotiated compromises which permeate the teaching-learning process often hide within themselves – sometimes with difficulty and often only for a time – different views of what should be happening in a class and what should not. This suggests that, although the nature of interpersonal and intergroup relationships within the language classroom may be complex and changing, the researcher needs to uncover what these are if we wish to describe what happens in the class and further interpret this as it is experienced by those within the class. As researchers in the past, we have tended to be teacher-centred in our assuming that the major asymmetry in role and identity, and the likely location of dissonance in perceptions and effects, resides between the teacher and the rest. We have also perhaps underestimated the possible effects – both negative and positive – of asymmetry and dissonance within the classroom upon the language learning process.[10]

The culture of the classroom is inherently conservative

Perhaps one of the best ways of revealing the established culture of the classroom group is to try to introduce an innovation which the majority neither expects nor defines as appropriate. Most teachers have had direct experience of the effort to be radical in their approach with a class (be it through different material, tasks, or procedure, etc.) and have suffered the experience of at least initial rejection. A genuine culture is one in which its members seek security and relative harmony in a self-satisfactory milieu. As such things take time to develop, anything which the group perceives as change will also take time to be absorbed or it will be resisted as deviant. (This does not mean that harmony will necessarily reign in the classroom, for even apparent anarchy – as long as it is the preferred ethos of that group – may be quite consistent with a definition of classroom life for some seemingly unsocialised collection of learners!). In essence, a classroom group seeks a particular social and emotional equilibrium just as soon as it can – even one which may seem to be antithetical to learning. It will subsequently resist any threat to the newly established order. The individual learner risks ostracisation from the group if he does not – overtly at least – conform, and the teacher risks rebellion in various forms if he does not honour the conventions expected by the collective definition of what a language teacher should be. Although this conservative spirit has its origins in the prior educational experiences of the learners, each new classroom group reinvents "the rules of the game" in ways which both reflect and form the classroom-culture assumptions of the particular participants who are suddenly sharing each others' company. It has to be said, of course, that a teacher may participate in this conservatism and, indeed, work *through* it in order to help develop group harmony, security and efficient ways of working. And teachers are certainly familiar with the dilemma of wishing to innovate whilst being cautious of disruption. This means that the very presence of a researcher, or even the awareness within the group that they are the focus of apparently objective evaluation and study will mobilise change. Our personal experience of having someone visit our home for the first time and then looking at it with them, as if seeing it through their eyes, can remind us of the effect of intrusion. In a sense, the classroom changes in the eyes of those within it and, therefore, *will* change in certain ways. This is, of course, the truism of observer effect. But there is also the observer's paradox in that the classroom we now see will be in a state of disequilibrium: it will not be the same classroom as yesterday and we will be investigating a classroom group which is newly adapting in a number of subtle ways. This phenomenon can be either bad news or good news for the researcher. It will render short-term, one-shot investigations into classroom language learning largely invalid and unreliable. If, on the other hand, we approach studies of classroom language learning on a longitudinal basis, then we may be able to explore the process of re-establishment of social and emotional equilibrium which our initial arrival challenged. In other words, we may uncover more precisely the "rules of the game" which represent the self-maintaining culture of that particular working group.

The culture of the classroom is jointly constructed

Whilst we may accept the truism that all knowledge is socially constructed – most especially if we are working with the knowledge of a language and how it is used between people – we need to consider how classrooms *re-construct* knowledge. In a language class, the classroom group together not only freshly evolves the new language (the content of lessons), but together also jointly constructs the lessons (the social procedures of teaching and learning). Whether or not the teacher plans a lesson in advance, the actual working out of that lesson in the class demands joint endeavour. The lesson-in-process is most often different from that which either the teacher or the learners anticipated before the lesson began. The social dynamic of the group insists that lessons evolve, through explicit or implicit negotiation. In whatever ways the lesson may be perceived by those who participate in it, the route it takes will be drawn by the joint contributions of most, if not all, of the members of the class. Teachers and learners are well aware that lessons are rarely straightforward journeys but are punctuated by hesitant starts, diversions, momentary losses of momentum, interesting side tracks, and unexpected breakdowns. That it may be better to plan classroom learning in advance has little to do with this entirely normal and creative evolution of lessons.[11]

Several important implications for the researcher result from the fact that the content and process of language classes are jointly constructed. First, any teacher-centred (or researcher-centred) perspective on lessons is partial. Second, the researcher's background knowledge of the actual language being worked upon in a class can be a serious handicap because it potentially blinds us to the process of re-invention of that language which teacher and taught engage in together. (This implication warns us against relying on external linguistic criteria alone in assessing the nature of comprehensible input, for example.) The problem reminds us of a similar gap between the teacher's definition of the new language and the different learners' definitions. There are likely to be as many versions of the new language, and changing versions of it, as there are people in the room. Third, the researcher has to be continually wary of being dazzled by what *seems* salient in classroom life. For example, even the most passive or non-contributory learner in a class can be a poltergeist on the proceedings. Silence, encouraged or not, is a characteristic part of the culture of the classroom and it has great significance. Silence or withdrawal can change a lesson just as powerfully as their opposites, and not just for the person who withdraws, but also for all the others who sense it. The fourth implication of the joint construction of the content and process of a language class is particularly significant for researchers who wish to examine the effects of classroom language learning. The fact that lessons-in-process are communal endeavours means that *any learning outcome*, for any member of the class, has been socially processed. The actual nature of individual achievements has been communally moulded. The culture of the classroom inevitably mediates between a new language and a learner in class. The culture of a particular class will shape what is made available for learning, will work upon what is made available in particular ways, will evolve its own criteria for progress and achievement, and will attain specific and various objectives. (It is worth emphasising here that linguistic input is only a part of the first of these classroom-based phenomena.) What someone learns in a language class will be a dynamic synthesis of individual *and* collective experience. Individual definitions of the new language, of what is to be attended to as worth learning, of how to learn, and personal definitions of progress will all *interact with* the particular classroom culture's definitions of each of these things. If strictly individualised or autonomous language learning is desirable or even possible then the classroom is necessarily antithetical towards it. The language I learn in a classroom is a communal product derived through a jointly constructed process.

The culture of the classroom is immediately significant

What is overtly done in a classroom and what can be described by an observer are *epiphenomena*; they are reductions of classroom reality. How things are done and why things are done have particular psychological significance for the individual and for the group. The particular culture of a language class will socially act in certain ways, but these actions are extensions or manifestations of the psychology of the group, its collective consciousness and subconscious. Individual perceptions and definitions will, of course, feed into and evolve from those of the group. However, the socio-cognitive world of the class – its culture – will be a world other than the sum of the individual worlds within it. What is *significant* for learners (and a teacher) in a classroom is not only their individual thinking and behaviour nor, for instance, a longer-term mastery of a syllabus, but the day-to-day interpersonal rationalisation of what is to be done, why, and how. The immediate significance of the experience of classroom language learning resides in how individual priorities (teacher and learner definitions of what, why, and how) can be given social space here and now. It is precisely this interplay between the individual, the individual as group member, and the group which represents and generates the social and psychological *nexus* which I have proposed as the culture of the language classroom. Most often the flow of classroom life is actually under the surface. What is observable is the rim of a socio-cognitive coral reef! Classroom life *seems* to require that many learners spend surprising amounts of time doing little, whilst a teacher spends equally surprising amounts of time trying to do too much. As researchers we can describe such overt peculiarities, but we also need to explain them. We have to ask whether or not such phenomena are true, and we must doubt the integrity of the observable. If we do, then we are led towards discovering what is, in fact, immediately significant for the group of people we started to observe. The search for the significance which a person, learner or teacher, invests in moments of classroom life (and for the significance granted to these moments by the classroom culture) is neither trivial nor avoidable, though it may be complex and subtle. We will never understand classroom language learning unless we explore its lesson-by-lesson significance for those who undertake it.

Reviewing the classroom as culture

I have offered brief descriptions of eight features of the genuine culture of the language classroom in order to achieve two purposes. First, to illustrate the potential of classroom life itself, its social and psychological richness. The particular features I have selected are offered with no evaluative intent. I would not wish to suggest here that such features are "good" or "bad" aspects of a classroom. They are the inevitable characteristics of the social event in which most people learn a foreign language. My second purpose has been to draw attention to significant social and psychological variables which we seem to be neglecting in our current research in language learning. My main argument would be that, if we wish to investigate language learning, these variables must be contained in whatever metaphor we have for that special social location from which a great deal of language learning actually derives.[12]

My practical purpose in exploring the metaphor of the classroom as culture has been to seek to offer a possible means for *relating social and cognitive variables* which may influence language learning; to suggest a particular frame through which we may come to understand language learning in a more contextually valid way. The culture of the class resembles a single person through its integration of psychological and social factors. A teacher or a learner is not *either* individual mind *or* social actor when participating in lessons. Each is at once cognitive and social, and so are the classroom realities which each perceives. Current language learning research tends to examine psychological change in an asocial way or social events in a non-cognitive way. Either approach implies distinctiveness of psychological and social dimensions of learning and, thereby, risks offering both a partial account and a simplistic causal explanation of the relations between social phenomena and individual development. The metaphor of the classroom as culture allows us to perceive the two dimensions as irrevocably linked and mutually engaged. The metaphor also captures the classroom group as a socio-cognitive dynamic which is an *extension* of the individual within it. Because the classroom culture is a human enterprise, it provides the researcher with a living subject, an informant, not unlike a single learner. When investigating an individual's learning process, we may endeavour to account for the particular permutation of attributes and activities of that learner which may influence the learning. Similarly, the study of a language class as culture can provide us with a holistic and integrated framework which incorporates the experimental and discoursal attributes of a classroom, but which also locates these attributes within a richer cluster of typical characteristics.

The eight features I have described are selective, and there are further features which reflect and create the socio-cognitive realities of a language class. A classroom group will achieve interaction, collectivism, or significance in its own ways. But all of the features overlap and interrelate, and a class will evolve particular permutations of features over time. Just as each feature will vary as the life of the class proceeds, there will also be changes in the patterning and interaction of all the features. Although I would suggest that the classroom as culture and the features which represent its cultural nature are *universal* to language classrooms wherever they may be, a particular classroom will evolve both individual features and a synthesis of features in particular ways at particular times. And it is the synthesis of features which is the specific culture of a classroom group. If such proposals are acceptable and valid, what do they imply for undertaking research with a language class? Also, what does the metaphor of classroom as culture offer to the language teacher? I wish to conclude by briefly outlining some major deductions for researching and teaching.

Researching within the classroom as culture

A researcher's sympathies with what I have argued so far may be strained by the seeming complexity suggested for methods of investigation. If our goal is to move closer to the realities of language learning and to understand the experience of discovering a new language in a classroom group, then such an audacious inquiry demands anthropological sensitivity. The culture of the language class will resist exposure from a single source – a sampled informant or a special moment perhaps – or through a single investigatory lens. Cautious triangulation has to be married with longitudinal patience! We are required to enter a cultural world – as if from Mars, perhaps – and intrude upon a relatively unique socio-cognitive process, unavoidably participating within as many realities as there are people in the room. In essence, we have to critically reexamine our own assumptions and familiar ways of collecting information. We will be obliged to employ what Garfinkel referred to as *methods of understanding*.[13] And such methods will lead us in the following directions:

1   An initial questioning of our own well-established perceptions of the classroom situation – its purposes, its subject matter, capacities, and social and psychological processes. (If we have learned or taught a language, or if we know the language being taught for example, we are unlikely to be objectively innocent.)

2   A recurrent reasonable doubt about the integrity of the observable, and an insistent curiosity for learner and teacher points of view.

3   An uncovering of the intentions and interpretations invested in classroom activities and content by its participants. A search for what is significant in the immediate and existential (historical) experiences of the classroom for those within it.

4   A socio-cognitive frame of reference which will give access to mutual relationships between social activity and psychological changes. An investigatory template which can reveal social behaviour as mentally motivated and thinking and learning as socially shaped.

5   An anthropological exploration of what, how, and why things are done within the classroom from the perspectives of all the members of the group (and including the researcher's perspective). A discovery, over time, of the subjective realities which that classroom contains and the distinctive intersubjective world of the group which is evolved by them but which is also other than the sum of individual definitions of the situation.

6   An evaluation of change and progress which accounts for individual and collective contributions, achievements, and failures. Evaluation which seeks the interactions between individual and collective and which can be based upon criteria derived directly from individual expectations and the group's emerging norms and values.

7   A study of the interpersonal and inter-group relationships, the roles and identities generated and maintained, and the rights and duties which are entailed (and including the researcher's location in these relationships).

8   A description and explanation of the specific culture of the classroom group which accounts for all the features of classroom life which generate the language learning context for that group. A profile of features *and* their dynamic permutations which avoids the partiality of the isolation and comparison of a few selected variables.

9   A research approach which honestly grapples with 'observer effects' so that we can move from intrusion towards a reciprocity of trust and helpfulness; becoming *within* the classroom culture over time and being seen as contributing as much to the group as we receive from it.

If the above objectives are seen to be difficult or impossible to attain, then our future investigations into classroom language learning will need to acknowledge more explicitly those things which we have not accounted for.

Teaching within the classroom as culture

As direct participants in the culture of their language classes, teachers are very likely to be highly sensitive to the nuances of the features of classroom life which I have tried to describe. However, the metaphor of the classroom as culture suggests two major implications for the language teacher. The first relates to the special task of teaching a language, and the second relates to the teacher's direct concern with the process of learning in classrooms.

1. How can the culture of the classroom be exploited as a resource for the development of linguistic and communicative knowledge and abilities? Although a classroom is an

apprenticeship for later authentic communication and any use of the new language primarily serves the learning and teaching of that language, any group of language learners has two significant contributions to make to the development of the new language: first, individual prior definitions and experiences of language and communication, of learning, and of working in classrooms: second, the capacity to be metalinguistic and metacommunicative, to talk about, to explore collectively, and to reconstruct jointly language and its use. The language class has the communicative potential for a dialogue about subjective definitions of language, how language may be best learned, and how the classroom context may be best used. The positive and explicit use of the interactive, collective, normative, and jointly constructed nature of lessons can be a *means* to uncovering and sharing what individual learners and the teacher perceive as significant for them in learning a language together. And what is revealed can, in turn, provide the starting points for later interaction, collective endeavour, agreed evaluation, and the joint construction of subsequent lessons. Put simply, a language class may be a place where the underlying culture of that class can be mobilised and engaged more overtly. I do not have space here to detail the practicalities of mobilising the culture of the classroom for language learning, but I would suggest two pedagogic motivations for such a proposal.[14] First, a gathering of people in a classroom provides a reservoir of prior knowledge and experience – both reflective or abstract and concrete – of language and communicating from which any new knowledge and experience must flow. Second, the teaching-learning process requires decisions to be made, and decision-making has high communicative potential. The sharing of decision-making in a language class will generate communication which has authentic roots in getting things done here and now.

2. How can the culture of the classroom help the teacher to facilitate *classroom* language learning? The culture of the class has the potential to reveal to the teacher the language learning process as it is actually experienced. In this way, teaching language and investigating language learning may be seen to be synonymous. Teachers and learners already undertake research in classrooms, but their joint investigation tends to focus upon subject matter – the new language and its use. An additional focus of investigation could be the language learning process as it actually unfolds and as it is directly experienced in the class. Many teachers and learners already undertake such action research, but it is sometimes rather implicit and accorded little space and significance. I am suggesting here that genuine classroom language learning research may progress to the extent that those people who are immediately involved in its everyday realities also become explicitly engaged in a methodical reflection upon their own learning and teaching. The *pedagogic* motivation would be that teacher–learner research has the potential to facilitate a delicate understanding and refinement of language development *within* the classroom itself. If this pedagogic purpose may be seen as valuable, then the researcher can offer knowledge and skills to a classroom rather than act only as a recipient of its riches.[15]

Learning within the classroom as culture

I have briefly argued for the explicit use of shared decision making and for teacher–learner research in the language class because both seem to me pedagogically appropriate within classrooms devoted to the discovery and development of *a new language* and its use. However, both proposals derive from considering the potential of the culture of the classroom *for* language teaching. Both also derive from the wish to bring research in language learning and the classroom experience of language learning closer together. The research approach suggested earlier requires participating investigators and longitudinal involvement (at least), and it could lead to a positive erosion of the distinctions between doing research, doing teaching, and learning.

This paper is not intended as some Rousseauesque appeal for a return to the primitive savagery of classroom life, in reaction, perhaps, to a vision of finely-tuned classrooms wherein learners might be discoursally programmed. Nor is it intended as a rejection of the metaphors of classroom as experimental laboratory or classroom as discourse. Classrooms *are* experiments and they are places where the discourse symbolizes significant actions and thoughts of those participating. And classrooms are specific cultures. All three metaphors seem to me to be true, but all three are also partial. I have tried to show that the classroom as culture embraces variables which we may have formerly neglected in research. The metaphor can allow us to see the classroom more distinctly and to re-explore its potential more precisely. However, we still need to develop, during the research process, sufficiently sensitive methods of investigation so that the culture of the language class may be less of a metaphor and more of a revelation.

I am pleased to be able to end with one of Edward Sapir's enlightening observations because he expressed, sixty years ago, a crucial consideration regarding the relationship between scientific efficiency and genuine culture. Sapir comments on his important distinction between human progress and cultural experience:

> We have no right to demand of higher levels of sophistication that they preserve to the individual his manifold functioning, but we may well ask whether, as a compensation, the individual may not reasonably demand an *intensification in cultural value*, a spiritual heightening of such functions as are left him.[16]
>
> (1949: 97 [my emphasis])

In this paper, I have tried to argue that our professional concern with one of the individual's most socially motivated functions – learning how to communicate with members of another social group, another culture – requires us to understand how the individual may best achieve this. And if the individual undertakes the task in a classroom, we need to understand the socio-cognitive experience made available through the meeting of individual and classroom group. The classroom may be a relatively inefficient environment for the methodical mastery of a language system, just as it is limited in providing opportunities for real world communication in a new language. But the classroom has its own communicative potential and its own authentic metacommunicative purpose. It can be a particular social context for the intensification of the cultural experience of *learning*.

Notes

1   This tendency has been captured by Kuhn's (1962) analysis of scientific research. Research exemplifying the first view I wish to explore is represented in the excellent anthologies of Hatch (1978), Felix (1980), Scarcella and Krashen (1983) and Baily, Long, and Peck (1984). The second prevalent view is implied by recent studies of classroom language learning, fairly represented in the valuable collections of Larsen-Freeman (1980), Seliger and Long (1983) and Færch and Kasper (1983). Of course, much language learning research makes no reference to the classroom and several researchers do not assume the perspectives discussed in this paper. My emphasis is upon currently influential views of language learning and what these imply for the functions of the classroom.

2 Paradoxically, the features of optimal input were initially derived from (1) the order of emergence of certain linguistic features in the production of language learners and (2) the characteristics of simple codes used by people other than learners – e.g., motherese, foreigner talk, talk to foreigners, etc. Neither phenomenon has been shown to have any necessary relationship with learning language. (On the relationship between motherese and learning, for example, see Newport, Gleitman, and Gleitman 1977; Shantz 1982.) Most work on learning strategies has tended to be individual case studies undertaken outside classrooms or through simulated tasks. These points are not intended critically but suggest limitations in relating research findings on learning to the language classroom.

3 To try to teach learning strategies seems to me an inappropriate interpretation of the investigations of, inter alia, Naiman, Fröhlich, Stern, and Todesco (1978), Rubin (1981), and Cohen and Hosenfeld (1981). Apart from the major problem of the researcher having to *infer* strategies from retrospections (Mann 1982) or from communication strategies (Færch and Kasper, 1983), we need to maintain clear distinctions between the act of learning and the influences of teaching. Language learning research currently lacks an approach to learning strategies and styles which accounts for key intervening variables – such as the context in which the learner works and how the learner strategically reacts to that context. Examples of a more comprehensive analysis can be found in Gibson and Levin (1975), Mann (1983) and Marton, Hounsell, and Entwistle (1984).

4 Although SLA research evolved from work in L1 acquisition, it has persisted in a narrow focus upon linguistic and mentalistic variables whilst the last decade of L1 research has been characterised by its concern with social, contextual and interactive variables also (Waterson and Snow, 1978; Lock, 1978). The significant theoretical synthesis provided to SLA research by Krashen (1981, 1982) has encouraged this asocial perspective. However, a paradox thrives at present wherein it is fashionable in some quarters to belittle Krashen's invaluable contributions to the SLA paradigm whilst many researchers unquestioningly assume his hypotheses proven as the starting point of their own investigations. Both positions seem equally unjustifed.

5 See Mueller's (1979) historical analysis of the "science" of psychology. In this paper, I will argue for a *socio-cognitive* perspective on language learning. Current influential approaches to the social psychology of language learning seem to me too narrowly focused upon motivational and attitudinal factors (Gardner, 1979) and, although social psychology grants significance to relationships between the individual and social context, its prevailing tradition is non-cognitive and somewhat deterministic in its evaluation of the effects of social experience. A socio-cognitive perspective allows us to identify variables of learning both within the social situation *and* within the active cognition of the learner (Forgas, 1981). It also encourages seeking relationships between learner cognition and situations and implies the need to understand, to see through language learning in ways cogently argued by Ochsner (1979).

6 Allwright (1983), Gaies (1983) and Long (1983) provide excellent reviews of classroom-oriented research.

7 Sapir (1949) and Hymes (1972) are, of course, emphasising collective meanings and values. Other scholars, notably Goffman (1959) and Cicourel (1973), would also assert the significance of *personal* intentions and interpretations within social events. I will argue that we need to account for both *and* their interrelationships.

8 The notion of "genuine culture" derives from Sapir's discussion of "Culture, Genuine and Spurious" (1949). In referring to Malinowski's (1935) study, I do not wish to imply that we adopt a narrow social anthropological approach to the classroom; rather one which *relates* social experience and psychological change in the tradition of Margaret Mead, Ruth Benedict, and Clyde Kluckhohn (see, for example, Beattie's 1964 overview of social anthropology). Perhaps the study of the classroom group might resemble Oscar

Lewis's investigations of family life in Mexico (1959) but with a particular focus upon the relationships between classroom life and language development.

9   "Interactive" is becoming a much-used term in language teaching circles and is, thereby, expanded to encompass many assumptions and diverse meanings (as has been the fate of "functional," "communicative," "negotiation," and, when applied to pedagogy, "natural"). Ambiguity resides in the fact that human interaction can be both interpersonal and intra-personal; both overtly social and covertly mental. Allwright's (1982, 1984a) fruitful identification of interactive work as a defining feature of classrooms clearly relates to the interpersonal. However, interactive work also occurs in the recreative relating of mind to external phenomena (Neisser, 1976). But interaction is more comprehensive than (1) overt behaviour between people and (2) covert perception and reconstruction of perceptions and experiences. We also need to regard social interaction as having psychological roots and outcomes (Rommetveit 1981) and mental interaction as being subject to social forces (Gauld and Shotter, 1977; Harré, 1978; Shotter, 1978). Thus, interaction is also (3) a socio-cognitive process which continually relates social action and experience to the content and capabilities of the mind, and vice versa.

10   Over the past twenty years there have been a number of interesting studies of classroom relationships and roles within the school system. Jackson's (1968) seminal investigation is complemented by Hargreaves (1972) and Woods (1979) – the more recent works echoing Goffman's (1961) revelations of the effects upon the perceptions and activities of people in situations which maintain asymmetrical relationships. Learner experiences and judgements have been studied by Taylor (1962), Nash (1974), Meighan (1977), and Hargreaves (1977), whilst teacher perspectives are considered by Morrison and MacIntyre (1969).

11   A well-established tradition within the sociology of knowledge argues that most of our learning is socially constructed. Berger and Luckmann's (1966) justification of such a view is based upon a phenomenological approach to human experience. (Douglas, 1973, and Luckmann, 1978, offer a range of studies whilst Filmer, Phillipson, Silverman, and Walsh, 1972, provide an overview.) Perhaps the two major influences upon recent endeavours to relate social experience and knowledge have been Schultz (1962–66, 1967) and Husserl (1965, 1967). Investigations directly concerned with the joint construction of classroom life are exemplified within Hargreaves (1977), Nash (1973), Stubbs and Delamont (1976), Woods and Hammersley (1977), and Woods (1980a, b).

12   The eight essential features which I describe are based on my own experience as a teacher and the shared experiences of many teachers from most countries of the world with whom I have worked. The features are also influenced by my interpretation of a number of scholars. Willard Waller's (1932) evaluation of the teaching process is still the most comprehensive, whilst the studies of teaching and learning referred to in notes 10 and 11 provide strong justification for seeing the classroom group as a special culture. (A helpful overview of classroom research within general education is provided by Cohen and Manion 1981.)

13   Garfinkel asserts the need for methods of understanding the everyday life of the group we may be investigating through an ethnomethodological approach. (Douglas, 1971, Turner 1974, and Douglas, 1973 provide examples of this approach, whilst Hughes, 1980, offers a humanistic interpretation of ethnomethodology.) For a broader critical consideration of methods of investigation, see Taylor (1971). Interesting examples of current research in classroom language learning which adopt various methods of understanding are found in Dingwall (1982), Wenden (1983), Murphy-O'Dwyer (1983), Allwright (1984b), and Bonamy, Cherchalli, Johnson, Kubrusly, Schwerdtfeger, Soule-Susbielles (all 1984):

14   In Breen (1982), I examine the practical realities of classroom language and procedures.

The more explicit involvement of learners is considered in Breen (1983), whilst syllabus planning through shared decision making is discussed in Breen (1984).

15   This implies that my proposals for the researcher may also be directly relevant to the teaching-learning process itself. If the culture of the group is explicitly mobilised for sharing decisions and for reflective investigation, then the generalisability of what may be derived from *that* classroom may seem to be undermined. But more may be gained from participatory research than might be lost. We have failed, as yet, to discover actual relationships between the classroom situation and language learning. We simply do not know *what* the classroom contributes to the developmental process. Research which implies that phenomena unique to classrooms must be *the* contributions to learning which only classrooms can offer is trapped in its own circularity. Objective investigations – through discourse analysis or the quantification of selected variables of classroom life, for example – represent little more than a *researcher*'s inferencing and, thereby, remain only relatively objective. Yet we cling onto a faith in the chasteness of neutral impartiality which is assumed to be synonymous with non-participant data collection and analysis. Validity of classroom data and its interpretation demands direct teacher-learner intervention *in* the research process, whilst the researcher can facilitate their exploration by contributing rigourous and established research methods and criteria.

16   Sapir (1949: 97), my emphasis.

References

Allwright, R.L. (1982) *Interactive work for input in the language classroom*. Keynote paper at the Second Language Research Forum, Los Angeles.

—— (1983) 'Classroom-centered research on language teaching and learning: A brief historical overview' *TESOL Quarterly* 17: 191–204.

—— (1984a) 'The importance of interaction in classroom language learning' *Applied Linguistics* 5: 156–71.

—— (1984b) *Making sense of classroom instruction*. Presentation at the Symposium on Classroom-centred Research, AILA 7th World Congress, Brussels.

Bailey, K., Long, M.H. and Peck, S. (eds) (1984) *Second language acquisition studies*. Rowley, MA: Newbury House.

Beattie, J. (1964) *Other cultures: Aims, methods and achievements in social anthropology*. London: Routledge and Kegan Paul.

Berger, P. and Luckmann, T. (1966) *The social construction of reality*. Harmondsworth: Penguin.

Bonamy, D. (1984) 'Perceptions of saliency in a language classroom'. Unpublished M.A. thesis. University of Lancaster.

Breen, M.P. (1982) 'Authenticity in the language classroom'. *Bulletin of the Canadian Association of Applied Linguistics* (ACLA) 4: 7–23.

—— (1983) 'How would we recognise a communicative classroom?', in B. Coffey (ed.) *Teacher training and the curriculum*, pp. 132–54. London: The British Council.

—— (1984) 'Process syllabuses for the language classroom', in C.J. Brumfit (ed.) *General English syllabus design*, pp. 47–60. Oxford: Pergamon Press/The British Council.

Cherchalli, S. (1984) *Asking learners about language learning*. Presentation at the Symposium on Classroom Research, University of Lancaster.

Cicourel, A.V. (1973) *Cognitive sociology*. Harmondsworth: Penguin.

Cohen, A.D. and Hosenfeld, C. (1981) 'Some uses of mentalistic data in second language research'. *Language Learning* 31: 285–313.

Cohen, L. and Manion, L. (1981) *Perspectives on classrooms and schools*. London: Holt, Rinehart and Winston.

Cole, M., Gay, J., Click, J.A. and Sharp, D.W. (1971) *The cultural context of learning and thinking*. London: Methuen.

Cole, M. and Scribner, S. (1974) *Culture and thought*. New York: Wiley.

Dingwall, S.D. (1982) 'Critical self-reflection and decisions in doing research', in Dingwall, S.D., Mann, S.J. and Katamba, F.X. (eds) *Methods and problems in doing applied linguistic research*, pp. 3–26. University of Lancaster.

Douglas, J.D. (ed.) (1971) *Understanding everyday life*. London: Routledge and Kegan Paul.

Douglas. M. (ed.) (1973) *Rules and meanings*. Harmondsworth: Penguin.

Færch, C. and Kasper, G. (eds) (1983) *Strategies in interlanguage communication*. London: Longman.

Felix, S.W. (ed.) (1980) *Second language development: trends and issues*. Tübingen: Gunter Narr.

Filmer, P., Phillipson, M., Silverman, D. and Walsh, D (1972) *New directions in sociological theory*. London: Collier Macmillan.

Forgas, J.P. (ed.) (1981) *Social cognition*. New York: Academic Press.

Gaies, S.J. (1983) 'The investigation of language classroom processes', *TESOL Quarterly* 17: 205–17.

Gardner, R.C. (1979) 'Social psychological aspects of second language acquisition', in Giles, H. and St. Clair, R. (eds) *Language and social psychology*, pp. 193–200. London: Basil Blackwell.

Gauld, A. and Shotter, J. (1977) *Human action and its psychological investigation*. London: Routledge and Kegan Paul.

Gibson, E.J. and Levin, H. (1975) *The psychology of reading*. Cambridge, MA: M.I.T. Press.

Goffman, C.E. (1959) *The presentation of self in everyday life*. Harmondsworth: Penguin.

—— (1961) *Asylums*. Harmondsworth: Penguin.

Hargreaves, D.H. (1972) *Interpersonal relations and education*. London: Routledge and Kegan Paul.

—— (1977) 'The process of typification in classroom interaction'. *British Journal of Educational Psychology* 47: 274–84.

Harré, R. (1978) 'Accounts, actions and meanings: The practice of participatory psychology', in M. Brenner *et al.* (eds) *The social contexts of method*. London: Croom Helm.

Hatch, E.M. (ed.) (1978) *Second language acquisition*. Rowley, MA: Newbury House.

Hughes, J. (1980) *The philosophy of social research*. London: Longman.

Husserl, E. (1965) *Phenomenology and the crisis of philosophy*. New York: Harper.

—— (1970) *Cartesian meditations*. The Hague: Nijhoff.

Hymes, D. (1972) 'Models of the interaction of language and social life', in Gumperz, J.J. and Hymes, D. (eds) *Directions in sociolinguistics. The ethnography of communication*, pp. 35–71. New York: Holt Rinehart and Winston.

Jackson, P.W. (1968) *Life in classrooms*. New York: Holt Rinehart and Winston.

Johnson, P. (1984) *Oral communication between non-native English speakers in the ESL practicum class*. Paper at the Symposium on Classroom-centred Research, AILA 7th World Congress, Brussels.

Krashen, S.D. (1981) *Second language acquisition and second language learning*. Oxford: Pergamon Press.

—— (1982) *Principles and practice in second language acquisition*. Oxford: Pergamon Press.

Kubrusly, M.H. (1984) 'Does the teacher make a difference?'. Unpublished M.A. thesis, University of Lancaster.

Kuhn, T.S. (1962) *The structure of scientific revolutions*. Chicago: University of Chicago Press.

Larsen-Freeman, D. (ed.) (1980) *Discourse analysis in second language research*. Rowley, MA: Newbury House.

Lewis, O. (1959) *Five families: Mexican case studies in the culture of poverty*. New York: Basic Books.

Lock, A. (ed.) (1978) *Action, gesture and symbol: The emergence of language*. New York: Academic Press.

Long, M.H. (1983) 'Does second language instruction make a difference? A review of research'. *TESOL Quarterly* 17; 359–82.

Luckmann, T. (ed.) (1978) *Phenomenology and sociology*. Harmondsworth: Penguin.

Malinowski, B. (1935) *Coral gardens and their magic*. London: Allen and Unwin (2nd edition, 1966).

Mann, S.J. (1982) 'Verbal reports as data: A focus on retrospection', in Dingwall, S.D., Mann, S.J. and Katamba, F.X. (eds) *Methods and problems in doing applied linguistic research*, pp. 87–105. University of Lancaster.

—— (1983) *Problems in reading and how they may be solved by the reader*. Paper at the 17th Annual TESOL Convention, Toronto.

Marton, F., Hounsell, D.J. and Entwistle, N.J. (eds) (1984) *The experience of learning*. Edinburgh: Scottish Academic Press.

Meighan, R. (1977) 'The pupil as client: The learner's experience of schooling'. *Educational Review* 29: 123–35.

Morrison, A. and MacIntyre, D. (1969) *Teachers and teaching*. Harmondsworth: Penguin.

Mueller, C. (1979) 'Some origins of psychology as a science'. *Annual Review of Psychology* 30: 9–20.

Murphy-O'Dwyer, M. (1983) 'Teachers in training: A diary study during an in-service course'. Unpublished M.A. thesis, University of Lancaster.

Naiman, M., Frolich, M., Stern, H.H. and Todesco, A. (1978) *The good language learner*. Toronto: Ontario Institute for Studies in Education.

Nash, R. (1973) *Classrooms observed*. London: Routledge and Kegan Paul.

—— (1974) 'Pupil's expectations for their teachers'. *Research in Education*, November 1974: 46–71.

Neisser, U. (1976) *Cognition and reality*. New York: W.H. Freeman.

Newport, E.L., Gleitman, H. and Gleitman, L.R. (1977) 'Mother I'd rather do it myself: Some effects and non-effects of maternal speech style', in Snow, C.E. and Ferguson, C.A. (eds) *Talking to children: Language input and acquisition*. Cambridge: Cambridge University Press.

Ochsner, R. (1979) A poetics of second language acquisition. *Language Learning* 29: 53–80.

Rommetveit. R. (1981) 'On meanings of situations and social control of such meanings in human communication', in Magnussen, D. (ed.) *Toward a psychology of situations: An interactional perspective*, pp. 151–67. Hillsdale, NJ: Lawrence Erlbaum Associates.

Rubin, J. (1981) 'The study of cognitive processes in second language learning'. *Applied Linguistics* 2:117–31.

Sapir, E. (1949) *Culture, language and personality: Selected essays*. Berkeley: University of California Press.

Scarcella, R. and Krashen, S.D. (eds) (1983) *Research in second language acquisition*. Rowley, MA: Newbury House.

Schutz, A. (1962, 64, 66) *Collected Papers Vols 1–3*. The Hague: Nijhoff.

—— (1967) *The phenomenology of the social world*. Chicago: Northwestern University Press.

Schwerdtfeger, I.C. (1984) *Exercises in the foreign language classroom: The pupils' point of view*. Paper at the Symposium on Foreign Language learning under Classroom Conditions, AILA 7th World Congress. Brussels.

Shatz, M. (1982) 'On mechanisms of language acquisition: Can features of the communicative environment account for development?', in Wanner, E. and Gleitman, L.R. (eds) *Language acquisition: The state of the art*, pp. 102–27. Cambridge: Cambridge University Press.

Shotter, J. (1978) 'Towards a social psychology of everyday life: A standpoint "in action"', in Brenner, M. *et al.* (eds), pp. 33–43.

Soule-Susbielles, N. (1984) *Pupils analyse their own classroom behaviour*. Paper at the Symposium on Classroom-centred Research, AILA 7th World Congress, Brussels.

Stubbs, M. and Delamont, S. (eds) (1976) *Explorations in classroom observation*. London: Wiley.

Taylor, C. (1971) 'Interpretation and the sciences of Man'. *Review of Metaphysics* xxv: 3–51.

Taylor, P.H. (1962) 'Children's evaluations of the characteristics of a good teacher'. *British Journal of Educational Psychology* 32: 258–66.

Turner, R. (ed.) (1974) *Ethnomethodology*. Harmondsworth: Penguin.

Waller, W. (1932) *The sociology of teaching*. New York: Wiley.

Waterson, N. and Snow, C.E. (eds) (1978) *The development of communication*. London: Wiley.

Wenden, A.L (1983) 'The process of interaction'. *Language Learning* 33: 103–21.

Woods, P. and Hammersley, M. (eds) (1977) *School experience*. London: Croom Helm.

Woods, P. (1979) *The divided school*. London: Routledge and Kegan Paul.

Woods, P. (ed.) (1980a) *Pupils' strategies*. London: Croom Helm.

—— (1980b) *Teachers' strategies*. London: Croom Helm.

PART TWO

Strategies and goals in the classroom context

Chapter 8

Paul Knight

THE DEVELOPMENT OF EFL
METHODOLOGY

Introduction

WHEN PLANNING THIS CHAPTER I CONSIDERED my own UK-based training as an EFL teacher and the fact that it contained virtually no explanation of the practices I was trained in. Further training informed me how Communicative Language Teaching had superseded Audio-Lingualism, but it was not until later that further studies made me aware that the field of foreign language teaching has a long and rich methodological tradition.

Ways of teaching English have been shaped by developments in many disciplines including linguistics, psychology and education. They have been informed by empirical research, purely theoretical developments and the practical hands-on experience of classroom teachers. In order to take part in the current methodological debates, an understanding of these influences is necessary. I hope this chapter can help foster that understanding by presenting an overview of the debates and issues, illustrated by reference to a variety of approaches, practices and materials.

First, it is important to remember that most second language learning, both in the past and today, has not been influenced by any of the methodologies that I will review here. Outside of the UK and North America, the prevalence of multilingualism across the globe shows that monolingualism is the exception rather than the norm. Most second languages are still learnt informally. Formal methodologies have tried to copy certain features of informal second language learning and this is something to look out for as we proceed.

While the term 'method' might be used to describe any practical procedure for teaching a language, the term 'methodology' implies the existence of a set of procedures related by an underlying rationale or theory of teaching and learning language. The approaches I will look at have all been thought of by their advocates as constituting a 'methodology in that sense. I will examine each of them by considering three questions:

1   What is the desired outcome?
2   What model of language is it based on?
3   What model of learning is it based on?

Historical/Pre-World War II

In my experience, few modern EFL teachers have looked at the history of their profession and the methodological practices of the past. The common perception is that until the advent of Audio-Lingualism, language teaching methodology consisted simply of the grammar–translation method, and the reform movement at the end of the nineteenth century was simply a reaction against this. However, as we shall see, methodological debates have characterised the profession for much longer.

Howatt records the use of materials to teach both French and Latin in the middle ages which were based on the study of dialogues (Howatt 1984). He notes the development of methods by teachers like Bellot and Holyband in the 16th and 17th centuries which included substitution tables, dialogues based on common situations and an emphasis on spoken proficiency. Describing Webbe's 'anti-grammar' stance in the 17th century, Howatt observes that:

> there is . . . every reason to suppose that Webbe was proposing a form of 'direct method' of language teaching without the use of reference grammars, which would depend heavily on spoken interaction . . .' (Howatt 1984: 37)

By the 19th century, grammar–translation was the dominant methodology. This was because of the importance given to the study of Greek and Latin in public schools. The study of Latin and Greek at this time focused on accessing their literature, something which was thought to be best achieved by consciously memorising the grammatical rules and lexical items of the target language. The basic unit of study was the sentence and, as the name of the methodology would suggest, learners spent a lot of their time translating both into and from the target language. Such techniques were not only thought to help learning, but also to instill 'mental discipline' (Stern 1983).

The 19th century saw a gradual disillusionment with the grammar–translation method, which led to a number of observations which were to change language teaching. Marcel, Prendergast and Gouin each drew on children's language learning to inform new theories (Richards and Rogers 1986: 5). Marcel argued for a focus on meaning; Prendergast noted the use of contextual factors in furthering comprehension and Gouin argued for the importance of context and that language learning was facilitated by 'using language to accomplish events' (Richards and Rogers 1986: 5 & 6).

By the end of the 19th century ideas which previously had only had a limited impact became more widely promoted. Central to this was the Reform Movement, an international movement which grew out of the formation of the International Phonetic Association in 1886. Its most significant British member was Henry Sweet, who argued for a scientific approach to the practice of language teaching in his *The Practical Study of Languages* in 1899. The key principles of the Reform Movement were:

> the primacy of speech, the centrality of the connected text as the kernel of the teaching–learning process, and the absolute priority of an oral methodology in the classroom. (Howatt 1984: 171)

It is important to note that it is not just the ideas of the Reform Movement which are significant; its approach also shaped developments which followed. It was the first truly scientific approach to language learning and can be seen as an important step in the development of the disciplines of linguistics and applied linguistics.

This challenge to grammar-translation in the 19th century and the increasing interest in child language learning led to the development of natural approaches to language teaching. Sauver's focus on oral interaction and avoidance of the mother tongue in his language school in the later part of the century became known as the Natural Method, the theoretical principles of which were outlined by Franke in 1884. This led to what became known as the Direct Method, which was in turn popularised as the 'Berlitz Method' by Maximilian Berlitz.

In the first decades of the 20th century, the forerunners of today's applied linguists started to take the ideas of the Reform Movement further. In the United States the foundations of Audio-Lingualism were being laid, while in the UK the Oral Approach was developed by Palmer, Hornby and others. The Oral Approach proposed principles of selection, gradation and presentation which had been lacking in the Direct Method (Richards and Rogers 1986: 33). The principle that language should be introduced and practised in situations, that is, it should be contextualised, led to the Oral Approach becoming known as Situational Language Teaching. This did not mean that a situational syllabus was proposed, rather that references should be made to the real world in order to teach a structural syllabus, e.g. by using pictures, realia and actions (see Figure 8.1 for example). By the 1950s this was the standard British approach to language teaching. It shared with Audio-Lingualism both a structural view of language and a belief in behaviourist models of learning, but its focus on situations made it distinct.

Audio-Lingualism

The Second World War and its aftermath provided a great spur to language teaching, especially in the USA. The Army Specialized Training Program (ASTP) was established in 1942 to provide the large number of foreign language speakers required by the military. This programme influenced the development of what became known as Audio-Lingualism and was a focus of attention amongst applied linguists long after it was wound up by the military.

Audio-Lingualism saw itself as the first 'scientific' language teaching methodology. Charles Fries, when he outlined the 'Oral Approach', a forerunner of Audio-Lingualism, saw the success of teaching as depending not only on classroom methodology, but also:

> fundamentally upon having satisfactory materials selected and arranged in accord with sound linguistic principles. (Fries 1945)

The principles he is referring to here were those of structural linguistics, whose main tenets were that language is primarily oral, and that it is a rule-governed system understandable in terms of increasing levels of complexity. These principles were most famously outlined by Bloomfield in a number of works between 1914 and 1942 (Bloomfield 1914, 1933, 1942).

The other important strand underlying Audio-Lingualism was that of behaviourist psychology. Behaviourist models of learning essentially saw language as a behavioural skill where learners receive a stimulus (such as a cue in a drill), respond (by providing the correct utterance) and then have correct responses reinforced. Error was not tolerated or investigated as it was thought that this will lead to the errors being reinforced and 'bad habits' engendered. Language had been viewed in terms of habit-formation before; in 1921 Palmer outlined a theory based on what would later have been called behaviourist principles

UNIT A ONE

THEY DO vs. THEY ARE DOING

OFTEN/NEVER, etc. Questions and Negatives

1   DOES vs. IS DOING

Problem Situations

i.   Mr. Collins is a businessman. He gets "The Financial Times" every day and always finds it very interesting. At the moment, he is in his office. His copy of "The Financial Times" is in his overcoat pocket.

1. Where is Mr. Collins?
2. What does he do?
3. Does he read "The Financial Times"?
4. Is he reading it?
5. Where is his copy of "The Financial Times"?

ii   Jack Carlton is a famous football-player. At the moment he is at the dinner-table. There is a large beefsteak in front of him.

1. Who is Jack Carlton?
2. Where is he?
3. Does he play football?
4. What is he doing?

2   **Illustrative Situations**

i.   John Dallas is a film director. At the moment he is in a plane over the Atlantic. He is on his way to Hollywood. There is a glass of champagne in his hand, a smile on his face, and a pretty girl opposite him.
Question: What DOES HE DO?
The only answer is: HE DIRECTS FILMS
or: HE IS A FILM DIRECTOR
Question: What IS HE DOING
Answer: HE IS FLYING TO HOLLYWOOD
HE IS DRINKING A GLASS OF CHAMPAGNE
HE IS SMILING AT A PRETTY GIRL

Question Prompts:
1. Ask and answer these questions about John Dallas:
   (a) Who (b) Where
2. Use DOES HE DO?
3. or IS HE DOING? in these questions:
   (a) films (b) a glass of champagne
   (c) to Hollywood (d) at a pretty girl

ii.   Arthur Docker is on the same plane. He is a very rich man. He drives a Rolls Royce, often eats caviar, plays roulette at Monte Carlo, hunts lions and elephants in Africa, and smokes large Havana cigars. At the moment he is having a nap.
Question: What IS HE DOING?
The only answer is: HE IS HAVING A NAP
Question: What are some of the things he DOES
Answers: HE DRIVES A ROLLS ROYCE.
HE PLAYS ROULETTE. HE HUNTS LIONS AND ELEPHANTS. HE SMOKES HAVANA CIGARS.

Questions and Question Prompts:
1. Is he smoking a Havana cigar?
2. Does he smoke Havana cigars?
3. What is he doing?
4. Ask and answer questions with these words:
   (a) roulette (b) lions and elephants
   (c) a Rolls Royce (d) caviar

Figure 8.1 Situational language teaching material

(Palmer 1921). However, it is Skinner who is generally credited as laying down the most complete theoretical basis for this assumption in his *Verbal Behavior*, where he asserted that:

> We have no reason to assume . . . that verbal behaviour differs in any fundamental respect from non-verbal behaviour. (Skinner 1957: 10)

The role of the learner in Audio-Lingualism came to be portrayed as that of an 'empty vessel' who needs do no more than take part in the drills organised by his/her teacher to learn the target language (see Figure 8.2 for example). This is to some degree unfair; it was certainly not what the exponents of the method had in mind. Fries outlines the role of the student as an active one:

> The student must be willing to give himself whole-heartedly to the strenuous business of learning the new language. (Fries 1945)

What's your job?

Exercise 1

Look at 13.	Look at 14.	Look at 15.	Look at 16.
What's his job?	What's her job?	What are their jobs?	...............?
He's a manager.	She's a receptionist.	They're waiters.	....

Look at 17.	Look at 18.	Look at 19.	**Use these words:**
...............?	...............?	...............?	**cleaners**
....	....	....	**cook**
			secretary
			porter

Figure 8.2 A typical audio-lingual drill

Subsequent attacks on Audio-Lingualism claimed that it promoted mindless repetition over communication. This is rather unfair as it saw communication as being its goal and saw this as being facilitated by learners not having to translate or recall rules, the target language having become 'habit' (Kleinjans 1961).

An important tenet of Audio-Lingualism was that the degree of similarity between the target language and the learners' first language would influence language learning either positively or negatively. Lado described these influences as 'facilitation' and 'interference' (Lado 1964). This meant that skilled linguists were needed to prepare materials based on a contrastive analysis of the first and target languages.

Although the audio-lingual classroom was very teacher-centred, the degree of teacher autonomy could be minimal. Teachers were regarded as models of the target language, judges of the students' output and managers of classroom activities (O'Connor and Twaddell, 1960). This often meant using prescribed materials within a very rigid syllabus; diversions from the prescribed path were frowned upon, as Richards and Rogers (1986) note: 'Failure to learn results only from improper application of the method'.

The language laboratory was a development of the audio-lingual method. It was seen as the ideal tool with which to apply behaviourist principles as it allowed self-monitoring, reinforcement of correct learner responses and the correction of errors without undue attention being drawn to them (Mueller 1959). Although the language laboratory has been demonised by proponents of more communicative approaches to language learning, it is important to remember that it marked an important departure from book-based learning, being an attempt to apply the principle that language is primarily oral.

From these roots, Audio-Lingualism developed into a system which is still used in many parts of the world today. The continued publication and success of textbooks based to a large degree on audio-lingual principles, such as the *Streamline* series (Hartley and Vine 1978), show that Audio-Lingualism has not disappeared. However, Audio-Lingualism as a coherent self-contained system has few, if any, proponents today. Even before the method approached its heyday, its theoretical basis was being demolished. Chomsky exposed the inadequacies of Audio-Lingualism when he showed that language is not just a learnt habit but something created by the speaker using an innate language facility (Chomsky 1957, 1966 etc.), thereby casting into doubt both Audio-Lingualism's model of language and of language learning. Parallel to these theoretical attacks was an increasing sense of the method's limited practical value amongst teachers and learners.

Humanistic methodologies

During the 1970s a number of methodologies appeared which have been broadly labelled as 'Humanistic'. Broadly speaking, this label applies to those methodologies which see the learner as a 'whole' person and the classroom as an environment where more than the transfer of 'knowledge' occurs (Moskowitz 1978). Although none of the humanistic methods have become widely popular, they are worthy of some attention as they are attempts to approach language learning from directions other than linguistic. We will look at four methodologies: The Silent Way, Community Language Learning, Suggestopedia and Total Physical Response.

The Silent Way

Caleb Gattengo proposed the Silent Way in two publications in the 1970s (Gattengo 1972 and 1976). The Silent Way's goals are self-expression in the target language, learner independence and the development of the learner's own facility to assess correctness. These goals are typical of modern language methodologies; it is the way they are to be achieved that is unique. The roles of teachers and learners are the key to this.

Teachers, although silent much of the time, should be constantly monitoring the learners as learners' errors are used to shape future input. Learners are expected to be responsible for their own learning, to make their own generalisations from the language presented to them and to self-assess their own output. Peer correction is encouraged, so learners are expected to become comfortable with each other. It is also thought that learners can 'learn' what they have been exposed to while they are sleeping.

Silent Way lessons are characterised by the use of Cuisenaire rods (coloured wooden rods of different lengths), Fidel charts (colour-coded pronunciation charts), vocabulary charts and the fact that the teacher is silent whenever possible. Typically, the teacher will model an utterance using the rods and charts and elicit student responses to it, which the teacher will accept or ask to be rephrased.

The Silent Way takes an essentially traditional structural view of language. It does, however, see the spoken language as paramount. Reading and writing are not explicitly taught, but are seen to follow from the spoken language.

Community Language Learning

Community Language Learning (CLL) is the name given to a teaching methodology developed by Charles Curran in the 1970s based on psychological counselling techniques (Curran 1972, 1976). The teacher acts as the 'counsellor', and the learners are the 'clients'. In practice this means that the teacher provides a translation of what the learners wish to say from their L1 to the target language, thus allowing the learners to interact using the target language. Dialogues developed in this way then form the basis for further study.

It is a crucial part of the teacher's job to create an unthreatening supportive atmosphere within the classroom as this is seen to be crucial for successful learning. In addition, teacher–learner interaction should not be limited to the exchange of 'information' but should include the discussion of the learners' feelings about the learning process. This relationship has been compared to that of a parent helping a child attain greater levels of independence (Richards and Rogers 1986).

The desired outcome of CLL is not only that the learner should be able to communicate in the target language, but also that he/she should learn about his/her own learning and take increasing responsibility for it (Larsen-Freeman 1986).

Initially CLL was not based on any new theories of language; La Forge, Curran's successor in promoting CLL, saw the learners' job as being to master the sound and grammatical systems of the language (La Forge 1983), which suggests a traditional structural syllabus. However, he later went on to suggest a theory of language which sees language as a social process. This seems more consistent with the wider foundations of CLL as it focuses on the interactional nature of language, something mentioned earlier by Curran but not expanded upon.

Suggestopedia

Suggestopedia, the system espoused by Georgi Lozanov, is perhaps the best-known humanistic method due to the media interest it attracted and the extent of the claims made by its proponents (Lozanov 1978). It is famous for its use of music to create a non-threatening atmosphere conducive to learning.

It is this focus on creating the appropriate mental state to facilitate learning that makes Suggestopedia an interesting methodology. Lozanov claimed that language learning based on his method could be 25 times more effective than other methods (Lozanov 1978). Amid such claims it is not surprising that Suggestopedia has also had equally ardent critics, most famously Scovel (Scovel 1979).

Suggestopedia's target is conversational proficiency in the language being studied. Although Suggestopedia is not based on a model of language, it usually describes language in terms of its vocabulary and grammatical system. In other words, the underlying model of language appears to be structural. Lozanov does say that Suggestopedia directs learners to 'acts of communication' (Lozanov 1978: 109), but goes no further towards a communicative model of either language or language learning.

It is its model and conditions of learning that characterise Suggestopedia – the creation of the right learning environment and the fact that learners are expected to have faith in the system and accept that they are in a childlike situation where they follow the teacher/parent. In this way learners are expected to 'absorb' what is presented to them without critically engaging with it. Teachers, who should also have complete faith in the method, are expected to facilitate the creation of the right environment for learning to occur.

Total Physical Response

Total Physical Response (TPR) is a language teaching methodology proposed by James Asher throughout the second half of the 1960s and 1970s (Asher 1965, 66, 69, 77). Its distinguishing feature is the linking of language learning with physical movement. Asher was not the first person to propose a link between physical activity and learning. Since the early part of the century, several psychological models of learning had argued for a link between physical activity and learning, including language learning (Palmer and Palmer 1925). TPR also draws on models of first language acquisition, in particular the ideas that comprehension comes before output and that early learning is usually associated with the concrete rather than the abstract.

Typically, learners respond physically to commands given by the teacher. Learner output is not required until the learner feels he/she is ready. The limitations of the method mean that it is rarely used beyond beginner level. This has meant, however, that the method has been used more widely than the other humanistic methodologies described here. Many teachers have been happy to borrow its techniques and use them with lower level classes as a prelude to moving on to more mainstream practices, usually CLT. Asher acknowledges this and considers it a positive trend (Asher 1977).

TPR is not based on a particular model of language. Simple structures are usually selected and vocabulary is selected for its relevance to learners' needs. Although this might suggest a structural view of language, TPR proponents would claim that the linking of the language with a physical response shows that meaning is considered paramount.

In the TPR classroom the teacher is expected to direct the lesson. The material to be taught and the actual classroom activities are all selected by the teacher. The learner is required to listen and act upon the instructions given. The degree of reflection on the content is not specified, and the method clearly has some links with habit-formation theories of language learning.

The teacher-centredness and apparently formulaic responses of the learners might not appear 'humanistic', however, these practices are believed to reduce the stress that TPR proponents claim accompanies learning a language.

Communicative Language Teaching

Communicative Language Teaching (CLT) can be said to be the current dominant methodology. Even in countries where CLT has not been adopted in the state sector, most ministries of education appear to be moving in its direction. Many of its practitioners, however, would espouse it on intuitive rather than theoretical grounds. It has become an umbrella term which covers a wide range of classroom practices. Many teacher training courses teach the classroom practices without explaining the underlying principles, which has led to a mistrust of theory among many teachers. However, it is the theoretical basis of CLT which is original; many of the classroom practices with which it is associated are found elsewhere (see Figure 8.3 for example).

If we look at the questions asked at the beginning of this chapter, we can answer the first, about the desired outcome, by saying that for CLT the desired outcome is that the learner can communicate successfully in the target language in real situations, rather than have a conscious understanding of the rules governing that language. (It should be remembered that this was also the outcome sought by Audio-Lingualism.)

Our second question looked at the model of language. For CLT the model of language is one which considers language as it is used rather than as an abstract system. The concept of 'communicative competence' is the key to this (Widdowson 1978, Hymes 1971, Canale and Swain 1980). A theoretical model of language was developed to include ideas about how language is actually used to communicate in real life situations. Chomsky had already proposed a distinction between 'competence' and 'performance', the former being what the speaker knows and the latter being what the speaker actually does, with both seen in purely linguistic terms. This idea was developed to include ideas of appropriacy and the social use of language, giving rise to the concept of 'communicative competence'. In order to define communicative competence, Hymes proposed a four point model concerned with what a speaker both knows and is able to use (Hymes 1971). The points of this model are as follows: what is formally possible in a language, what is feasible given the means of implementation, what is appropriate given the context, and lastly, what is in fact done.

In an environment where the existing orthodoxy of Audio-Lingualism had been discredited, the concept of communicative competence helped shape new models of language teaching and learning. CLT has been described as:

> an approach that aims to (a) make communicative competence the goal of language teaching and (b) develop procedures for the teaching of the four language skills that acknowledge the interdependence of language and communication. (Richards and Rogers 1986: 66)

These basic principles have been applied in a variety of ways. However, Richards and Rogers have isolated three key elements which they feel characterise CLT classroom practice and the theory of learning underlying it:

> One such element might be described as the communication principle: Activities that promote real communication promote learning. A second element is the task principle: Activities in which language is used for carrying out meaningful tasks promote learning. A third element is the meaningfulness principle: Language that is meaningful to the learner supports the learning process. (Richards and Rogers 1986: 72)

LISTENING AND SPEAKING

Leaving home

Pre-listening task

Discuss the following questions in groups.

1 Do you live in the capital city of your country?

  a. If you do
  — do you like it?
  — what are its attractions?
  — is it safe?

  b. If you don't
  — would you like to?
  — have you visited your capital city?
  — what attractions does it have that your town doesn't have?

2 What is the population of your capital city? What is special about it?

3 When you go away from home (for a short or a long time), do you *keep in touch*? How?

Jigsaw listening

Divide into two groups.

T.2a Group **A** You will hear David Snow, who lives in the north-west of England, talking about his only daughter, Jackie.

T.2b Group **B** You will hear Jackie, David Snow's daughter, talking about her life in London.

Figure 8.3 CLT materials which encourage groupwork and participation (continued opposite)

Read and answer the questions below as you listen.
(You can't answer them all!)

Comprehension check

1 Why did Jackie come to London?
2 When did she come?
3 Where is she living?
4 Who is she living with?
5 What's she doing in London?
6 What does her boyfriend do?
7 What does she do at the weekend?
8 What does she think of living in London?
9 How often does she keep in touch?
10 What does she think of her parents?

When you have answered your questions, find a partner from the other group.
Compare your answers and swap information.

What do you think?

1 Is Jackie's father right to be so worried about his daughter? Was Jackie right to leave home at eighteen?

2 Use your dictionary to find out what *generation gap* means. Is there a generation gap between you and your parents? Between you and your children?

3 In your country, at what age

  – can people get married? – can they smoke?
  – can they vote?   – can they drive?

It has been observed that CLT exists in both a 'weak' and a 'strong' version (Howatt 1984). Howatt suggests that:

> The weak version, which has become more or less standard practice in the last ten years, stresses the importance of providing learners with opportunities to use their English for communicative purposes and, characteristically, attempts to integrate such activities into a wider programme of language teaching. (Howatt 1984: 297)

Whilst the 'strong' version:

> advances the claim that language is acquired through communication, so that it is not merely a question of activating an existing but inert knowledge of the language, but of stimulating the development of the language system itself. (Howatt 1984: 297)

He concludes:

> If the former could be described as 'learning to use' English, the latter entails 'using English to learn it'. (Howatt 1984: 297)

Our third question, concerning learner and teacher roles, is perhaps the most open. We can see that in all strands of CLT the learner is expected to interact actively both with other learners and the material. A strong cooperative element is also present in many classroom activities. Within CLT the definition of the learners' roles varies in the degree to which learners direct their own learning and interact as themselves rather than in roles assigned by a teacher. Nunan analysed this question and discerned a trend towards increasing learner independence within CLT (Nunan 1989).

Breen and Candlin identify three key roles for the CLT teacher – facilitator of the communication process, participant within the learning–teaching group, and researcher–learner (Breen and Candlin 1980). They also see these roles as including those of organiser and guide. The CLT teacher is often more autonomous than the audio-lingual teacher because classroom practices are usually less predictable, and in his/her role as facilitator of communication the teacher often interacts with the learners in ways which mirror interaction outside the classroom, e.g. by asking real questions about the learner's background, opinions, etc.

One new role for teachers that has arisen from CLT is that of 'needs analyst', i.e. someone who can analyse their learners' language needs. Although such a role had been present to a greater or lesser degree in earlier methodologies, its focus within CLT on functions rather than structures and its elevation by writers such as Munby to a formal rather than an ad-hoc process make this a significant change (Munby 1978). For individual teachers in collaboration with their learners to decide on the content of courses was very different to the audio-lingual tradition where it was thought that it was the job of structural linguists to prescribe course content. The realisation that learner needs vary can be seen as a precursor of the trend towards learner-centredness and negotiated syllabuses that followed (Nunan 1988).

Immersion programmes and the Natural Approach

Parallel to the development of CLT in the late 1970s and early 1980s another methodology was being developed which had at its base a model of language learning partly based on studies of students in Canadian immersion programmes. This methodology was called the Natural Approach and its proponents were Steven Krashen and Tracy Terrell.

The Canadian immersion programme dates back to the 1960s, but really became widespread in the 1970s and 1980s. It marked a move away from the formal teaching *of* French in Canadian schools to the teaching *in* French of other subjects. It was felt that while the content would be clear to the students through the context, they would acquire the target language through exposure. This process has been described as the partial 'deschooling' of language (Stern 1992: 12).

Canadian French immersion programmes seem to have had interesting but mixed results. Surveying the various studies into their effectiveness, Ellis notes that they do not seem to have had a negative impact on the students' proficiency in English, their L1, and that they have also tended to break down ethnolinguistic stereotypes. He also notes that they have led to high levels of proficiency in the target language, French, in the areas of discourse and strategic competence. They have not, however, been as successful in promoting grammatical proficiency and it has been observed that a fossilised non-standard variant of the target can result (Ellis 1994).

In 1983 Krashen and Terrell published *The Natural Approach*, which essentially contained Krashen's theoretical perspectives, developed in earlier publications (Krashen 1981 and 1982), and Terrell's guidelines for their classroom application (Krashen and Terrell 1983).

Krashen and Terrell saw the Natural Approach as 'similar to other communicative approaches being developed', and it can be seen as sharing the same goals as CLT (Krashen and Terrell 1983: 17).

The Natural Approach's uniqueness lies in its model of learning. Krashen drew a distinction between conscious learning and 'acquisition', which parallels L1 development. Only language which is 'acquired' is seen as being available for natural language use. Language which has been 'learnt' can be used to monitor and correct output based on 'acquired' learning, but that is all; a function which has obvious time constraints in natural language processing.

Learners 'acquire' new language by being exposed to 'comprehensible input'. Such input is defined by Krashen as being comprehensible to the learner but containing language just above the learner's current level. According to Krashen it is only comprehensible input which facilitates acquisition, learner output is essentially irrelevant. Also according to Krashen learners are only able to acquire new grammatical structures in a certain order. This is called the Natural Order Hypothesis and is based on studies of children learning their L1 which suggested a certain order of acquisition. This focus on grammatical structures, usually individual morphemes, suggests a grammatical view of language more in keeping with the audio-lingual tradition than CLT (Richards and Rogers 1986: 130).

Krashen also thought that learning was influenced by the learner's emotional state, an idea shared by humanistic approaches. Krashen argued that an 'Affective Filter' existed, which meant that learners who weren't very motivated, lacked confidence or who were anxious would not do as well as those who were motivated, confident and relaxed.

The breadth of Krashen's model obviously attracted a lot of attention, and it would not be unreasonable to say that a lot of the claims on which it was based have been overturned. McLaughlin has shown that the acquisition/learning differentiation is hard to support and that there is no need to postulate a 'monitor' based upon it (McLaughlin, 1987).

Krashen's ideas concerning comprehensible input have also led to a great deal of debate. It has been clearly argued that comprehensible input is not the only, or even the most important, factor in language learning (McLaughlin, 1987; White, 1987). The Natural Order Hypothesis and Affective Filter Hypothesis have also been subjected to criticism (McLaughlin, 1987). In the case of the former for methodological reasons concerning the collection of data; in the case of the latter because it is unclear exactly how such a filter would work, and alternative models seem better able to explain the evidence.

It would be unfair to leave our discussion of the Natural Approach on such a critical note without acknowledging its role in increasing our understanding of the language learning process. Krashen's model of language learning was an attempt to find a broad universal framework and although it is not widely accepted now, it has acted as a spur for a great deal of subsequent thinking and debate.

Task based learning (TBL)

Task based learning of languages is currently attracting a lot of attention. However, as with CLT, the definition of this methodology is not fixed. In general though it can be said that TBL methodologies:

> share a common idea: giving learners tasks to transact, rather than items to learn, provides an environment which best promotes the natural language learning process (Foster 1999)

Long and Crookes have identified three approaches to TBL, including their own: Prabhu's, which they regard as a procedural syllabus; Breen and Candlin's, which they regard as a process syllabus, and their own, which they regard as a true task based syllabus (Long and Crookes 1992).

Until recently most classroom teachers were only likely to have encountered TBL in reference to the Bangalore Project, the name by which the Bangalore/Madras Communicational Teaching Project (CTP) in India is commonly known. This project was established by N.S. Prabhu in 1979 and formed the basis of his *Second Language Pedagogy* (Prabhu 1987). It was a conscious attempt to compare different methodological approaches to the teaching of English.

Prabhu's version of TBL was built around a syllabus which contained no linguistic specifications but 'instead contained a series of tasks in the form of problem-solving activities' (Beretta and Davies 1985). When evaluating the project, Beretta and Davis conclude that the results of their investigation: 'provide tentative support for the CTP claim that grammar construction can take place through a focus on meaning alone'.

Prabhu's approach focuses on the input the students receive and the cognitive processing which they are required to carry out. Unlike the other TBL approaches we will look at, it does not focus on interaction as a facilitator of acquisition. Groupwork is allowed in the classroom, but not actively encouraged; the argument being that language can be consolidated in this way but not acquired (Prabhu 1987: 82). Prabhu outlines suitable types of tasks and a procedure for their use, including guidelines for the selection and grading of tasks (see Figure 8.4 for example). He found that the best activities were 'reasoning-gap activities', which 'involve deriving some new information from given information through processes of inference, deduction, practical reasoning, or a perception of relationships or patterns' (Prabhu 1987: 46).

Long and Crookes criticise Prabhu's approach for failings deriving from its being based on a procedural syllabus (Long and Crookes 1992: 37). Thus they claim that no rationale exists for the syllabus content; grading and sequencing of tasks appear arbitrary and the syllabus doesn't address specific language acquisition issues (Long and Crookes 1992: 37). We could say that the Bangalore Project has proved influential because of the questions it has raised rather than the questions it has answered.

During the 1980s Breen and Candlin started outlining their own TBL proposals, which were based on educational and psychological rather than psycholinguistic principles (Long and Crookes 1992: 37). They argued for a negotiated syllabus with both teachers and learners selecting the content of a course built upon social and problem-solving interaction. Its aim would be to increase the students' capacity for communication rather their declarative knowledge about the target language, although the teacher would be expected to ensure that sufficient breadth of language content was included in the course (Breen 1984, 1987; Breen and Candlin 1980; Candlin 1984, 1987; Candlin and Murphy 1987).

This approach has been criticised because it requires highly competent teachers and self-aware students in order to be successful. It also requires the production and banking of a large amount of materials if real choice is to exist. These are not insurmountable problems. However, Long and Crookes feel that there are four possible theoretical problems with this approach (Long and Crookes 1992: 40–41). First, the lack of preselection of materials means that learners' needs might not be adequately assessed or addressed. Secondly, although the basis of materials selection is discussed, it is not sufficiently outlined. Thirdly, 'no explicit provision is made for a focus on language form' (Long and Crookes 1992: 41). Finally, the model's lack of a clear psycholinguistic foundation makes it difficult to assess according to current models of language acquisition.

Pallavan Transport Corporation
(Madras City)

a Students can buy and use bus tokens for a month, buying a ticket for each bus journey.

b The cost of tokens is as follows:

30 tokens	Rs 7.50
60 tokens	Rs 15.00
90 tokens	Rs 22.50
120 tokens	Rs 30.00

c A student has to buy at least 30 tokens a month. He/she cannot buy more than 120 tokens a month.

d One token is equal to one bus ticket: the student has to give a token to the conductor of the bus, instead of buying a ticket from him.

e Tokens should be used only for the purpose of travelling between one's home and the school or college where one is studying.

f Tokens should be bought each month between the 1st and the 15th. They can be used only between the 16th of that month and the 15th of the next month.

g No money will be refunded on unused tokens.

h Only full-time students of a school, college, or university can buy and use bus tokens. They have to produce a certificate from the head of the institution to show that they are full-time students.

i Tokens cannot be transferred from one person to another.

j If a student misuses his/her tokens, he/she will not be allowed to buy any more tokens during that year.

Pre-task After a glossing, at the students' request, of some words (for example 'refunded', 'misused') and a preliminary discussion, involving questions, about the nature of some rules (for example on the point that tokens can be bought only in multiples of thirty and that a direct bus from home to school involves the use of a single token while a change of buses involves using one token on each bus), the following case is discussed as the pre-task:

Raman is a student of the Government Arts College in Nandanam. He lives in T. Nagar. He has classes from Monday to Friday each week and eats his lunch at the college canteen. There are direct buses from T. Nagar to Nandanam.

1 How many bus tokens does Raman need each week?
2 How many tokens does he need for a month (i.e. 4 weeks, by convention)?
3 A bus ticket from T. Nagar to Nandanam costs Rs 0.50. How much does Raman save by buying tokens?
4 How many tokens should he buy each month? Why? How many will he actually use?
5 Raman's brother goes to a High School in Saidapet. Can he use Raman's extra tokens? How do you know?

> **6** Raman goes to see his uncle in K. K. Nagar every Sunday. Can he use his tokens to go to K. K. Nagar? How do you know?
>
> *Task* Balan studies at the Higher Secondary School in Nungambakkam. His home is in Adyar. He has classes only in the afternoons, from Monday to Saturday. There are direct buses from Nungambakkam to Adyar and a ticket costs one rupee.
>
> **1** How many tokens does Balan need each month?
> **2** How many tokens should he buy each month? How much money does he save?
> **3** He bought 60 tokens in July. His school had some holidays in August, so he used only 30 tokens up to 15 August.
>   **a** Can he go on using the remaining 30 tokens? How do you know?
>   **b** Can he return the remaining 30 tokens and get back the money? How can you tell?

Figure 8.4 A typical Prabhu task

Having used Long's and Crookes' analysis of TBL, we now come to the model that they propose, known as task-based language teaching (TBLT). They argue that this model is soundly based on SLA research, on classroom-centred research and on principles of syllabus and course design (Long and Crookes 1992: 41). A distinctive feature of this model is that it encourages a 'focus on form'. This is not a traditional structural syllabus approach, but an acknowledgement that acquisition can be accelerated if learners' attention is drawn to specific linguistic features of the target language (Long 1991). In developing the model of TBLT further, Long has outlined those features which should characterise a 'task' and attempted to provide a solid theoretical framework for an approach based on them (Long 1996, *et al.*).

However, there are still questions TBLT needs to address. Long and Crookes acknowledge this when they compare it to other TBL approaches (Long and Crookes 1992: 46). Its research base is still small and no complete programmes have yet been undertaken to access it. The question of sequencing tasks is still an issue, as is the question of producing a taxonomy of tasks. Finally, the degree of reduced learner autonomy could invite criticism. Long and Crookes' model has also never actually been realised in terms of materials development or classroom practice, in contrast to Prabhu's model or Breen and Candlin's.

Overall, TBL looks like a very exciting area and one which is already strongly influencing thinking in the field of language teaching methodology. It is not just limited to those models described here; other models are being proposed and specific questions of task definition and design are also being examined (Skehan 1996, 1998; Nunan 1989, etc.).

Text-based teaching

Another new post-CLT approach to language teaching has been text-based teaching (also known as genre-based). Unlike TBL, which we saw is based on a model of learning, text-based learning grew out of a model of language, namely Systemic-Functional Grammar. It is an approach which has been summarised in the following observation:

> Language occurs as whole texts which are embedded in the social contexts in which they are used.
> People learn language through working with whole texts. (Feez 1998)

This approach is perhaps better known and more widely applied in Australia, where much of the theory was developed, than elsewhere. Its development there has primarily occurred within the provision of English as a second language for migrants, as well as more generally in language and literacy programmes. English for Academic Purposes (EAP) programmes have also been influenced by its innovations.

Systemic-Functional Grammar describes language not only in terms of linguistic systems, but relates these to the social interaction they are used to undertake and the wider culture in which they are used. This model of language was first proposed by Halliday and also greatly influenced CLT (Halliday 1973).

The model of learning upon which this method is based is informed by research in first language acquisition. Learning is seen as a process of acculturisation into the 'culture' of the target language with learners perceive as going through an 'apprenticeship' process as they learn more and increase in independence. The degree to which learners are expected to develop declarative knowledge about the target language has been debated by proponents of text-based methodologies and, in general, some declarative knowledge is seen as desirable, in other words, learners are expected to become, to some degree, language analysts (see Figure 8.5 for example). This contrasts with both the ideas of Audio-Lingualism and CLT, where declarative knowledge is not seen as a necessary outcome of learning.

This brings us to the question of learner and teacher roles within this approach. Text-based approaches can be seen as more teacher-centred than other current methodologies as the role of teacher as 'expert' is central. Typically, the teacher would lead the initial exploration of a text type, then the teacher and learners jointly construct a text, followed by sole production by the learners. This model is based on first language acquisition parent-child roles, as well as Vygotskian notions of the social interactional nature of communication and learning.

It will be interesting to see this methodology develop further as more materials based on it become available and it becomes taken up more widely.

Conclusion

How does one conclude an outline of a process which has been underway for centuries – namely the search for better ways to teach languages? This search has probably never been as intense as it is today, with universities, classroom teachers and publishers all active. The realisation that this is an 'on-going' process is perhaps the first step. This might make us approach more critically the claims of researchers and publishers who are trying to promote particular solutions. Instead, with a sense of historical perspective, we should assess each new development ourselves. This assessment should draw on the disciplines which inform our field, not only second language acquisition theory, but psychology and general education as well. Our three questions from the introduction that we have used to examine the methodologies presented here can provide a starting point. We should not ignore our own experience either; classroom-centred research has been one of the most important steps forward in recent years. In this way the field of language teaching methodology will remain vibrant and exciting.

**UNIT OF WORK
CASUAL CONVERSATION**

Goal

To enable learners to participate in a casual conversation in a workplace.

Learner objectives

The learners will:
- understand the purpose of casual conversation in Australian workplace culture
- know which conversation topics are appropriate in Australian workplaces
- recognise and use the key features of a casual conversation, i.e. greetings and closures, feedback, clarification, managing topic shifts
- recognise and use conversation chunks such as comments, descriptions or recounts
- take turns appropriately within simple exchanges ie question/answer, statement, agreement, statement/disagreement
- use language appropriate to casual conversation including politeness strategies, informal language, idiom
- build pronunciation and paralinguistic skills and strategies, specifically in the areas of intonation and gesture

Teacher objectives

The teacher will:
- provide authentic listening materials
- provide conversation practice through scaffolded roleplay
- record learner language for analysis

Achievement assessment

The unit will enable students to achieve the following curriculum outcome, eg CSWE III Competency 7.

Figure 8.5 An example of unit objectives within a text-based approach

References

Anthony, E.M. (1963) 'Approach, method and technique'. *English Language Teaching*: 63–7.

Asher, J. (1965) 'The strategy of the total physical response: an application to learning Russian'. *International Review of Applied Linguistics 3*: 291–300.

—— (1966) 'The learning strategy of the total physical response: a review'. *Modern Language Journal 50*: 79–84.

—— (1969) 'The total physical response approach to second language learning'. *Modern Language Journal 53*: 3–17.

—— (1977) *Learning Another Language Through Actions: The Complete Teacher's Guide Book*. Los Gatos, Calif.: Sky Oaks Productions Inc.

Beretta, A. and Davies, A. (1985) 'Evaluation of the Bangalore Project'. *ELT Journal 39/2*.

Bloomfield, L. (1914) *An Introduction to the Study of Language*. New York: Holt.

—— (1933) *Language*. New York: Holt.

—— (1942) *Outline Guide for the Practical Study of Foreign Languages*. Baltimore: Linguistic Society of America.

Breen, M.P. (1984) 'Process syllabuses for the language classroom', in C.J. Brumfit (ed.), *General English syllabus design*. (ELT Documents No. 118, 47–60). London: Pergamon Press & The British Council.

—— (1987) 'Learner contributions to task design', in C.N. Candlin and D. Murphy (eds) *Lancaster Practical Papers in English Language Education: Vol 7. Language learning tasks*. Englewood Cliffs, NJ: Prentice Hall.

Breen, M.P. and Candlin, C.N. (1980) 'The essentials of a communicative curriculum in language teaching'. *Applied Linguistics, 1 (2)*. 89–112.

Canale, M. and Swain, H. (1980) 'Theoretical bases of communicative approaches to second language teaching and testing'. *Applied Linguistics 1 / 1*. 1–7

Candlin, C.N. (1984) 'Syllabus design as a critical process', in C.J. Brumfit (ed.) *General English syllabus design*. (ELT Documents No. 118, 29–46). London: Pergamon Press and The British Council.

—— (1987) 'Towards task-based language learning', in C.N. Candlin and D. Murphy (eds) *Lancaster Practical Papers in English Language Education: Vol 7. Language learning tasks*. Englewood Cliffs, NJ: Prentice Hall.

Candlin, C.N. and Murphy, D. (eds) (1987) *Lancaster Practical Papers in English Language Education: Vol 7. Language learning tasks*. Englewood Cliffs, NJ: Prentice Hall.

Chomsky, N. (1957) *Syntactic Structures*. The Hague: Mouton.

Chomsky, N. (1966) *Aspects of the Theory of Syntax*. Boston: MIT Press.

Curran, C.A. (1972) *Counseling-Learning: A Whole-Person Model for Education*. New York: Grune and Stratton.

—— (1976) *Counseling-Learning in Second Languages*. Apple River, Ill.: Apple River Press.

Ellis, R. (1994) *The Study of Second Language Acquisition*. Oxford: Oxford University Press.

Feez, S. (1998) *Text-based Syllabus Design*. Sydney: NCELTR, Macquarie University.

Foster, P. (1999) 'Task-based learning and pedagogy'. *ELT Journal 53 / 1*. 69–70.

Fries, C. (1945) *Teaching and Learning English as a Foreign Language*. Michigan: Michigan University Press.

Gattengo, C. (1972) *Teaching Foreign Languages in Schools: The Silent Way* (2nd ed.). New York: Educational Solutions.

—— (1976) *The Common Sense of Teaching Foreign Languages*. New York: Educational Solutions.

Halliday, M.A.K. (1973) 'Towards a sociological semantics'. *Explorations in the Functions of Language*. London: Edward Arnold

Hartley, B. and Vine, P. (1978) *Streamline English*. Oxford: Oxford University Press.

Howatt, A.P.R. (1984) *A History of English Language Teaching*. Oxford: Oxford University Press.

Hymes, D.H. (1971) *On communicative competence*. Philadelphia: University of Philadelphia Press.

Kleinjans, E. (1961) 'From Mim-Mem to Communication'. *Studies in Descriptive and Applied Linguistics: Bulletin of the Summer Institute in Linguistics* Vol 1.

Krashen, S.D. (1981) *Second Language Acquisition and Second Language Learning*. Oxford: Pergamon.

—— (1982) *Principles and Practices in Second Language Acquisition*. Oxford, Pergammon.

Krashen, S.D. and Terrell, T. (1983) *The Natural Approach: Language Acquisition in the Classroom*. Oxford, Pergamon.

La Forge, P.G. (1983) *Counseling and Culture in Second Language Acquisition*. Oxford: Pergamon.

Lado, R. (1964) *Language Teaching: A scientific approach*. New York: McGraw-Hill.

Larsen-Freeman, D. (1986) *Techniques and Principles in Language Teaching*. Oxford: Oxford University Press.

Long, M.H. (1991) 'Focus on form: A design feature in language teaching methodology', in

Foreign language research in cross-cultural perspective, K. de Bot, D. Coste, R. Ginsberg and C. Kramsch (eds). Amsterdam: John Benjamins.

—— (1996) 'The role of the linguistic environment in second language acquisition', in *Handbook of Second Language Acquisition*, W.C.B. Ritchie (ed.). T K, Academic Press.

Long, M.H. and Crookes, G. (1992) 'Three Approaches to Task-Based Syllabus Design'. *TESOL Quarterly 26:1*: 27–55.

Lozanov, G. (1978) *Suggestology and Outlines of Suggestopedy*. New York: Gordon and Breach.

McLaughlin, B. (1987) *Theories of Second-Language Learning*. London: Edward Arnold.

Moskowitz, G. (1978) *Caring and Sharing in the Foreign Language Class*. Rowley, Mass.: Newbury House.

Mueller, T. (1959) 'Psychology and the Language Arts'. *School and Society 87*.

Munby, J. (1978) *Communicative Syllabus Design*. Cambridge: Cambridge University Press.

Nunan, D. (1988) *The Learner-Centred Curriculum*. Cambridge: Cambridge University Press.

—— (1989) *Designing Tasks for the Communicative Classroom*. Cambridge: Cambridge University Press.

O'Connor, J.C. and Twaddell, W.F. (1960) 'Intensive Training for an Oral Approach in Language Teaching'. *The Modern Language Journal Vol XLIV 2:2*.

Palmer, H.E. (1921) *The Oral Method in Teaching Languages*. Cambridge: Heffer.

Palmer, H.E. and Palmer, D. (1925) *English Through Actions*. Toyko: IRET. Republished by Longmans, Green, 1959.

Prabhu, N.S. (1987) *Second Language Pedagogy*. Oxford: Oxford University Press.

Richards, J.C. and Rogers, T.S. (1986) *Approaches and Methods in Language Teaching*. Cambridge: Cambridge University Press.

Scovel, T. (1979) 'Review of "Suggestology and Outlines of Suggestopedy"'. *TESOL Quarterly 13*. 255–266.

Skehan, P. (1996) A framework for the implementation of task-based instruction. *Applied Linguistics 17:1* : 38–62.

—— (1998) *A Cognitive Approach to Language Learning*. Oxford: Oxford University Press.

Skinner, B.F. (1957) *Verbal Behavior*. New York: Appleton-Century-Crofts.

Stern, H.H. (1983) *Fundamental Concepts of Language Teaching*. Oxford: Oxford University Press.

Stern, H.H. (1992) *Issues and Options in Language Teaching*. Oxford: Oxford University Press.

White, L. (1987) 'Against Comprehensible Input'. *Applied Linguistics 8*: 95–109.

Widdowson, H.G. (1978) *Teaching Language as Communication*. Oxford: Oxford University Press.

Chapter 9

Jack C. Richards

BEYOND METHODS

METHODOLOGY IN TEACHING IS THE ACTIVITIES, tasks, and learning experiences used by the teacher within the teaching and learning process. Methodology is seen to have a theoretical basis in the teacher's assumptions about (a) language and second language learning, (b) teacher and learner roles, and (c) learning activities and instructional materials. These assumptions and beliefs provide the basis for the conscious or unconscious decision making that underlies the moment-to-moment processes of teaching. Methodology is not therefore something fixed, a set of rigid principles and procedures that the teacher must conform to. Rather it is a dynamic, creative, and exploratory process that begins anew each time the teacher encounters a group of learners. Teaching as an exploratory process is different from the approach to teaching seen in many teacher preparation programs or language teaching programs, where particular instructional methods, such as the Silent Way, Total Physical Response, or the Natural Approach, are presented as models to be imitated and internalized. In this chapter, these two approaches to teaching will be explored in more depth. The use of methods as the basis for instructional processes in a second language program will be compared with one that moves beyond methods and focuses on exploring the nature of effective classroom teaching and learning.

Approaching teaching in terms of methods

For many centuries the goal of language teachers has been to find the right method (Kelly 1969). The history of language teaching in the last hundred years has done much to support the impression that improvements in language teaching will result from improvements in the quality of methods, and that ultimately an effective language teaching method will be developed. Some breakthrough in linguistic theory or in second language acquisition research, it is assumed, will eventually unlock the secrets of second and foreign language learning. These will then be incorporated into a new supermethod that will solve the language teaching problem once and for all. Some believe that the supermethod has already been found, and that adoption of a method such as the Silent Way, Suggestopedia, or the Natural Approach will bring about dramatic improvements in language learning.

Common to all methods is a set of specifications for how teaching should be accomplished, derived from a particular theory of the nature of language and second language learning. Differences in the instructional specifications reflect differences in the theories underlying the methods. Some methods advocate an early emphasis on speaking as a basis for establishing basic language patterns. Others recommend that speaking be delayed until the learner has built up a receptive competence in the language. Some make use of memorized dialogues and texts; others require that learners attempt to communicate with each other as soon as possible using their own language resources. Common to all methods is a set of prescriptions on what teachers and learners should do in the language classroom. Prescriptions for the teacher include what material should be presented and when it should be taught and how, and prescriptions for learners include what approach they should take toward learning. Specific roles for teachers, learners, and instructional materials are hence established (Richards and Rodgers 1986). The teacher's job is to match his or her teaching style as well as the learners' learning styles to the method. Special training packages and programs are available for some methods to ensure that teachers do what they are supposed to do and teach according to the method.

Despite the appeal of methods, their past history is somewhat of an embarrassment. Studies of the effectiveness of specific methods have had a hard time demonstrating that the method itself, rather than other factors, such as the teacher's enthusiasm or the novelty of the new method, was the crucial variable. Likewise, observers of teachers using specific methods have reported that teachers seldom conform to the methods they are supposed to be following. Swaffar, Arens, and Morgan (1982), for example, investigated differences between what they termed rationalist and empiricist approaches to foreign language instruction. By a rationalist approach they refer to process-oriented approaches in which language is seen as an interrelated whole, where language learning is a function of comprehension preceding production, and where it involves critical thinking and the desire to communicate. Empiricist approaches focus on the four discrete language skills. Would classroom practices reflect such differences? "One consistent problem is whether or not teachers involved in presenting materials created for a particular method are actually reflecting the underlying philosophies of these methods in their classroom practices" (Swaffar et al. 1982: 25). Swaffar et al. found that many of the distinctions used to contrast methods, particularly those based on classroom activities, did not exist in actual practice:

> Methodological labels assigned to teaching activities are, in themselves, not informative, because they refer to a pool of classroom practices which are used uniformly. The differences among major methodologies are to be found in the ordered hierarchy, the priorities assigned to tasks. (1982: 31)

Methods hence make assumptions about the nature of teaching that are not based on study of the process of teaching. The findings of Swaffar et al. account for the difficulty teacher supervisors often have in recognizing which method a teacher is following. Nevertheless, the future for methods continues to look good. Several new ones have appeared in recent years, and at conferences where salespersons for the new methods are present, teachers flock to hear presentations on the current supermethods. Yet there are serious limitations in conceptualizing teaching in terms of methods.

The basic problem is that methods present a predetermined, packaged deal for teachers that incorporates a static view of teaching. In this view specific teacher roles, learner roles, and teaching/learning activities and processes are imposed on teachers and learners. Studies of classroom events, however, have demonstrated that teaching is not static or fixed in time but is a dynamic, interactional process in which the teacher's "method" results from the processes of interaction between the teacher, the learners, and the instructional tasks and activities over time (Chall 1967; Dunkin and Biddle 1974; Swaffar et al. 1982). Attempts to find general methods that are suitable for all teachers and all teaching situations reflect an essentially negative view of teachers, one which implies that since the quality of teachers cannot be guaranteed, the contribution of the individual teacher should be minimized by designing teacher-proof methods. The assumption that underlies general, all-purpose methods is hence essentially this: Teachers cannot be trusted to teach well. Left to their own devices, teachers will invariably make a mess of things. A method, because it imposes a uniform set of teaching roles, teaching styles, teaching strategies, and teaching techniques on the teacher, will not be affected by the variations that are found in individual teaching skill and teaching style in the real world.

Researchers who have investigated the nature of teaching, however, have proposed a different view of teaching (Good 1979; Elliot 1980; Tikunoff 1985). They begin with the assumption that teachers (rather than methods) do make a difference; that teachers work in ways that are, to an extent, independent of methods; and that the characteristics of effective teaching can be determined. Other researchers have turned their attention to learners and sought to determine what characterizes effective learning. This requires a different approach to teaching, one in which teachers are involved in observing and reflecting upon their own teaching as well as the learning behaviors of their students.

The nature of effective teaching

Teacher strategies

Every teacher aims to be an effective teacher. The concept of effective teaching is a somewhat elusive one, however. Can it be determined from the teacher's behavior, the learner's behavior, classroom interaction, or the results of learning? Researchers have attempted to operationalize the notion of effective teaching by describing it as teaching that produces higher-than-predicted gains on standardized achievement tests (Good 1979). Studies of teacher effectiveness have dealt mainly with first language classrooms and with the teaching of reading and math. One major study has dealt with effective teachers in bilingual programs (Tikunoff *et al.* 1980). These studies are characterized by detailed observation of teachers performing instructional activities in the classroom in an attempt to isolate the qualities and skills of effective teachers.

In a comprehensive survey of the research on effective schooling, Blum (1984: 3–6) summarizes effective classroom practices as follows:
1   Instruction is guided by a preplanned curriculum.
2   There are high expectations for student learning.
3   Students are carefully oriented to lessons.
4   Instruction is clear and focused.
5   Learning progress is monitored closely.
6   When students don't understand, they are retaught.
7   Class time is used for learning.
8   There are smooth and efficient classroom routines.
9   Instructional groups formed in the classroom fit instructional needs.
10   Standards for classroom behavior are high.
11   Personal interactions between teachers and students are positive.
12   Incentives and rewards for students are used to promote excellence.

Several dimensions of teaching have been found to account for differences between effective and ineffective instruction (Doyle 1977; Good 1979). These include classroom management, structuring, tasks, and grouping.

Classroom management

Classroom management refers to the ways in which student behavior, movement, and interaction during a lesson are organized and controlled by the teacher to enable teaching to take place most effectively. Good managerial skills on the part of the teacher are an essential component of good teaching. In a well-managed class, discipline problems are few, and learners are actively engaged in learning tasks and activities; this contributes to high motivation and expectations for success. Evertson, Anderson, and Brophy (1978) found that it was possible to identify teachers with managerial problems in the first few days of the school year, that such problems continued throughout the year, and that managerial skills in the classroom were related to levels of student involvement.

Structuring

A lesson reflects the concept of *structuring* when the teacher's intentions are clear and instructional activities are sequenced according to a logic that students can perceive. Classroom observations and studies of lesson protocols indicate that sometimes neither the teacher nor the learners understood what the intentions of an activity were, why an activity occurred when it did, what directions they were supposed to follow, or what the relationship between one activity and another was. Hence, it may not have been clear what students needed to focus on to complete a task successfully. Fisher *et al.* (1980) conclude that students "pay attention more when the teacher spends time discussing the goals or structures of the lesson and/or giving directions about what the students are to do" (p. 26). Berliner (1984) likewise suggests that "structuring affects attention rate: it is sometimes not done at all, sometimes it is done only minimally, and sometimes it is overdone" (p. 63).

Tasks

Tasks, or activity structures, refer to activities that teachers assign to attain particular learning objectives. For any given subject at any given level, a teacher uses a limited repertoire of tasks that essentially define that teacher's methodology of teaching. These might include completing worksheets, reading aloud, dictation, quickwriting, and practicing dialogues. According to Tikunoff (1985), class tasks vary according to three types of demands they make on learners: *response mode demands* (the kind of skills they demand, such as knowledge, comprehension, application, analysis/synthesis, evaluation); *interactional mode demands* (the rules governing how classroom tasks are accomplished, such as individually, in a group, or with the help of the teacher); and *task complexity demands* (how difficult the learner perceives the task to be).

Teachers have to make decisions not only about the appropriate kinds of tasks to assign to learners, but also about the *order of tasks* (the sequence in which tasks should be introduced); *pacing* (how much time learners should spend on tasks); *products* (whether the product or result of a task is expected to be the same for all students); *learning strategies* (what learning strategies will be recommended for particular tasks); and *materials* (what sources and materials to use in completing a task) (Tikunoff 1985).

The concept of tasks has been central to studies of effective teaching. The amount of time students spend actively engaged on learning tasks is directly related to learning (Good and Beckerman 1978). For example, Teacher A and Teacher B are both teaching the same reading lesson. In Teacher A's class, learners are actively engaged in reading tasks for 75% of the lesson, the remaining time being occupied with noninstructional activities such as taking breaks, lining up, distributing books, homework, and making arrangements for future events. Students in Teacher B's class, however, are actively involved in reading for only 55% of the lesson. Not surprisingly, studies of time-on-task have found that the more time students spend studying content, the better they learn it. In one study (Stallings and Kaskowitz 1974), the students with the highest levels of achievement in a reading program were spending about 50% more time actively engaged in reading activities than the children with the lowest achievement gains. Good teaching is hence said to be task oriented. Effective teachers also monitor performance on tasks, providing feedback on how well tasks have been completed.

Grouping

A related dimension of effective teaching is the *grouping* of learners to carry out instructional tasks, and the relation between grouping arrangement and achievement. An effective teacher understands how different kinds of grouping (such as seat work, pair work, discussion, reading circle, or lecture) can impede or promote learning. Webb (1980) found that the middle-ability child suffers a loss of achievement, while the low-ability child shows some gains in achievement in mixed-ability groups, compared with what would be expected if both were in uniform-ability groups. Tikunoff (1985) cites Good and Marshall's findings on groupings.

> Good and Marshall (1984) found that students in low-ability reading groups in the early grades received very little challenge, thus perceiving of themselves as unable to read. In addition, a long-range result of interacting most frequently with only other students of low-ability in such groups was an inability to respond to the demands of more complex instructional activities. Ironically, Good pointed out that the very strategy used to presumably help low-ability youngsters with their reading problems – pull-out programs in which teachers worked with small groups of these students outside the regular classroom – exacerbated the problem. Demands in the special reading groups were very different from those in the regular classroom and at a much lower level of complexity, so low-ability students were not learning to respond to high level demands that would help them participate competently in their regular classrooms. (p. 56)

The research findings suggest therefore that effective teaching depends on such factors as time-on-task, feedback, grouping and task decisions, classroom management, and structuring. Although the concept of effective teaching evolved from studies of content teaching, Tikunoff's (1983) major study of effective teaching in bilingual education programs has examined the extent to which it also applies to other contexts, such as bilingual and ESL classrooms.

Effective teaching in bilingual classrooms

Tikunoff (1983) suggests that three kinds of competence are needed for the student of limited English proficiency (LEP): *participative competence*, the ability "to respond appropriately to class demands and the procedural rules for accomplishing them" (p. 4); *interactional competence*, the ability "to respond both to classroom rules of discourse and social rules of discourse, interacting appropriately with peers and adults while accomplishing class tasks" (p. 4); and *academic competence*, the ability "to acquire new skills, assimilate new information, and construct new concepts" (p. 4). Furthermore, to be functionally proficient in the classroom, the student must be able to utilize these competences to perform three major functions: (a) to decode and understand both task expectations and new information; (b) to engage appropriately in completing tasks, with high accuracy; and (c) to obtain accurate feedback with relation to completing tasks accurately (p. 5).

In his Significant Bilingual Instructional Features (SBIF) descriptive study, Tikunoff (1983) collected data to find out how effective teachers in bilingual education programs organize instruction, structure teaching activities, and enhance student performance on tasks. Teachers were interviewed to determine their instructional philosophies, goals, and the demands they would structure into class tasks. Teachers were clearly able to specify class task demands and intended outcomes and to indicate what LEP students had to do to be functionally proficient. Case studies of teachers were undertaken in which teachers were observed during instruction, with three observers collecting data for the teacher and for four target LEP students. Teachers were interviewed again after instruction.

> An analysis of data across the case studies revealed a clear linkage between (1) teachers' ability to clearly specify the intent of instruction, and a belief that students could achieve accuracy in instructional tasks, (2) the organization and delivery of instruction such that tasks and institutional demands reflected this intent, requiring intended student responses, and (3) the fidelity of student consequences with intended outcomes. In other words, teachers were able to describe clearly what instruction would entail, to operationalize these specifications, and to produce the desired results in terms of student performance. (p. 9)

This approach to teaching is one in which methodological principles are developed from studying the classroom practices and processes actually employed by effective teachers. Good teaching is not viewed as something that results from using Method X or Method Y, or something that results from the teacher modifying teaching behaviors to match some external set of rules and principles. Rather, it results from the teacher's active control and management of the processes of teaching, learning, and communication within the classroom and from an understanding of these processes. The classroom is seen as a place where there is ongoing and dynamic interaction between the teacher's instructional goals, learners' purposes, classroom tasks and activities, the teacher's instructional activities and behaviors, student behaviors in completing assigned tasks, and learning outcomes.

In the bilingual classrooms observed in Tikunoff's study, effective teaching was found to reflect the degree to which the teacher is able to successfully communicate his or her intentions, maintain students' engagement in instructional tasks, and monitor students' performance on tasks. In classrooms where different instructional goals are present and different aspects of second language proficiency are being addressed, the characteristics of effective teaching in those settings cannot be inferred merely from reading about the theoretical principles underlying the method or approach the teacher is supposed to be following. Rather, classroom observation of teachers who are achieving higher-than-predicted levels of achievement in their learners, or who are assessed as performing at high levels of effectiveness according to other criteria, provides the data from which profiles of effective teachers in listening, reading, writing, speaking, and other kinds of classes can be developed.

Learner strategies

The approach to teaching in which methodology is developed from study of classroom practices attributes a primary role to the teacher in the teaching/learning process. Successful learning is viewed as dependent upon the teacher's control and management of what takes place in the classroom. However, what the teacher does is only half of the picture. The other half concerns what learners do to achieve successful learning, or *learner strategies*. Prompted by the awareness that learners may succeed despite the teacher's methods and techniques rather than because of them, researchers as well as teachers have begun to look more closely at learners themselves in an attempt to discover how successful learners achieve their results (O'Malley *et al.* 1985a, b; Willing 1985).

Studies of learner strategies attempt to identify the specific techniques and strategies learners use to facilitate their own learning (Oxford 1985b). The focus is on the particular cognitive operations, processes, procedures, and heuristics that learners apply to the task of learning a second language. Given any language learning task, such as understanding a lecture, reading a text, writing a composition, understanding the meaning of a new grammatical or lexical item, or preparing a written summary of a text, a number of strategies are available to a learner to help carry out the task. But what is the practical value of knowing which particular strategies a learner employed?

Just as research on effective teaching has identified the kinds of teaching behaviors that appear to account for superior teaching, so research on effective learning seeks to identify the kinds of learning behaviors that can best facilitate learning. Good language learners seem to be successful because they have a better understanding of and control over their own learning than less successful learners. Use of inappropriate learning strategies has been found to account for the poor performance of learners on many classroom learning tasks (Hosenfeld 1979). It should therefore be possible to improve student performance on learning tasks by identifying successful approaches to learning and by directing learners toward these kinds of strategies. Research on learner strategies in second language learning hence seeks to identify the strategies employed by successful learners and then to teach those strategies to other learners in order to improve their language learning capacities (Hosenfeld 1977; Cohen and Aphek 1980; Chamot and O'Malley 1984). The premises underlying Cohen and Aphek's work, for example, are:

Some language learners are more successful than others.
Some aspects of the learning process are conscious and others are not.
Less successful learners can use successful strategies consciously to accelerate learning.
Teachers can promote the use of learning strategies.
Learners can become the best judges of how they learn most effectively, both in and out of
    classes.

The field of learner strategy research in second language learning is hence now an important domain of classroom research, and differs substantially from previous research in this area. Earlier work on learning strategies lacked a sound theoretical basis and consisted largely of lists of features that good language learners were assumed to possess. These lists were developed from interviews with successful language learners (e.g., Rubin 1975, 1981; Stern 1975; Naiman *et al.* 1978). Willing (1987: 275) points out that "while such generalizations have their usefulness as a help in understanding the process of language learning from the point of view of the learner, they do not immediately yield prescriptions for teaching."

More recent work on learner strategies has attempted to yield more usable results by making use of data obtained from a broader range of sources, such as classroom observation, "think-aloud" procedures (in which learners record their thoughts and observations as they perform different tasks), interviews, self-reports employing note-taking and diaries, questionnaires, as well as controlled experimental studies designed to investigate specific cognitive processes (e.g., Heuring 1984). These kinds of approaches are yielding information of greater practical value. For example, Cohen (cited in Oxford 1985a) lists six strategies used by successful language learners:

1 Attention-enhancing strategies, such as responding silently to tasks asked of other students in class
2 Use of a variety of background sources, including knowledge of the world, knowledge of the given topic, awareness of stress and tone of voice of the speaker, perception of the speaker's body language, and cues from earlier parts of the conversation in the effort to decode communicative meaning
3 Oral production tricks, such as avoiding unfamiliar topics, paraphrasing, and asking for help
4 Vocabulary learning techniques, such as making associations, attending to the meaning of parts of the word, noting the structure of the word, placing the word in a topical group with similar words, visualizing or contextualizing it, linking it to the situation in which it appears, creating a mental image of it, and associating some physical sensation to it
5 Reading or text-processing strategies, such as clarifying the communicative purpose of the text, distinguishing important points from trivia, skipping around to get an overall conceptual picture, using substantive and linguistic background knowledge, reading in broad phrases rather than word for word, relying on contextual clues, making ongoing summaries, and looking for emphasis and cohesion markers in the text
6 Writing techniques such as focusing on simply getting ideas down on paper instead of trying for perfection right away; purposefully using parallel structures and other means of enhancing cohesion; and writing multiple drafts.

Willing (1987: 278–9) notes that strategies are essentially "methods employed by the person for processing input language information in such a way as to gain control of it, thus enabling the assimilation of that information by the self." Strategies are hence viewed as ways of managing the complex information that the learner is receiving about the target language.

Wenden (1983) interviewed adult language learners about how they organized their language learning experiences and found that they asked themselves eight kinds of questions.

Question	Decision
1 How does this language work?	Learners make judgments about the linguistic and sociolinguistic codes.
2 What's it like to learn a language?	Learners make judgments about how to learn a language and about what language learning is like.
3 What should I learn and how?	Learners decide upon linguistic objectives, resources, and use of resources.

4 What should I emphasize?	Learners decide to give priority to special linguistic items.
5 How should I change?	Learners decide to change their approach to language learning.
6 How am I doing?	Learners determine how well they use the language and diagnose their needs.
7 What am I getting out of this?	Learners determine if an activity or strategy is useful.
8 How am I responsible for learning? How is language learning affecting me?	Learners make judgments about how to learn a language and about what language learning is like.

O'Malley *et al.* have investigated the use of strategies by ESL learners both in and out of classrooms (O'Malley *et al.* 1985a, b; O'Malley and Chamot 1989). ESL students and their teachers were interviewed about the strategies learners used on specific language learning tasks, and the learners were observed in ESL classrooms. They were also asked about their use of English in communicative situations outside the classroom. A total of twenty-six different kinds of learning strategies were identified.

In a follow-up study, high school ESL students were given training in the use of particular strategies in order to determine if it would improve their effectiveness as language learners and their performance on vocabulary, listening, and speaking tasks. Strategies were compared across proficiency levels and with learners of different language backgrounds. Students were given training in the use of specific strategies for particular language learning tasks. Results supported the notion that learners can be taught to use more effective learning strategies (O'Malley *et al.* 1985a, b):

> Strategies training was successfully demonstrated in a natural teaching environment with second language listening and speaking tasks. This indicates that classrooms instruction on learning strategies with integrative language skills can facilitate learning. (O'Malley *et al.* 1985a: 577)

Phillips (1975) investigated how learners approach reading tasks and identified strategies employed by good and poor readers. She employed a "think-aloud" procedure to investigate readers' strategies in dealing with unknown vocabulary. From her students' descriptions Phillips found that strategies used by efficient readers included categorizing words grammatically, interpreting grammatical operations, and recognizing cognates and root words. Hosenfeld (1977, 1984) used similar techniques in studying processes employed by foreign language readers when encountering unfamiliar words. In one study (Hosenfeld 1977), some of the differences between those with high and low scores on a reading proficiency test were these: High scorers tended to keep the meaning of the passage in mind, read in broad phrases, skip unessential words, and guess meanings of unknown words from context; low scorers tended to lose the meaning of sentences as soon as they decoded them, read word by word or in short phrases, rarely skip words, and turn to the glossary when they encountered new words. In addition successful readers tended to identify the grammatical categories of words, could detect word-order differences in the foreign language, recognized cognates, and used the glossary only as a last resort (Hosenfeld 1984: 233). Hosenfeld found that unsuccessful readers could be taught the lexical strategies of successful readers, confirming Wenden's observation that "ineffective learners are inactive learners. Their apparent inability to learn is, in fact, due to their not having an appropriate repertoire of learning strategies" (1985: 7).

Studies of how learners approach writing tasks have also focused on the effectiveness of the processes learners employ (Raimes 1985). Lapp (1984) summarizes some of the research findings on differences between skilled and unskilled writers with respect to rehearsing and prewriting behaviors (what a writer does before beginning writing), drafting and writing processes (how the writer actually composes a piece of writing), and revising behaviors (revisions and corrections the writer makes).

Research findings on learner strategies in reading and writing classes (e.g., Heuring 1984) suggest that teachers need to evaluate their teaching strategies on an ongoing basis, to determine if they are promoting effective or ineffective learning strategies in learners. Many commonly employed techniques in the teaching of writing, such as outlining or writing from a rhetorical model, might well inhibit rather than encourage the development of effective writing skills, because they direct the learner's attention to the form and mechanics of writing too early in the writing process.

In order to present information about learning strategies to students, strategies need to be operationalized in the form of specific techniques (see Fraser and Skibicki 1987); however, there is no consensus yet concerning how to approach the teaching of learning strategies. As with other aspects of language teaching, the issue of whether strategies are best "learned" or "acquired" is a central one. Some researchers advocate a direct approach. This involves explicit training in the use of specific strategies and teaching students to consciously monitor their own strategies (e.g., O'Malley *et al.* 1985a, b; Russo and Stewner-Manzanares 1985). Others favor a more indirect approach in which strategies are incorporated into other kinds of learning content. Fraser and Skibicki (1987) describe the development of self-directed learning materials for adult migrant learners in Australia, which focus on specific strategies in different skill areas. A related issue concerns whether the focus of teacher intervention should be to provide additional strategies to learners or merely to help the learner develop a better awareness of and control over existing strategies. Willing (1987: 277) observes that despite the recent amount of attention to learning strategies, some serious issues still await resolution:

1   Current notions of learning strategies lack conceptual coherence . . .
2   Learning strategies as currently described have been identified more or less in isolation and on a purely empirical and arbitrary basis and have not been related to an overall view of learning . . .
3   There has been little systematic work on placing learning strategies within a broader description of the nature and meaning of learning itself . . .
4   There has been little effort to relate the notion of learning strategies (within a general learning theory) to current ideas about second language acquisition.

In addition, there has been little attempt to relate theories of learning strategies to more general theories of teaching, such as the one discussed previously.

Summary

Two approaches to language teaching have been discussed and contrasted. One conceptualizes teaching as application of a teaching method, in which both the teacher and the learner are approached on the terms of the method promoter, educational theorist, or applied linguist. The assumptions or theory underlying the method provide the starting point for an instructional design that is subsequently imposed on teachers and learners. An attempt is then made to make the teacher's and learner's classroom behaviors match the specifications of the method. This can be contrasted with an approach that starts with the observable processes of classroom teaching and learning, from which methodological principles and practices in language teaching are derived. Observation can yield two categories of information:

1   The study of effective teaching provides information about how effective teachers organize and deliver instruction. This relates to classroom management skills, and to the strategies teachers use to present instructional goals, structure learning tasks and activities, monitor learning, and provide feedback on it.
2   The study of effective learning provides information about the learning strategies effective learners apply to the process of using and learning a second and foreign language.

However, a word of caution is in order, since the goal of this approach is not simply to arrive at a set of general principles that can be taught to teachers and learners. This of course would be to come full circle, and would simply replace one "method" with another. The approach advocated here starts with the assumption that the investigation of effective teaching and learning strategies is a central and ongoing component of the process of teaching. This is the core of a process-oriented methodology of teaching.

This approach implies a redefinition of the role of the teacher. Teachers are not viewed merely as "performers," who carry out the role prescribed by the method or apply an externally derived set of principles to their teaching. Teachers are seen rather as investigators of both their own classroom practices and those of the learners. Much of the effort to determine what constitutes effective teaching and learning is initiated by the teacher. Through regular observation of their own classes and through analysis and reflection, teachers can obtain valuable feedback about the effectiveness of their own teaching. At the same time they can develop a better understanding of the principles that account for effective teaching and learning in their own classrooms. In the domain of learning strategies, the teacher also has an important role to play. The teacher is initially an observer and investigator of the learners' learning behaviors and subsequently provides feedback on the kind of strategies that are most successful for carrying out specific learning tasks. Relevant concerns for the teacher thus focus not on the search for the best method, but rather on the circumstances and conditions under which more effective teaching and learning are accomplished.

References

Berliner, D.C. (1984) 'The half-full glass: a review of research on teaching', in P.L. Hosford (ed.) *Using What We Know about Teaching*, pp. 51–77. Alexandria, Va.: Association for Supervision and Curriculum Development.

Blum, R.E. (1984) *Effective Schooling Practices: A Research Synthesis*. Portland, Ore.: Northwest Regional Educational Laboratory.

Chall, J. (1967) *Learning to Read: The Great Debate*. New York: McGraw-Hill.

Chamot, A.U., and O'Malley, J.M. (1986) *A Cognitive Academic Language Learning Approach: An ESL Content-Based Curriculum*. Rosslyn, Va.: National Clearinghouse for Bilingual Education.

Cohen, A.D., and Aphek, E. (1980) 'Retention of second-language vocabulary over time: investigating the role of mnemonic associations'. *System 8:* 221–35.

Doyle, W. (1977) 'Paradigms for research on teacher effectiveness', in L.S. Shulman (ed.) *Review of Research in Teacher Education*, Vol. 5, pp. 163–98. Itasca, Ill.: Peacock.

Dunkin, M., and Biddle, B. (1974) *The Study of Teaching*. New York: Holt, Rinehart and Winston.

Elliot, J. (1980) 'Implications of classroom research for professional development', in E. Hoyle and J. Megarry (eds) *World Yearbook of Education, 1980*, pp. 308–24. London: Kogan Page.

Evertson, C.M., Anderson, L.M. and Brophy, J.E. (1978) *The Texas junior high school study: report of process-product relationships*. University of Texas, Research and Development Center for Teacher Education, Austin.

Fisher, C.W., Berliner, D.C., Filby, N.N., Marliave, R.S., Cahen, L.S. and Dishaw, M.M. (1980) 'Teaching behaviors, academic learning time and academic achievement: an overview', in C. Denham and A. Lieberman (eds) *Time to Learn*, pp. 7–32. Washington, D.C.: U.S. Department of Education, National Institute of Education.

Fraser, H., and Skibicki, A. (1987) 'Self-directed learning strategies for adult Vietnamese learners of ESL'. *Prospect 3*, 1: 33–44.

Good, T.L. (1979) 'Teacher effectiveness in the elementary school'. *Journal of Teacher Education 30*, 2: 52–64.

Good, T.L., and Beckerman, T.M. (1978) 'Time on task: a naturalistic study in sixth grade classrooms'. *Elementary School Journal 78*: 193–201.

Good, T.L., and Marshall, S. (1984) 'Do students learn more in heterogeneous or homogeneous groups?', in P. Peterson, L.C. Wilkinson and M. Hallinan (eds) *The Social Context of Instruction: Group Organization and Group Processes*. New York: Academic Press.

Heuring, D.L. (1984) 'The revision strategies of skilled and unskilled ESL writers: five case studies. Master's thesis. University of Hawaii at Manoa.

Hosenfeld, C. (1977) 'A preliminary investigation of the reading strategies of successful and non-successful second language learners'. *System 5*: 110–23.

—— (1979) 'A learning-teaching view of second language instruction'. *Foreign Language Annals 12*, 1: 51–4.

—— (1984) 'Case studies of ninth grade readers', in J.C. Alderson and A.H. Urquhart (eds), *Reading in a Foreign Language*, pp. 231–49. London: Longman.

Kelly, L. (1969) *Twenty-five Centuries of Language Teaching*. Rowley, Mass.: Newbury House.

Lapp, R. (1984) 'The process approach to writing: towards a curriculum for international students'. Master's thesis. Working Paper available from Department of English as a Second Language, University of Hawaii.

Naiman, N., Fröhlich, M., Stern, H.H. and Todesco, A. (1978) *The Good Language Learner*. Toronto: Ontario Institute for Studies in Education.

O'Malley, J., and Chamot, A.U. (1989) *Learner Strategies in Second Language Acquisition*. New York: Cambridge University Press.

O'Malley, J., Chamot, A.U., Stewner-Manzanares, G., Russo, R.P. and Kupper, L. (1985a) 'Learning strategy applications with students of English as a second language'. *TESOL Quarterly 19*, 3: 557–84.

O'Malley, J., Chamot, A.U., Stewner-Manzanares, G., Kupper, L. and Russo, R.P. (1985b) 'Learning strategies used by beginning and intermediate ESL learners'. *Language Learning 35*, 1.

Oxford, R. (1985a) *A New Taxonomy of Second Language Learning Strategies*. Washington, D.C.: Center for Applied Linguistics.

—— (1985b) 'Second language learning strategies: what the research has to say'. *ERIC/CLL News Bulletin 9*, 1.

Phillips, J. (1975) 'Second language reading: teaching decoding skills'. *Foreign Language Annals* 8: 227–30.

Raimes, A. (1985) 'What unskilled ESL students do as they write: a classroom study of composing'. *TESOL Quarterly 19*, 2: 229–59.

Richards, J. C., and Rodgers, T. (1986) *Approaches and Methods in Language Teaching*. New York: Cambridge University Press.

Rubin, J. (1975) 'What the good language learner can teach us'. *TESOL Quarterly 9*, 1: 41–51.

—— (1981) 'Study of cognitive processes in second language learning'. *Applied Linguistics 11*, 2: 117–31.

Russo, R. P., and Stewner-Manzanares, G. (1985) 'The training and use of learning strategies for English as a second language in a military context'. Paper presented at the annual meeting of the American Educational Research Association, Chicago.

Stallings, J. A., and Kaskowitz, D.H. (1974) *Follow through Classroom Observation Evaluation, 1972–1973*. Menlo Park, Cal.: Stanford Research Institute.

Stern, H. H. (1975) 'What can we learn from the good language learner?' *Canadian Modern Language Review 31*: 304–18.

Swaffar, J.K., Arens, K. and Morgan, M. (1982) 'Teacher classroom practices: redefining method as task hierarchy'. *Modern Language Journal 66*, 1: 24–33.

Tikunoff, W.J. (1983) 'Utility of the SBIF features for the instruction of limited English proficient students'. Report No. SBIF-83-R.15/16 for NIE Contract No. 400-80-0026. San Francisco: Far West Laboratory for Educational Research and Development.

—— (1985) *Applying Significant Bilingual Instructional Features in the Classroom*. Rosslyn, Va.: National Clearinghouse for Bilingual Education.

Tikunoff, W.J., Ward, B.A., Fisher, C.A., Armendariz, J.C., Parker, L. Dominguez, V.J.A., Mercado, C., Romero, M. and Good, R.A. (1980) 'Review of the literature for a descriptive study of significant bilingual instructional features'. Report No. SBIF-81-D.1.1. San Francisco: Far West Laboratory for Educational Research and Development.

Webb, N.M. (1980) 'A process-outcome of learning in group and individual settings'. *Educational Psychologist 15*: 69–83.

Wenden, A. (1983) 'A literature review: the process of intervention'. *Language Learning 33*, 1: 103–21.

—— (1985) 'Learner strategies'. *TESOL Newsletter* (October).

Willing, K. (1985) *Helping Adults Develop Their Learning Strategies*. Sydney: Adult Migrant Education Service.

—— (1987) 'Learner strategies as information management'. *Prospect 2*, 3: 273–92.

Chapter 10

Michael H. Long

FOCUS ON FORM: A DESIGN FEATURE IN LANGUAGE TEACHING METHODOLOGY

Against methods

LANGUAGE TEACHER EDUCATION PROGRAMS PERSIST in presenting classroom options to trainees in terms of methods. While many have stopped pretending that any one method is a panacea or at least that they know which one is, most nevertheless continue to use method as a unit of analysis in their professionally oriented courses, and some even give college credit for training in particular methods taught by their developers or licensed acolytes. Books on methods sell very well, books surveying methods do even better, and expensive one-day "seminars" offering training in particular methods are rarely short of customers. Yet it is no exaggeration to say that language teaching methods do not exist – at least, not where they would matter, if they did, in the classroom.

There are at least four reasons for avoiding the methods trap. First, even as idealized by their developers, groups of methods overlap considerably, prescribing and proscribing many of the same classroom practices. For example, while one method may have teachers provide feedback on error using hand-signals, and one verbally, both prescribe "error correction". Almost all methods in fact advocate error correction (Krashen and Seliger 1975).

Second, when third parties analyze lesson transcripts – records of what teachers and learners actually do, as opposed to what methodologists tell them to do – brief excerpts can occasionally be identified as the product of this or that method, but the classifications usually have to be made on the basis of one or two salient but (as far as we know) trivial features, e.g. whether students are informed of the commission of error verbally or non-verbally. Quite lengthy excerpts are often impossible to distinguish, especially if taken from real classes, as opposed to staged demonstration lessons (Dinsmore 1985; Nunan 1987).

Third, studies that have set out to compare the effectiveness of supposedly quite different methods (e.g. Scherer and Wertheimer 1964; Smith 1970; Von Elek and Oskarsson 1975) have typically found little or no advantage for one over another, or only local and usually short-lived advantages. One interpretation of such results is that methods do not matter. Another is that methods do not exist, among other reasons, because most teachers tend to do much the same things (many methods require this, after all), whatever they are supposed to be doing, especially over time. The absence of a systematic observational component in most of the comparative methods studies makes either interpretation problematic. However, the second view is supported retrospectively by descriptive studies which have found the same classroom practices surviving differences not only in "methods" (Nunan 1987), but also in professional training (Long and Sato 1983), materials (Phillips and Shettlesworth 1975; Long, Adams McLean and Castanos 1976; Ross, to appear), teaching generations (Hoetker and Ahlbrand 1969) and teaching experience (Pica and Long 1986).

Fourth, method may or may not be a useful analytic construct for teachers in training, but it is not a conceptual basis for how they operate in practice. Numerous studies of the ways content teachers plan lessons and recall them afterwards show that they think of what transpires in the classroom in terms of instructional activities, or tasks (for review, see Shavelson and Stern 1981; Crookes 1986). The same appears to be true of FL teachers. Swaffer, Arens and Morgan (1982) conducted a six-month comparative methods study ("comprehension" and "four skills" approaches) of German teaching at the University of Texas. Classroom observations and debriefing interviews with teachers at the end of the study showed that, despite the teachers having received explicit training in the methods and (supposedly) having each used one or the other for a semester, there was no clear distinction between them in their minds or in the classroom practices used across groups.

For these and other reasons, it is clear that "method" is an unverifiable and irrelevant construct when attempting to improve classroom FL instruction. Worse, it may actually do harm by distracting teachers from genuinely important issues. Saying that methods do not exist and so do not matter at the classroom level does not mean, after all, that what goes on in classrooms does not matter. On the contrary, there is growing evidence of the importance of classroom processes, of pedagogic tasks, and of qualitative differences in classroom language use for success and failure in FLs (for review, see Chaudron 1988). Rather than focus on method as the key, however, we would do better to think in terms of psycholinguistically relevant design features of learning environments, preferably features which capture important characteristics of a wide range of syllabus types, methods, materials, tasks, and tests. It is to one of these, *focus on form*, that we now turn.

Focus on form in language teaching

Many developments in foreign language syllabus design, materials writing, methodology and testing during the past 30 years reflect the tension between the desirability of communicative use of the FL in the classroom, on the one hand, and the felt need for a linguistic focus in language learning, on the other. However, while discussion has occurred in staff-rooms and journals alike, it has generally concerned how best to achieve such a focus, not whether or not to have one. Most applied linguists and pedagogues continue to advocate teaching and testing isolated linguistic units of one kind or another in one way or another. Thus, while procedural, process and task-based alternatives are available (see Prabhu 1987; Breen 1987; Long and Crookes 1989), the overwhelming majority of syllabi are still structural, notional-functional or a hybrid, and superficially different "methods", like ALM, TPR and the Silent Way, all teach one linguistic item at a time (or assume they do), in building-block fashion. Pervasive classroom practices, such as grammar and vocabulary explanations, display questions, fill-in-the-blanks exercises, dialog memorization, drills and error correction, all entail treatment of the language as object, and so do discrete-point language tests.

There have always been a few dissenting voices. Newmark (1966), Newmark and Reibel (1968), Corder (1967) and Allwright (1976), among others, have argued strongly against "interfering" with language learning. While differing considerably both in the detail of their own proposals and in the rationales offered for them, each has claimed that the best way to learn a language, inside or outside a classroom, is not by treating it as an object of study, but by experiencing it as a medium of communication.

More recently, some non-interventionist positions have been espoused on the basis of second language acquisition (SLA) theory and research findings (see e.g. Dulay and Burt 1973; Ellis 1984; Felix 1981; Krashen and Terrell 1983; Prabhu 1987; Wode 1981). Most often cited in this context are the well attested *developmental sequences* in interlanguage (IL), such as those for Swedish negation, English relative clauses and German word order. These sequences are fixed series of overlapping stages, each characterizable by the relative frequency of IL structures, which learners apparently have to traverse on the way to mastery of the target language system. (For the most comprehensive study of this phenomenon, see Johnston 1985.)

Numerous studies show, for instance, that ESL negation has a four-stage sequence (for review, see Schumann 1979):

Stage	Sample utterances
1 *No + X*	No is happy / No you pay it
2 *no / not / don't V*	They not working / He don't have job
3 aux. -neg.	I can't play / You mustn't do that
4 analyzed *don't*	I didn't see her / She doesn't live there

At stages 1 and 2, not just Spanish speakers, whose L1 has pre-verbal negation, but also Japanese learners, whose native system is post-verbal, initially produce pre-verbally negated utterances in ESL (Gillis and Weber 1976; Stauble 1981), although the Japanese abandon the strategy sooner (Zobl 1982). Pre-verbal negator placement appears to reflect strong internal pressures, for it is widely observed in studies of both naturalistic and instructed SLA. Turkish speakers receiving formal instruction, for example, start with pre-verbal negation in Swedish, even though both L1 and L2 have post-verbal systems (Hyltenstam 1977).

With minor variations, the evidence to date suggests that the same developmental sequences are observed in the ILs of children and adults, of naturalistic, instructed and mixed learners, of learners from different L1 backgrounds, and of learners performing on different tasks. L1 differences occasionally result in additional sub-stages and swifter or slower passage through stages, but not in disruption of the basic sequence by skipping stages (for review, see Ellis 1985; Larsen-Freeman and Long, in press; Zobl 1982).

Passage through each stage, in order, appears to be unavoidable, and obligatoriness has been incorporated into the definition of "stage" in SLA (Meisel, Clahsen and Pienemann 1981; Johnston 1985). As would be predicted if this definition is accurate, it also seems that developmental sequences are impervious to instruction. It has repeatedly been demonstrated that morpheme accuracy orders and developmental sequences do not reflect instructional sequences (Lightbown 1983; Ellis 1989), and tuition in a German SL word order structure beyond students' current processing abilities has been shown not to result in learning (Pienemann 1984).

The results for developmental sequences, together with related findings of common (although not invariant) naturalistic and instructed morpheme accuracy orders, show that language learning is obviously at least partly governed by forces beyond a teacher's or textbook writer's control. This realization has in turn led some theorists to conclude that classrooms are useful to the extent that they provide sheltered linguistic environments for beginners, but that it does not help for teachers to focus on linguistic form. An inference that could easily be drawn from such interpretations is that there are only two options in this area of course design: either (1) a linear, additive syllabus and methodology whose content and focus is a series of isolated linguistic forms (sound contrasts, lexical items, structures, speech acts, notions, etc.), or (2) a program with no overt focus on linguistic forms at all. While this turns out to be a false dichotomy, *focus on form* is a potentially important design feature for distinguishing instructional methodologies and settings.

Focus on form is a feature which reveals an underlying similarity among a variety of (a) teaching "methods", e.g. ALM, TPR, Grammar Translation and Silent Way, (b) syllabus types, e.g. structural, notional-functional, lexical, and (c) program types, e.g. submersion, immersion, sheltered subject-matter, which on the surface appear to differ greatly. Groups (a) and (b) all utilize an overt focus on form; Group (c) does not. It also allows generalizations across traditional boundaries, identifying a link between the program types in group (c) and in theory, at least, a linguistically non-isolating teaching "method", such as the Natural Approach (Krashen and Terrell 1983). At the classroom process level, techniques, procedures, exercises and pedagogic tasks can also be categorized as to whether or not they either permit or require a focus on form. Display questions, repetition drills and error correction, for example, all overtly focus students on form; referential questions, true/false exercises and two-way tasks do not. Finally, while many potentially relevant design features will distinguish some methods, syllabi, tasks and tests from others, few have the valency of focus on form. It appears to be a parameter one value or another of which characterizes almost all language teaching options.

Five caveats are in order. First, it is not being suggested that whether or not a program type, syllabus, method, task or test focuses on form is the only relevant design characteristic or that important differences will not exist among members of groups which share the feature, and *vice versa*. Second, while most programs, syllabi, methods, tasks and tests either do or do not overtly focus on form, some within the former group differ in the *degree* to which they isolate linguistic structures, not to mention as to how they do so; there are, in other words, relative as well as absolute, within-group as well as inter-group, differences. Third, it is likely that students will often focus on form when teachers or materials designers intend them not to, and ignore form when they are supposed to concentrate on it. Fourth, some degree of awareness of form and a focus on meaning may not be mutually exclusive on some tasks (for review, see Schmidt 1990). Fifth, the fact that the distinction can be made does not mean that it should; whether it is important is a theoretical and/or an empirical matter.

Focus on form: a psycholinguistic rationale

The practice of isolating linguistic items, teaching and testing them one at a time, was originally motivated by advances in behaviorist psychology and structuralist linguistics. Combined with the advent of a world war and a sudden need for fluent foreign language speakers, these events led to the growth of ALM and its many progeny. As distinct from a focus on *form*, to which we return below, structural syllabi, ALM, and variants thereof involve a focus on *forms*. That is to say, the content of the syllabus and of lessons based on it is the linguistic items themselves (structures, notions, lexical items, etc.); a lesson is designed to teach "the past continuous", "requesting" and so on, nothing else.

Arguments abound against making isolated linguistic structures the content of a FL course, that is, against a focus on *forms*. Of the hundreds of studies of interlanguage (IL) development now completed, not one shows either tutored or naturalistic learners developing proficiency one linguistic item at a time. On the contrary, all reveal complex, gradual and inter-related developmental paths for grammatical subsystems, such as auxiliary and negation in ESL (Stauble 1981; Kelley 1983), and copula and word order in GSL (Meisel, Clahsen and Pienemann 1981). Moreover, development is not unidirectional; omission/suppliance of forms fluctuates, as does accuracy of suppliance.

Although most syllabi and methods assume the opposite, learners do not move from ignorance of a form to mastery of it in one step, as is attested by the very existence of developmental sequences like that for ESL negation. Typically, when a form first appears in a learner's IL, it is used in a non-target-like manner, and only gradually improves in accuracy of use. It sometimes shifts in function over time as other new (target-like and non-target-like) forms enter (Huebner 1983). It quite often declines in accuracy or even temporarily disappears altogether due to a change elsewhere in the IL (see, e.g. Meisel, Clahsen and Pienemann 1981; Huebner 1983; Lightbown 1983; Neumann 1977), a phenomenon sometimes describable as U-shaped behavior (Kellerman 1985). Further, attempts to teach isolated items one at a time fail unless the structure happens to be one the learner can process and so is psycholinguistically ready to acquire. In Pienemann's (1984) terminology, learnability determines teachability. Finally, as language teachers, employers and learners alike will attest, there is a great difference between structural knowledge of a language, when that is achieved, and ability to use that knowledge to communicative effect.

As noted earlier, facts about IL development like these have led some to advocate that teachers abandon not just a focus on *forms*, but a focus on *form*, i.e. any attention to language as object, as well. Flaws in this reasoning are obvious. Further, reviews of studies of the effects of instruction on IL development (Harley 1988; Long 1988) find clear evidence of some beneficial effects of a focus on *form*, and suggestive evidence of others. Briefly, while it is true that instruction does not seem capable of altering *sequences* of development, it does appear to offer three other advantages over either naturalistic SLA or classroom instruction with no focus on form. (1) It speeds up the *rate* of learning (for review, see Long 1983). (2) It affects acquisition *processes* in ways possibly beneficial to long-term accuracy (Lightbown 1983; Pica 1983). And most crucially, on the basis of preliminary data, (3) it appears to raise the *ultimate level of attainment*. Further, as White (1987, 1989) has argued, *in*comprehensible input and drawing learners' attention to *in*admissable constructions in the L2 (two kinds of negative evidence) may be necessary when learning from positive evidence alone will be inadequate. To illustrate, an L1 may allow placement of adverbs of manner more flexibly than an L2. "He drinks every day coffee" and "He drinks coffee every day" are both acceptable in French, for example, but not in English. Both will be communicatively effective in English, however, with the result that the French learner of English (but not the English learner of French) will need negative input (e.g. error correction) on this point.

Whereas the content of lessons with a focus on *forms* is the *forms* themselves, a syllabus with a focus on *form* teaches something else – biology, mathematics, workshop practice, automobile repair, the geography of a country where the foreign language is spoken, the cultures of its speakers, and so on – and overtly draws students' attention to linguistic elements as they arise incidentally in lessons whose overriding focus is on meaning, or communication. Views about how to achieve this vary. One proposal is for lessons to be briefly "interrupted" by teachers when they notice students making errors which are (1) systematic, (2) pervasive and (3) remediable. The linguistic feature is brought to learners' attention in any way appropriate to the students' age, proficiency level, etc. before the class returns to whatever pedagogic task they were working on when the interruption occurred. (For details and a rationale, see Crookes and Long 1987; Long, in press).

An example of the probable effect of instruction on ultimate attainment comes from work on the acquisition of relative clauses in a SL. Several studies (e.g., for English: Gass 1982; Gass and Ard 1980; Pavesi 1986; Eckman, Bell and Nelson 1988; for Swedish: Hyltenstam 1984) have shown that both naturalistic and instructed acquirers develop relative clauses in the order predictable from the noun phrase accessibility hierarchy (Keenan and Comrie 1977; Comrie and Keenan 1979; see Figure 10.1), although with occasional reversals of levels 5 and 6.

---

least marked

1. subject (The man that stole the car . . .)
2. direct object (The man that the police arrested . . .)
3. indirect object (The car that he paid nothing for . . .)
4. object of a preposition (The man that he spoke to . . .)
5. possessive/genitive (The man whose . . .)
6. object of a comparative (The man that Joe is older than . . .)

most marked

Figure 10.1 Noun phrase accessibility hierarchy

Of particular interest in the present context, Pavesi (1986) compared relative clause formation by instructed and naturalistic acquirers. The former were 48 Italian high school students, ages 14–18, who had received from 2 to 7 years (an average of 4 years) of grammar-based EFL instruction and who had had minimal or (in 45 of 48 cases) no informal exposure to English. The untutored learners were 38 Italian workers (mostly restaurant waiters), ages 19–50, who had lived in Scotland anywhere from 3 months to 25 years (an average of 6 years), with considerable exposure to English at home and at work, but who had received minimal (usually no) formal English instruction.

Relative clause constructions were elicited using a set of numbered pictures and question prompts: ("Number 7 is the girl who is running", and so on). Implicational scaling showed that both groups' developmental sequences correlated significantly with the noun phrase accessibility hierarchy. There were two other kinds of differences, however. First, naturalistic learners produced statistically significantly more full nominal copies than the instructed learners (e.g. "Number 4 is the woman who the cat is looking at the woman"), whereas instructed learners produced more pronominal copies ("Number 4 is the woman who the cat is looking at her"). Given that neither English nor Italian allow copies of either kind, this is further evidence of the at least partial autonomy of IL syntax, a claim also supported by the developmental sequence itself, of course. Interestingly, the relative frequencies of the different kinds of copies suggest that the instructed learners had "grammaticized" more, even in the errors they made, a result consistent with findings by Pica (1983) and Lightbown (1983). Second, more instructed learners reached 80 percent criterion on all of the five lowest NP categories in the hierarchy, with differences attaining statistical significance at the second lowest (genitive) level and falling just short (p. 06) at the lowest (object of a comparative) level. More instructed learners (and very few naturalistic acquirers) were able to relativize out of the more marked NPs in the hierarchy. In considerably less average time, that is, instructed learners had reached higher levels of attainment.

Pavesi's study is a non-equivalent control groups design, so causal claims are precluded. There are also no data on whether or not the high school students were ever actually taught relative clauses, or if so, which ones. We know simply that they received something like a grammar-translation course. The findings are nonetheless suggestive of the kind of effects a focus on form may have on ultimate SL attainment. Two other studies, furthermore, have shown that structurally focused teaching of relative clause formation can accelerate learning, also that, at least as far down as level 4 (object of a preposition) in the hierarchy, instruction in a more marked structure will generalize back up the implicational scale to less marked structures (Gass 1982; Eckman *et al.* 1988; and see also Zobl 1985).

SLA research findings like those briefly described here would seem to support two conclusions. (1) Instruction built around a *focus on forms* is counter-productive. (2) Instruction which encourages a systematic, non-interfering *focus on form* produces a faster rate of learning and (probably) higher levels of ultimate SL attainment than instruction with *no focus on form*. If correct, this would make [+ focus on form] a desirable design feature of FL instruction. Programs exist which have this feature, alternating in some principled way between a focus on meaning and a focus on form. (One example is task-based language teaching. See Long 1985; Crookes and Long 1987; Long and Crookes 1989; Long, in press). Programs with a focus on form need to be compared in carefully controlled studies with programs with a focus on forms and with (e.g. Natural Approach) programs with no overt focus on form.

Further research

True experiments are needed which compare rate of learning and ultimate level of attainment after one of three programs: *focus on forms, focus on form*, and *focus on communication*. Preliminary research in this area has produced mixed results, two studies finding positive relationships between the amount of class time given to a focus on *forms* and various proficiency measures (McDonald, Stone and Yates 1977, for ESL; Mitchell, Parkinson and Johnstone 1981, for French FL), and a third study of ESL (Spada 1986, 1987) finding no such effects. (For detailed review, see Chaudron 1988.) All three studies were comparisons of intact groups which differed in *degree* of focus on *forms*, it should be noted. Research has yet to be conducted comparing the unique program types.

Studies of this kind should be true experiments, employing a pretest/post-test control group design, and should also include a process component to monitor implementation of the three distinct treatments. They should utilize multiple outcome measures, some focusing on accuracy, some on communicative ability or fluency, thereby avoiding (supposed) bias in favour of one program or another. The post-tests should include immediate and delayed measures, since at least one study (Harley 1989) has found a short-term advantage for students receiving form-focused instruction disappeared (three months) later. Some of the measures should further reflect known developmental sequences and patterns of variation in ILs, appropriate for the developmental stages of the subjects as revealed on the pretests. A distinction should be maintained between constructions which are in principle learnable from positive instantiation in the input and constructions which in principle require negative evidence. (For further details and desirable characteristics of such studies, see Long 1984, forthcoming; Larsen-Freeman and Long 1989.)

Several additional issues need to be addressed, either as separate studies of the *focus on form* design feature or as sub-parts of the basic study outlined above. Many interesting questions remain unanswered, after all. It will be useful to ascertain which structures require focus and/or negative evidence, and which can be left to the care of "natural processes" (White 1987). Other possibilities include studies motivated by implicational markedness relationships designed to determine the principles governing maximal *generalizability* of instruction (see, e.g. Eckman *et al.* 1988). Similarly, one can envisage studies inspired by current models of UG designed to test the claimed potential of certain structures to trigger instantaneous (re-)setting of a parameter. An example would be Chomsky's (1981) work on the pro-drop parameter, and the claimed triggering effects of expletives with *it* and *there* as dummy subjects (Hyams 1983; Hilles 1986). Finally, further theoretically motivated work, like that of Pienemann (1984) and Pienemann and Johnston (1987), is clearly needed on the *timing* of instruction. Research of these and other kinds will establish the validity and scope of *focus on form* as a design feature in language teaching methodology.

References

Allwright, R.L. (1977) "Language learning through communication practice." *ELT Docs* 76/3.2–14.

Breen, M.P. (1987) "Contemporary paradigms in syllabus design." *Language Teaching* 20/2.81–92, and 20/3.157–174.

Chaudron, C. (1988) *Second Language Classrooms. Research on Teaching and Learning*. Cambridge: Cambridge University Press.

Chomsky, N. (1981) *Lectures on Government and Binding*. Dordrecht: Foris.

Comrie, B. and Keenan, E.L. (1979) "Noun phrase accessibility revisited". *Language* 55.649–664.

Corder, S.P. (1967) "The significance of learners' errors." *International Review of Applied Linguistics* 5.161–170.

Crookes, G. (1986) *Task classification: a cross-disciplinary review* (Technical Report 4.) Honolulu: Center for Second Language Classroom Research, Social Science Research Institute, University of Hawaii at Manoa.

Crookes, G. and Long, M.H. (1987) "Task-based language teaching. A brief report". *Modern English Teaching* (Part 1) 8.26–28 + 61, and (Part 2) 9.20–23.

Dinsmore, D. (1985) "Waiting for Godot in the EFL classroom." *ELT Journal* 39.225–234.

Dulay, M. and Bert, H. (1973) 'Should we teach children syntax?' *Language Learning* 24/2.245–258.

Eckman, F.R., Bell, L. and Nelson, D. (1988) "On the generalization of relative clause instruction in the acquisition of English as a second language." *Applied Linguistics* 9/1.1–20.

Ellis, R. (1984) "The role of instruction in second language acquisition." *Language Learning in Formal and Informal Contexts* ed. by D.M. Singleton and D.G. Little, 19–37. Dublin: IRAAL.

—— (1985) *Understanding Second Language Acquisition*. Oxford: Oxford University Press.

—— (1989) "Are classroom and naturalistic acquisition the same? A study of the classroom acquisition of German word order rules." *Studies in Second Language Acquisition* 11/3.305–328.

Felix, S.W. (1981) "The effect of formal instruction on second language acquisition." *Language Learning* 31/1.87–112.

Gass, S.M. (1982) "From theory to practice." *On TESOL '81* ed. by M. Hines and W. Rutherford, 129–139. Washington, DC: TESOL.

Gass, S.M. and Ard, J. (1980) "L2 data: their relevance for language universals." *TESOL Quarterly* 14/4.443–452.

Gillis, M. and Weber, R. (1976) "The emergence of sentence modalities in the English of japanese-speaking children." *Language Learning* 26/1.77–94.

Harley, B. (1988) "Effects of instruction on SLA: issues and evidence." *Annual Review of Applied Linguistics* 9.165–178.

—— (1989) "Functional grammar in French immersion: a classroom experiment." *Applied Linguistics* 10/3.331–359.

Hilles, S. (1986). "Interlanguage and the pro-drop parameter." *Second Language Research* 2/1.33–52.

Hoetker, J. and Ahlbrand, W.P. (1969) "The persistence of the recitation." *American Educational Research Journal* 6/1/145–167.

Hyams, N. (1983) "The pro-drop parameter in child grammars." *Proceedings of the West Coast Conference on Formal Linguistics* ed. by M. Barlow, D. Flickinger and M. Westcoat. Stanford, CA: Stanford University, Department of Linguistics.

Hyltenstam, K. (1977) "Implicational patterns in interlanguage syntax variation." *Language Learning* 27/2.383–411.

—— (1984) "The use of typological markedness conditions as predictors in second language acquisition: the case of pronominal copies in relative clauses." *Second Languages. A Cross-Linguistic Perspective* ed. by R.W. Andersen, 39–58. Rowley, MA: Newbury House.

Johnston, M. (1985) *Syntactic and morphological progressions in learner English*. Canberra, Australia: Commonwealth Department of Immigration and Ethnic Affairs.

Keenan, E. and Comrie, B. (1977) "Noun phrase accessibility and universal grammar." *Linguistic Inquiry* 8.63–99.

Kellerman, E. (1985) "If at first you *do* succeed . . . " *Input in Second Language Acquisition* ed. by S. Gass and C. Madden, 345–353. Rowley, MA: Newbury House.

Krashen, S.D. and Seliger, H.W. (1975) "The essential contributions of formal instruction in adult second language learning." *TESOL Quarterly* 9/12.173–183.

Krashen, S.D. and Terrell, T. (1983) *The Natural Approach*. New York: Pergamon Press.

Larsen-Freeman, D. and Long, M.H. (1989) *Research Priorities in Foreign Language Learning and Teaching*. Washington, DC: Johns Hopkins University, National Foreign Language Center.

Larsen-Freeman, D. and Long, M.H. (1991) *An Introduction to Second Language Acquisition Research*. London: Longman.

Lightbown, P.M. (1983) "Exploring relationships between developmental and instructional sequences." *Classroom-Oriented Research on Second Language Acquisition* ed. by H.W. Seliger and M.H. Long, 217–243. Rowley, MA: Newbury House.

Long, M.H. (1983) "Does instruction make a difference? A review of research." *TESOL Quarterly* 17/3.359–382.

—— (1984) "Process and product in ESL program evaluation." *TESOL Quarterly* 18/3.409–425.

—— (1985) "A role for instruction in second language acquisition: task-based language teaching." *Modelling and Assessing Second Language Acquisition* ed. by K. Hyltenstam and M. Pienemann, 77–99. Clevedon, Avon: Multilingual Matters.

—— (1988) "Instructed interlanguage development." *Issues in Second Language Acquisition. Multiple Perspectives* ed by L.M. Beebe, 115–141. New York: Newbury House.

—— (1991) "The design and psycholinguistic motivation of research on foreign language learning." *Foreign Language Acquisition Research and the Classroom* ed. by B. Freed. Boston: D.C. Heakin.

—— (2001) *Task-Based Language Teaching*. Oxford: Basil Blackwell.

Long, M.H., Adams, L., McLean, M. and Castanos, F. (1976) "Doing things with words: verbal interaction in lockstep and small group classroom situations." *On TESOL. '76* ed. by J.F. Fanselow and R. Crymes, 137–153. Washington, DC: TESOL.

Long, M.H. and Crookes, G. (1989) *Units of analysis in syllabus design*. Ms. Department of ESL, University of Hawaii at Manoa.

Long, M.H. and Sato, C.J. (1983) "Classroom foreigner talk discourse: forms and functions of teachers' questions." *Classroom-Oriented Research in Second Language Acquisition* ed. by H.W. Seliger and M.H. Long, 268–285. Rowley, MA: Newbury House.

McDonald, F.J., Stone, M.K. and Yates, A. (1977) *The effects of classroom interaction patterns and student characteristics on the acquisition of proficiency in English as a second language*. Princeton, NJ: Educational Testing Service.

Meisel, J.M., Clahsen, H. and Pienemann, M. (1981) "On determining developmental stages in natural second language acquisitions." *Studies in Second Language Acquisition* 3/2.109–135.

Mitchell, R., Parkinson, B. and Johnstone, R. (1981) *The foreign language classroom: an observational study*. (*Stirling Educational Monographs* 9.) Stirling: Department of Education, University of Stirling.

Neumann, R. (1977) *An attempt to define through error analysis an intermediate ESL level at UCLA*. M.A. in TESL thesis. Los Angeles, CA: UCLA.

Newmark, L. (1966) "How not to interfere with language learning." *International Journal of American Linguistics* 32/1.77–83.

Newmark, L. and Reibel, D.A. (1968) "Necessity and sufficiency in language learning." *International Review of Applied Linguistics* 6.145–164.

Nunan, D. (1987) "Communicative language teaching: making it work." *ELT Journal* 41/2.136–145.

Pavesi, M. (1986) "Markedness, discoursal modes, and relative clause formation in a formal and an informal context." *Studies in Second Language Acquisition* 8.138–55.

Phillips, D. and Shettlesworth, C. (1975). "Questions in the design and implementation of courses in English for specialized purposes." *Proceedings of the 4th International Congress of Applied Linguistics (Volume 1)* ed. by G. Nickel, 249–264. Stuttgart: Hochschule Verlag.

Pica, T. (1983) "Adult acquisition of English as a second language under different conditions of exposure." *Language Learning* 33/4.465–497.

Pica, T. and Long, M.H. (1986) "The linguistic and conversation performance of experienced and inexperienced teachers." *"Talking to learn": Conversation in Second Language Acquisition* ed. by R.R. Day, 85–98. Rowley, MA: Newbury House.

Pienemann, M. (1984) "Psychological constraints on the teachability of languages'." *Studies in Second Language Acquisition* 6/2.186–214.

Pienemann, M. and Johnston M. (1987) "Factors influencing the development of language proficiency." *Applying Second Language Acquisition Research* ed. by D. Nunan, 45–141. Adelaide. SA: National Curriculum Resource Centre.

Prabhu, N.S. (1987) *Second Language Pedagogy*. Oxford: Oxford University Press.

Ross, S. (1992) "Program-defining evaluation in a decade of eclecticism." In Alderson C. and Beretta, A. (eds). *Evaluating Second Language Education*. Cambridge: Cambridge University Press.

Scherer, G. and Wertheimer, M. (1964) *A Psycholinguistic Experiment in Foreign Language Teaching*. New York: McGraw-Hill.

Schmidt, R.W. (1990) "The role of consciousness in second language learning" *Applied Linguistics* 11/2.17–45.

Schumann, J.H. (1979) "The acquisition of English negation by speakers of Spanish: a review of the literature." *The Acquisition and Use of Spanish and English as First and Second Languages* ed. by R.W. Andersen, 3–32. Washington, DC: TESOL.

Smith, P. (1970) *A Comparison of the Cognitive and Audiolingual Approaches to Foreign Language Instruction: The Pennsylvania Foreign Language Project*. Philadelphia: Center for Curriculum Development.

Spada, N. (1986) "The interaction between types of content and types of instruction: some effects on the L2 proficiency of adult learners." *Studies in Second Language Acquisition* 8/2.181–199.

—— (1987) "Relationships between instructional differences and learning outcomes: a process-product study of communicative language teaching." *Applied Linguistics* 8.137–161.

Stauble, A.-M. (1981) *A comparative study of a Spanish-English and Japanese-English second language continuum: verb phrase morphology*. Unpublished Ph.D. dissertation, UCLA.

Swaffer, J.K., Arens, K. and Morgan, M. (1982) "Teacher classroom practices: redefining method as task hierarchy." *Modern Language Journal* 66.24–33.

Von Elek, T. and Oskarsson, M. (1975) *Comparative Methods Experiments in Foreign Language Teaching*. Department of Educational Research. Gothenburg, Sweden: Molnda School of Education.

White, L. (1987) "Against comprehensible input: the Input Hypothesis and the development of second-language competence." *Applied Linguistics* 8/2.95–110.

White, L. (1989) 'The principle of adjacency in second language acquisition: do learners observe the subset principle?' Paper presented at the Child Language Conference Boston MA. March.

Wode, H. (1981) "Language-acquisitional universals: a unified view of language acquisition." *Native Language and Foreign Language Acquisition*. (*Annals of the New York Academy of Sciences* 379) ed. by H. Winitz, 218–234. New York: New York Academy of Sciences.

Zobl, H. (1982) "A direction for contrastive analysis: the comparative study of developmental sequences." *TESOL Quarterly* 16. 169–183.

—— (1985) "Grammars in search of input and intake." *Input in Second Language Acquisition* ed. by S.M. Gass and C. Madden, 329–344. Rowley, MA: Newbury House.

Chapter 11

David Nunan

TEACHING GRAMMAR IN CONTEXT

Introduction

FROM A GRAMMATICAL PERSPECTIVE, MANY foreign language programmes and teaching materials are based on a linear model of language acquisition. This model operates on the premise that learners acquire one target language item at a time, in a sequential, step-by-step fashion. However, such a model is inconsistent with what is observed as learners go about the process of acquiring another language. In this chapter I argue for an alternative to the linear model which I call, for want of a better term, an organic approach to second language pedagogy. In the first part of the chapter I shall contrast both approaches, and look at evidence from second language acquisition and discourse analysis which supports the organic view. In the second part I shall outline some of the pedagogical implications of the organic approach, illustrating them with practical ideas for the classroom.

Metaphors for second language acquisition

A strictly linear approach to language learning is based on the premise that learners acquire one grammatical item at a time, and that they should demonstrate their mastery of one thing before moving on to the next. For example, in learning English, a student should master one tense form, such as the simple present, before being introduced to other forms, such as the present continuous or the simple past. Metaphorically, learning another language by this method is like constructing a wall. The language wall is erected one linguistic 'brick' at a time. The easy grammatical bricks are laid at the bottom of the wall, providing a foundation for the more difficult ones. The task for the learner is to get the linguistic bricks in the right order: first the word bricks, and then the sentence bricks. If the bricks are not in the correct order, the wall will collapse under its own ungrammaticality.

When we observe learners as they go about the process of learning another language, we see that, by and large, they do not acquire language in the step-by-step, building block fashion suggested by the linear model. It is simply not the case that language learners acquire target items perfectly, one at a time. Kellerman (1983), for example, notes the 'u-shaped behavior' of certain linguistic items in learners' interlanguage development. Accuracy does not increase in a linear fashion, from 20% to 40% to 100%; at times, it actually decreases. It appears that, rather than being isolated bricks, the various elements of language interact with, and are affected by, other elements to which they are closely related in a functional sense. This interrelationship accounts for the fact that a learner's mastery of a particular language item is unstable, appearing to increase and decrease at different times during the learning process. For example, mastery of the simple present deteriorates (temporarily) at the point when learners are beginning to acquire the present continuous. Rutherford (1987) describes this process as a kind of linguistic metamorphosis.

The adoption of an 'organic' perspective can greatly enrich our understanding of language acquisition and use. Without this perspective, our understanding of other dimensions of language such as the notion of 'grammaticality' will be piecemeal and incomplete, as will any attempt at understanding and interpreting utterances in isolation from the contexts in which they occur. The organic metaphor sees second language acquisition more like growing a garden than building a wall. From such a perspective, learners do not learn one thing perfectly, one item at a time, but numerous things simultaneously (and imperfectly). The linguistic flowers do not all appear at the same time, nor do they all grow at the same rate. Some even appear to wilt, for a time, before renewing their growth. The rate of growth is determined by a complex interplay of factors related to speech processing constraints (Pienemann and Johnston 1987), pedagogical interventions (Pica 1985), acquisitional processes (Johnston 1987), and the influence of the discoursal environment in which the items occur (Nunan 1993).

Language in context

In textbooks, grammar is very often presented out of context. Learners are given isolated sentences, which they are expected to internalize through exercises involving repetition, manipulation, and grammatical transformation. These exercises are designed to provide learners with formal, declarative mastery, but unless they provide opportunities for learners to explore grammatical structures in context, they make the task of developing procedural skill – being able to use the language for communication – more difficult than it needs to be, because learners are denied the opportunity of seeing the systematic relationships that exist between form, meaning, and use.

As teachers, we need to help learners see that effective communication involves achieving harmony between functional interpretation and formal appropriacy (Halliday 1985) by giving them tasks that dramatize the relationship between grammatical items and the discoursal contexts in which they occur. In genuine communication beyond the classroom, grammar and context are often so closely related that appropriate grammatical choices can only be made with reference to the context and purpose of the communication. This, by the way, is one of the reasons why it is often difficult to answer learners' questions about grammatical appropriacy: in many instances, the answer is that it depends on the attitude or orientation that the speaker wants to take towards the events he or she wishes to report.

If learners are not given opportunities to explore grammar in context, it will be difficult for them to see how and why alternative forms exist to express different communicative meanings. For example, getting learners to read a set of sentences in the active voice, and then transform these into passives following a model, is a standard way of introducing the passive voice. However, it needs to be supplemented by tasks which give learners opportunities to explore when it is communicatively appropriate to use the passive rather than the active voice. (One of my favourite textbook instructions is an injunction to students, in a book which shall remain nameless, that 'the passive should be avoided if at all possible'.)

We need to supplement form-focused exercises with an approach that dramatizes for learners the fact that different forms enable them to express different meanings; that grammar allows them to make meanings of increasingly sophisticated kinds, to escape from the tyranny of the here and now, not only to report events and states of affairs, but to editorialize, and to communicate their own attitudes towards these events and affairs. Unfortunately, many courses fail to make clear the relationship between form and function. Learners are taught about the forms, but not how to use them to communicate meaning. For example, through exercises such as the one referred to in the preceding paragraph, they are taught how to transform sentences from the active voice into the passive, and back into the active voice; however, they are not shown that passive forms have evolved to achieve certain communicative ends – to enable the speaker or writer to place the communicative focus on the action rather than on the performer of the action, to avoid referring to the performer of the action. If the communicative value of alternative grammatical forms is not made clear to learners, they come away from the classroom with the impression that the alternative forms exist merely to make things difficult for them. We need an approach through which they learn how to form structures correctly, and also how to use them to communicate meaning. Such a methodology will show learners how to use grammar to get things done, socialize, obtain goods and services, and express their personality through language. In other words, it will show them how to achieve their communicative ends through the appropriate deployment of grammatical resources.

Some practical implications

In the rest of this chapter I shall focus on the implications of an organic approach to language teaching. Such an approach offers exciting opportunities for teachers and students to look at language in a new way — as a vehicle for taking voyages of pedagogical exploration in the classroom and beyond.

There are many different ways of activating organic learning, and many 'traditional' exercise types can, with a slight twist, be brought into harmony with this approach, particularly if they are introduced into the classroom as exploratory and collaborative tasks. (For examples, see Wajnryb's (1990) 'grammar dictation' tasks, and Woods' (1995) gap and cloze exercises.)

In my own classroom, I try to activate an organic approach by:

- teaching language as a set of choices;
- providing opportunities for learners to explore grammatical and discoursal relationships in authentic data;
- teaching language in ways that make form/function relationships transparent;
- encouraging learners to become active explorers of language;
- encouraging learners to explore relationships between grammar and discourse.

Teaching language as a set of choices

As indicated in the preceding section, one of the reasons why it is difficult to give learners hard-and-fast grammatical rules is that, in many instances, once grammar is pressed into communicative service, decisions about which forms to use will be determined by the meanings learners themselves wish to make. For example, if learners wish to give equal weight to two pieces of information, they can present the information in a single sentence, using co-ordination. If they wish to give one of these pieces of information greater weight, they can use subordination.

In order to help learners see that alternative grammatical realizations exist in order to enable them to make different kinds of meanings, and that ultimately it is up to them to decide exactly what they wish to convey, I often begin my language courses with 'ice-breaker' tasks such as Example 1. In completing this task, learners come to fashion their own understanding of the functional distinctions between contrasting forms. They also come to appreciate the fact that in many instances it is only the speaker or writer who can decide which of the contrasting forms is the appropriate one.

Example 1

In groups of 3 or 4, study the following conversational extracts. Focus in particular on the parts of the conversation in italics. What is the difference between what Person A says and what Person B says? When would you use one form, and when would you use the other?

1 A: *I've seen Romeo and Juliet twice.*
   B: Me too. *I saw it last Tuesday, and again on the weekend.*
2 A: Want to go to the movies?
   B: No. *I'm going to study tonight.* We have an exam tomorrow, you know.
   A: Oh, in that case, *I'll study as well.*
3 A: Looks wet outside. I'm supposed to go to Central, but I don't have an umbrella. *If I went out without one, I'd get wet.*
   B: Yes, I went out a while ago. *If I'd gone out without an umbrella, I'd have got wet.*
4 A: *I finished my essay* just before the deadline for submission.
   B: Yes, *mine was finished* just in time as well.
5 A: *My brother, who lives in New York, is visiting me here in Hong Kong.*
   B: What a coincidence! *My brother, who is visiting me in Hong Kong, lives in New York,* too.
6 A: I need you to look after the kids. You'll be home early tonight, *won't you?*
   B: Oh, you'll be late tonight, *will you?*
7 A: I won *a prize* in the English-speaking competition.
   B: Yeah? I won *the prize* in the poetry competition.
8 A: *The baby was sleeping* when I got home.
   B: So, *he'll be sleeping* when I get home, then?
9 A: Are you hungry?
   B: No, *I've already eaten.*
   A: Well, *I'll have already eaten* by the time you get home.

Compare explanations with another group. What similarities and differences are there in your explanations?

Providing opportunities for learners to explore grammatical and discoursal relationships in authentic data

Non-authentic texts are meant to make language easier to comprehend but an unvarying diet of such texts can make language learning more, not less, difficult for learners. Authentic language shows how grammatical forms operate in the 'real world', rather than in the mind of a textbook writer; it allows learners to encounter target language items – such as the comparative adjectives and adverbs in Example 2 – in interaction with other closely related grammatical and discoursal elements. What learners need is a balanced diet of both types of text.

Example 2

Study the following extracts. One is a piece of genuine conversation, the other is taken from a language teaching textbook. Which is which? What differences can you see between the two extracts? What language do you think the non-authentic conversation is trying to teach? What grammar would you need in order to take part in the authentic conversation?

Text A[1]

A: Excuse me, please. Do you know where the nearest bank is?

B: Well, the City Bank isn't far from here. Do you know where the main post office is?

A: No, not really. I'm just passing through.

B: Well, first go down this street to the traffic light.

A: OK.

B: Then turn left and go west on Sunset Boulevard for about two blocks. The bank is on your right, just past the post office.

A: All right. Thanks!

B: You're welcome.

Text B[2]

A: How do I get to Kensington Road?

B: Well you go down Fullarton Road . . .

A: . . . what, down Old Belair, and around . . .?

B: Yeah. And then you go straight . . .

A: . . . past the hospital?

B: Yeah, keep going straight, past the racecourse to the roundabout. You know the big roundabout?

A: Yeah.

B: And Kensington Road's off to the right.

A: What, off the roundabout?

B: Yeah

A: Right.

Teaching language in ways that make form/function relationships transparent

This principle can be activated by creating pedagogical tasks in which learners structure and restructure their own understanding of form/function relationships through inductive and deductive tasks. Example 3, taken from Badalamenti and Henner-Stanchina (1993: 105), is useful for exploring a range of structures, including 'there + be', articles, yes/no questions, and conjunctions. The teacher can determine which form/function relationships are focused on by giving the learners certain types of prompts, for example: Whose apartment is this? How much can you tell about the person who lives here? Is the person poor? Why is the person fit?

Encouraging learners to become active explorers of language

By exploiting this principle, teachers can encourage their students to take greater responsibility for their own learning. (A striking example of this principle, in an ESL setting, can be found in Heath (1992).) Students can bring samples of language into class, and work together to formulate their own hypotheses about language structures and functions. I sometimes give my students a Polaroid camera, and get them to walk around the campus taking photographs, either of signs and public notices which they believe are ungrammatical, or of signs which they think are interesting, or puzzling, or which contain language they would like to know more about. The photographs then become the raw material for our next language lesson. In fact, the last time I did this, the lesson culminated in the students writing a letter to the university estates office pointing out the errors and suggesting amendments.

Example 3

Look at the picture. Whose apartment is this? Make guesses about the person who lives here. Circle your guesses and then explain them by circling the clues in the picture.

1.	The person is	a man / a woman
2.	The person	has a baby / doesn't have a baby
3.	The person	has a pet / doesn't have a pet
4.	The person is	athletic / not athletic
5.	The person is	a coffee drinker / not a coffee drinker
6.	The person is	well-educated / not well-educated
7.	The person is	a smoker / not a smoker
8.	The person is	middle class / poor
9.	The person is	a music lover / not a music lover
10.	The person is	on a diet / not on a diet

Classrooms where the principle of active exploration has been activated will be characterized by an inductive approach to learning in which learners are given access to data and provided with structured opportunities to work out rules, principles, and applications for themselves. The idea here is that information will be more deeply processed and stored if learners are given an opportunity to work things out for themselves, rather than simply being given the principle or rule.

Encouraging learners to explore relationships between grammar and discourse

Tasks exploiting this principle show learners that grammar and discourse are inextricably interlinked, and that grammatical choices (for example, whether to combine two pieces of information using co-ordination or subordination) will be determined by considerations of context and purpose. Such tasks help learners to explore the functioning of grammar in context, and assist them in deploying their developing grammatical competence in the creation of coherent discourse.

Example 4

Consider the following pieces of information about nursing.

The nursing process is a systematic method.
The nursing process is a rational method.
The method involves planning nursing care.
The method involves providing nursing care.

These can be 'packaged' into a single sentence by using grammatical resources of various kinds:

> The nursing process is a systematic and rational method of planning and providing nursing care.

Task 1   Using the above sentence as the topic sentence in a paragraph, produce a coherent paragraph incorporating the following information. (You can rearrange the order in which the information is presented.)

The goal of the nursing process is to identify a client's health status.
The goal of the nursing process is to identify a client's health care problems.
A client's health care problems may be actual or potential.
The goal of the nursing process is to establish plans to meet a client's health care needs.
The goal of the nursing process is to deliver specific nursing interventions.
Nursing interventions are designed to meet a client's health care needs.
The nurse must collaborate with the client to carry out the nursing process effectively.
The nurse must collaborate with the client to individualize approaches to each person's particular needs.
The nurse must collaborate with other members of the health care team to carry out the nursing process effectively.
The nurse must collaborate with other members of the health care team to individualize approaches to each person's particular needs.

Task 2 Compare your text with that written by another student. Make a note of similarities and differences. Can you explain the differences? Do different ways of combining information lead to differences of meaning?

Task 3 Now revise your text and compare it with the original. [This is supplied separately to the students.]

(Adapted from Nunan 1996)

Conclusion

In this chapter, I have argued that we need to go beyond linear approaches and traditional form-focused methodological practices in the grammar class, and that while such practices might be necessary, they do not go far enough in preparing learners to press their grammatical resources into communicative use. I have suggested that grammar instruction will be more effective in classrooms where:

- learners are exposed to authentic samples of language so that the grammatical features being taught are encountered in a range of different linguistic and experiential contexts:
- it is not assumed that once learners have been drilled in a particular form they have acquired it, and drilling is seen only as a first step towards eventual mastery:
- there are opportunities for recycling of language forms, and learners are engaged in tasks designed to make transparent the links between form, meaning, and use:
- learners are given opportunities to develop their own understandings of the grammatical principles of English by progressively structuring and restructuring the language through inductive learning experiences which encourage them to explore the functioning of grammar in context:
- over time, learners encounter target language items in an increasingly diverse and complex range of linguistic and experiential environments.

In making a case for a more organic approach to grammar teaching, I hope that I have not given the impression that specially written texts and dialogues, drills, and deductive presentations by the teacher, have no place in the grammar class. What we need is an appropriate balance between exercises that help learners come to grips with grammatical forms, and tasks for exploring the use of those forms to communicate effectively.

In seeking to explore alternative ways of achieving our pedagogical goals, it is important not to overstate the case for one viewpoint rather than another, or to discount factors such as cognitive style, learning strategy preferences, prior learning experiences, and the cultural contexts in which the language is being taught and learnt. However, while there are some grammatical structures that may be acquired in a linear way, it seems clear from a rapidly growing body of research that the majority of structures are acquired in complex, non-linear ways.

Notes

1   I have not acknowledged the source of this extract, because I do not wish to appear to be criticizing the text from which it was taken. It is cited here for contrastive purposes only.
2   Source: D. Nunan (1993).

Acknowledgement

The author and the publisher would like to thank Heinle and Heinle for their kind permission to reproduce copyright material from Badalamenti and Henner-Stanchina (1993).

References

Badalamenti, V. and Henner-Stanchina, C. (1993) *Grammar Dimensions One*. Boston: Heinle and Heinle.

Ellis, R. (1994) *The Study of Second Language Acquisition*. Oxford: Oxford University Press.

Halliday, M.A.K. (1985) *An Introduction to Functional Grammar*. London: Arnold.

Heath, S.B. (1992) 'Literary skills or literate skills? Considerations for ESL/EFL learners' in Nunan (1992).

Johnston, M. (1987) 'Understanding learner language' in Nunan (1987).

Kellerman, E. (1983) 'If at first you do succeed . . . , in S. Gass and C. Madden (eds) *Input in Second Language Acquisition*. Rowley, Mass.: Newbury House.

Larsen-Freeman, D. and Long, M. (1991) *An Introduction to Second Language Acquisition Research*. London: Longman.

Nunan, D. (ed.) (1987) *Applying Second Language Acquisition Research*. Adelaide: NCRC.

—— (1992) *Collaborative Language Learning and Teaching*. Cambridge: Cambridge University Press.

Nunan, D. (1993) *Introducing Discourse Analysis*. London: Penguin.

—— (1996) *Academic Writing for Nursing Students*. Hong Kong: The English Centre. University of Hong Kong.

Pica, T. (1985) 'The selective impact of classroom instruction on second language acquisition'. *Applied Linguistics* 6/3: 214–22.

Pienemann, M. and Johnston, M. (1987) 'Factors influencing the development of language proficiency' in Nunan (1987).

Rutherford, W. (1987) *Second Language Grammar: Teaching and Learning*. London: Longman.

Wajnryb, R. (1990) *Grammar Dictation*. Oxford: Oxford University Press.

Woods, E. (1995) *Introducing Grammar*. London: Penguin.

Chapter 12

Anne Burns

GENRE-BASED APPROACHES TO WRITING AND BEGINNING ADULT ESL LEARNERS

Introduction

COMMUNICATIVE LANGUAGE TEACHING (CLT) HAS played its part in revolutionising narrowly conceived theories of language learning and most language teachers would say they no longer equate the learning of a second language with the learning of traditional grammar. At the same time, CLT has given rise to a sometimes confusing array of methodologies, some of which claim to be 'the method' by which second languages will be acquired and all of which call themselves 'communicative'. This has often led to a state of affairs in the language classroom which seems to derive much of its pedagogical base from intuition.

More and more, researchers and educators have begun to question some of the assumptions implicit in communicative approaches to second-language teaching which have failed to take into account a well-formulated theory of language. Cope (1989) has argued that what is needed is an 'authoritative' pedagogy for the 1990s which will replace what he terms the 'progressive' curriculum which has existed since the mid-1970s. Because of its discovery learning, ego-centred base, progressive ESL pedagogy has failed to make explicit to learners the knowledge they need to gain access to socially powerful forms of language. It has emphasised inquiry learning, process and naturalism but has neglected to offer learners systematic explanations of how language functions in various social contexts.

In recent years much attention has been given to socially based theories of language and in Australia work drawing on systemic linguistics and notions of genre and register developed by Michael Halliday (e.g. Halliday 1985; Halliday and Hasan 1985) has provided a model for explaining language in relation to the context in which it is used, while at the same time taking into account language at the levels of whole text. I would also argue that systemic-functional approaches to language learning and teaching fit well with Communicative Language Teaching, as they provide teachers and learners with a means of exploring language use within a framework of cultural and social purpose.

Although genre-based language theories have application to both spoken and written language, much of the work done in educational settings has related to literacy development in the schools context (Martin and Rothery 1980, 1981; Martin 1985). The Adult Migrant Education Program (AMEP) Literacy Project organised throughout the National Centre for English Language Teaching and Research (NCELTR) described by Hammond (1989) has drawn on this work as well as on work done by the Sydney Metropolitan East Disadvantaged Schools Program (Callaghan and Rothery 1988).

The NCELTR Literacy Project: a genre-based approach

As one of the teachers involved in the Project, I was particularly interested in investigating how genre-based approaches could be applied to adult second-language learners at the early stages of learning. Typically in beginning ESL classes, reading and writing are consigned to second place and the focus is on the development of speaking and listening. In addition, assumptions are frequently made that beginning learners are unable or not ready to cope with the development of reading and writing in English, even though there is a frequent reliance on written materials to support spoken language development. Teachers sometimes maintain that learners do not have well-developed skills in first-language literacy and therefore it will be difficult to provide instruction in a second language where oral skills are almost non-existent also. This may be true, but many beginning learners do have well-developed literacy skills in first language and those who do not will generally wish to acquire them in English.

I would argue that these beliefs prevent learners from gaining access to opportunities to develop their literacy skills in second language and from understanding and responding to the written texts which will be of value to them in furthering their learning and in extending their ability to cope with a range of tasks common in the wider community, many of which depend on the ability to read and write.

In the schools context the range of genres dealt with in the classroom is fairly restricted, as they will be those which are pedagogical in their purpose and powerful within the context of the school curriculum. In the adult context the choice is more open-ended, as texts will be drawn from a larger number of social, vocational and work-related genres. At present, teachers working with beginning adult ESL learners have few guidelines to direct them to appropriate texts. This has meant that teachers involved in the NCELTR Literacy Project have, to a certain extent, become classroom researchers trying out a variety of genres based on needs expressed by their learners, to discover which are appropriate and relevant at different stages of learning.

Beginning learners and a genre-based approach

Within the group of Literacy Project participants was one teacher who was working on a class for beginning learners. Because part of the participants' involvement in the project was the recording of classroom interaction and the documenting of any written texts used, she agreed that I would work collaboratively with her, collecting and recording the classroom data as she taught the class. The 19 learners were all within their first year of settlement as permanent immigrants to Australia and had all been rated as less than 1.0 on a seven-point oral rating scale (AMES, Speaking Proficiency Descriptions, Brindley 1979). Twelve of them had completed high school and, of these, six had some post-high school education. Of the others, two had primary school education only, while six had received varying levels of high school education. They came from a wide variety of first-language backgrounds, some of which used non-Roman script.

One of the genres identified as important by the learners, in consultation with the teacher, was job applications, and the writing of a letter of application was used by the teacher to structure a unit of work. During the theoretical input sessions at the beginning of the project, Jennifer Hammond had proposed a teaching-learning cycle (Callaghan and Rothery 1988), an adaptation of which (Hammond 1990) is presented in Figure 12.1 below, which could be used to inform the planning of classroom activities.

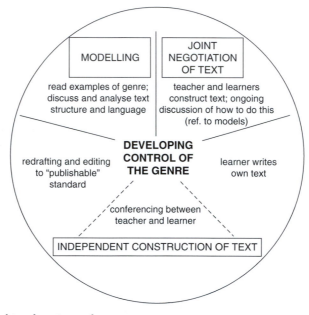

Figure 12.1 The teaching–learning cycle
Source: Hammond (1990)

This cycle incorporates different classroom activities which move the learners through various spoken and written tasks related to the genre being taught. The teacher can begin the cycle at any point, but for genres being taught for the first time it is preferable for the teacher to work through all stages. For this particular class, the teacher decided to work in the following sequence of stages:

1   Modelling
2   Joint Negotiation of Text
3   Independent Construction.

Modelling involved discussion of the cultural and social purpose of the genre and the sharing of experience within that context, followed by examples of a model text. At this point the teacher and learners discussed the staging of the text and the distinctive language features which realised the text. The stage *Joint Negotiation* involved the teacher and learners in a joint construction of a text in the same genre, followed by the joint construction of another text by the learners working in groups. The final stage, *Independent Construction*, comprised the teacher and learners working together to discuss and revise the group's jointly constructed texts and the learners' construction of their own independent texts.

Putting theory into practice

The rest of this paper describes part of a lesson which focuses on the stage where the teacher gave a presentation of a model and the learners followed up with joint construction of a similar text. At the beginning of the lesson, the teacher and learners again discussed a model job-application letter which had been presented to them the previous day:

Text 1: Model job application letter

11 Cotten Avenue
Kensington
NSW 2033
7th December 1989

The Personnel Officer
Elfex Ltd
High Street
North Ryde
NSW 2113

Dear Sir or Madam

Re: Receptionist's Job

I am writing for the job of receptionist advertised in The Sydney Morning Herald today.
I have worked as a receptionist for three years in a dentist's consultancy and I am very experienced in answering the telephone, writing letters and preparing accounts.
I am 20 years old and I have my Higher School Certificate. I speak and write fluent English and Greek and consider myself a most suitable candidate for the job.
I have enclosed a reference from my last job. Please contact me at home on 370 2915 any time in the evening.

Yours sincerely
(Signature)

The teacher's aim was to help the learners develop a metalanguage to describe the schematic structure of this text, which would assist them during the joint construction activity which was to follow. The following extract from the classroom illustrates how this was done:

Classroom transcript 1

T: All right, have a look at the letter we wrote together yesterday. In fact I'm going to read it to you so that we can recall what we did. At the top right hand corner we put the . . .?

LL: Address . . . address . . . date.

T: Address . . . OK and date. Then on the left underneath we put . . .?

L: Who . . . and address.

T: OK . . . to whom and the address. Then 'Dear Sir or Madam'. Why did we put 'Sir or Madam'?

L: Because I don't know man or woman.

T: You don't know if it is a man or a woman. 'Re: Receptionist's job'. What does 're' mean?

L: About . . . about . . .

T: 'I am writing to apply for the job of the receptionist advertised in The Sydney Morning Herald today.' So the first thing you should say in the letter is what the letter is about. 'I'm writing to apply for the job. I have worked as a receptionist for three years in a dentist's consultancy and I am very experienced in answering the phone, writing letters and preparing accounts. So, the second part, what is that . . .?

L: Experience . . .

T: Right. Two is the experience (writing on board next to number 2). What was one? What would you put for one?

LL: (*Unintelligible*)

T: What is the first thing in the letter? 'I am writing . . .'?

L: Address?

LL: No . . . no . . .

T: 'I am writing to apply . . .' What could we put there?

L: The problem . . .

T: Not a problem . . .

L: No . . . information

LL: No . . . about me . . .

T: The main information in the letter . . . OK? (writes on board next to number 1).

As can be seen from this extract, the teacher builds up a description of the schematic staging of the text by eliciting from the learners metalinguistic labels, which they can draw up to guide their own construction of a similar letter and to increase their awareness of the text as an object of study. Although the descriptions of the staging may not be very sophisticated at this level of language proficiency, they provide a guiding framework which is accessible to the learners. The result was the following description of the schematic structure:

Text 2: Schematic structure of job application letter

1   Address
2   Date
3   Who to and address
4   Dear
5   Re (about)
6   Main Information
7   Experience
8   About me (relevant to job)
9   Ending
10   Reference
11   Contact
12   Yours sincerely
13   Signature.

The teacher followed this by discussing with the learners some of the distinctive features of the text, such as the predominant use of the present tense, the focus on an individual participant and the use of primarily 'being' and 'having' clauses. At the end of this segment of the lesson, the learners were asked to construct their own letters in response to Commonwealth Employment Service (CES) advertisements, which had also been read and discussed in a previous lesson. Each group was given a sample advertisement (see Text 3 below) and asked to choose a scribe who would record the text as it was produced. The account which follows described how one group of three learners went about constructing their text.

The group was composed of three female learners; Katia, who was Chilean; Zorka, who was Yugoslav; and Susanna, a Czech. All three were in their 20s and had post-high school education, two having been nurses and one a teacher in her own country. They had all indicated that job-seeking was a priority for them and were highly motivated to improve their language skills so that they could eventually find employment. Susanna was nominated to scribe the jointly negotiated text and what she wrote was closely monitored by the two other members of the group. The letter they wrote was in response to the following advertisement:

Text 3: CES job advertisement

Mechanic	6052–a/531 kcs
Woolloomooloo	Motor repairs
General Repair Work on Jaguars	
8 a.m. – 5 p.m.	
$Award – Negotiable	
Age: 25+	
Tradesman Mechanic	
Exp. On Jaguars	

Despite their limited proficiency in English, the group employed a wide range of strategies during the joint construction activity. The following extract illustrates how they collaborated to produce their text:

Classroom transcript 2

Su: I am writing to apply . . . (writing)
Ka: Of the job . . .
Zo: Excuse me
Su: About the job . . .
Zo: Of ? Of the job?
Su: About
Ka: About . . . about . . . of . . . of . . .
Zo: No . . . for the . . . for the job
Su: For the job . . . (writing)
Zo: Of . . .
Ka: Motor mechanic

(Susanna writes, then reads aloud)

Su: I am writing to apply for the job . . . (compares with model) in the CES today . . .
Ka: In the service station . . . in the newspaper . . . Spanish . . . newspaper

Su: Oh (laughs) . . . (looks at job advertisement) . . . In the CES . . . C . . . (writes)
Ka: (watches as Susanna writes) C . . . E . . . S . . .

This extract illustrates how the learners:

- referred to the model
- transferred language from the model to the situational context of their own text
- offered suggestions for constructing the text
- collaborated to produce what they believed to be correct versions of the text
- monitored what was being written
- used the model to check their version of the text
- read aloud to 'try out' the text on each other
- used each other as resources for writing
- exchanged cross-cultural information about the social context of the genre.

The final version of the letter by this group of learners is reproduced below and is representative of similar texts completed by other groups in the class during this activity.

Text 4: Jointly negotiated letter of application

It can be observed that the learners have drawn upon the model provided by the teacher to structure the text appropriately in terms of layout and overall presentation. In addition they have used appropriate schematic staging, with the heading and statement of general purpose coming as an introduction, followed by accounts of previous experience, qualifications and personal details. They have also written a suitable conclusion which refers to the reference and includes a contact number.

Although these learners are at the beginning stage in their second-language development, they have been able to produce a fairly effective text approximating the genre, 'letter of job application'. I believe that this was made possible because the approach taken here, based on systemic linguistics and the notions of genre and register, provides an explicit account of the schematic structure, organisation and language features of the genre upon which they were focusing.

Even at early stages in second-language learning, learners can, and must, be assisted to begin the process of acquiring and extending skills in reading and writing. As there is no reason to suppose that written language acquisition in a second language cannot be developmental in the same way that spoken language acquisition is generally agreed to be, it is vital that in a technologically oriented and highly literate society, adult learners are given instruction in written language as early as possible and in a principled way. A genre-based approach provides them with learning activities presented within a social contextual framework, which encourage them to focus on language and which assist them to become more independent and analytical learners.

Note

I am grateful to the other participants in the NCELTR Literacy Project and in particular to Jenny Hammond and Eileen Lustig for their advice and contributions to the writing of this paper.

References

Brindley, G. (1979) *The Assessment of Speaking Proficiency Through the Oral Interview*. Sydney: AMES.

Callaghan, M. and Rothery, J. (1988) *Teaching Factual Writing: A Genre Based Approach*. Report of the DSP Literacy Project, Metropolitan East Region. Sydney: NSW School Education Department.

Cope, W. (1989) *A historical background to current curriculum changes and the shift to genre*. Presentation at the First LERN Conference, Sydney.

Halliday, M.A.K. (1985) *An Introduction to Functional Grammar*. London: Edward Arnold.

Halliday, M.A.K. and Hasan, R. (1985) *Language, context and text: Aspects of language in a social semiotic perspective*. Geelong, Victoria: Deakin University Press.

Hammond, J. (1989) 'The NCELTR Literacy Project.' *Prospect* 5, 1: 23–30.

—— (1990) *Collaborating in Literacy Teaching and Research*. Paper presented at 26th Annual TESOL Convention, San Francisco.

Martin, J.R. (1985) *Factual Writing: Exploring and Challenging Social Reality*. Geelong, Victoria: Deakin University Press.

Martin, J.R. and Rothery, J. (1980) *Writing Project, Report No. 1, Working Papers in Linguistics No. 1*. University of Sydney: Department of Linguistics.

—— (1981) *Writing Project, Report No. 2, Working Papers in Linguistics No. 2*. University of Sydney: Department of Linguistics.

Chapter 13

A. Suresh Canagarajah

CRITICAL ETHNOGRAPHY OF A SRI LANKAN CLASSROOM: AMBIGUITIES IN STUDENT OPPOSITION TO REPRODUCTION THROUGH ESOL

Introduction

THIS CHAPTER ARGUES THAT THE way in which domination is experienced and oppositional tendencies are formed in classroom life has to be observed closely rather than conceived abstractly. This ethnographic study of 22 tertiary-level Tamil students following a mandatory English for general purposes (EGP) course reveals that whereas the lived culture displays opposition to the alienating discourses inscribed in a U.S. textbook, the students affirm in their more conscious statements before and after the course their strong motivation to study ESOL. Interpreting this contradiction as reflecting the conflict students face between cultural integrity, on the one hand, and socioeconomic mobility, on the other, the study explains how students' desire for learning only grammar in a product-oriented manner enables them to be somewhat detached from cultural alienation while being sufficiently examination oriented to pass the course and fulfill a socioeconomic necessity. However, this two-pronged strategy is an ideologically limiting oppositional behavior that contains elements of accommodation as well as resistance and unwittingly leads students to participate in their own domination.

The recent introduction of poststructuralist perspectives on language and radical theories of schooling that view language teaching as a political act is a long-awaited development in TESOL. Such theories enjoy much currency in L1 circles, almost becoming the orthodoxy in areas like composition teaching, with words like *discourse* and *empowerment* becoming clichéd and posing the danger that they might have lost their critical edge. TESOL, on the other hand, while being a far more controversial activity, has managed to see itself as safely "apolitical" due to its positivistic preoccupation with methods and techniques.

In recent issues of the *TESOL Quarterly*, scholars such as Pennycook (1989) and Peirce (1989) have deconstructed dominant methods and the idea of method itself in order to expose the ideologies that inform TESOL. Though their papers perform a pioneering function, the force with which they are compelled to present their theses also involves some simplification. Whereas Pennycook's delineation of ideological domination through TESOL appears overdetermined and pessimistic, Peirce's characterization of the possibilities of pedagogical resistance appears too volitionist and romantic. We should now turn to the sober task of analyzing the complexities of domination and resistance as they are played out in ESOL classrooms and the confusing manner in which they are often interconnected.

Pennycook (1989) is generally convincing when, after a detailed analysis of the socially constructed nature of the concept of method, he asserts, "The power of the Western male academy in defining and prescribing concepts . . . plays an important role in maintaining inequities between, on the one hand, predominantly male academics and, on the other, female teachers and language classrooms on the international power periphery" (p. 612). This scenario is so true that, ironically, even pedagogies of resistance (of those like Pennycook and Peirce) have to reach us in the periphery from the West. However, in stretching the effects of the political economy of textbook publishing and research at the macrolevel to language classrooms, Pennycook is making too wide a leap – especially because his paper does not focus on classroom realities. What Pennycook overlooks in the process is that the classroom is a site of diverse discourses and cultures represented by the varying backgrounds of teachers and students such that the effects of domination cannot be blindly predicted. Such classroom cultures mediate the concepts defined and prescribed by the Western academy as they reach the periphery. It is possible that various modes of opposition are sparked during this encounter. Although Pennycook himself eventually exhorts teachers and academics to envision a more democratic social environment, this will not be possible if a space is not created for such resistance by acknowledging the relative *autonomy* of the school from other social institutions and processes. Through this term, Henry Giroux (1983) posits that the different social institutions and cultural sites "are governed by complex ideological properties that often generate contradictions both within and between them" (p. 102), that a specific institution like the school is not ruled inexorably by the interests of the state and economy, although necessarily influenced by them. Giroux (1983) in fact criticizes reproductive perspectives of schooling, such as those of Althusser (1971), Bowles and Gintis (1976), and Bourdieu and Passeron (1977) for deterministically conceiving the school as serving to inculcate only the culture, ideologies, and social relations necessary to build and sustain the status quo.

If Pennycook has to attend the noun in the term *relative autonomy*, Peirce has to note the adjective. That is, the attitudes, needs, and desires of minority communities and students are only partially free from the structures of domination in the larger social system. Hence, whereas Peirce (1989) makes a powerful case for how 'the teaching of English can open up possibilities for students by helping them to explore what might be *desirable*, as well as "appropriate," uses of English' (p. 401), she assumes too much in considering "People's" English as what will be unanimously desired by the "minority" students of South Africa. This is not to slight the importance of developing such pedagogies of resistance, that is, politically conscious approaches to learning/teaching which critically interrogate the oppressive tendencies behind the existing content and forms of knowledge and classroom relations to fashion a more liberating educational context that would lead to student empowerment and social transformation (see Giroux, 1983). They are certainly a pressing concern in TESOL and a much needed corrective to deterministic theories of schooling. However, with remarkable balance, Giroux (1983) also criticizes one-sided pedagogies of resistance for "not giving enough attention to the issue of how domination reaches into the structure of personality itself" (p. 106). Minority students may then display a complex range of attitudes towards domination with a mixture of oppositional and accommodative tendencies which have to be critically examined.

Pennycook and Peirce are unable to attend to the complexities of the classroom culture in the face of domination because their papers are broadly theoretical, focus on the politics of TESOL-related macrostructures, and only assume implications for language classrooms rather than reporting empirical observations of the classroom itself for how domination is experienced and oppositional tendencies are formed there. We can understand the "ambiguous areas" (Giroux, 1983, p. 109) of student response, where a confusing range of accommodative and oppositional tendencies are displayed, only if we take a closer look at the day-to-day functioning of the classroom and the lived culture of the students. It is by doing so that we can attain a realistic understanding of the challenges as well as the possibilities for a pedagogy of resistance in TESOL. The objective of this chapter is not to outline one more pedagogy of resistance, but to interrogate the range of behaviors students display in the face of domination – the awareness of which should precede and inform any development of such pedagogies. The ethnographic study below of an ESOL classroom in Sri Lanka creatively complicates the perspectives on domination and resistance presented by Pennycook and Peirce.

Contextualizing the study

Ever since the British colonial power brought the whole island of (then) Ceylon under its control in 1796 and instituted English education to create a supportive lower administrative work force, English has functioned as a valued linguistic capital over the local Sinhala and Tamil languages to provide socioeconomic advantages for native Lankans. Although since 1956 (8 years after independence), "leftist" governments have professed to raise the status of Sinhala (and, to a limited extent, Tamil), it is the English-speaking bilinguals who have dominated the professions and social hierarchy. On the other hand, the democratization or popularization of English promised by "rightist" governments has only amounted to providing limited mobility into lower-middle-class rungs for aspirants whose newly acquired English is marked as a nonprestige "sub-standard Sri Lankan English" (see Kandiah, 1979). These developments have historically disgruntled the monolingual majority to make them perceive English as a double-edged weapon that frustrates both those who desire it as well as those who neglect it (Kandiah, 1984). Similarly, in the Tamil society, whereas the emergent militant nationalism has unleashed a Tamil-only and even "pure Tamil" movement, such parallel developments as the exodus to the West or the cosmopolitan capital as economic and political refuges have bolstered English to assure the dominance of English bilinguals and to attract monolinguals.

As for English language teaching, the teachers, administrators, and general public in Sri Lanka agree that English language teaching is a "colossal failure" (de Souza, 1969, p. 18) considering the vast resources expended on this enterprise by the state and Western cultural agencies. Though all identify the problem as one of student motivation, they differ as to why students are unmotivated. Hanson-Smith (1984), a U.S. TESOL consultant, and Goonetilleke (1983), a local professor of English, fault the educational system. In the university, for instance, they perceive that the requirements for English are not stringent enough to motivate students to take the subject as seriously as other subjects. Both, however, are in agreement that English does a world of good for Sri Lankan students: "English is learned not primarily to communicate with other Lankans . . . but to converse with the world at large – and not just the world of technology and machines, but also of dreams, aspirations and ideals" (Hanson-Smith, 1984, p. 30). Because Kandiah (1984), on the other hand, is of the view that the dreams encouraged by English are illusory (as English learning does not challenge but in fact perpetuates inequality) and its ideals are suspected by students of resulting in cultural deracination, he sees the problem of motivation differently: "[The] reasons why they lack this motivation are socioeconomic-political" (p. 132). The present study developed as an attempt to arbitrate between these divergent approaches to the problems of motivation with empirical data because the papers of the above scholars were largely impressionistic and simply imputed to students attitudes neither systematically observed nor elicited.

Method

The methodological orientation and fieldwork techniques developed by ethnography enable us to systematically study the students' own point of view of English language teaching in its natural context. Though ethnography is noted for its intensive, detailed focus on the local, contextualized, and concrete, the challenge in this study is to analyze how the attitudes formed by students in daily classroom life are impinged upon by the more abstract sociopolitical forces outside the walls of the classroom. However, current ethnography is taking up the challenge of "how to represent the embedding of richly described local cultural worlds in larger impersonal systems of political economy" (Marcus and Fischer, 1986, p. 84). This new orientation in the fieldwork and writing of ethnography is inspired by a more complex, politicized view of culture in both anthropology and political economy. Such developments account for a small but growing body of ethnographic literature that looks at the culture of classrooms and student communities in relation to social conflict and political domination (see Bourdieu and Passeron, 1977; Ogbu, 1986; Weis, 1985; Willis, 1977).

In order to conduct such politically motivated ethnography, we have to go beyond the dominant *descriptive ethnography* that is practiced today in TESOL circles (see, e.g., Benson, 1989) and theorized in definitive terms for TESOL practitioners by Watson-Gegeo (1988). What we need in its place is a *critical ethnography* – an ideologically sensitive orientation to the study of culture that can penetrate the noncommittal objectivity and scientism encouraged by the positivistic empirical attitude behind descriptive ethnography and can demystify the interests served by particular cultures to unravel their relation to issues of power (see Marcus and Fisher, 1986). Willis (1978), whose 1977 study of working-class black students in an urban British school is a pioneering and sophisticated example of this orientation, defines the project of critical ethnography thus:

> We must interrogate cultures, ask what are the missing questions they answer, probe the invisible grid of context, inquire what unsaid propositions are assumed to the invisible and surprising external forms of cultural life. If we can supply the premises, dynamics, logical relations of responses which look quite untheoretical and lived out "merely" as cultures, we will uncover a cultural politics. (p. 18)

Practicing such a committed, value-laden ethnography does not mean that we can ignore Watson-Gegeo's (1988) warning that "true ethnographic work is systematic, detailed and rigorous, rather than anecdotal or impressionistic" (p. 588). Hence, an intensive participant observation of the ESOL class I taught 6 hr/week was carried out for an academic year (November 1990 to July 1991). Though it is possible that my dual roles as teacher and researcher could create certain tensions (as could be expected in any observation by a participant), my teaching also created certain advantages which I would have lacked as a detached observer. My daily interaction with the students in negotiating meanings through English and participating in the students' successes and failures, with the attendant need to revise my own teaching strategy, provided a vantage point to their perspectives. Moreover,

I enjoyed natural access to the daily exercises and notes of the students and the record of their attendance without having to foreground my role as researcher. As the teaching progressed, I stumbled into other naturalistic data that provided insights into students' own point of view of the course, such as the comments students had scribbled during class time in the margins of the textbook (which, due to frequent losses, was distributed before each class and collected at the end).

To add a chronological dimension to the study, I situated the other methods of data collection at significant points in the progression of the course. During the first week of classes, I conducted a free recall procedure, asking the students to jot down their impressions of English. I also gave a detailed questionnaire covering their social and linguistic background to be completed at home. At the end of the course, but before their final examination, I conducted an oral interview with the students in my office to analyze their responses to the course, textbook, and learning English in general. Though I invited the students for a 15-min interview, eventually each interview ranged from 70 to 90 min. Because some students preferred to converse with me in the company of another classmate, I permitted them to meet me in pairs. Even then, 7 students, all females, failed to turn up – probably reflecting the taboo on close interpersonal relations between the sexes in Tamil society. The interview, like the questionnaire, was in Tamil so that students could express themselves freely. (Such data is presented below, in translation, unless otherwise stated. The original Tamil is cited only when discursively significant.)

The questionnaire and the interview modules were constructed in such manner as to enable cross-checking of students' opinions. In the questionnaire, the first part surveyed students' educational backgrounds and exposure to English. The second part surveyed the educational and socioeconomic background of the parents. The third part provided a set of true/false statements to test more obliquely students' attitudes toward the use of English. The final part contained open-ended questions that further sampled their attitudes, allowing comparison of these with their previous statements. Though the final interview was prestructured, I shifted topic freely according to the flow of conversation. Questions 1–3 queried the attitude of the students towards English in relation to their other courses; Questions 4–7 checked their response to the organization and cultural content of the textbook; 8 and 9 sampled the effects of English learning on their thinking and identity; 10–12 invited a critique of the pedagogy and curriculum; 13–15 explored their use of English outside the class; and 16–18 solicited their recommendations for the improvement of the course. Some of the similar questions in the interview then enabled me to compare the motivation and attitudes of the students with their opinions stated in the questionnaire in the beginning of the course. The other modes of data collection, too, enabled me to authenticate the data more effectively through triangulation (see Denzin, 1970). For instance, the lived culture of the students (as recorded in my field notes and students' comments in the textbook) was at odds with their stated opinions in the interview and questionnaire, compelling me to reconstruct more complex hypotheses to explain their attitudes.

The course

The class that I observed consisted of 22 first-year students in the arts and humanities at the University of Jaffna. The ESOL course is mandatory for all students of the faculty of arts. A pass is required in ESOL to qualify for admission to the second year. For eligibility to specialize in a specific subject from the second year onwards, students are required to score at least a B on the ESOL exam in the first sitting. It is from the second year that English teaching is structured into English for specific purposes (ESP), catering to the different subject specialties. The first-year course is based on English for general purposes (EGP), providing practice in all four skills.

Because the course is structured around a core text, it is necessary to discuss the organization of *American Kernel Lessons (AKL): Intermediate* (O'Neill, Kingbury, Yeadon, and Cornelius, 1978). We have to remember that such prepackaged material, which comes with a teachers' manual, testing kit, and audiotapes for listening comprehension, represents "a direct assault on the traditional role of the teacher as an intellectual whose function is to conceptualize, design and implement learning experiences suited to the specificity and needs of a particular classroom experience" (Aronowitz and Giroux, 1985, p. 149). Although teachers in the University of Jaffna realize these problems, the limitations of time, funds, stationery, and printing facilities in war-torn Jaffna eventually drive them to use texts such as *AKL* which have been amply gifted by Western agencies such as the Asia Foundation. If existing books become dated, teachers have to simply wait for the next consignment of material.

As the title implies, the text is targeted towards intermediate-level students and focuses on the tenses, using eclectic methods organized around a predominantly situational approach (see Richards and Rodgers, 1986). Each unit contains five parts. Part A introduces the grammatical item for that unit through a set of "situations," accompanied by visuals. Part B, labeled Formation and Manipulation, introduces the grammatical item more overtly and provides pattern practice. Part C is a serialized detective story that introduces new vocabulary in addition to providing practice in reading/listening comprehension. Part D presents a conversation for role playing, whereas the final part contains guided composition. The last two parts also provide grammar revision exercises. Though grammar is presented overtly in some sections, in most others, students are encouraged to formulate their own hypotheses inductively through active use of the language in specific skills.

It is also necessary to analyze the ideologies that structure the text in order to place in context the attitudes and responses of the students to the course. What stands out in the note, "To the Student and Teacher," in the beginning of the text is the concern with providing adequate "practice" so that students will "progress" in the "fundamentals of English" which intermediate students "still cannot seem to use correctly, easily and as automatically as they would like" (O'Neill *et al.*, 1978, p. vi). The language echoes behaviorism and assumes that with sufficient drill, students can be made to display habit-oriented automatic responses. Furthermore, the fundamentals of English are considered autonomous, value-free grammatical structures (in the fashion of U.S. structuralism), ignoring the culture and ideologies that inform the language or the textbook. The students themselves are isolated from their social context, and there is no consideration of how their own linguistic and cultural backgrounds can affect or enhance their learning. In its concern with correctness (which, of course, is based on standard U.S. English rather than on the Englishes students bring with them), the textbook empowers the teacher as the sole authority in the classroom to regulate, discipline, and arbitrate the learning process. Such assumptions amount to what Giroux (1983) has identified as instrumental ideology (p. 209). Though *AKL* acknowledges the need to make learning an "enjoyable experience" and also provides opportunities for collaborative pair work, these attempts provide only occasional relief from the largely positivistic pedagogy.

In fairness to *AKL*, we have to note that certain sections are influenced by the notion of communicative competence with advice to students that "the situations themselves are more important than isolated words" (O'Neill *et al.*, 1978, p. v). However, the interactions and the discourse employed in such situations assume an urbanized, technocratic, Western culture that is alien to the students. Even such simple speech activities as conversations are conducted in a strictly goal-oriented manner (see Unit 2d), whereas Tamil discourse values the "digression" and indirection typical of oral communities. The values that emerge through the situations are not hard to decipher, such as upward social mobility and consumerism (4d). The work ethic (12a) and routine of factory life (13a) are presented positively, whereas strikes and demonstrations (5a) and the lifestyle of blacks (in the story of Jane and her boyfriends) are not. The potential of the textbook to influence students with certain dominant values of U.S. society is subtly effective because *AKL* disarms its users by presenting language learning as a value-free, instrumental activity.

The class

The class consisted of 13 female and 9 male native Tamil students, of whom 3 were Roman Catholics and the rest Hindus. These students had failed the initial placement test in English and fared among the worst among the new entrants for that academic year. They were enrolled in a range of subjects related to the humanities and social sciences besides the mandatory ESOL. A majority of these students were from rural communities and from the poorest economic groups. Except for 4 students whose parents were in clerical or teaching professions (thus earning the relatively decent sum of 1000 rupees, or US$25 a month!), the other parents did not have steady jobs or salaries. In the latter group, some were tenant farmers, and others were seasonal casual laborers. The families of the students had also had limited education. Only one student's parents had proceeded beyond Grade 10. The parents of 5 others had not completed an elementary school education.

Furthermore, the students came from backgrounds in which English held limited currency. Only 8 students said their parents had managed to study some elementary English in school. Of these, 3 reported that their parents might listen to English programs on the multilingual television or radio. Five reported that their parents could be expected to utter some English words if they encountered foreigners or if need arose in their workplace. None of them could read or write English. Considering the students themselves, although 18 had sat for the Grade 10 English language test, only 10 had managed to score a simple pass (i.e., a grade of 40%). Three students reported that they had read English newspapers/books or seen English films – although they could not remember the titles of any. Fourteen reported that they might occasionally switch on some English programs on radio or television. The same number said they might code-mix English with friends or when they needed a link language.

Contextualizing classroom life

Precourse determination

When the university reopened belatedly for the academic year, it was after much doubt as to whether it would continue to function at all because renewed hostilities between the Sinhala government and Tamil nationalists had brought life to a standstill in the Tamil region. Yet students trickled in from jungles where they had taken refuge from the fighting – in some cases, trekking hundreds of miles by foot. In a country where only a small percentage of all those who annually qualify for tertiary education do get admission, the students valued their university degrees sufficiently to turn up for classes. As a grim reminder of the violence and tension that would continue to loom behind their studies, government fighter jets screamed overhead and bombed the vicinity of the university while the students were taking the English placement test during the opening week of classes.

Despite these problems or because of them, students were highly motivated for studies (including English), as is evident in an initial questionnaire I gave them. Asked whether they wanted to study English at the university, all of the students replied in the affirmative. However, the intensity of the feelings that accompanied their motivation is conveyed through some of the other data in which students enjoyed more scope for free expression. Thiru wrote the following personal note at the end of his free recall procedure:

> It is difficult to study English in the village. And I am from Kaddaiparichchan in Mutur. There was no English from Grade 3 to 7. I lacked opportunities. But I *really* (extremely) *desire* learning English (Please don't reveal this to anybody else in the class: Here in Jaffna there are a lot of opportunities, and I am presently studying English from a private tutor also).

Students from remote villages profoundly regretted not having enjoyed opportunities to learn English earlier and admitted that it was belatedly that they had realized the need for the language. Some of the male students including Thiru caught me alone a couple of times in the first month (while I walked back to my office after class) to impress upon me their previous frustrations with the language and their present desire to master it in the university.

The reasons for learning English however seemed predominantly utilitarian. In the questionnaire, 76.1% stated "educational need" as their first preference (including 61.9% who considered this their sole choice). "Job prospects" was cited by 19.2%, and "social status" by 4.7%. "To travel abroad" was cited by none. But the categories students themselves proffered suggest motives that are more pragmatic or idealistic as they emerge through a relatively open-ended later question. Students needed English (a) because ESOL is mandatory in the university, 5.8%; (b) because a pass is required in the first-year test, 5.8%; (c) to pursue postgraduate studies, 5.8%; (d) to understand other cultures, 11.7%; (e) to interact with a wider group of people, 14.7%; (f) to gather more information, 20.8%; (g) to know an international language, 23.5%; (h) "to become a complete person," 11.7%. Although Motives a–c show a narrowly pragmatic view of education, Motives d–g are less so. And the final reason, which is the most idealistic stated, suggests that students are not always purely utilitarian in their perspective. Some, like Lathan, insisted, "Through English a student becomes a *mulu manithan* [i.e., a complete man]." In fact, when the question was reframed as "What are the disadvantages of being a Tamil monolingual?" students expressed a paralyzing sense of powerlessness in the face of diverse peoples and circumstances.

Such high notions as Lathan's about the functions of English are confirmed in the students' attitudes toward English as a language. Although students would be expected to resist English at a time of heightened linguistic nationalism and purism in the community with political leaders daily condemning English, students' attitudes were, on the contrary, quite positive. Except for one student (i.e., Supendran – whose remarkably consistent opposition will be discussed later), the rest disagreed with the statement "Studying English as a second language would create damage for Tamil language and culture." Similarly, for the more personalized variant of this statement, "What are the social/personal disadvantages that would occur to you by your use of English," all answered "none." Such a favorable attitude on the part of the students is partly explained by a phrase that kept recurring in their responses: English as a *pothu moli* (i.e, common language). It was evident that students were not using this synonymously with *sarvathesa moli* or *akila ulaka moli* (i.e., international language) with its usual connotations. When they used *pothu moli* in addition to the latter terms, they seemed to use it with the meaning that it was an "unmarked" language that transcended the specific cultures and ideologies of different nations. So Gnani stated, "Although it is the language of a particular nation, it is a common language for all people and nations."

Although the relatively more spontaneous impressions of the students in the free recall procedure largely confirm their positive attitudes toward English, they are also tinged with fears and inhibitions. Hence, though a majority of the students associated English with development, progress, learning, civilization, literacy, culture, social respect, and personality, one can also detect other comments which suggest that students are not unaware of the sociopsychological damage and politics of the language. Shanthi wrote:

> British mother tongue. We were forced to study it because of colonialism. If we have a knowledge of this language we can live in whichever country we want. Brings to mind the developed life of the white people. A language that everybody should know.

Though conflicting impressions are mixed in Shanthi's stream of consciousness, what is remarkable is that she remains detached from the negative features and fails to take a perspective on them. The fact that students are probably consciously rationalizing their fears or suppressing their inhibitions is evident from Ratnam's comments. He argued, "Since the dominance of English is uncontestable, the best strategy is to exploit its resources to develop our own language and culture."

Midcourse resistance

The inhibitions towards English which lay partly suppressed during the initial period of the course in the conscious responses of the students, came into relief in their largely unconscious lived culture as the course proceeded. It is evident from the record of daily attendance that students faced problems in the course. Although students recorded an impressive 94% daily turn out for most of the first 2 months, at the end of the second month, attendance fell to 50%. Students began to miss classes for the slightest reason: to write tutorials for another subject, to prepare for a test, to attend funerals of friends' relatives. At times intense fighting in the district or the imposition of curfew also affected attendance. But none of this deterred 90% of the students from attending from the eighth month as the final examination was approaching, demanding that past test papers be done and revision undertaken.

The comments, drawings, and paintings students had penned in the textbook are more subtle evidence of the flagging interest of students. Because students had written these during class time, this activity suggested that topics other than English grammar had preoccupied them while teaching was going on. Although students had appeared to be passively observing or listening to the teacher, as required by the instrumental pedagogy in the class, the glosses in the text suggest a very active underlife. Unknown to the teacher, students were communicating with each other or sometimes with themselves through these glosses. The glosses suggest the discourses and themes that seem to have interested the students more than those in the textbook. In one sense, these are the discourses which mediate for the students the situations, grammar, and language taught by the textbook. In another sense, these are students' counterdiscourses that challenge the textual language, values, and ideology. Hence, they deserve close examination.

Many of the glosses are inspired by the ongoing nationalist struggle for a separate Tamil state. For this reason, in Unit 1c, the picture of Fletcher (the protagonist in the detective story) as he is seated in a prison cell is modified in a couple of textbooks. He has been painted with a traditional *thilakam* (a mark on one's forehead symbolizing a Saiva identity), given a mustache and spectacles, and referred to below as *Thileepan* (i.e., the name of a popular Tamil resistance fighter who had fasted unto death protesting against the Indian "occupation" forces in 1987). Two police officers talking to each other after setting up a roadblock to arrest an escaping convict (in Unit 10c) have been referred to as LTTE and PLOTE – two rival Tamil militant groups. When Fred joins the army in Unit 25a, the guns in the background are labeled AK–47 and T–57 – the arms typically used by Tamil fighters. There are also refrains from Tamil resistance songs penned all over the textbook which talk about the domination of the Tamil nation and the need to resist.

Other glosses seem to seek cultural relevance from the situations and pictures. Jane and Susan are painted with a *thilakam* and *kondai* (i.e., a traditional hairdo) to resemble Tamil women. Some other characters are drawn with traditional dress to Tamilize them. Tamil proverbs and aphorisms comment on the moral of some of the situations presented in the textbook. Other situations are glossed by tides of films and refrains from cinema songs, reflecting the important place cinema occupies in Tamil popular culture. Bruce's success story, in Unit 4a, from a factory worker to a factory owner, accompanied by the purchase of a bigger car, bigger house, having another child, and eventually a second marriage is aptly satirized by romantic film titles at each stage of the development.

Romance and sex, which are glorified by university students, inform other glosses. Because these experiences are often associated with a liberal Western culture (different from the conservative Tamil ethos), most of these comments, interestingly, are written in English. Fletcher driving with Marilyn in Unit 14c is a target for many such comments. In one book Fletcher is presented as saying, "I love you darling." In another it is Marilyn who says, "My dear lover." Susan, whispering to Joe in a concert in Unit 9a, is made to say, "Love me," while Laura leaning towards Bruce says, "Kiss me." There are also comments through which students send messages to each other: "Meena loves Sugirthan." Ironically, though students find it difficult to produce correct sentences in transformation exercises and pattern practice, in these comments they produce fairly complex sentences which have not been taught in the class: "I love all of the girls beautiful in the Jaffna University." "Reader! I love you. Bleave me" has been replied to by another student: "I don't love you because I do not believe you. You are terrible man."

The sexual component gets expressed when the private parts of characters in the textbook are highlighted with ink. There are also different postures of the sex act drawn all over the book. Such drawing would create much sensation in a mixed class of students in a conservative society. However, it is impossible to avoid the impression that some of the drawings deliberately vulgarize sex. Perhaps they are aimed at insulting the English instructors, or the publishers of the textbook, or the U.S. characters represented.

While the cultural distance of the textbook from the discourses of the students is dramatized by these glosses, it intrudes more directly into the daily lessons to affect the learning process. Although the textbook expects teachers to use its visual aids to help students formulate interpretive schemata for comprehension passages, such exercises in fact end in frustration as the attempts of students are complicated by the cultural difference. After reading the first episode of the serialized story in which Fletcher, an ex-army officer, is presented in a federal penitentiary, I asked the students to reconstruct what they had heard with the help of the picture. (In the conversation below, reproduced from field notes, the contribution of the students was in Tamil):

(a)   Teacher: Where do you think Fletcher is? . . . Shanthi!
(b)   Shanthi: In the army barracks.

(c) Teacher: Army? What makes you say that?
(d) Shanthi: He is wearing a uniform.
(e) Teacher: Well . . . Indran?
(f) Indran: He is in the hospital. . . . He is seated on a bed.
(g) Teacher: But what about the bars? . . . Don't you see the bars? He is actually in prison.
(h) Shanthi: Okay, but he is wearing good clothes. He is wearing shoes.
(i) Indran: And he is said to be going to the library and having regular meals. . . . And he is seated alone in the room.
(j) Teacher: (Explains in detail the difference between prison life in Sri Lanka and the U.S.)

The students' image of prison life as overcrowded, dirty, and more repressive (based on Sri Lankan conditions) interferes with their interpretation. The other situations visually represented, such as an orchestra playing, air travel, department store shopping, and apartment living, also confused the students. Such cultural estrangement created an additional layer of problems to the linguistic ones students were already confronted with.

Other tensions in the course resulted from the styles of learning desired by the students. The students seemed uncomfortable with a collaborative approach to learning whenever it was encouraged. Because the textbook specified pairwork occasionally, and I myself wanted to create more linguistic interaction among students, I insisted that the desks be arranged in a circle. But before each class, the students rearranged the desks into a traditional lecture-room format, with the teacher's desk in front of the room and their own in horizontal rows. Thus, students minimized interaction among themselves and failed to take initiative in the flow of classroom discourse. As the conversation cited above suggests, typical interactions follow the features of traditional teacher-centered classroom discourse (see Mehan, 1985; Stubbs, 1976), in which the teacher regulates and dominates talk. Turn taking follows the tripartite Structure of Question (see Turn a above), Answer (Turn b), and Evaluation (Turn c); such sequences follow in c–d–e, e–f–g. Turns for students are assigned by the teacher (see Turns a and e); for each single turn by the student, the teacher takes two, thus dominating the quantity of talk. The questions asked are display questions for which the teacher already knows the answer. In a quite atypical move here, Shanthi and Indran attempt to contradict the teacher's explanation; significantly, these were not framed as questions but simply as casual asides. It was only Supendran who asked for clarifications or challenged my explanations more explicitly. For most of the time, the rest preferred to sit, pen in hand, and write down whatever was on the board or simply listen to the teacher's lecture (as in Turn j). Ironically, one of the glosses above an interactive pair-work exercise said, "This is a job for the jobless."

Accompanying this desire for teacher-centered learning, students made learning a product rather than process. Students expected to be provided with the abstract forms and rules of language deductively or prescriptively for them to store in memory rather than to inductively formulate the rules for themselves through active use of the language in communicative interactions. Disregarding activities, students demanded notes. Whenever charts or grammatical paradigms were presented, the students eagerly wrote them down. They demanded more written work rather than speech or listening exercises because they felt that they could retain it for personal study and revision before tests. My diary records much time taken in discussing the importance of "use rather than rules." But the slogan failed to create changes in their attitude. Gradually students noted my practice of reserving the 2–hr classes for activities and 1–hr slots for the more overtly grammar-oriented sections of the textbook and attended the latter while cutting the former.

Students also resisted the active use of English as a medium for instruction or interaction in the classroom. During the first week when I asked students to introduce themselves in English by making use of simple syntactic structures I had written on the board, they simply giggled and found it embarrassing to do so. Students responded in Tamil even though I used English for questions, commands, and explanations, whether in formal or informal situations. Thiru displayed the most paralyzing sense of inhibition. It was simply impossible for him to produce a single word of English from the textbook or by himself. The long moments of silence would become embarrassing as the class waited patiently for Thiru to open his mouth when his turn came to do an exercise or read a passage orally. Although Thiru was very voluble in class in Tamil about matters related to university policies and regulations, in English he was simply tongue-tied.

Much of the stress seemed to result from the implications of English for the identity and group solidarity of the students. A particularly trying time was the correction of pronunciation as required by the textbook. Because Tamil lacks syllable-initial fricatives, the students pronounced *he* and *she* as /ki/ and /si/. The discomfort of the students in my repeated attempts to correct such pronunciation was explained by their later comments that revealed their awareness of such pronunciation being identified as "nonstandard" Sri Lankan English. These students had been the target of insults by middle-class speakers of "educated" Sri Lankan English. Not only pronunciation but the very language was a class marker. Supendran said that he simply avoided contexts in which students (from "better backgrounds") used English with him because he felt that they were flaunting their knowledge of the language in order to make him look ignorant. English then provided unfavorable subject positions to such students, making them feel disadvantaged, helpless, inferior, and uneducated. Students also felt that the use of English for interactions would be interpreted by their peers as an attempt to discard their local rural identity and pass off as an anglicized bourgeois or even a foreigner. It was probably for this reason that in the questionnaire, although 50% stated that they would use English "with a foreigner who also knew Tamil," all except one rejected the possibility of using English "with a Tamil who also knew English."

The conflicts English created for the representation of their identity become more explicit in the conversation pieces students had to role-play in each unit. Students typically uttered their parts in a flat reading intonation when they were asked to dramatize the dialogue in front of the class. My model renditions with an eye for realism only increased their inhibition. Students said that it was "funny" or "unbecoming of themselves" to speak in such manner. It soon became apparent that the discourse behind these dialogues was itself so alien to these students that they had difficulty entering into the roles specified. One such conversation was between Joe and Susan in Unit 4d while they budgeted their weekly expenses: Joe's casual remark that he has to hold a party soon for 35 people in his office to celebrate his promotion irks Susan because of insufficient notice and the amount of additional expenses involved when they have just purchased a new house. When, as usual, students found it difficult to imaginatively enter into the situation, I tried to construct local situations where such dialogue could be expected to occur. Students however pointed out that the genre of "money talk" or "budgeting conversation" was alien to their peasant background. "We spend as we earn," according to one student, was their lifestyle. Even the consumerism, thrift, delayed gratification, and drive for social mobility assumed by the conversation turned out to be alien. It was not surprising then that such role-playing exercises were purely of academic interest to them and, therefore, nothing better could be employed for these other than the reading intonation for descriptive prose. Indran's notes in his notebook at the end of the class were a telling comment on his attitude to the exercise. He had simply jotted down Tamil synonyms for new lexical items like *adding, tradition*, and *promotion* and identified some examples of count/noncount structures which the unit was supposed to teach: "How many employees are at the bank? How much money did you spend last week?" Indran had simply filtered out the necessary grammatical and vocabulary items from the supposedly interesting conversation.

What the lived culture of the students suggests is a dual oppositional trend. On the one hand, they oppose the alien discourses behind the language and textbook. On the other hand, they oppose a process-oriented pedagogy and desire a product oriented one. Indran's notebook suggests that both trends could be connected: Seeing little possibility of relating what they learned to their sociocultural background, students saw little meaning for the course other than the formal, academic one of acting through the examination and satisfying the English requirements of the institution.

Postcourse contradiction

Although the final interview with the students soliciting their own impressions of the content and organization of the course confirmed some of the observations on their lived culture, it also contradicted many findings – at least at face value. Asked which subjects they had enjoyed most and which they had worked hardest in, students mentioned their different subjects of specialization for the former but unanimously cited English for the latter. When I pointed out the flagging attendance in English and contradicted their claim, I was confronted with a surprising piece of evidence. The majority of the students in the class had been going for private instruction in English outside the university. As Indran put it conclusively, "For no other subject in the university do we go for tutoring, thus spending additional time and money on it. The fact that we do this only for English proves our motivation to master the language." The students continued to affirm, as they had done at the beginning of the course, the need for English and the priority they had given to it.

The admission that students had sought help outside the class was potentially an indictment of the university ESOL course. I then began exploring what it was that the students were getting in their private instruction that they were not getting in the university. It appeared that the tutors were using Sri Lankan or Indian textbooks – if they used any at all. But it was not the cultural relevance that students seemed to value in these courses as much as the grammar instruction. In fact, the texts and pedagogy were overtly grammar oriented and were rarely contextualized. Tharma praised his tutor (using lexical borrowings from English): "He 'cleared' the 'grammar.'"

Other questions in the interview confirm the desire of the students for grammar-oriented instruction. When asked which section of the textbook they had enjoyed and which they had found useful (13 out of the 15 interviewed) replied that they found the grammar tables and exercises (Sections b and e) useful although they had variously enjoyed the serialized story, conversation, and listening sections. Some conflated these distinctions: Jeyanthi said that she enjoyed the grammar section "because it is useful for the test." Statements such as Jayanthi's revealed that the desire of the students to learn the rules of grammar prescriptively was related to an examination-oriented motivation. In fact, the final 3–hr written test featured mostly discrete-item questions on formal aspects. Later, asked specifically what the students had initially hoped to achieve through this course and the extent to which the course had fulfilled their expectations, Siva said, "I expected that the course would prepare me for the test . . . that is, cover the necessary grammar comprehensively." It was not surprising, then, when all eventually agreed that the course had failed to satisfy their expectations.

The recommendations of the students for a more effective ESOL course that would also successfully motivate Tamil students was quite predictable. Tharma argued that a more grammar-based textbook should replace *AKL*. Vilvan expounded, "Grammar should be given primacy and covered first since this is crucial for other areas like listening, reading, or speaking." Most students agreed that grammar has to be taught first before "wasting time" on skills and activities. Other recommendations also confirmed a product-oriented, examination-based motivation: "More notes should be provided . . . more homework should be given to retain grammar . . . allow textbooks to be taken home for personal study . . . teach more slowly . . . " Only a couple also added: "Provide more communicative tasks . . . get more culturally relevant textbooks."

Moving on to the attitudes of the students to the cultural content of the textbook, here again some observations on their lived culture were contradicted. Students did not perceive any threats stemming from the foreign culture. Some students disclosed that they had actually enjoyed learning about life in the U.S. In fact, because students failed to understand the force of my questions, I often had to reframe the questions to highlight the issue of the damage U.S. values and lifestyle could do to their subjectivity or culture. When I pointed to instances where details of people, places, and situations had confused them, students agreed that these had created some confusion especially at the beginning of the course but added that these difficulties were outweighed by the new and interesting information that they could gather from the textbook. They went on to state that *AKL* was "interesting," although not "useful" – perhaps from the examination point of view.

Discussing next their impressions of U.S. society, they listed a variety of both positive and negative features with typical academic poise. Although they observed the individual freedom, technological development, comfort, and liberal relationship between the sexes, they also stressed the subtle forms of racism, social inequality, "decadence," and imperialism (although it was not clear where in the text they saw the last feature displayed). Asked how these had influenced their own values and behavior, students displayed a remarkable detachment towards this clash of cultures. Jeyanthi said, "We don't have to accept everything: We can take the good and leave out the bad." It has to be observed that the students' relaxed attitude toward U.S. culture (at least in their statements) might result from making culture, too, a product – something to be learnt for its information value and stored in memory.

Although the retrospective statements of most students are at tension with their lived culture, it was Supendran who displayed a remarkable consistency. Supendran, who came from a remote rural community and whose nonliterate parents lacked any formal education, entered the university relatively late after working as a teacher in his community. He did not go for private tutoring – partly due to lack of finances. Rather than being examination oriented or desiring grammar-based instruction, Supendran wanted English to equip him to serve his own community: "to enable me to help my village folk to draft official letters to institutions, to read documents we receive from the state, to understand foreign news broadcasts, to read labels on fertilizers and farm equipment." Therefore, Supendran was the only student who categorically stated "*AKL* has to go." He wanted a textbook and pedagogy that was not just communicative, but also based on local culture: "Rather than talking about apples, talk about mangoes; rather than talking about apartment houses, talk about village huts. Are we all emigrating to America? No! Some of us will continue to live here." Being the single student who consistently stated that English posed a cultural threat, he sought deep social relevance from the teaching and textbook.

Before concluding the story of our classroom life, it is necessary to provide at least sufficient information to enable a consideration of how my own subject positions could have contributed to the construction of student attitudes and classroom culture. Young (in my early 30s), male, "progressive," Christian, culturally Westernized, middle class, native Tamil, bilingual, director of English teaching at the university are the identities that I believe were most salient for the students. So students' insistence on the use of Tamil in the classroom, for example, is motivated by my being a bilingual Tamil. If there had been a native-English-speaking teacher, students would have been compelled to use English. Additionally, use of English with me would have been perceived to violate our Tamil in-group solidarity. (However, my class and cultural identities separate me from the rural poor and would likely have increased students' inhibitions in using their marked English.) Our common Tamil identity would likely have also forced students to sound more nationalistic, especially as the present communalist mood tends not to tolerate neutrality. In this context, however, their affirmation of English is daring. On the other hand, because I was in an institutionally powerful role, instances of opposition to English (as their falling attendance) are significant. The same identity, however, would have motivated students to affirm the language, textbook, and the course. (In a sense, then, my multiple subject positions seem to qualify each other.) Although the uniqueness of each teacher/researcher-student interaction should not be slighted in favor of the generalizability of this study, we have to note that almost all Sri Lankan ESOL teachers are Westernized, middle-class, bilingual, native Lankans like me.

Contextualizing student opposition

At face value, the findings of the study seem inconclusive, if not contradictory. On the one hand, students seemed to gradually lose motivation in the course, as it was most objectively displayed in their record of attendance. There is reason to believe that this drop in motivation was related to an oppositional response to the threats posed by the discourse inscribed in the language, pedagogy, and the textbook. At the very least, students were experiencing a tension or discomfort in the confrontation between the discourse they preferred and the discourses informing the ESOL course. But, on the other hand, students insisted that they worked hardest in English compared to all the other subjects (which is true because they had been attending private classes as well). They maintained, as they did in the beginning of the course, the importance of English and the high priority given to learning the language. They went further to insist that they enjoyed learning Western culture and using the U.S. textbook (although they did not find them useful from the examination point of view). In general, the oppositional attitude was manifested in the largely unreflected, untheorized lived culture of the students emerging from their glosses in the textbooks and my field notes; the receptive attitude emerges from the more conscious expression of their views in the questionnaires and interviews.

As a way of reconciling this tension, we have several options: We can suppress one set of data in favor of the other; we can judge the students as confused and contradicting themselves; or we can simply fault the methodology. Not seeing valid reasons to do any of this, I find it challenging to preserve both sets of data and consider how both attitudes of the students display a complex response to the learning of English. It appears that these dual attitudes simply dramatize the conflict students faced in the course between the threats of cultural alienation experienced intuitively or instinctively and the promises of a socioeconomic necessity acknowledged at a more conscious level. The students experienced discomfort in the face of the alien discourses, although they do not theorize about it. But this experience has to be juxtaposed with their awareness of the powerful discourses which glorify the role of English (such as those of policymakers Goonetilleke, 1983, and Hanson-Smith, 1984), the pressure from the educational system to display proficiency in English, the promise of social and economic advancement English holds, and (especially for Tamil students today) the uses of English as a buffer against Sinhala nationalism and passport for exodus as political or economic refugees abroad.

The grammar-based, product-oriented learning which students alternatively desired (as exemplified in the lived culture as well as their statements) is one way for them to reconcile this conflict. That is, grammar learning enabled the students to be detached from the language and the course, avoid active use of the language which could involve internalization of its discourses, and thereby continue their opposition to the reproductive tendencies of the course. At the same time, this strategy enabled them to maintain the minimal contact necessary with the language in order to acquire the rules of grammar – which in their view was the most efficient preparation for getting through the examination. This strategy while enabling them to preserve their cultural integrity (however tenuously) also enabled them to accommodate the institutional requirement of having to pass English and thus bid for the socioeconomic advantages associated with the language.

Although noting that grammar learning functions as a possible strategy to negotiate the conflicts students face in the ESOL classroom, we have to realize that there are significant historical and cultural reasons which motivate them to adopt this strategy. The popular demand for grammar among all Sri Lankan university students is attested to by the chairperson for English Language Teaching Centres in the country (R. Raheem, personal communication, September 28th, 1991). Students' desire to be simply given the abstract rules of the language by the teacher could be influenced by traditional styles of learning in Tamil society (or, for that matter, Sri Lankan society), which have been largely product oriented and teacher centered. Although it is hard to generalize about the different institutions of learning that have existed historically (such as *thinnai*, or "house front," and temple schools), it can be said that typically the teacher (always male) passed on his stock of received knowledge orally to the disciple at his feet (see Jeyasuriya, no date; Sirisena, 1969; Somasegaram, 1969). The disciples had to cultivate the art of listening meditatively and memorizing accurately the huge stock of information to be preserved without corruption. The reverence paid to the guru, as to the knowledge he transmitted, was almost religious in character. This tradition is directly inherited by private institutes in contemporary Tamil society, enjoying immense popularity among parents and students (and pitted by my own students as a corrective to the university ESOL course), which intensively prepare passive students for competitive examinations.

Moreover, traditional descriptions of language and pedagogies of language teaching display a penchant for prescriptive, deductive, and formalistic methods. Although the well-known Dravidian scholar Emeneau (1955) outlines the fundamental influence of Hindu linguistic tradition on Western descriptive linguistics, he also notes: "Intellectual thoroughness and an urge toward ratiocination, intellection, and learned classification for their own sakes should surely be recognized as characteristic of the Hindu higher culture. . . . They become grammarians, it would seem, for grammar's sake" (pp. 145–146). Similarly, as late as the colonial period, the teaching of local languages to European administrators was primarily based on studying and memorizing learned grammatical treatises (see Wickramasuriya, 1981).

Anthropological approaches based on a narrowly conceived egalitarianism would encourage us to fashion a method of language teaching that resembles the native tradition of a community (see, e.g., a description of the KEEP project in Watson-Gegeo, 1988). However, the grammar-focused tradition of Tamils – which resembles the now disreputed grammar-translation method in TESOL – drives to a reductio ad absurdum such attempts. Critical ethnography would posit that native learning traditions have to be interrogated for the interests they serve because minority cultures are steeped in traditions of domination as well as resistance. Without delving too much into how this favored pedagogy of Tamils traditionally bolstered their caste structure and religious hierarchy, we can proceed to its contemporary implications for the students discussed in this study. We must remember that such a pedagogy encourages a teacher-controlled, nondialogic, "banking" style of learning that is known to reproduce the dominant values and social relations of an oppressively stratified society (see Freire, 1970; Giroux, 1983).

Furthermore, though a formalistic approach to the abstract rules of "standard English" might appear to preserve students from the more obvious cultural content associated with the communicative orientation of the course, it in no way saves them from other forms of domination: It disconfirms the Englishes students bring with them; it prevents students from interrogating their own culture and society through literacy; it fails to alter the unfavorable subject positions belonging to monolingual and English-incompetent Lankans. Nor does the formalistic approach enable students to effectively internalize the rules of the language or progress rapidly in fluent language use. In the in-course assessments carried out to monitor their progress, the majority of the students continued to score below the passing grade. They remained with the smattering of "marked" English they brought with them. What all this implies is that these students will continue to occupy the marginalized position accorded to the monolingual, poorly educated, rural poor in a social system dominated by the English-speaking, bilingual, urban middle class (see Kandiah, 1984). Ironically, the desire for grammar-oriented learning only influences students to accept these limitations more uncritically and give in to social reproduction.

Hence, although on one level the grammatical approach – which is a culturally mandated, indigenous form of learning – enables students to somewhat resist the ideological thrusts of the foreign language and textbook, it is doubtful whether we can glorify this as a form of radical "resistance" as Kandiah (1984) implies. This is not to deny that the study sympathizes with Kandiah's explanation of lack of motivation in ESOL students as being a result of the sociopolitical implications of English in Sri Lanka; the study also refutes the alternative explanations of Goonetilleke (1983) and Hanson-Smith (1984) that this is simply a consequence of the educational policy which makes students give more time to rival subjects even though students are convinced of the benefits of English. Yet Kandiah fails to grapple with the complexity of students' opposition which has to be qualified by their belief in the benefits of English, resulting in examination-oriented motivation. This tension results eventually in their giving in to social and ideological reproduction through English.

It becomes important therefore to unravel the ambiguous strands of students' behavior with the help of Giroux (1983) who warns that the concept of resistance must not be allowed to become a category indiscriminately hung over every expression of "oppositional behavior" (p. 109). Thus, Giroux distinguishes between *resistance*, which he sees as displaying ideological clarity and commitment to collective action for social transformation from mere *opposition*, which is unclear, ambivalent, and passive. Having analyzed the effects of classroom behavior in the larger historical and social contexts, we can say that the responses and attitudes of the students do not fall under Giroux's definition of radical resistance. Students fail to sustain consciousness-raising or collective critical action. Theirs is largely a vague, instinctive oppositional behavior which, due to its lack of ideological clarity, ironically accommodates to their reproductive forces. It is perhaps in Supendran we see any signs of conscious resistance that display potential for the development of a radical pedagogy for the Lankan context. The behavior of most other students in the class is an ambivalent state which contains elements of accommodation as well as opposition in response to the conflicting pulls of socioeconomic mobility, on the one hand, and cultural integrity on the other.

However, the prospects for a pedagogy of resistance for such students is not all that bleak. Giroux (1983) is quick to point out:

> On the other hand, as a matter of radical strategy *all* forms of oppositional behavior, whether they can be judged as forms of resistance or not, need to be examined in the interests being used as a basis for critical analysis and dialogue. Thus oppositional behavior becomes the object of theoretical classification as well as the basis for possible radical strategy considerations. (p. 110)

The foregoing study has been conducted in the same spirit and for the same objectives. It attempts to disentangle the conflicting strands in the classroom culture of marginalized students, to expose the accommodative impulses and encourage the potential for resistance, in order to fashion a pedagogy that is ideologically liberating as well as educationally meaningful for such students.

References

Althusser, L. (1971) 'Ideology and ideological state apparatuses', in *Lenin and philosophy and other essays* (pp. 121–173). London: New Left Books.

Aronowitz, S., and Giroux, H. (1985) *Education under siege: The conservative, liberal and radical debate over schooling*. South Hadley, MA: Bergin and Garvey.

Benson, M. J. (1989) 'The academic listening task: A case study'. *TESOL Quarterly, 23*(3), 421–445.

Bourdieu, P., and Passeron, J-P. (1977) *Reproduction in education, society and culture*. London: Sage.

Bowles, S., and Gintis, H. (1976) *Schooling in capitalist America*. New York: Basic Books.

de Souza, D. (1969, April) 'The teaching of English'. *The Ceylon Observer*, pp. 18–29.

Denzin, W. (1970) *The research act*. Chicago: Aldine.

Emeneau, M. B. (1955) 'India and linguistics'. *Journal of the American Oriental Society, 75*, 145–153.

Freire, P. (1970) *Pedagogy of the oppressed*. New York: Herder and Herder.

Giroux, H. (1983) *Theory and resistance in education: A pedagogy for the opposition*. South Hadley, MA: Bergin and Garvey.

Goonetilleke, D.C.R.A. (1983) 'Language planning in Sri Lanka'. *Navasilu*, 5, 13–18.

Hanson-Smith, E. (1984) 'A plan for the improvement of English instruction in Sri Lanka'. *Navasilu*, 6, 26–30.

Jeyasuriya, J. E. (no date) 'The indigenous religious traditions in education', in *Educational policies and progress during British rule in Ceylon* (pp. 4–23). Colombo, Sri Lanka: Associated Educational Publishers.

Kandiah, T. (1979) 'Disinherited Englishes: The case of Lankan English'. *Navasilu*, 3, 75–89.

Kandiah, T. (1984) '"Kaduva": Power and the English language weapon in Sri Lanka', in P. Colin-Thome, and A. Halpe (eds) *Honouring E. F. C. Ludowyk* (pp. 117–154). Colombo, Sri Lanka: Tisara Prakasayo.

Marcus, G.E., and Fischer, M.M.J. (1986) *Anthropology as cultural critique: An experimental moment in the human sciences*. Chicago: University of Chicago Press.

Mehan, H. (1985) 'The structure of classroom discourse', in T. A. van Dijk (ed.) *Handbook of discourse analysis* (Vol. 3, pp. 119–131). London: Academic.

Ogbu, J. (1986) 'Class stratification, racial stratification and schooling', in L. Weis (ed.) *Race, class and schooling* (pp. 10–25). Buffalo, NY: Comparative Education Center.

O'Neill, R., Kingbury, R., Yeadon, T., and Cornelius, E.T. (1978) *American kernel lessons: Intermediate*. New York: Longman.

Peirce, B.N. (1989) 'Toward a pedagogy of possibility in the teaching of English internationally: People's English in South Africa'. *TESOL Quarterly, 23*(3), 401–420.

Pennycook, A. (1989) 'The concept of method, interested knowledge, and the politics of language teaching'. *TESOL Quarterly, 23*(4), 589–618.

Richards, J. C., and Rodgers, T.S. (1986) *Approaches and methods in language teaching: A description and analysis*. Cambridge: Cambridge University Press.

Sirisena, U.D.I. (1969) Editorial introduction in *Education in Ceylon* (Pt. 1, pp. xxv–xvii). Colombo, Sri Lanka: Ministry of Education and Cultural Affairs.

Somasegaram, S.W. (1969) 'The Hindu tradition', in U.D.I. Sirisena (ed.) *Education in Ceylon* (Pt. 3, pp. 1131–1144). Colombo, Sri Lanka: Ministry of Education and Cultural Affairs.

Stubbs, M. (1976) *Language, schools and classrooms*. London: Methuen.

Watson-Gegeo, K. A. (1988) 'Ethnography in ESL: Defining the essentials'. *TESOL Quarterly, 22*(4), 575–592.

Weis, L. (1985) *Between two worlds: Black students in an urban community college*. Boston: Routledge.

Wickramasuriya, S.(1981) 'James de Alwis and second language teaching in Sri Lanka'. *Navasilu, 4*, 11–29.

Willis, P. (1977) *Learning to labour: How working class kids get working class jobs*. Manchester, England: Saxon House.

—— (1978) *Profane cultures*. London: Routledge.

Chapter 14

J. Keith Chick

SAFE-TALK: COLLUSION IN APARTHEID EDUCATION

Introduction

Background to the study

THERE IS WIDESPREAD AGREEMENT AMONGST observers about what were the essential characteristics of interactions in schools for black people in South Africa under the former apartheid system: highly centralised, with teachers adopting authoritarian roles and doing most of the talking, with few pupil initiations, and with most of the pupil responses taking the form of group chorusing. Schlemmer and Bot (1986: 80) report a senior African school inspector as stating that black pupils were discouraged from asking questions or participating actively in learning and explain that it was regarded as impolite and even insubordinate to ask questions or make suggestions in class. Thembela (1986: 41) refers to classroom practice being characterised by rote learning and teacher-centred instruction.

Most observers, moreover, agree that the educational consequences of such interaction styles were unfortunate. Schlemmer and Bot (1986) and Thembela (1986), for example, argue that the use of such styles oppressed creativity, initiative and assertiveness. MacDonald (1988) claims that there are aspects of metacognition and disembedded thinking crucial to advanced learning and to effective functioning in a technological society which these styles of interacting and learning did not promote.

I became very aware of the possible negative educational consequences of the overwhelming preference for such styles of interaction in schools for black people in South Africa, through my involvement with in-service teacher education projects which had, as one of their primary objectives, the fostering of communicative approaches to the teaching of English in KwaZulu schools. (KwaZulu was a patchwork of geographical areas on the eastern seaboard of South Africa which, in terms of apartheid policy, was designated a 'homeland' for Zulu people. At the time of the study reported here, the total population of native speakers of Zulu was almost seven million; they thus constituted the largest language group in South Africa. Zulu speakers live in many parts of South Africa, but at that time approximately five million of them lived in KwaZulu.)

A number of the implementors of the in-service teacher education projects complained about the reluctance of many of the teachers, and even some of the students, to adopt the more egalitarian, de-centralised ways of interacting associated with these approaches to language teaching. This reluctance was pervasive enough to make at least some of those involved with the in-service projects, including myself, question whether the choice of communicative language teaching as a goal was an appropriate one. Given that communicative language teaching approaches had their origins chiefly in Europe and the USA, contexts very different from those which obtained in KwaZulu, I began to wonder whether our choice of communicative language teaching as a goal was possibly a sort of naive ethnocentricism prompted by the thought that what is good for Europe or the USA had to be good for KwaZulu. I reasoned that, in order to discover whether the goal of communicative language teaching was appropriate or not, it would be necessary to discover why students and teachers in KwaZulu schools found it so difficult to transfer to styles compatible with communicative language teaching. With this goal in mind, I encouraged Marianne Claude – who, under my supervision, was engaged in action research/in-service education with teachers in a peri-urban area of KwaZulu – to collect, by means of participant observation, interviews and discussions with the teachers, relevant ethnographic data, including classroom interactional data. I supplemented this with my own participant observation and discussions with teachers during visits to classrooms elsewhere in KwaZulu. In this chapter, I report on my analysis and interpretation of some of this data.

My thinking at this stage was heavily influenced by the findings of research I had completed earlier, working within the interactional sociolinguistic framework developed by scholars such as Gumperz (see, for example, 1982a, 1982b) and Erickson (see, for example, 1975 and 1976). In analysing interethnic encounters between a white South African English-speaking academic and Zulu graduate students at the University of Natal (see Chick 1985) I had identified putative culturally-specific Zulu-English interactional styles. These styles are characterised, amongst other things, by the preference by higher status speakers in asymmetrical encounters (i.e. those in which there are marked differences in the relative status of the participants) for what Scollon and Scollon (1983) term solidarity politeness, including the politeness or face-preserving strategy of volubility (much talking), and by lower status speakers for what they term deference politeness, including the strategy of taciturnity (avoidance of talking). I hypothesised that KwaZulu teachers and students found it difficult to transfer to styles compatible with communicative language teaching because these styles, which call on students to be voluble, differ markedly from those which predominate in a wide range of domains within the Zulu-speaking community, and which are transferred to their use of English in academic and other settings.

Incidentally, to avoid misinterpretation, I need to clarify that I am using 'preference' not in its lay sense of speaker's or hearer's individual preferences. Rather, I am borrowing a technical term from ethnomethodology, a branch of sociology concerned with investigating how people organise and make sense of social activities. As Levinson (1983: 307) explains, 'preference' is not a psychological notion but a structural notion that corresponds closely to the linguistic concept of markedness, according to which certain linguistic features are more basic and conventional and occur more frequently ('unmarked') than other features (referred to as 'marked'). Thus, when Zulus who have relatively low status choose deferential politeness, it is not because they like behaving deferentially, or that they 'feel' deferential, but rather because such behaviour is conventional, or as Lakoff expresses it, 'targeted'. She explains (1979: 69) that each culture has implicitly in its collective mind a concept of how a good human being should behave: 'a target for its members to aim at and judge themselves and others by'.

Organisation of the study

Most research reports imply that the research which they are reporting on proceeded in very orderly and logical ways, and that the researchers, from the outset, were more knowledgeable and insightful than they actually were. The false starts, the partial understandings and the dead ends do not feature. In this chapter I will be departing from this tradition, and sharing with my readers the often tortuous paths I followed in exploring the significance of interactional styles widely employed in schools for black people in South Africa.

To begin with, I report on my micro-ethnographic analysis of an episode in a lesson in a KwaZulu classroom. The general goal of micro-ethnographic analysis is to provide a description of how interlocutors set up or constitute contexts that allow them to make sense of one another's messages. My specific purpose was to try to establish why teachers and students in such classrooms found it difficult to transfer to styles compatible with communicative language teaching. The analysis reveals interactional behaviour consistent with the putative Zulu-English interactional styles identified in the interethnic encounters referred to above. More significantly, it reveals that such styles served valuable social functions for students and teachers alike. This could account for why teachers and students were reluctant to abandon such styles, despite the fact that the academic consequences of such preference were probably unfortunate.

I then explain how my growing awareness of the limitations of micro-ethnographic research in general, and explanations of pervasive school failure amongst dominated groups in terms of culturally-specific interactional styles in particular, prompted me to re-examine my classroom interactional data. Critics have pointed out that micro-ethnographic studies often take insufficient account of how pervasive values, ideologies and structures in the wider society (macro context) constrain what takes place at a micro level. Accordingly, I give an account of the historical, structural circumstances which contributed to making primary school education for most teachers and students in so-called black education in apartheid South Africa such a traumatic experience. Finally I offer a reinterpretation of the analysed data. I suggest that what is most significantly displayed in this episode is not culturally-specific Zulu interactional styles, but styles consistent with interactional norms which teachers and students interactionally constituted as a means of avoiding the oppressive and demeaning effects of apartheid ideology and structures. Following McDermott and Tylbor (1987) I see the teacher and her students as *colluding* in preserving their dignity by hiding the fact that little or no learning is taking place. While serving the short-term interests of teachers and students, such strategies, I suggest, contributed to the widely documented high failure rate in black education in apartheid South Africa, and made teachers and students resistant to educational innovation. The strategies thus served to reinforce and reproduce the inequalities between the various population groups which characterised apartheid society.

Culturally-specific interactional styles as barriers to innovation and learning

With the goal, then, of trying to establish why many teachers and students in KwaZulu schools resisted the adoption of egalitarian, decentralised ways of interacting, I carried out a fine-grained micro-ethnographic analysis of an episode in a video-recorded mathematics lesson, initially with the help of Marianne Claude (who had observed the lesson while it was taking place) and, later, independently. I selected this episode from the corpus collected by Marianne Claude because it contains features that I had observed in many lessons taught by teachers who were highly regarded either by students or by school authorities in the KwaZulu educational system. In other words, I chose part of a 'good' lesson. I did this to ensure that I would be analysing conventional 'targeted' behaviour in Lakoff's sense. I chose a content subject rather than an English lesson so as to lessen the chance that the teacher's style might have been influenced by Marianne Claude's intervention.

I based the analysis on methods developed by interactional socio-linguists (see, for example, Gumperz 1982a) who, rather than impose their own categories, attempt to access the interpretative or inferential processes of the participants by repeatedly playing the video or sound recordings to the participants and/or informants who share their cultural backgrounds, and by eliciting interpretations from them about progressively finer details of the discourse. I make use of transcription conventions which highlight the nature of turn exchange and which provide information about the supra-segmental phonology of the episode. Latch marks (|__) are used to show smooth exchange of turns without overlap, while square brackets are used to signify simultaneous speech ([ ). Underlining is used to signify phonological prominence such as stress or marked pitch movement. The 'shape' of the pitch movement is indicated above the part of the utterance where this occurs, and so (´) signifies rising tone.

Relevant contextual information is that the class consisted of 38 students of both sexes who were native speakers of Zulu, whose average age at the time was fourteen years, and who were in their seventh year of schooling (the fourth year of the Senior Primary phase). The teacher, whom I shall refer to as Mrs Gumbi, also a native Zulu speaker, was 32 years of age and had completed ten years of schooling and two years of teacher training. Mrs Gumbi conducted the entire lesson from the front of the classroom, making considerable use of the board. The students were crowded into multiple-seat wooden desks arranged in rows facing the board. The lesson took place through the medium of English. (In KwaZulu schools English served as the medium of instruction across the curriculum after the first four years of schooling through the medium of Zulu.)

As the video-recording shows, the focus of the lesson was 'elements which form the union set'. At the start of the lesson Mrs Gumbi introduced the notion of elements of a union set with the aid of the board. Elements were written on the board, and common elements pointed to. She individually nominated one student to answer a question but, significantly, only after the information to be provided had been written on the board. The few other student responses took the form of teacher-initiated group chorusing.

The lesson continued:

```
1     Mrs Gumbi: but I know that these two elements are common
2     because they are found in set B as well as in set C do you get
3     that
4                 Students: |yes
5     Mrs Gumbi:                        | now now a let us form the universal set the
6     univers I mean sorry union set is the set which
7     has the elements of both sets get it B ánd        [ C
8                                      Students:        [ C
9                                      Mrs Gumbi:          collect
10    the elements of those two sets and write them together
11    all them they will form union  [ set
12                           Students: [ set
13                    Mrs Gumbi:   |can you try to to list
```

14   the elements of the union set
15   Student A: |two [three
16   Mrs Gumbi: [that is twó
17   Student A: |three
18   Mrs Gumbi: |thrée
19   Student A: |four
20   Mrs Gumbi: |fouŕ
21   Student A: |five
22   Mrs Gumbi: |fíve
23   Student A: |six
24   Mrs Gumbi: |śix
25   Student A: |seven
26   Mrs Gumbi: |seVen
27   Student A: |eight
28   Mrs Gumbi: |eíght and eight . . .
29   what type of set is this now . . . it is á [union set
30   Students: [union set
31   Mrs Gumbi: |it is a
32   union set because we have been listing now at the elements
33   of set B together with the elements of sét   [C
34   Students: [C
35   Mrs Gumbi: |to form one
36   set which called what . . . a uńion [set
37   Students: [set
38   Mrs Gumbi: |but remember
39   when you list the union set the elements for for the union set
40   do not repeat those elements which are written twice do you get that
41   Students: |yes
42   Mrs Gumbi: |do not repeat them list them once OK
43   Students: |yes
44   Mrs Gumbi: |do you understand this
45   Students: |yes
46   Mrs Gumbi: |do you understand this
47   Students: |yes

What is immediately striking about this episode (as also the lesson as a whole) is the coincidence of teacher volubility and student (particularly individual student) taciturnity, characteristics of interactions in the formerly segregated schools for black people in South Africa, which, as I noted above, have been commented upon by many observers. Mrs Gumbi in this extract, as elsewhere in the lesson, does most of the talking. Indeed, of the total 19 minutes duration of the lesson as a whole, five seconds short of 16 minutes consists of teacher talk. Also the students' opportunities to talk (with one or two exceptions) are reduced to group chorusing.

Volubility on the part of the teacher, which Scollon and Scollon (1983) regard as a solidarity strategy, and taciturnity on the part of the students, which they regard as a deference strategy, is consistent with the culturally-specific interactional styles I had found evidence for in my analysis of interethnic encounters between Zulu-English speakers and South African (white) English speakers (Chick 1985). This finding might, therefore, be seen as lending credence to the notion that the interactional styles employed in KwaZulu classrooms were similar to those used in a wide range of domains within the Zulu-speaking community.

A problem for this interpretation is that teacher volubility and student taciturnity have been shown to be characteristic of classroom discourse in many parts of the world including white, middle class European (see, for example, Sinclair and Coulthard 1975) and USA classrooms (see, for example, Mehan 1979). Indeed Ellis (1987: 87) suggests that teacher-centred instruction, which has been so pervasive in black education in South Africa, is derived from classroom practices common in pre-war European schools. An equally, if not more plausible interpretation, is that teacher volubility and student taciturnity are features of institution-specific rather than culturally-specific discourse. According to this interpretation, the source of teacher volubility and student taciturnity is the asymmetrical distribution of social power and knowledge between teachers and students evident in educational institutions throughout the world.

What is not found, however, in classroom discourse throughout the world is the chorusing behaviour evident in this episode, which is why I chose to focus on it in my analysis. Closer examination revealed that two kinds of cues to chorusing are provided by Mrs Gumbi. The one kind of cue involves the use of a set of yes/no questions: 'do you understand this?' (lines 44 and 46); 'do you get that?' (lines 2–3 and 40); 'OK' (line 42); 'isn't it?' and 'do you see that?'; 'can I go on?' (elsewhere in the lesson). The second kind of cue involves the use of rising tone on accented syllables (e.g. lines 7, 11, 29, 33, 36). This cue is also used as a prompt to individual student responses in a sequence (lines 16, 18, 20, 22, 24, 26 etc.). What this suggests is the operation of a relatively simple prosodic system in which a restricted set of prosodic cues is used for a wide range of prosodic functions. Interestingly, this observation is consistent with my finding in a study of interethnic encounters (see Chick 1985) that Zulu-English speakers rely less than do white South African English speakers on prosodic cues to signal (together with kinesic, paralinguistic, lexical and syntactic cues) the relationship between different parts of the text, the relative importance of information units, speaker transition points and so on. This may be related to the fact that the prosody of Zulu, a tone language, is very different from that of English.

The closer examination of the chorusing behaviour in this episode points to a possible explanation for the difficulty which teachers and students in KwaZulu schools have in transferring from the putative culturally-specific Zulu-English styles (of which the system of prosodic cues is apparently a distinctive feature) to styles compatible with communicative language teaching. I examined, first, the possibility that the chorusing elicited by the one kind of cue (rising tone), in certain cases, serves the academic function of reinforcing certain key information items and, perhaps, helping the students to become more familiar with (to memorise?) technical terms (e.g. lines 29–30). However, further analysis revealed that it is often not *new* information that students are asked to chorus, but information already available to the students before the lesson (e.g. in lines 12 and 37 the students are required to supply the word SET rather than the name of the set that they have learnt about in the lesson). Elsewhere in the lesson the rising tone prompts them merely to complete words (e.g. intersecTION; we are looking for the unKNOWN). The fact that the information value of items chorused is often low prompted me to investigate the possibility that the primary function of the chorusing elicited by this kind of cue is social rather than academic.

I also examined the possibility that the chorusing elicited by the other kind of cue (the set of questions) serves the academic function of enabling Mrs Gumbi to access the level of her students' understanding so that she can know whether or not to recycle her explanation at a lower level of abstraction. However, I discovered that the chorused responses are without exception 'yes'. This suggests that the questions are not really open questions, and that their function is to signal participation rather than level of understanding, i.e. it is again social rather than academic in purpose.

The social function of chorusing became even more clearly evident when I examined the lesson as a whole. I discovered that the students are required, in response to both kinds of cue, to provide mainly confirmative one- or two-word responses, or responses which repeat information on the board or information which has been recycled again and again by Mrs Gumbi. This suggests that chorusing gives the students opportunities to participate in ways that reduce the possibility of the loss of face associated with providing incorrect responses to teacher elicitations, or not being able to provide responses at all. It is interesting to note that the chorusing is more evident at the beginning of the lesson than later on. Once responses have been well rehearsed, so that the chance of being wrong publicly is reduced, more individual responses are elicited, and at the end students are even invited to leave their desks and carry out the very public act of writing their responses on the board.

There is, of course, nothing unusual about teachers needing to resort to face-saving strategies, since the asymmetrical role relations between teachers and students to be found in most parts of the world ensure that the risk of face-threat is great. As Cazden (1979: 147) explains, 'teachers, by the very nature of their professional role, are continuously threatening both aspects of their students' face constraining their freedom of action; evaluating, often negatively, a high proportion of student acts and utterances; and often interrupting student work and student talk'. To reduce this risk, teachers employ face-saving strategies such as expressing directives indirectly by means of interrogatives, e.g. 'Can you open your books, please?' This strategy reduces the sense of imposition associated with the directive by suggesting that the students are free to decide whether or not to comply. However, the need to resort to face-saving strategies is particularly great in KwaZulu classrooms because the asymmetry in the relative status of teachers and students is marked. This reflects the marked asymmetry in the relative status of adults and children in the wider community. According to Marianne Claude's informants (see Chick and Claude 1985), an adult in that community has the right to ask any child, who may well be a stranger, to do errands for them (i.e. take a message to someone; buy something at the shop) and may even chastise a child not their own.

Another striking feature of this episode is the remarkably rhythmic manner in which teacher and students synchronise their verbal and prosodic behaviours, particularly in accomplishing the chorusing sequences. Context analysts (e.g. Scheflin 1973; Condon 1977; Kendon 1973, 1979; McDermott, Gospodinoff and Aaron 1978) have demonstrated that participants in conversations organise their behaviours in co-operative, reciprocal, rhythmically co-ordinated ways in signalling to one another and negotiating the context of their talk. This enables them to make sense of what it is that they are doing together. In the episode such interactional synchrony is possible, presumably, because the teacher and her students are able to draw on their shared, implicit knowledge of the discourse conventions associated with conventional interactional styles. I suggest that this synchrony contributes to the perception that purposeful activity and learning are taking place.

To sum up, the micro-ethnographic analysis of this episode reveals interactional behaviour consistent with Zulu-English interactional styles identified in a study of interethnic encounters (see Chick 1985). Particularly noteworthy features of the discourse are the chorusing behaviour and the remarkably rhythmic manner in which the participants synchronise their interactional behaviours in accomplishing the chorusing sequences. Analysis revealed that these putative styles serve social rather than academic functions. For example, they help the students to avoid the loss of face associated with being wrong in a public situation, and provide them with a sense of purpose and accomplishment. Something not examined here, but equally important, is that these styles also help teachers avoid the loss of face associated with displays of incompetence. This is because they ensure that the lesson develops along predetermined lines, and that the opportunities for students to raise issues and problems that teachers may not be competent to handle are few. It is for such reasons that I refer to discourse associated with these styles as 'safe-talk'.

What this analysis suggests is that the task of making a transition – from the culturally-preferred interactional styles employed conventionally in KwaZulu classrooms to the styles associated with the more egalitarian relationships required by the communicative language teaching approach – was likely to be fraught with risk for both teachers and students. They all resisted innovation because they had vested interests in the maintenance of 'safe-talk'.

Limitations of explanations of school failure in terms of culturally-specific styles

One of the advantages of doing sociolinguistic research within the context of apartheid South Africa was that one was constantly prompted to reconsider one's interpretations. Many scholars in this context were very suspicious of sociolinguistic research which had an ethnographic orientation, and indeed of ethnography in general. As Kuper, writing during the apartheid era, explained, 'almost by its very nature, ethnographic research may appear to provide some support for the ideological assumptions underpinning apartheid, notably the belief that "traditional" and "tribal" institutions remain viable, and command respect' (1985: 1). It was in part the negative reaction of such critics to my analysis and interpretation of the episode referred to above which prompted the reinterpretation outlined below.

Another advantage of researching within the context of apartheid South Africa was that the discriminatory legislation tended to make visible what is normally hidden in democratic societies, namely the mechanisms in the wider (macro) society through which groups and individuals exercise power and deny it to others. It was the visibility of those mechanisms that had prompted me in an earlier study (see Chick 1985) to try to account for how macro-level factors, such as segregation, constrain what takes place at a micro level of interethnic communication. I was, therefore, open to the suggestion that a limitation of my original analysis of the episode was that I had not adequately contextualised my data; that I had not taken sufficient account of the effect on classroom discourse of such factors as the differential funding of the racially segregated school systems, differential teacher-student ratios, levels of teacher training and so on.

I was also familiar with the claim of such critics of micro-ethnography as Singh, Lele and Martohardjono (1988) that, because micro-ethnographers fail to show how the pervasive values, ideologies and structures of the wider society constrain micro-level behaviour, they come perilously close to being apologists for the systems they are investigating. Along similar lines, Karabel and Halsey (1977: 8) are critical of the neglect of macro factors in interactional accounts of the pervasive school failure of minority groups. They point out that:

> Teachers and pupils do not come together in a historical vacuum: the weight of precedent conditions the outcome of 'negotiation' over meaning at every turn. If empirical work is confined to observation of classroom interaction, it may miss the process by which political and economic power set sharp bounds to what is negotiable.

Ogbu (1981), too, while not denying that micro-ethnographic studies have a role in explaining how interaction acts as an immediate cause of a particular child's failure, argues that it is essential also to study how these classroom events are built up by forces emanating from outside these micro settings.

Influenced by such thinking, I concluded that my micro-ethnographic analysis of the episode from the mathematics lesson needed to be informed by a macro-ethnographic account of the schooling provided for black students in KwaZulu. This account, along lines suggested by Ogbu (1981), would be one that showed how the school system was related to social organisation, economy, political organisation, belief system and values, change and so on.

In the section which follows, I provide information about the macro context of schooling for blacks in South Africa during the apartheid era, which I identified as potentially relevant to the reinterpretation of this episode. Since the lesson occurred in a Senior Primary school (fourth to eighth years of schooling) I focus on this phase of the schooling system. I focus also on the role of English as medium of instruction, since research suggests (see, for example, MacDonald 1990) that difficulties associated with the transfer from mother tongue to English in the first year of this phase constrain classroom behaviour in powerful ways.

The macro context of schooling for black people in apartheid South Africa

As most people are aware, *apartheid*, an Afrikaans word meaning literally 'apartness' or separateness, refers to the policy of the Nationalist Party, which, subsequent to its coming to power in 1948, was implemented as a massive programme of social engineering. Racial segregation had been a feature of South African society ever since the arrival of whites in the 17th century. However, after 1948, segregation on racial and even, within racial groups, on ethnic lines, in every sphere of life, was implemented on a scale unprecedented in human history. Not merely were separate institutions such as educational institutions established for different race and ethnic groups, but geographical separation was attempted through the creation of ethnic 'homelands', of which KwaZulu was one.

Exemplifying as it does the classic divide-and-rule strategy, the apartheid policy admirably served the goal of the Nationalist Party of consolidating and increasing the newly-won hegemony of Afrikanerdom. Segregation also served to maintain and increase the privileged status that whites had enjoyed since the 17th century, by facilitating the systematic discrimination against people of colour.

In education, systematic discrimination was evident in the differential per capita expenditure on education for the various population groups. Towards the end of the apartheid era, there were attempts by the government to narrow the gaps between the provision for the various groups. However, as recently as the financial year 1986/7, the per capita expenditure on education for whites was R2508. That for blacks (i.e. Africans rather than Asians or so-called 'coloureds') was only R476, whilst that for blacks in the homelands was still lower; for example, in KwaZulu it was only R359 (South African Institute of Race Relations (SAIRR) Survey 1987/88).

One of the consequences of this differential expenditure, which probably played a role in determining what styles of interaction were possible, was differential teacher-student ratios. In 1987, whereas the student-teacher ratio for whites was 16 to 1, that for blacks in so-called white areas was 41 to 1, and for KwaZulu primary schools 53 to 1 and KwaZulu secondary schools 37 to 1 (SAIRR Survey 1987/88). It is very difficult for teachers, who are responsible for large numbers of students and who usually have to cope with overcrowded classrooms, to facilitate more egalitarian, decentralised ways of interacting.

The more long-term discriminatory effects of segregated education were evident, also, in the differential levels of professional qualification of teachers in schools for the various population groups. According to Du Plessis, Du Pisani and Plekker (1989) whereas, in 1989, 100% of teachers in schools for whites were professionally qualified in the sense of having at least matriculation or higher academic qualifications, as well as a teachers' certificate or diploma, only 20% of teachers in black primary schools and 10% in black secondary schools were professionally qualified.

Of particular relevance to the constraints of macro factors upon classroom discourse is another factor, namely, how apartheid ideology was translated into language medium policy in black education. Hartshorne (1987) reports that, until the Nationalists came to power, the position of English as sole medium of instruction after the first few years of schooling was unchallenged. He reports, further, that the Nationalists:

> made of Afrikaans a symbol of exclusiveness and separateness, and the struggle for Afrikaans became part of the 'mission' to control and rule South Africa. In education this expressed itself in a commitment to separate schools and rigid mother-tongue education policy. (Hartshorne 1987: 88)

This commitment eventually translated into mother-tongue instruction in primary education with English and Afrikaans as compulsory subjects from the first year of schooling, and with both Afrikaans and English as media of instruction in secondary education (half the subjects through English and half through Afrikaans). It was the inflexible and doctrinaire implementation of this policy, and the deafness to the protests of the black community, that sparked the Soweto uprising of 1976. This spread to the rest of the country, almost assuming the proportions of a full-scale civil war. As a consequence of the conflict, the government was forced to concede to the black community the right to choose *either* English *or* Afrikaans as medium in the high schools. In response to further pressure from the community, this right to choose was extended to the higher primary phase. English became overwhelmingly the chosen medium in black education after the first three years of schooling. In 1988, for example, only 20 primary schools (including some very small farm schools) and no high schools used Afrikaans as medium (SAIRR 1988/89).

Though the choice of English as medium represented the will of the people, as MacDonald (1990) explains, in primary education at least, it added to the burdens of teachers and students. She points out (1990: 39) that the apartheid system ensured that most of the teachers in so-called black education did not speak English with confidence or fluency, used outmoded materials, and had almost no contact with English speakers. Also, following the major shift to English as medium in primary education from 1979 onwards, no changes were made to the syllabus for English to prepare the ground linguistically and conceptually for its use across the curriculum. As a consequence, black primary school students were not adequately prepared for the sudden transition to English in the fourth year of schooling concurrently with the curriculum broadening into ten subjects. Nor were most of the teachers equipped to explain effectively in English the new concepts in the various content subjects such as mathematics.

MacDonald and her fellow researchers found that there was a considerable gap between the English competence required for the reading of content subject textbooks in the fourth year of schooling, and the English competence that might have been expected if a student had benefited optimally from English as a second language teaching materials then used in junior primary schools. They also found that there was also a very large gap between this hypothesised optimal competence and the level of competence students actually reached. They estimated, for example, that the vocabulary requirements in English increased by 1000% in the fourth year of schooling. They calculated that a student who had learnt optimally from the ESL materials in the junior primary phase might have encountered not more than half the vocabulary, and might have been unfamiliar with syntactic elements in up to 60% of sentences in science textbooks used in the fourth year of schooling. Moreover they might have been so ignorant of the conventions of expository writing as to experience what is referred to as 'register shock' when reading those texts.

As a consequence, the fourth year of schooling was a time of trauma for both teachers and students; a trauma reflected in the high drop-out rate in black schools at the end of that year (64, 100 or 8.9% of the total outflow in 1987 according to the SAIRR Report 1988/89). The researchers found that the effect of those conditions was what they termed 'the loss of meaning'. 'The children are likely to be alienated by what they have to learn, and only dimly perceive the implications and linkages between the concepts they are presented with' (MacDonald 1990: 141). Faced with these odds, teachers tended to resort to providing notes that the students were required to memorise. This gave the impression of real learning taking place, but as MacDonald (1990: 143) points out, the students often learnt what they did not understand, and were usually unable to use what they had learnt because this mode of education did not allow the integration of new information with what had been learnt before.

A reinterpretation: safe-talk as the outcome of collusion between teachers and students

Reexamining my micro-ethnographic analysis of the episode in a mathematics lesson in a KwaZulu classroom, I was struck by the similarity between MacDonald's account of the teachers' response to the trauma experienced in the early years of senior primary schooling and my interpretation of the interactional behaviour in the episode as 'safe-talk'.

My thinking was also strongly influenced by two studies that attempt to trace the relationship between the structure of classroom discourse and the macro context in which it occurs, including the ideologies that are promoted in them. In the first of these studies, Collins (1987) argues that the ideology of ability grouping promoted in school systems in the United States leads students in low ability groups and their teachers to socialise one another into systematic departures from the norms of classroom discourse. Behaviour consistent with these 'emergent' norms (see Mehan 1979: 90) interferes with the reading practice which members of these groups so badly need. Collins argues, further, that the ideology of prescriptivism also promoted in the United States school system results in evaluation being made on the basis of cultural background rather than on academic aptitude. This leads to the systematic exclusion of minority students from opportunities to learn and practise forms of literary discourse.

In the second of these studies, McDermott and Tylbor (1987) analyse an episode in which teachers and students do interactional work to make the illiteracy of one of the students, Rosa, not noticeable. In the process Rosa does not get a turn to practise her reading. They show that while evaluation is constantly taking place, teachers and students collude in evaluating overtly only when the evaluation is positive, while, at the same time, making covert, unspoken, negative evaluations. Such collusion hides the unpleasant fact that schooling is structured in such a way as to provide access to opportunities for learning for some students and to deny it to others.

These two studies show how features of the macro context, namely the institutional ideologies and bureaucratic structures, constrain what takes place at a micro level. They also show the participants working together to reshape the structure of their discourse and to socialise one another into a set of sociolinguistic norms that enable them to meet their immediate needs. As Collins (1987: 313) explains:

> Institutional ideologies and bureaucratic organisation forms do not entirely constrain participants; people still strive to make sense of their situation, to avoid or resist that which is demeaning or oppressive.

It was these insights that enabled me to recognise that the 'safe-talk' which I had identified in my analysis of the episode of the mathematics lesson does not represent the inappropriate use of culturally-specific Zulu-English interactional styles. Rather, it represents styles which the participants interactionally developed and constituted as a means of coping with the overwhelming odds they faced in their segregated schools. I suggest that these styles enabled them to collude in hiding unpleasant realities. Thus, for example, the rhythmically co-ordinated chorusing prompts and responses enabled the teacher and students in the episode to hide their poor command of English; to obscure their inadequate understanding of academic content; and to maintain a façade of effective learning taking place. In this way they were able to preserve their dignity to some extent. In terms of this interpretation, commonalities between 'safe-talk' and the putative Zulu-English styles identified in an earlier study (Chick 1985) are features of conventional Zulu interactional styles that survived the process of constituting a new set of norms of interaction. In doing the interactional work involved in constituting these norms, the participants inevitably started by making use of interactional styles most familiar to them.

Unfortunately, as Collins (1987: 313) notes, 'solutions achieved to local problems may have unforeseen consequences which are quite damaging'. 'Safe-talk' has proved to be a barrier both to learning and to educational innovation in South Africa. As such it served to reinforce the inequalities that gave rise to it in the first place.

Conclusion

To sum up, in this chapter I have explored the significance of interactional styles that were widely employed in schools for black people in South Africa. The fine-grained analysis of an episode from a lesson which exemplifies such styles revealed that they served important social functions for teachers, but probably did not promote efficient learning. They also provided support for the hypothesis that teachers and students in KwaZulu classrooms were often reluctant to adopt more egalitarian, decentralised ways of interacting advocated in in-service education because they had vested interests in 'safe-talk'.

A richer contextualisation of the classroom data in terms of the ideology and structures of the wider apartheid society facilitated a reinterpretation of my findings. According to this reinterpretation, 'safe-talk' represents styles consistent with norms of interaction which teachers and students constituted as a means of avoiding the oppressive and demeaning constraints of apartheid educational systems.

One implication of this study is that teaching innovation at the micro level which is not accompanied by appropriate structural change at the macro level is unlikely to succeed. For those like myself who have been engaged in the difficult task of educational innovation within the constraints imposed by the apartheid society, it has been exciting to experience the dismantling of apartheid structures and the assembling of alternative structures. Hopefully, the latter will make it less necessary for teachers and students to engage in 'safe-talk'.

Acknowledgement

I wish to acknowledge the contribution of Marianne Claude, who recorded the interactional data and assisted in the analysis of it, and that of my colleagues Ralph Adendorff and Nicole Geslin for their insightful comments and suggestions.

References

Cazden, C. (1979) 'Language in education: variation in the teacher-talk register', in J.E. Alatis and G.R. Tucker (eds) *Language in Public Life*, 144–62. Washington D.C.: Georgetown University Press.

Chick, J.K. (1985) 'The interactional accomplishment of discrimination in South Africa. *Language in Society* 14(3): 229–326.

Chick, J.K., and Claude, M. (1985) 'The Valley Trust English Language Project: research in progress'. *Proceedings of the Fourth National Conference of the Southern African Applied Linguistics Association*. Johannesburg: University of the Witwatersrand.

Collins, J. (1987) 'Conversation and knowledge in bureaucratic settings'. *Discourse Processes* 10: 303–19.

Condon, W. (1977) 'The relation of interactional synchrony to cognitive and emotional processes', in M. Key (ed.) *The Relationship of Verbal and Nonverbal Communication*, 50–65. The Hague: Mouton.

Du Plessis, A., Du Pisani, T. and Plekker, S. (1989) *Education and Manpower Development*. Bloemfontein: Research Institute for Education Planning.

Ellis, R. (1987) 'Using the English medium in African Schools', in D. Young (ed.) *Bridging the Gap between Theory and Practice in English Second Language Teaching*, 82–99. Cape Town: Maskew Miller Longman.

Erickson, F. (1975) 'Gatekeeping and the melting pot: interaction in counselling encounters'. *Harvard Educational Review* 45 (1): 44–70.

—— (1976) 'Gatekeeping encounters: A social selection process', in P.R. Sanday (ed.) *Anthropology and the Public Interest: Fieldwork and Theory*, 111–45. New York: Academic Press.

Gumperz, J. (1982a) *Discourse Strategies* (Studies in interactional sociolinguistics 1). Cambridge: Cambridge University Press.

—— (1982b) *Language and Social Identity* (Studies in interactional sociolinguistics 2). Cambridge: Cambridge University Press.

Hartshorne, K. (1987) 'Language policy in African education in South Africa 1910–1985, with particular reference to the issue of medium of instruction', in D. Young (ed.) *Language: Planning and Medium of Education*. Rondebosch: Language Education Unit and SAALA.

Karabel, J. and Halsey, A.H. (Eds) (1977) *Power and Ideology in Education*. New York: Oxford University Press.

Kendon, A. (1973) 'The role of visible behaviour in the organization of social interaction', in M. Von Cranach and I. Vine (eds) *Social Communication and Movement*, 3–74. New York: Academic Press.

—— (1979) 'Some theoretical and methodological aspects of the use of film in the study of social interaction', in G. Ginsberg (ed.) *Emerging Strategies in Social Psychological Research*, 67–91. New York: John Wiley.

Kuper, A. (1985) *South Africa and the Anthropologist*. London/New York: Routledge and Kegan Paul.

Lakoff, R. (1979) 'Stylistic strategies with a grammar of style', in J. Oraisainn, M. Slater and L. Loeb Adler (eds) *Annals of the New York Academy of Sciences* 327: 53–78.

Levinson, S.C. (1983) *Pragmatics*. Cambridge: Cambridge University Press.

MacDonald, C. (1988) 'Teaching primary science in a second language: two teaching styles and their cognitive concomitants', in A. Weideman (ed.) *Styles of Teaching and Styles of Learning*. Bloemfontein: SAALA.

—— (1990) *Crossing the Threshold into Standard Three*. Report of the Threshold Project. Human Sciences Research Council.

McDermott, R., Gospodinoff, K. and Aaron, J. (1978) 'Criteria for an ethnographically adequate description of the concerned activities and their contexts'. *Semiotica* 24: 245–75.

McDermott, R. and Tylbor, H. (1987) 'On the necessity of collusion in conversation', in L. Kedar (ed.) *Power through Discourse*. Norwood, N.J.: Ablex.

Mehan, H. (1979) *Learning Lessons: Social Organization in the Classroom*. Cambridge, Mass.: Harvard University Press.

Ogbu, J. (1981) 'School ethnography: a multi-level approach'. *Anthropology and Educational Quarterly* pp. 3–29.

Scheflin, A.E. (1973) *Communicating Structures: Analysis of a Psychotherapy Transaction*. Bloomington: Indiana University Press.

Schlemmer, L. and Bot, M. (1986) 'Education and race relations in South Africa', in G. Kendal (ed.) *Education and the Diversity of Cultures*. Pietermaritzburg: University of Natal.

Scollon, R. and Scollon, S. (1983) 'Face in interethnic communication', in J.C. Richards and R.W. Schmidt (eds) *Language and Communication*, 156–88. London: Longman.

Sinclair, J.McH. and Coulthard, M. (1975) *Towards an Analysis of Discourse*. London: Oxford University Press.

Singh, R., Lele, J. and Martohardjono, G. (1988) 'Communication in a multi-lingual society: some missed opportunities'. *Language in Society* 17: 43–59.

South African Institute of Race Relations (SAIRR) Reports 87/88; 88/89.

Thembela, A. (1986) 'Some cultural factors which affect school education for blacks in South Africa', in G. Kendall (ed.) *Education and the Diversity of Cultures*, 37–43. Pietermaritzburg: University of Natal.

PART THREE

Analysing teaching and learning

Chapter 15

Neil Mercer

LANGUAGE FOR TEACHING A LANGUAGE

Introduction

THIS CHAPTER IS ABOUT THE use of language as a medium for teaching and learning, with special relevance to the teaching of English. However, many of the issues I will deal with, especially those in the early parts of the chapter, are not specific to the use of any particular language in the classroom, or the teaching of any particular curriculum subject. Of course, languages of instruction and curricula vary from country to country, region to region and even from school to school. Teachers differ in their style and approach, and their classes are made up of individuals of various personal characteristics and cultural backgrounds, who differ in the ways they respond to teachers and particular styles of teaching. But, as I will explain, observational research suggests that some ways that language is used in interactions between teachers and students are common features of classroom life throughout the world. I will illustrate some of these features of classroom language with real-life examples, and discuss their possible educational functions. In the latter part of the chapter, I will use the theoretical perspective of socio-cultural psychology to relate the earlier analysis of classroom language to a consideration of the nature and quality of classroom education. In these ways, I hope to demonstrate the practical educational value of a careful analysis of the interactive process of teaching-and-learning.

Language and teaching

Wherever they are and whatever they are teaching, teachers in schools and other educational institutions are likely to face some similar practical tasks. They have to organize activities to occupy classes of disparate individuals, learners who may vary considerably in their aims, abilities and motivations. They have to control unruly behaviour. They are expected to teach a specific curriculum, a body of knowledge and skills which their students would not normally encounter in their out-of-school lives. And they have to monitor and assess the educational progress the students make. All these aspects of teachers' responsibilities are reflected in their use of language as the principal tool of their responsibilities. As examples of this, I would like you now to consider two transcribed sequences of classroom talk, Sequences 1 and 2 overleaf. For each in turn, consider:

1   Can you identify any recurring patterns of interaction in the talk between teacher and pupils?

2   What would you say were the main functions of the teacher's questions in each of the sequences? Do the sequences differ at all in this respect?

I have made my own comments after both the sequences.

(Note: in the transcriptions words spoken particularly emphatically are underlined. Words which were unclear during transcription are in curled brackets { }. The onset of simultaneous speech is marked with a square bracket [.)

Sequence 1: Toy animals

This sequence was recorded in an English lesson in a Russian primary school. The teacher has just set up a collection of soft toy animals in front of the class.

T: Have you got any toy animals at home? Be quick. Raise your hand (*she raises her own hand*) and show me. Have you got any toy animals? S-{Name of child}
S: (*Standing up*) I have got a cat, a
T: No, sit down, in your place.
S: Yes, I have.
T: I have got many?
S: Toys at home.
T: Toy <u>animals</u> at home.

Sequence 2: Personal qualities

This next sequence comes from a TESOL class for young adults in a college in London. A little earlier, the teacher had asked each of the students to list their own personal qualities, both positive and negative.

T: Who would like to tell the class about their personal qualities? Dalia?
D: I am polite, friendly, organized, trustworthy, responsible but sometimes I am impatient and unpunctual. Sometimes (*laughs*).
T: Good, isn't it? (*Addressing the class*) Thank you, Dalia. That was good. Now can you tell me the positive qualities you have just said.
D: Yeah?
T: That is, friendly, um, organized.
D: {Right}
T: How is it helping you . . .
D: Yeah?
T: . . . with your friends [in the class?
D: [It help me to get along with people and to understand them and help them.
T: That's good. And what about the, the not very positive ones [like punctual
D: [Sometimes
T: What happens then?
D: Sometimes I lose my friend basically of that because I lose my temper very quickly.
T: And what happens with me? I don't smile at you that much do I?

Comments on Sequences 1 and 2

Sequence 1 illustrates some patterns which typify most classroom talk. First, the teacher took longer turns at speaking than any students. Second, she asked all the questions. Observational research has shown that in classroom conversations teachers usually ask the great majority of questions, usually – as in this case – to elicit some kind of participatory response from the students. She then *evaluates* the replies they give. She is also using questions to direct the topic or content of the talk towards issues that she wishes to focus attention on. Looking more carefully at Sequence 1, we can see that there is a structural pattern to the talk: a *teacher's question* is followed by a *student response*, followed in turn by some *teacher feedback or evaluation*. This structural element of classroom talk was first described by the linguists Sinclair and Coulthard (1975; see also Mehan, 1979; Van Lier, Chapter 5 of this book) and usually known as an Initiation-Response-Feedback (IRF) exchange. For example:

T:	. . . Have you got any toy animals? S-{Name of child}	I
	S: (*Standing up*) I have got a cat, a	R
	T: No, sit down, in your place.	F

IRF exchanges can be thought of as the archetypal form of interaction between a teacher and a pupil – a basic unit of classroom talk as a continuous stretch of language or 'text'. They do not typify the pattern of talk in all classroom activities; other kinds of talk involving different patterns of exchanges (e.g. in which students ask questions of teachers, or of other students) may happen too. And outside the most formal and traditional of classrooms, they may not often be found in their classic, simple form. But IRFs have been observed as a common feature in classrooms the world over, and in other languages besides English.

In Sequence 1, the IRF exchanges are being used to perform a common function in classrooms, one that is almost certainly familiar to you from your own schooldays: a teacher is eliciting from learners their knowledge of the relevant curriculum subject (in this case, English). Research shows that this particular kind of use of question-and-answer by a teacher – asking questions to which the teacher knows exactly what answers she seeks – is the most common function of IRFs in classrooms. Here students are essentially trying to provide the information that the teacher expects them to know. As the classroom researchers Edwards and Westgate say:

> Most classroom talk which has been recorded displays a clear boundary between knowledge and ignorance . . . To be asked a question by someone who wants to know is to be given the initiative in deciding the amount of information to be offered and the manner of telling. But to be asked by someone who already knows, and wants to know if you know, is to have your answer accepted, rejected or otherwise evaluated according to the questioner's beliefs about what is relevant and true. (1994, p 48)

Teachers need to check students' understanding of procedural, factual matters, and that is commonly the function of IRF exchanges. Sequence 1 illustrates also how 'feedback' from a teacher may also be used to control students' behaviour. These are quite legitimate functions of teacher-talk, and all teachers might expect to use language in this way quite frequently. But the danger of relying heavily and continuously on traditional, formal question-and-answer reviews for guiding learning is that students then get little opportunity for using language in more creative ways – such as experimenting with new types of language constructions.

As in much classroom talk, in Sequence 2 we can also see IRF exchanges occurring, though here as slightly more complex, linked structures, in which the student interjects during the teacher's elicitations, perhaps seeking clarification which the teacher provides. And if we consider the content and function of the question-and-answer exchanges in the two sequences, we can see that something rather different is going on in each of them. In Sequence 1, the teacher is asking her primary school pupils to produce English sentences which conform to the models she has in mind. The children respond by trying to provide these 'right answers'. The teacher in Sequence 2 is not doing that. Instead, she is asking questions to encourage the students to elaborate, in English, on what they have written. In this way, the teacher is not so much trying to elicit particular forms or structures of English, but rather encouraging the student to use English in a practical, communicative manner. I am not suggesting that either teacher is using their questioning techniques to better or worse effect, but simply illustrating the fact that IRF exchanges can be made to serve a variety of pragmatic, educational functions.

Techniques for teaching

Having identified the archetypal structure of teacher-student talk, I will next describe some specific ways of interacting with students which are commonly used by teachers. I call these 'techniques', because I believe that they represent teachers attempting to shape language into a set of suitable tools for pursuing their professional goals. I will illustrate each technique and consider how they can contribute to the process of teaching-and-learning. The techniques are summarised in Table 15.1 below.

Table 15.1 Some techniques that teachers use

. . . to elicit knowledge from learners
Direct elicitations
Cued elicitations

. . . to respond to what learners say
Confirmations
Rejections
Repetitions
Reformulations
Elaborations

. . . to describe significant aspects of shared experience
amplifications
explanations
'we' statements
recaps

Eliciting knowledge from learners

We have seen that when a teacher initiates an IRF sequence, this usually has the function of eliciting information from a student. If this is simply a straightforward request, we can describe the teacher's verbal act as a *direct elicitation*. But teachers also often engage in what can be called *cued elicitation*, which is a way of drawing out from learners the information they are seeking – the 'right' answers to their questions – by providing visual clues and verbal hints as to what answer is required. Here is an example recorded in an English lesson in a Zimbabwean primary school. The teacher has set up a number of objects on her desk, and also has a set of cards on which various consonants ('b', 'f', 'j' etc.) are written. The children have to come to the front of the class and match the consonants to the name of an object.

Sequence 3: say the sound

Teacher: (*to child*):   Say the sound.
Child: b-b-b
Teacher: b-b-b is for?

(*Child does not answer. Teacher waves her hand over the nearest objects, one of which is a book*)

Child: b-b-b is for book.
Teacher: Well done!

The use of cued elicitation as a teaching technique is widespread. It can be traced to the Socratic dialogues constructed by Plato (Edwards, 1988). By using this technique, the teacher avoids simply giving the child the right answer. Sequence 3 also illustrates how non-verbal communication – the use of gestures and other signs – can be an important component of classroom talk.

Responding to what learners say

As illustrated by the sequences above, one of the ways that teachers sustain dialogues with their students is to use what students say as the basis for what they say next. In this way, the learners' own remarks are incorporated into the teaching-learning process. The most obvious way of doing this is through *confirmation* (as, for example, a teacher's 'Yes, that's right' to a pupil's answer). *Repetitions* of things learners say are another way, one which allows the teacher to draw to the attention of a whole class an answer or other remark which is judged by the teacher to have educational significance.

Teachers often paraphrase or *reformulate* a pupil's remark, usually so as to offer the class a revised, tidied-up version of what was said which fits in better with the point that the teacher wishes to make or the form of response being sought. For example, in this extract from Sequence 1:

S: Yes, I have.
T: I have got many?
S: Toys at home.
T: Toy <u>animals</u> at home.

There are also *elaborations*, when a teacher picks up on a cryptic statement made by a pupil and expands and/or explains its significance to the rest of the class. Wrong answers or unsuitable contributions may be explicitly *rejected* by a teacher. But we should also note a popular technique that teachers have for dealing with wrong answers – simply ignoring them.

Describing shared experience

Classroom activities often rely on students reading instructions, whether in print or on a computer screen. It is important that they understand properly what is expected of them, if the activity is to succeed. Teachers therefore often *amplify* instructions with the intention of making them clearer and less ambiguous. Other texts may also contain information which students need to make sense of before they continue any further. In classrooms it is common to hear teachers *explaining* these texts to students as either a preliminary to activities or if some confusion about them seems to arise. For example, in this extract from a Spanish lesson for adult students:

Sequence 4: *Ser and Estar*

Teacher: It says (*reading from text*) ' This is one of the main difficulties for English speaking learners' meaning the two verbs *ser* and *estar* which both, uh, translate as 'to be' in English. (*Reading again*) '*Ser* means to exist while *estar* means to be situated'. That sounds horribly complicated, I think to start by thinking of *ser* as being about permanent things and *estar* as temporary ways of being. *Vamos a ver . . . (He continues in Spanish*)

An important task for a teacher is to help learners see how the various activities they do, over time, contribute to the development of their understanding. Education cannot be merely the experience of a series of consecutive events, it must be a developmental process in which earlier experiences provide the foundations for making sense of later ones. For those involved in teaching and learning, continuous shared experience is one of the most precious resources available. There are many ways that teachers try to create continuities in the experience of learners – by sequencing activities in certain ways, by dealing with topics in order of difficulty, and so on. Teachers can help learners perceive *continuity* in what they are doing. Through language there is the possibility of repeatedly revisiting and reinterpreting that experience, and of using it as the basis for future talk, activity and learning.

'*We*' *statements* (as in a teacher saying to a class 'last week we learned how to measure angles') are often used when teachers are trying to represent past experience as relevant to present activity. They show how teachers help learners see that they have significant past experience in common and so have gained shared knowledge and collective understanding which can be drawn upon to progress further. Teachers also often *recap* shared classroom experience from earlier in a lesson, and from previous lessons, usually emphasising the points or events they consider of most educational significance.

I have described and illustrated each of the techniques as separate items, each with an obvious function; but this is a simplification, for the sake of clarity of exposition, of the relationship between language form, function and context. An analyst of classroom discourse has to recognize that (a) any particular utterance can perform more than one function (so that, as in the first part of Sequence 3, a *repetition* can also be an *elicitation*); (b) any particular technique can serve more than one pedagogic purpose, and be used effectively or otherwise; and (c) the functional meaning of any interaction for participants may be shaped by contextual factors not available to the analyst (such as information gained from their shared past experience of interaction; see Breen, Chapter 7, for further discussion of such matters). However, despite these caveats, I have found the identification of these techniques a useful, practical aid to analysis.

Interaction in bilingual and multilingual settings

In the next part of the chapter I will consider some aspects of teacher–student interaction in classrooms where English is being used as a classroom language, but is not the first language of the children. I hope to show through these examples some of the qualities these bilingual settings have in common with monolingual classrooms, while also pointing out some of the special interactional features they may generate. There are two main sorts of situation which can be included here. The first occurs in countries where English is not the usual everyday language and the mother tongue of most of the children is not English. The second is where pupils whose mother tongue is not English enter schools in a predominantly English speaking country. I will provide examples from both of these types of situation.

In any situation where English is used as a classroom language but is not the main language of children's home or community, teachers may have the multiple task of teaching (a) the English language, (b) the educational ground rules for using it in the classroom, and (c) any specific subject content. Jo Arthur (1992) carried out observational research on teaching and learning in primary school classrooms in Botswana. English was used as the medium of education, but it was not the main language of the pupils' local community. She observed that when teachers were teaching mathematics, they commonly used question-and-answer sessions as opportunities for schooling children in the use of appropriate 'classroom English' as well as maths. For example, one primary teacher commonly insisted that pupils reply to questions 'in full sentences', as shown below:

Sequence 5: How many parts?

Teacher:	How many parts are left here (first pupil's name)?
First pupil:	Seven parts.
Teacher:	Answer fully. How many parts are there?
Pupil:	There are . . . there are seven parts.
Teacher:	How many parts are left? Sit down my boy. You have tried. Yes (second pupil's name)?
Second pupil:	We are left with seven parts.
Teacher:	We are left with seven parts. Say that (second pupil's name).
Second pupil:	We are left with seven parts.
Teacher:	Good boy. We are left with seven parts.

(Arthur, 1992, pp. 6–7)

Sequence 5 is made up of a linked series of IRF exchanges. For example:

How many parts are left here? [Initiation]
Seven parts [Response]
Answer fully [Feedback/Evaluation]

The Botswanan students therefore needed to understand that their teacher was using these exchanges not only to evaluate their mathematical understanding, but also to test their fluency in spoken English and their ability to conform to a 'ground rule' that she enforced in her classroom – 'answer in full sentences'. Arthur comments that for pupils in this kind of situation, the demands of classroom communication are complicated because their teacher is attempting to get them to focus on both the medium (English) and the message (maths).

Arthur reports that such dual focus is common in Botswanan classrooms, as the following sequence from another lesson shows:

Sequence 6: the continent of Africa

T: In which continent is your country? In which continent is your country? Give an answer
P1:   In Africa is my country
T: He says in Africa is my country. Who could frame her sentence? In Africa is my country
P2:   Africa is my continent
T: My question was in which continent is your country?
P3:   Its continent is in Africa
T: It is in the continent of Africa. everybody
Ps: It is in the continent of Africa

(Arthur, 1992, p. 13)

Bilingual code-switching in the classroom

In circumstances where one language is being used as a classroom language, but where the pupils' first language is a different one, a teacher may sometimes 'code-switch' to the first language if they judge it necessary. (We saw this kind of switch taking place between Spanish and English in Sequence 4 above). Sometimes the first language may be used only for asides, for control purposes or to make personal comments. However, when code-switching amounts to translation by the teacher of the curriculum content being taught, its use as an explanatory teaching strategy is somewhat controversial. On the one hand, there are those who argue that it is a sensible, common-sense response by a teacher to the specific kind of teaching and learning situation. Thus in studying its use in English-medium classrooms in Hong Kong, Angel Lin (Chapter 17 of this book) explains a particular teacher's use of code-switching as follows:

> by always starting in L1, Teacher D always starts from where the student is – from what the student can fully understand and is familiar with. (p. 282)

Researchers of bilingual code-switching (as reviewed by Martyn-Jones, 1995) have often concluded that it is of dubious value as a teaching strategy, if one of the aims of the teaching is to improve students' competence in English. Thus Jacobson comments:

> the translation into the child's vernacular of everything that is being taught may prevent him/her from ever developing the kind of English language proficiency that must be one of the objectives of a sound bilingual programme (Jacobson, 1990, p. 6.)

It seems, however, that teachers often use code-switching in more complex ways than simply translating content directly into another language. On observing classrooms in Hong Kong, Johnson and Lee (1987) observed that the switching strategy most commonly employed by teachers had a three-part structure as follows:

1   'Key statement' of topic in English
2   Amplification, clarification or explanation in Cantonese
3   Restatement in English

They comment that 'direct translation was comparatively rare; the general effect was of a spiralling and apparently haphazard recycling of content, which on closer examination proved to be more organised than it appeared.' (1987, p 106). The implication here is that such teachers are pursuing the familiar task of guiding children's understanding of curriculum content through language, but using special bilingual techniques to do so.

An interesting study of code-switching in bilingual classrooms in Malta was carried out by Antoinette Camilleri (1994). She showed that code-switching was used as a teaching technique by teachers in a variety of ways. Look for example at these two extracts from the talk of a teacher in a secondary school lesson about the production and use of wool, and based on a textbook written in English. The teacher begins by reading part of the text (*A translation of talk in Maltese is given in the right hand column*)

Sequence 7: Wool

Extract 1
England Australia New Zealand and
Argentina are the best producers of wool
dawk l-aktar li għandhom farms *li j*
rabbu n-nagħaġ għas-suf O.K. England
tgħiduli minn licma post England
għandhom Scotland *magħrufin tant*
*għall-*wool *u ġersijiet tagħhom* O.K.

they have the largest number of farms
and the largest number of sheep for wool
O.K. England where in England we really
mean Scotland they are very well-known
for their woollen products

Extract 2
wool *issa* it does not crease but it has to be
washed with care *issa din importanti*
ma għidtilkomx illi jekk ikolli nara xagħra jew
sufa waħda under the microscope *għandha*
qisha ħafna scales *tal. ħuta issa jekk ma naħ*
*slux sewwa dawk l-*iscales *jitgħaqqdu ġo xulxin*
u indaħħ ġersi daqshekk ġol- washing
machine *u noħorġu daqshekk għax jixxrinkjali*
u jitgħaqqad kollu

now this is important didn't I tell you that
if I had a look at a single hair or fibre
it has many scales which if not washed
properly get entangled and I put a jersey
this size into the washing machine and it
comes out this size because it shrinks and
gets entangled

(Adapted from Camilleri, 1994)

Camilleri notes that the first extract shows the teacher using the switch from English to Maltese to expand or *amplify* the point being made, rather than simply repeat it in translation. In the second extract, she *explains* the English statement in Maltese, again avoiding direct translation. Camilleri comments that the lesson therefore is a particular kind of literacy event, in which these are 'two parallel discourses – the written one in English, the spoken one in Maltese' (p 12).

Studies of code-switching in classrooms have revealed a variety of patterns of bilingual use (Martyn-Jones, 1995). For example, Zentella (1981) observed and recorded events in two bilingual classes in New York schools, one a first grade class (in which the children were about six years old) and the other a sixth grade (in which the average age would be about 12). The pupils and teachers were all native Spanish speakers, of Puerto Rican origin, but the official medium for classroom education was English. One of the focuses of her analysis of teacher-pupil interactions was IRF sequences. Both Spanish and English were actually used by teachers and pupils in the classes, and Zentella was able to show that there were three recurring patterns of language-switching in IRF sequences, which seem to represent the use of certain 'ground rules' governing language choice. These are summarized below:

Rules governing language choice	teacher initiation	student reply	teacher feedback
1. Teacher and student: 'follow the leader'	English Spanish	Spanish Spanish	English Spanish
2. Teacher: 'follow the child'	English Spanish	Spanish English	Spanish English
3. Teacher: 'include the child's choice not yours'	English Spanish	Spanish English	both languages both languages

(Adapted from Zentella, 1981)

From this example, we can see that distinctive patterns of language use emerge in bilingual classrooms, but these can be interpreted as adaptations of the common IRF structure and language strategies used by teachers in monolingual settings. What is more, the distinctive patterns of switching which emerge in teacher-talk can be explained in terms of the special communicative resources that arise in a modern language classroom and the ways that teachers decide to respond to these special circumstances. The extent to which code-switching between English and another language occurs in a particular setting will therefore be influenced by factors such as (a) the degree of fluency in English that members of a particular class have achieved; (b) the bilingual competence of teachers (c) the specific teaching goals of teachers; and – crucially – (d) the attitudes of both children and teachers to the practice of code-switching and to the languages involved.

What learners have to understand about classroom language

When students enter an English medium or EFL classroom having grown up speaking another language, it may be difficult for both teachers and children to distinguish between two 'learning tasks' – acquiring a basic fluency in English and learning the social conventions of using English as a classroom language. Some patterns of classroom language – such as IRF sequences – are likely to be familiar to any student who has had experience of school, even if they had encountered them in another language. As I noted earlier, however (in the comparison of Sequences 1 and 2), IRFs can be used for different purposes, some of which may not be familiar to students from their previous educational experience (say, if they have arrived as immigrants in an English-speaking country having been educated elsewhere in another language). Depending on their experiences within their own language communities, students might also be unfamiliar with some other conventions or 'ground-rules' for using English that are associated with particular social settings inside and outside school.

For these reasons, it can be difficult for a teacher to tell whether a new pupil who is not fluent in English, and who appears to be having difficulties with using the language in the classroom, is struggling with general aspects of using English or having difficulties with grasping the 'local' ground rules for classroom language use. This kind of difficulty may arise in relation to the learning of written as well as spoken English, and is well illustrated by the research of Alex Moore (1995) who studied the progress of children of non-English speaking immigrant families entering secondary schools in Britain.

Because of his close and continuous involvement in classroom events as a kind of 'action researcher' (Elliot, 1991), Moore was able to observe, describe and analyse teaching and learning over several weeks or months in one class. One of his special 'case studies' was of the progress of a Sylheti boy of 15 who had been in Britain one year since coming from Bangladesh (where he had been educated in Bengali). Moore focused on Mashud's classroom education in writing English. Mashud had quite a few problems with 'surface features' of English such as handwriting, spelling and grammatical structures, but was an enthusiastic writer. However, Moore and Mashud's teacher (Mrs Montgomery) both noticed that:

> his work had a particular idiosyncrasy in that whenever he was set creative writing – or even discursive writing – assignments, he produced heavily formulaic fairy-story-style moral tales which were apparently – according to information volunteered by other Sylheti pupils in the class – translations of stories he had learnt in his native tongue. (Moore, 1995: 362)

Despite being a willing pupil, Mashud seemed unable to transcend this traditional style of genre, and write in the genres that his teachers knew would be required of him in the British education system and in wider society. Further consideration led Moore and Mrs Montgomery to some hypotheses about why this was so:

> It has to be said that neither Mrs Montgomery or I knew enough about Bangladeshi or Sylheti story-telling traditions to be able to expound with any degree of confidence on the cause of Mashud's particular way of going about things. The key to our future pedagogy, however [. . .] lay in Mrs Montgomery's very wise recognition that "<u>there could be</u> the most enormous difference between what Mashud has been brought up to value in narratives and what we're telling him he should be valuing". (Moore, 1995: 366)

This insight into Mashud's difficulties with genres of writing was supported by a more careful analysis of Mashud's texts, which had a linear, additive, chronological structure associated with oral, rather than literate cultural traditions (Ong, 1982). The outcome was the teacher designing activities for Mashud which would support or 'scaffold' (Bruner, 1986; Maybin, Mercer and Stierer, 1992) his development as a writer of English:

> If we responded appropriately, Mashud would, we hoped, learn something of what was valued in expressive writing in his new school, and how that was different from – though no better than – what he may have learned to value at school in Bangladesh. (Moore 1995: 368)

This approach proved successful, as during the remaining period of Moore's research Mashud showed clear progress in coming to understand and cope with the demands of writing in the genres of English required in the British school system. Describing research with children in a Spanish-English bilingual program in Californian schools, Moll and Dworin (1996) also highlight the important role of a teacher in helping learners make the best educational use of their bi-cultural language experience in developing their literacy skills in the second language.

A socio-cultural perspective on classroom interaction

I now wish to relate the above discussion of language as the medium of teaching-and-learning to a consideration of the quality of education. To do this, I will draw on a particular approach to human learning and development which is known as *sociocultural psychology*. This approach has emerged during the final decades of the twentieth century from a belated appreciation of the pioneering research on the relationship between language and cognitive development carried out by the Russian psychologist Lev Vygotsky (for example, Vygotsky, 1962). Vygotsky worked in Moscow in the 1920s and 30s, in an institution for children who had special educational needs, but his ideas on the process of teaching and learning have much broader educational relevance than the specific institutional settings in which he put them into practice. Vygotsky gave language a special, important role in human cognitive development, describing human individuals and their societies as being linked by language into a historical, continuing, dynamic, interactive, spiral of change. Led by the example of Jerome Bruner (1985, 1986), a considerable body of research has now emerged which uses a 'neo-Vygotskian', socio-cultural perspective in the analysis of educational processes. Some of the most significant and distinctive implications of adopting a socio-cultural perspective on classroom education are, I believe, as follows:

1   *Language is our most important pedagogic tool*. Although they do not necessarily make this explicit, I suggest that the most influential socio-cultural theorists of cognitive development (as represented by such as Bruner, 1986; Wertsch, 1991; Rogoff, 1990) ascribe three important functions to language: (a) as *a cognitive tool* whose acquisition enables children to gain, process, organize and evaluate knowledge; (b) as *a cultural tool*, by which knowledge is shared, stored and made available to successive generations; (c) as *a pedagogic tool* by which intellectual guidance is provided to children by other people. These roles are inextricably intertwined. To this specification of the roles of language we might add the comment: learning how to use language effectively as a cultural tool is an important educational goal for native speakers as well as second language learners. So language is both the tool for carrying out teaching-and-learning and also that which is meant to be learnt and taught.

2   *Education is a dialogical, cultural process*. The development of students' knowledge and understanding is shaped by their relationships with teachers and other students, and by the culture in which those relationships are located. (Newman, Griffin and Cole, 1989; Gee, 1996). The educational success students achieve is only partly under their own control, and only partly under the control of their teachers. This is where the sociocultural concept of 'scaffolding', which I mentioned briefly earlier, is useful. The essence of this concept, as developed by Bruner (1986), Wood (1988) and others, is that an effective teacher provides the kind of intellectual support which enables learners to make intellectual achievements they would never accomplish alone; and one way they do so is by using dialogue to guide and support the development of understanding.

3   *Language carries the history of classroom activity into its future*. The socio-cultural perspective suggests that if we want to understand the process of learning, we must study not only what a learner does but also the activities of parents, teachers, peers who create – indeed, constitute – the dynamic context of their learning experience (Edwards and Mercer, 1987; Hicks, 1996). Rogoff (1990) talks of children being involved in a process of 'guided participation' in the intellectual life of their communities, which implies the necessary involvement of others. For similar reasons,

I have described the process of teaching-and-learning as 'the guided construction of knowledge' (Mercer, 1995). This is a process which is carried on over time, so that, as the language researcher Janet Maybin (1994) has put it, the talk on any occasion between a teacher and their regular class of students can be considered part of the 'long conversation' of their relationship. Language is a tool for building the future out of the past: the meaningfulness of current and future joint activities of teachers and learners depends on the foundations of their common knowledge (Mercer, 2000).

4   *Classroom interaction follows implicit 'ground rules'.* The socio-cultural perspective emphasises that everyday human activity depends heavily on participants being able to draw on a considerable body of shared knowledge and understanding, based on their past shared experience or similar histories of experience. The conventions or 'ground rules' which ensure that speakers and listeners, writers and readers are operating within the same genres of language are rarely made explicit, but so long as participants can safely assume shared knowledge, the language of everyday interaction follows its conventional patterns. If the contextual foundations of shared knowledge are lacking – such as when students' home backgrounds have not prepared them well for making sense of the language and culture of the classroom – misunderstandings may easily arise and persist unresolved (Heath, 1983; LoCastro, 1997). Making the 'ground rules' of classroom activity explicit can help overcome misunderstandings and misinterpretations, and there is growing evidence that students' progress is significantly enhanced if teachers do so (Christie, 1990; Mercer, Wegerif and Dawes 1999).

Conclusion

Recordings and transcriptions of classroom talk, analysed from a socio-cultural perspective, offer us glimpses of the social, cultural, communicative process of education being pursued and, with varying degrees of success, accomplished. They may capture illustrations of the best practice, in which teachers enable students to achieve levels of understanding which might never, or at least not nearly so quickly, have been achieved without a 'scaffolding' guidance; they as often reveal misunderstandings being generated, and opportunities for guided development being squandered. As teachers, as well as researchers, we can learn much from what they reveal. It is of course unrealistic to expect any busy teacher to monitor and evaluate every interaction in their classroom; but recent research (in areas of the curriculum other than language teaching) has shown that through a better understanding of the use of language as a pedagogic tool, teachers can help students improve their curriculum-related learning and their use of language as a tool for constructing knowledge. (Brown and Palincsar, 1989; Wegerif, Rojas-Drummond and Mercer, 1999; Mercer, Wegerif and Dawes, 1999.) A socio-cultural perspective has only quite recently been brought to bear on teaching and learning in the modern language classroom (see Chapters 5, 16 and 19 of this book, by Van Lier, Gibbons and Breen), but I am convinced that its application will have significant practical implications for this field of educational endeavour.

References

Arthur, J. (1992) 'English in Botswana classrooms: functions and constraints'. *Centre for Language in Social Life Working Papers No. 46*. University of Lancaster, U.K.

Brown, A. and Palincsar A.S. (1989) 'Guided, cooperative learning and individual knowledge acquisition', in L. Resnick (ed.) *Knowing, Learning and Instruction*. New York: Lawrence Erlbaum.

Bruner, J.S. (1985) 'Vygotsky: a historical and conceptual perspective', in J.V. Wertsch (ed.) *Culture, Communication and Cognition: Vygotskian perspectives*. Cambridge: Cambridge University Press.

Bruner, J.S. (1986) *Actual Minds, Possible Worlds*. London: Harvard University Press.

Camilleri, A. (1994) 'Talking bilingually, writing monolingually'. Paper presented at the Sociolinguistics Symposium, Lancaster University, March 1994.

Christie, F. (1990) *Literacy for a Changing World*. Melbourne: Australian Council for Educational Research.

Edwards, A.D. and Westgate, D. (1994) *Investigating Classroom Talk (Second Edition)*. London: The Falmer Press.

Edwards, D. (1988) 'The Meno', in Billig, M., Condor, S., Edwards, D., Gane, M., Middleton, D. and Radley, A. (eds) *Ideological Dilemmas: a social psychology of everyday thinking*. London: Sage.

Edwards, D. and Mercer, N. (1987) *Common Knowledge: the development of understanding in the classroom*. London: Methuen/Routledge.

Elliot, J. (1991) *Action Research for Educational Change*. Milton Keynes: Open University Press.

Gee, J.P. (1996) 'Vygotsky and current debates in education: some dilemmas as afterthoughts to *Discourse, Learning and Schooling*', in D. Hicks (ed.) *Discourse, Learning and Schooling*. Cambridge: Cambridge University Press.

Heath, S.B. (1983) *Ways with Words: language, life and work in communities and classrooms*. Cambridge: Cambridge University Press.

Hicks, D. (1996) 'Contextual enquiries: a discourse-oriented study of classroom learning', in D. Hicks (ed.) *Discourse, Learning and Schooling*. Cambridge: Cambridge University Press.

Jacobson, R. (1990) 'Allocating two languages as a key feature of a bilingual methodology', in R. Jacobson and C. Faltis (eds) *Language Distribution Issues in Bilingual Schooling*. Clevedon: Multilingual Matters.

Johnson, R.K. and Lee, P.L.M. (1987) 'Modes of instruction: teaching strategies and students responses', in R. Lord and H. Cheng (eds) *Language Education in Hong Kong*. Hong Kong: The Chinese University Press.

LoCastro, V. (1997) 'Politeness and pragmatic competence in foreign language education'. *Language Teaching Research*, Vol.1, No.3, 239–268.

Martyn-Jones, M. (1995) 'Code-switching in the classroom', in L. Milroy and P. Muysken (eds) *One Speaker, two languages: cross disciplinary perspectives on code-switching*. Cambridge: Cambridge University Press.

Maybin, J. (1994) 'Children's voices: talk, knowledge and identity', in Graddol, D, Maybin, J. and Stierer, B. (eds) *Researching Language and Literacy in Social Context*. Clevedon: Multilingual Matters.

Maybin, J., Mercer, N. and Stierer, B. (1992) '"Scaffolding" learning in the classroom', in Norman, K. (ed.) *Thinking Voices*. London: Hodder and Stoughton.

Mehan, H. (1979) *Learning Lessons: social organization in the classroom*. Cambridge, Mass: Harvard University Press.

Mercer, N. (1995) *The Guided Construction of Knowledge: talk amongst teachers and learners*. Clevedon: Multilingual Matters.

—— (2000) *Words and Minds: how we use language to think together*. London: Routledge.

Mercer, N., Wegerif, R. and Dawes, L. (1999) 'Children's talk and the development of reasoning in the classroom'. *British Educational Research Journal*, 25, 1, 95–113.

Moll, L. and Dworin, J. (1996) 'Biliteracy development in classrooms: social dynamics and cultural possibilities', in D. Hicks (ed.) *Discourse, Learning and Schooling*. Cambridge: Cambridge University Press.

Moore, A. (1995) *The Academic, Linguistic and Social Development of Bilingual Pupils in Secondary Education: issues of diagnosis, pedagogy and culture*. Unpublished Ph.D. thesis, The Open University.

Newman, D., Griffin, P. and Cole, M. (1989) *The Construction Zone*. Cambridge: Cambridge University Press.

Ong, W. (1982) *Orality and Literacy*. London: Methuen.

Rogoff, B. (1990) *Apprenticeship in Thinking*. Oxford: Oxford University Press.

Sinclair, J. and Coulthard, M. (1975) *Towards an analysis of discourse: the English used by teachers and pupils*. London: Oxford University Press.

Vygotsky, L.S. (1962) *Thought and Language*. Cambridge, Mass.: MIT Press. (Originally published in Russian in 1934.)

Wegerif, R., Rojas-Drummond, S. and Mercer, N. (1999) 'Language for the social construction of knowledge: comparing classroom talk in Mexican pre-schools', *Language and Education*, Vol. 13, No. 2, pp. 133–150.

Wertsch, J. (1991) *Voices of the Mind: a socio-cultural approach to mediated action*. Cambridge, Mass.: Harvard University Press.

Wood, D. (1988) *How children think and learn*. Oxford: Basil Blackwell.

Zentella, A.C. (1981) '*Ta bien*, you could answer me in *cualquier idioma*: Puerto Rican code-switching in bilingual classrooms', in R. Duran (ed.) *Latino Language and Communicative Behavior*, pp 109–132. Norwood, N.J.: Ablex Publishing Corporation.

Chapter 16

Pauline Gibbons

LEARNING A NEW REGISTER IN A SECOND LANGUAGE

Introduction

FOR STUDENTS WHO ARE LEARNING English as a second language in an English medium school, English is both a target and medium of education: they are not only learning the dominant language but they are learning in it and through it as well. For these learners, the construction of curriculum knowledge must go hand in hand with the development of the second language.

This chapter illustrates how such integration can be achieved. In it I argue that learners' current understandings of a curriculum topic, and their use of familiar 'everyday' language to express these understandings, should be seen as the basis for the development of the more unfamiliar and academic registers of the school. I show how teacher-student talk, based on shared common experiences, leads to the development of new ways of meaning. I also suggest the usefulness of bringing together, for the purposes of classroom-based research, bodies of knowledge which have rarely overlapped; second language acquisition (SLA) research, neo-Vygotskian socio-cultural approaches to teaching and learning, and systemic functional linguistics (SFL)

The context for the study

The classroom from which the data derive is in an inner city school in Sydney. At the time of the study, twenty three languages were spoken by the children in the school. The class consisted of 30 children aged between 8–10, with all but two children in the class coming from homes where a language other than English was spoken. Many children had been born in Australia but entered school with little English, others were first generation migrants, including two children who had arrived in Australia within the last year. Generally, such children very quickly become adept at using English in face-to-face contexts, where the conversation relates to what is occurring around them. However, as Cummins (1996), Collier (1989) and McKay *et al.* (1997) have shown, children who appear 'fluent' in such contexts may still have difficulty in controlling the more written-like and subject specific registers of school, because these more academic registers usually require a much longer time for development. The focus of this paper is on the learning of a more academic register by students who are largely fluent in English in face-to-face, everyday communication.

The language model

Where the teaching of a new language is to be integrated with the teaching of subject content, then program planning needs to be informed by a model of language which relates language to meaning, and to the context in which it is used. This study draws on systemic functional grammar (Halliday, 1985) and related descriptions of register theory (Halliday and Hasan, 1985).

A major organising principle of the teaching program described was the construct of **mode** (which refers to the channel of the text, whether it is spoken or written) and the notion of a **mode continuum** (Martin, 1984), because it offers a linguistic framework against which teaching activities can be sequenced from most situationally-dependent (and thus for ESL learners the most easily understood), to least situationally-dependent. The following four texts illustrate this mode continuum, and show how certain linguistic features change as language becomes increasingly closer to written forms.

Text 1: (spoken by three 10-year-old students and accompanying action)

this . . . no it doesn't go . . . it doesn't move . . . try that . . . yes it does . . . a bit . . . that won't . . . won't work it's not metal . . . these are the best . . . going really fast.

Text 2: (spoken by one student about the action, after the event)

we tried a pin . . . a pencil sharpener . . . some iron filings and a piece of plastic . . . the magnet didn't attract the pin.

Text 3: (written by the same student)

Our experiment was to find out what a magnet attracted. We discovered that a magnet attracts some kinds of metal. It attracted the iron filings, but not the pin.

Text 4: (taken from a child's encyclopedia)

A magnet . . . is able to pick up, or attract, a piece of steel or iron because its magnetic field flows into the magnet, turning it into a temporary magnet. Magnetic attraction occurs only between ferrous materials.

Text 1 is typical of the kind of situationally-dependent language produced in face-to-face contexts. Because the visual context obviates the need to name the referent, exophoric reference is used (*this, these, that*), and there is a relatively low lexical density, or number of 'content' words per clause. In Text 2 the context changes, because the student is telling others what she learned, and no longer has the science equipment in front of her. She must now reconstruct the experience through language alone, and so makes explicit the participants (*we, pin, pencil sharpener, iron filings, piece of plastic*) and process (*attract*) she is referring to. Text 3 is a written text and, since the audience is now unseen, it cannot rely on shared assumptions, and so the writer must recreate experience through language alone – note, for example, the orientation which is needed to provide the context for what follows: *Our experiment was to* . . . In Text 4 the major participant (*a magnet*) is generic: its properties are those of all magnets. There is a further increase in lexical density, and the text includes a nominalisation, the coding of a process term as a noun (*attraction*) which is typical of much written text.

While spoken and written language obviously have distinctive characteristics, this continuum of texts illustrates that there is no absolute boundary between them. Technology increases this blurring. Leaving a detailed message on an answering machine, for example, may be quite linguistically demanding since, in the absence of two-way contact, and without (initially at least) the shared understandings and expectations which are implicit in two-way, face-to-face communication, we are required to 'speak aloud' the kind of language that would more usually be written. Thus in terms of the mode continuum it is perhaps more appropriate to describe texts as 'more spoken-like' or 'more written-like', and these are the terms which will be used here.

In many ways the continuum reflects the process of formal education itself, as students are required to move from personal everyday ways of making meanings towards the socially shared discourses of specific disciplines. A second language learner is likely to have fewer difficulties with producing something like text 1, where the situational context itself provides a support for meaning and there are thus fewer linguistic demands, than with more written-like texts, where more lexico-grammatical resources are required. It is worth noting, too, that when children are expected to write simply on the basis of personal experiences, they are being asked to take a very large linguistic step (as can be seen by comparing text 1 and 3), and one which is beyond the current linguistic resources of some second language learners.

In the classroom described here, a major focus is on students using spoken language in the way that text 2 illustrates, that is, language which, while spoken, is not embedded in the immediate situational context in which it occurs. This more 'written-like' spoken language can be seen as a bridge between the language associated with experiential activities and the more formal – and often written – registers of the curriculum.

The role of talk in learning

While the importance of talk in learning has long been recognised (Barnes 1976; Bruner 1978; Martin et al. 1976), a more recent focus, largely influenced by the work of Vygotsky, has been on the social and cultural basis for learning (Mercer 1994, 1995 and Chapter 15 of this book; Maybin, Mercer and Stierer 1992; Wells 1992, 1999). A socio-cultural or 'neo-Vygotskian' perspective places interactions and the broad social context of learning at the heart of the learning process; the classroom is viewed as a place where understanding and knowledge are jointly constructed, and where learners are guided or 'apprenticed' into the broader understandings and language of the curriculum and the particular subject discipline. The notion of apprenticeship into a culture is particularly relevant in an ESL school context, where, in order to participate in society, students must learn to control the dominant genres through which that culture is constructed (Martin 1986; Delpit 1988; Kalantzis, Cope, Noble and Poynting 1991).

SLA researchers have also shown the significance of interaction for second language learning (see for example, Ellis 1985, 1991, 1994; van Lier 1988, 1996 and Chapter 5 of this book; Swain 1995; Swain 2000). Of particular importance are the kinds of on-going modifications which occur as meaning is negotiated or clarified (Long 1983; Pica, Young and Doughty 1986; Pica 1994). Swain (1985, 1995) also argues for the need for 'comprehensible output', whereby learners pay attention to their own talk, and as a result produce more comprehensible, coherent, and syntactically improved discourse. This attention to output 'stretches' the learner, in that s/he is pushed to attend to syntactic as well as to semantic processing. The classroom implication for this, I suggest, is not that language 'form' per se should become a major teaching focus, but that it is important, at times, for learners to have opportunities to use stretches of discourse in contexts where there is a 'press' on their linguistic resources, and where, for the benefit of their listeners, they must focus not only on what they wish to say but on how they are saying it.

One clear teaching implication of these various studies is that the degree to which a classroom is facilitative of second language learning depends largely on how classroom discourse is constructed. Traditional classroom interactions consisting of sequences of initiation, response, and feedback moves (Sinclair and Coulthard 1975; Edwards and Mercer 1987) may, in fact, deprive learners of just those interactional features and interactive conditions which SLA research suggests are enabling factors in language learning. When teacher initiations lead to single word or single clause responses, there is little opportunity for learner language to be 'stretched', or for the production of comprehensible output. A classroom program which is supportive of second language learning must therefore create opportunities for more dialogic interactional patterns to occur (see van Lier 1996, for detailed discussion of these issues).

The data

The classroom context

Based on the science topic of magnetism, teaching and learning activities were planned to reflect points along the mode continuum, the assumption being that this would offer a logical development in terms of language learning. Thus students initially participated in small-group learning experiences where the language used was clearly situationally-embedded. This was followed by a teacher-guided reporting session, where, in interaction with the teacher, each group shared their learning with the whole class. Talking with the teacher about what had been learned, since this did not involve the use of the concrete materials, led to a mode shift towards more written-like language, and provided a bridge into the writing, which was the final activity of the cycle and linguistically the most demanding. This three-part cycle was repeated several times during the course of the development of the unit of work. The three stages are described below, together with representative texts from each stage. Taken as a sequence, they illustrate how language development can evolve through jointly constructed discourse.

Stage 1

In many primary schools it is usual for students to rotate through a number of activities over the course of one or two lessons. However, such an organisational structure may negate any authentic purpose for reporting back to others, since children are likely to share very similar experiences. Here, an attempt was made to set up a genuine communicative situation by having each group of children work at *different* (though related) science experiments; thus they held different information from other class members. In its communicative structure the classroom organisation was based on an important principle in second language task design: the notion of an information 'gap' and the need for information exchange (Long 1989).

One experiment consisted of a small polystyrene block into which a number of paddle-pop (ice-lolly) sticks had been inserted to enclose a bar magnet. The students were asked to test the effect of a second magnet. (When the second magnet is placed above the first in a position in which they are repelling, repulsion causes the second magnet to be suspended in mid-air.) The texts below (1.1 and 1.2) occurred as students were engaged in this activity. Prior to beginning the activity, they were told that they would later describe and attempt to explain what happened to the rest of the class ([. . .] marks an obvious pause).

Text 1.1

Hannah: try . . . the other way
Patrick: like that
Hannah: north pole facing down
Joanna: we tried that
Peter: oh!
Hannah: it stays up!
Patrick: magic!
Peter: let's show the others
Joanna: mad!
Peter: I'll put north pole facing north pole . . . see what happen
Patrick: that's what we just did
Peter: yeah . . . like this . . . look

The dialogue continues for several minutes longer as the students try different positions for the magnet, and then they begin to formulate an explanation.

Text 1.2

Hannah: can I try that? . . . I know why . . . I know why . . . that's like . . . because the north
          pole is on this side and that north pole's there . . . so they don't stick together
Peter: what like this? yeah
Hannah: yeah see because the north pole on this side . but turn it on the other . . . this side
          like that . . . turn it that way . . . yeah
Peter: and it will stick
Hannah: and it will stick because. look . . . the north pole's on that side because . . .
Peter: the north pole's on that side yeah

Stage 2

The overall aim of the teacher-guided reporting was to extend children's linguistic resources and focus on aspects of the specific discourse of science. As the teacher expressed it to the children: *we're trying to talk like scientists*. It was anticipated that the reporting stage would create a context for students to 'rehearse' language structures which were closer to written discourse. Before the reporting began, there had been a short teacher-led discussion focusing on the specific lexis the children would need to use, including the lexical item *repel*.

In the text below (Text 2), Hannah is explaining what she learned.

Text 2

STUDENTS	TEACHER
1	try to tell them what you learned . . . OK . . . (*to Hannah*) yes?

2	when I put/ when you put . . . when you put a magnet . . . on top of a magnet and the north pole poles are. . . *(7 second pause, Hannah is clearly having difficulty in expressing what she wants to say)*	
3		yes yes you're doing fine . . . you put one magnet on top of another . . .
4	and and the north poles are together er em the magnet . . . repels the magnet er . . . the magnet and the other magnet . . . sort of floats in the air?	
5	*(The teacher invites other contributions, and then asks Hannah to explain it again.)*	I think that was very well told . . . very well told . . . do you have anything to add to that Charlene?
6		now listen . . . now Hannah explain once more. . . alright Hannah . . . excuse me everybody *(regaining classes attention)* . . . listen again to her explanation
7	the two north poles are leaning together and the magnet on the bottom is repelling the magnet on top so that the magnet on the top is sort of . . . floating in the air	
8		so that these two magnets are repelling *(said with emphasis)* each other and . . . *(demonstrating)* look at the force of it.

Stage 3

After the students had taken part in the reporting session, they wrote a response in their journals to the question 'what have you learned?' These were later used as a source of information in the writing of more formal reports about magnets. The interest of the journals here, however, is that they provide some evidence of 'uptake', in that they reflect wordings which occurred in the process of jointly-produced student-teacher discourse. The texts below include Hannah's own entry, and an entry from another student who had listened to Hannah's talk with her teacher.

Text 3.1 (Hannah's journal entry)

I found it very interesting that when you stuck at least 8 paddle pop sticks in a piece of polystyrene, and then put a magnet with the North and South pole in the oval and put another magnet with the north and south pole on top, the magnet on the bottom will repel the magnet on the top and the magnet on the top would look like it is floating in the air.

Text 3.2 (another student's journal entry)

The thing made out of polystyrene with paddle pop sticks, one group put one magnet facing north and another magnet on top facing north as well and they repelled each other. It looked like the top magnet was floating up in the air.

Discussion

Stage 1 texts

The small group activities produced situationally embedded, 'here-and-now' language. Note, for example, the exophoric references: *like that; like this; that way* in text 1.1 (These references, of course, carry meanings which, in the absence of a visual context, must be realised in a different way, and it is precisely this aspect of discourse which causes Hannah, and many of the other students, difficulty in the later reporting session.)

Talk at this stage also foregrounds the interpersonal aspects of language. Students are concerned with directing each other's actions, rather than exchanging information. Text 1.1 is about social interaction as much as it is about magnets: subject specific language is simply not necessary for communication between the interactants because of the visual face-to-face context in which the discourse occurs. There are also personal comments indicating affect, such as the expression of attitude and feelings: in this text, *magic! mad!* Participants are generally human and frequently thematised, and they relate to the interactants themselves: *We tried that; I'll put north pole facing north pole.*

What is important about the activities, however, is that they allowed children to explore and develop together certain scientific understandings (the position of the poles is significant to the movement of the magnets). As the discourse progresses (text 1.2), individual utterances become longer and more explicit, and this occurs as the students begin to formulate explanations for what they see (note the logical connectives *so, because*). Interpersonal elements are reduced; there is now a non-human participant (*the north pole*) and this, rather than the interactants themselves, becomes the topic of conversation. The cognitive challenge inherent in the teacher's instruction to 'try to explain what you see' may have been significant here, since it extended the task from simply 'doing' to 'doing and thinking'. This explicit focus on thinking is an important one in the light of this type of teaching context, where a teacher must balance the need for suitably high levels of cognitive learning with learners' relatively low levels of English, and where learning activities aimed at development of the second language must also be linked to cognitive growth. Clearly within these texts there is evidence of children's learning of science: the beginnings of an understanding of why the magnets are behaving as they are, and attempts to hypothesise about the causal relations involved. Through the kind of exploratory talk which begins to be evident here in the small group work, "knowledge is made more publicly accountable and reasoning is more visible" (Wegerif and Mercer, 1996: 51).

From the point of view of second language learning, it is also important to note that the children developed some understandings about magnets before they were expected to understand and use more scientific discourse. For example, at the beginning of the reporting session, the teacher introduces the term *repel* at a time when students had already expressed this meaning in familiar everyday language, using terms such as *it pushes away; it feels like a strong wind*. There is some parallel here to the principle within bilingual programs which suggests that learning should occur first in L1 as a basis to learning in L2, but here the issue is one of register rather than language.

Stage 2 texts

Driver makes the important point about science education that 'activity by itself is not enough. It is the sense that is made of it that matters' (Driver, 1983: 49). In Stage 2 texts we see the teacher working with the children to 'make sense' of the activities in which they have been engaged, by helping them reconstruct their experiences and develop shared understandings through language. Wegerif and Mercer suggest that it is through being encouraged and enabled 'to clearly describe events, to account for outcomes and consolidate what they have learned in words' that children are helped to 'understand and gain access to educated discourse' (Wegerif and Mercer, 1996: 53). Text 2 illustrates one type of situation in which this process can occur.

The teacher's role in these episodes was crucial; the texts show how her interactions with individual students provided a 'scaffold' for their attempts, allowing for communication to proceed while giving the learner access to new linguistic data. In Text 2, the interaction between teacher and students is different in several small but important respects from the traditional IRF pattern, but these modifications appear to have significant effects on the interaction as a whole. Typically, the IRF pattern is realised in fairly predictable ways, frequently involving a teacher known-answer question, followed by a student answer (often brief), and followed by a teacher evaluation relating to the correctness or otherwise of the answer. In Text 2, the interactions approximate more closely what occurs in L1 adult–child interactions outside of the formal teaching context (see for example, Halliday 1975; Wells 1981; Painter 1985). The teacher begins the exchange with inviting students to relate what they have learned, rather than with a 'known answer' or display question. While teachers' questions are often framed in ways which do not allow for students to make extended responses (Dillon, 1990), here, by contrast, the teacher sets up a context where it is the students who initiate the specific topic of the exchange. As Ellis (1996) shows, when learners initiate what they wish to talk about, language learning is facilitated because they enter the discourse on their own terms, rather than responding to a specific request for information from the teacher. In this text, the student takes on the role of what Berry refers to as 'primary knower' (Berry 1981). Although of course it is the teacher who is in control of the knowledge associated with the overall thematic development of the unit of work, the individual exchanges locate that control in the student. The reciprocity and mutuality in the speaker roles leads to Hannah producing longer stretches of discourse than often occurs in classroom interaction. As is typical in these reporting sessions, the teacher 'leads from behind', and while following Hannah's lead and accepting as a valid contribution the information she gives, the teacher also recasts it, providing alternative linguistic forms to encode student meaning in more context-appropriate ways.

It is also clear that teacher-guided reporting encourages learner language to be 'pushed'. (As one student commented as she struggled to explain what she had done: *I can't say it Miss!*). Hannah is going beyond what is unproblematic for her but, because she is allowed a second attempt, she has an opportunity to produce more comprehensible output. Hannah's second attempt at her explanation is considerably less hesitant and syntactically more complete than her first, and is produced this time without the help of the teacher. Vygotsky's notion of the 'ZPD' is significant here. Vygotsky suggests that learning occurs, with support from those more expert, in the learner's 'zone of proximal development' (Vygotsky 1978), that is, at the 'outer edges' of a learner's current abilities. In 1.2, Hannah appears to have reached her own zone of proximal development for this task, since she hesitates for a considerable time, and can presumably go no further alone. The recasting and support she receives from the teacher (1.3) then appears to be precisely timed for learning to occur and to assist Hannah to continue.

As Text 2 illustrates, the reporting context also gives students opportunities to produce longer stretches of discourse which are more written-like than those which occurred in the small group work. Often this required the teacher to increase 'wait time', on occasions for as long as eight seconds. Research suggests that when teachers ask questions of students, they typically wait one second or less for the students to begin a reply, but that when teachers wait for three or more seconds, there are significant changes in student use of language and in the attitudes and expectations of both students and teachers (Rowe, 1986). We can surmise that the importance of wait time is increased for students who are formulating responses in a language they do not fully control. Perhaps equally important, students were able to complete what they wanted to say and as a result were positioned as successful interactants and learners. In addition, since it is the immediate need of the learner which is influencing to a large extent the teacher's choice of actual wording, it would seem likely that this wording will be more salient to the learner – more likely to be noticed – than if it had occurred in a context which was less immediate. (For discussion of the significance of 'noticing' in second language development, see Ellis, 1994).

Another significant mode shift occurred towards the end of most reporting sessions, where the teacher used children's personal knowledge to show how generalisations might be generated. Her questions at this point included, for example: *can you see something in common with all these experiences? what's the same about all these experiments?*

Such questions require the students to do more than simply produce a personal recount of what they did; they must now recontextualise this in terms of the teacher's question. What they say is now characterised by a shift towards generalisation, an increased use of field specific lexis, and the thematisation of field-related participants; the children themselves are no longer the 'actors' in the text:

> *the north pole of the magnet sticks . . . attracts . . . the second magnet . . . the south pole of the second magnet.*

> *if you put the south and north together then they will . . . attract but if you put north and north or south and south . . . together . . . they won't stick . . . attract.*

Thus the teacher again mediates between children's individual experiences and the broader knowledge and discourse into which they are being apprenticed, locating these experiences within a larger framework of meanings. Stage 2 texts, then, both in the way language is used, and in the kinds of knowledge which is constructed, serve to create a 'bridge' for learners between personal experiential ways of knowing and the public discourse of shared and socially constructed knowledge.

Stage 3 texts

Many of the journals reflected what had been said in the teacher-guided reporting sessions. Students included wording which they had used in interaction with the teacher, or which had been part of the teacher's recasting, and this was particularly evident when the students themselves had reformulated their own talk. Compare, for example, Hannah's written text (3.1) with what she says in interaction with the teacher. There is also evidence that the reporting back sessions influenced not only the interactants themselves but also those who listened to the interactions as part of the larger group: Text 3.2 was written by a student who had not taken part in this particular experiment herself.

Conclusions

While the research I have described illustrates the value of 'learning by doing' (especially for second language learners where concrete experiences help to make language comprehensible), it also illustrates the critical role of teacher-learner talk in children's learning and language development, and the way that such scaffolded interactions can begin to co-construct a new register. Teacher-guided reporting in particular appears to offer a rich potential for second language development.

The research also suggests that in analysing how interactions are made comprehensible to ESL students in the classroom context, we need to look further than the linguistic features of the interactions themselves (for example the simplicity or otherwise of syntactic structures), and examine the on-going context in which those interactions are situated. Of particular significance within the sequence of lessons was the scaffolding of new language. Occurring as this did *after* students had already developed some understanding of key concepts through the small group work, it allowed the teacher to use new wordings and ways of meaning – a new register – which were then more readily interpretable by the students. The broader principle is that language which would normally be beyond students' comprehension is likely to be understood when students can bring their experiences and understandings as a basis for interpretation. The degree to which interactions are comprehensible for ESL students should therefore be related not only to the interactional features themselves, and to the immediate situational context in which they occur, but also to what has preceded them – in this case the learning which the students had gained through participation in the small group work. For second language learners, the 'long conversation' (Maybin 1994; Mercer 1995) is an important part of the total teaching and learning context, because students and teacher 'relate discourse to context, and build through time a joint frame of reference' (Edwards and Mercer, 1995). As Wong-Fillmore states in her study of an ESL kindergarten class, "the prior experience becomes a context for interpreting the new experience . . . prior experiences serve as the contexts within which the language being used is to be understood" (Wong-Fillmore 1985).

The overall sequence of activities also presents a challenge to more traditional ways of sequencing teaching and learning activities in the second language classroom, where a unit very often *begins* with the pre-teaching of vocabulary or a grammatical structure. While this approach may be appropriate in some teaching contexts, it is underpinned by the notion that learners must first 'learn' language before they can 'use' it. Aside from questions about the nature of language and language learning which this sets up, it is also clear that it is an approach which cannot be easily applied to the school ESL context, where children must from the outset use their target language in specific social contexts and for specific purposes. In this class, students used their current language resources at the beginning of the unit while the focus on new language occurred at later stages, a sequence which allowed for students to build on their existing understandings and language, and to link old learning with new; in effect to move successfully towards target texts, rather than beginning with them.

The research I have described also indicates the significance for language learning of the intertextual nature of classroom language: how one text is understood or produced in relation to another. A wide range of intertextual relationships exist in all classrooms, between, for example, what a teacher says and what students are expected to read; what students listen to and what they are expected to write; the discourse of the lesson and the texts students are expected to work with for homework; and the familiar language or dialect of the home and the less familiar language of the school. A consideration of how these links are made intertextually – and recognising where linguistic 'bridges' are missing – might offer insights for the planning of school programs for all learners, and help to suggest the kind of linguistic support most relevant for students less familiar with the language of the classroom.

A final point concerns the model of language drawn on in my research. A language model which addresses the relationship between context and meaning, and which is concerned therefore with more than grammatical competence, provides a significant dimension to the planning of ESL programs and design and sequencing of learning activities.

Further classroom-based studies are needed into the language learning processes of school-aged ESL learners, if educators are to develop more theoretically informed and equitable curricula and pedagogy. This task requires researchers to take a more interdisciplinary approach to research in multilingual classrooms, one which draws on several theoretical and methodological lines of enquiry and which is underpinned by a social view of learning and a model of language-in-context.

References

Barnes, D. (1976) *From Communication to Curriculum*. Harmondsworth: Penguin.

Berry, M. (1981) 'Systemic linguistics and discourse analysis: a multi-layered approach to exchange structure', in M. Coulthard and M. Montgomery (eds) *Studies in Discourse Analysis*. London: Routledge and Kegan.

Bruner, J. (1978) 'The role of dialogue in language acquisition', in A. Sinclair, R. Jarvella, and W. Levelt (eds) *The Child's Conception of Language*. New York: Springer-Verlag.

Collier, V. (1989) 'How long? A synthesis of research in academic achievement in a second language'. *TESOL Quarterly, 23*, 509–531.

Cummins, J. (1996) *Negotiating Identities: Education for Empowerment in a Diverse Society*. Ontario CA: California Association for Bilingual Education.

Delpit, L. (1988) 'The silenced dialogue: power and pedagogy in educating other people's children'. *Harvard Educational Review, 58*(3), 280–298.

Dillon, J. (1990) *The Practice of Questioning*. London: Routledge.

Driver, R. (1983) *The Pupil as Scientist?* Milton Keynes: Open University Press.

Edwards, D., and Mercer, N. (1987) *Common Knowledge: The Development of Understanding in the Classroom*. London: Methuen.

Ellis, R. (1985) *Understanding Second Language Acquisition*. Oxford: Oxford University Press.

—— (1991) 'The interaction hypothesis: a critical evaluation', in E. Sadtono (ed.), *Language Acquisition and the Second/Foreign Language Classroom*. Singapore: Anthology Series 28, SEAMEO Regional Language Centre.

—— (1994) *The Study of Second Language Acquisition*. Oxford: Oxford University Press.

Halliday, M. (1975) *Learning How to Mean: Explorations in the Development of Language*. London: Arnold.

—— (1985) *An Introduction to Functional Grammar*. London: Edward Arnold.

Halliday, M., and Hasan, R. (1985) *Language, Context and Text*. Geelong Victoria: Deakin University Press.

Kalantzis, M., Cope, B., Noble, G., and Poynting, S. (1991) *Cultures of Schooling: Pedagogies for Cultural Difference and Social Access*. London: Falmer Press.

Long, M. (1983) 'Native speaker/non native speaker conversations and the negotiation of comprehensible input'. *Applied Linguistics*, 4, 126–141.

Martin, J. (1984) 'Language, register and genre', in F. Christie (ed.) *Children Writing, Study Guide*. Geelong, Victoria: Deakin University Press.

—— (1986) *Secret English: discourse technology in a junior secondary school*. Proceedings from the Working Conference on Language in Education, Macquarie University.

Martin, N., Williams, P., Wilding, J., Hemmings, S., and Medway, P. (1976). *Understanding Children Talking*. London: Penguin.

Maybin, J. (1994) 'Children's voices: talk, knowledge and identity', in D. Graddol, J. Maybin and B. Stierer (eds) *Researching Language and Literacy in Social Contexts*. Clevedon: Multilingual Matters.

Maybin, J., Mercer, N., and Stierer, B. (1992) 'Scaffolding learning in the classroom', in K. Norman (ed.) *Thinking Voices: The Work of the National Oracy Project*. London: Hodder and Stoughton.

McKay, P., Davies, A., Devlin, B., Clayton, J., Oliver, R., and Zammit, S. (1997) *The Bilingual Interface Project Report*. Canberra: Department of Employment, Education, Training and Youth Affairs.

Mercer, N. (1994) 'Neo-Vygotskian theory and classroom education', in B. Stierer and J. Maybin *Language, Literacy and Learning in Educational Practice*. Clevedon: Multilingual Matters.

—— (1995) *The Guided Construction of Knowledge: Talk Amongst Teachers and Learners*. Clevedon: Multilingual Matters.

Painter, C. (1985) *Learning the Mother Tongue*. Geelong, Victoria: Deakin University Press.

Pica, T. (1994) 'Research on negotiation: what does it reveal about second language learning conditions, processes and outcomes?' *Language Learning*, 44, 493–527.

Pica, T., Young, R., and Doughty, C. (1987) 'The impact of interaction on comprehension'. *TESOL Quarterly*, 21(4), 737–758.

Rowe, M. (1986) 'Wait time: slowing down may be a way of speeding up'. *Journal of Teacher Education*, 37, 43–50.

Sinclair, J., and Coulthard, R. (1975) *Towards an Analysis of Discourse: the English Used by Teachers and Pupils*. London: Oxford University Press.

Swain, M. (1985) 'Communicative competence: some roles of comprehensible input and comprehensible output in its development', in S. Gass and C. Madden (eds) *Input in Second Language Acquisition*. Cambridge MA: Newbury House.

Swain, M. (1995) 'Three functions of output in second language learning', in G. Cook and B. Seidlehofer (eds) *Principle and Practice in Applied Linguistics: Studies in Honour of H.G. Widdowson*. Oxford: Oxford University Press.

Swain, M. (2000) 'The output hypothesis and beyond: mediating acquisition through collaborative dialogue', in J. Lantolf (ed.) *Sociocultural Theory and Second Language Learning*. Oxford: Oxford University Press.

van Lier, L. (1988) *The Classroom and the Language Learner*. Harlow: Longman.

—— (1996) *Interaction in the Language Curriculum: Awareness, Autonomy and Authenticity*. London: Longman.

Vygotsky, L. (1978) *Mind in Society: The Development of Higher Psychological Processes*. London: Harvard University Press.

Wegerif, R., and Mercer, N. (1996) 'Computers and reasoning through talk in the classroom'. *Language and Education*, 10(1), 47–64.

Wells, G. (1981) *Learning through Interaction: the Study of Language Development*. Cambridge: Cambridge University Press.

—— (1992) 'The centrality of talk in education', in K. Norman (ed.) *Thinking Voices: The Work of the National Oracy Project*. London: Hodder and Stoughton.

—— (1999) *Dialogic Inquiry*. Cambridge: Cambridge University Press.

Wong-Fillmore, L. (1985) 'When does teacher talk work as input?', in S. Gass and C. Madden (eds) *Input in Second Language Acquisition*. Rowley MA: Newbury House.

Chapter 17

Angel M. Y. Lin

DOING-ENGLISH-LESSONS IN THE REPRODUCTION OR TRANSFORMATION OF SOCIAL WORLDS?

1 Introduction

THIS ARTICLE TELLS A STORY of four classrooms, situated in different socioeconomic backgrounds. Drawing on the theoretical notions of cultural capital, habitus, symbolic violence, and creative, discursive agency as analytic tools, the story unfolds witnessing the classroom dilemmas in which students and teachers found themselves, as well as the creative, discursive strategies which they used to cope with these dilemmas. The implications of their strategies are discussed with reference to the question of whether doing English lessons contributes to the reproduction or in the transformation of the students' social worlds.

Statements about the global spread of English and its increasing socioeconomic importance in the world have almost become clichés. On colorful banners celebrating the TESOL Annual Convention in Chicago streets in 1996 was written the eye-catching mission slogan, "Teaching English to the World". Indeed, English seems to have become a precious commodity increasingly demanded by the world, and TESOL practitioners and researchers seem to be striving to meet the demand of the world market with all our professionalism. In TESOL journals and annual conventions, practitioners and researchers share their findings about methods, approaches, material designs that are effective.

However, apart from the technical concern of efficiency in teaching and learning, it seems that a far more diverse range of questions needs to be addressed which includes questions such as whether, and if yes, how, English is implicated in the reproduction of social inequalities in different contexts in the world. As regards the global influence of English, Pennycook (1994) points out both the global dominant position of English and the socioeconomic, cultural and political embeddedness of English in the world. Access (or lack of it) to English often affects the social mobility and life chances of many children and adults not speaking English as their first or second language. The classroom in many places in the world is a key site for the reproduction of social identities and unequal relations of power (Martyn-Jones and Heller, 1996). It is also likely that many students in the world hold an ambivalent, want-hate relationship with English and the classroom becomes a site for students' struggles and oppositional practices which, however, often lead students to participate in their own domination (e.g. see Canagarajah, Chapter 13 of this book). This chapter is written for TESOL practitioners and researchers who want to listen to more of the lived stories of English in the world and who share a similar concern in exploring ways of doing TESOL that do not participate in the reproduction of student disadvantage.

2 A theoretical preamble: cultural capital, symbolic violence, and creative, discursive agency

Some theoretical notions that can serve as analytical tools for achieving a greater understanding of social phenomena of reproduction are discussed in this section. Given limited space, what goes below must be treated as a highly synoptic characterization and the interested reader is urged to consult the references themselves for a more detailed account.

Cultural capital

This is a concept from Bourdieu (Bourdieu, 1973; Bourdieu and Passeron, 1977; Bourdieu, 1977; Bourdieu, 1991) referring to language use, skills, and orientations/dispositions attitudes/schemes of perception (also called "habitus") that a child is endowed with by virtue of socialization in her/his family and community. Bourdieu's argument is that their familial socialization bestows on children of the socioeconomic elite the right kind of cultural capital for school success (i.e., their habitus becomes their cultural capital). A recurrent theme in Bourdieu's works is that children from disadvantaged groups, with a habitus incompatible with that presupposed in school, are not competing with equal starting points with children of the socioeconomic elite; hence the reproduction of social stratification. The notion of cultural capital has been used by educationists (e.g., Delpit, 1988; Luke, 1996) to describe the disadvantaged position of ethnic and linguistic minorities and to problematize the notion that state education in modern societies is built on meritocracy and equal opportunity.

Symbolic violence

Another recurrent theme in Bourdieu's works concerns how the disadvantaging effect of the schooling system is masked or legitimized in people's consciousness. School failure can be conveniently attributed to individual cognitive deficit or lack of effort and not to the unequal initial shares of the cultural capital both valued and legitimized in school:

> the dominated classes allow (the struggle) to be imposed on them when they accept the stakes offered by the dominant classes. It is an integrative struggle and, by virtue of the initial handicaps, a reproductive struggle, since those who enter this chase, in which they are beaten before they start, as the constancy of the gaps testifies, implicitly recognize the legitimacy of the goals pursued by those whom they pursue, by the mere fact of taking part. (Bourdieu, 1984: 165)

Symbolic violence, according to Bourdieu, is the imposition of representations of the world and social meanings upon groups in such a way that they are experienced as legitimate. This is achieved through a process of *misrecognition*. For instance, the recent "English Only" campaigns in the United States provide illustrations of the political struggles required to create and maintain a unified linguistic market in which only one language is recognized as legitimate and appropriate for discourse in official settings, and this "English = American" symbolic representation has numerous consequences for schooling and jobs (Collins, 1993). For another instance, many Hong Kong parents insist on fighting for a place for their children in English medium schools (often despite the fact that their children speak and understand little English) because of the "English medium schools = good schools" symbolic representation that they have steadfastly accepted even in a largely Chinese society and a post-1997 era (for some background to the symbolic domination of English in Hong Kong, see Lin, 1996, 1998; and more on this in section 3 below).

Creative, discursive agency

Bourdieu has often been accused of being overly deterministic and a theorist more of reproduction than transformation (e.g., Jenkins, 1992; Canagarajah in Chapter 13). Lemke, however, points out that Bourdieu is not limited to reproduction; what he does limit is the effectiveness of single agents in changing whole fields of valuation (Jay Lemke, personal communication). For instance, the legitimate prestige and value attached to English in Hong Kong cannot be changed by single agents unless there are systematic changes in the social selection mechanism (e.g., the medium of the universities and the professions; the language of the job market; see section 3 below). While the above seems true, an area in which Bourdieu offers few analyses is the creative, discursive agency of social actors who find themselves caught in dilemmas. As Collins points out:

> we need to allow for dilemmas and intractable oppositions; for divided consciousness, not just dominated minds; . . . for creative, discursive agency in conditions prestructured, to be sure, but also fissured in unpredictable and dynamic ways. (Collins, 1993: 134)

In section 4 below, we shall see some examples, and discuss the consequences, of teachers' and students' different creative discursive strategies in response to the classroom dilemmas posed by the larger social structures. However, before looking at the classrooms, let us first look at the larger social context of the classrooms.

3 Hong Kong: the setting of the story

Despite its international cosmopolitan appearance Hong Kong is ethnically rather homogeneous. About 97% of its population is ethnic Chinese, and Cantonese is the mother tongue of the majority. English native speakers account for not more than 3% of the entire population. They constituted the privileged class of the society until July 1, 1997 when Hong Kong's sovereignty was returned to China and Hong Kong became a Special Administrative Region (SAR) of China. The English-conversant bilingual Chinese middle class has, however, remained the socioeconomically dominant group in Hong Kong.

Notwithstanding its being the mother tongue of only a minority, English has been the language of educational and socioeconomic advancement; that is, the dominant symbolic resource in the symbolic market (Bourdieu, 1991) in Hong Kong. Even in the post-1997/colonial era, English has remained a socioeconomically dominant language in Hong Kong society. For instance, a 1998 survey on business corporations in Hong Kong found that the majority of business corporations said they would prefer employees with a good command of English to employees with a good command of Chinese (*Sing Tao Jih Pao*, May

21, 1998). Besides, English remains the medium of instruction in most universities and professional training programmes.

It can be seen that the symbolic market is embodied and enacted in the many key situations (e.g., educational and job settings) in which symbolic resources (e.g., certain types of linguistic skills, cultural knowledge, specialized knowledge and skills) are demanded of social actors if they want to gain access to valuable social, educational and eventually material resources (Bourdieu, 1991). For instance, a Hong Kong student must have adequate English resources to enter and succeed in the English-medium professional training programmes and in order to earn the qualifications to enter high-income professions.

To see how the larger social context can pose local dilemmas on teachers and students and how they can exercise their creative discursive agency in dealing with their dilemmas, let us compare and contrast four different classrooms.

4 A story of four classrooms

Taken from the database of the author's ethnographic and classroom discourse study of eight classrooms in seven schools from a range of socioeconomic backgrounds in Hong Kong, the following four classroom scenarios are meant to give the reader a sense of the diversity of discursive practices that can be found across even similarly constrained classrooms (e.g., Classrooms B, C, and D). To protect the anonymity of the schools and the participants, all names are pseudo-names and all identifying details of the schools and teachers are left out. In listening to these very different stories, however, you will sense a preoccupation with a recurrent question: To what extent are classroom participants shaped by the larger social structures such as sociocultural and familial background and to what extent are they free to transform their lot (and habitus)? We shall return to this question in section 5. For each classroom I shall first describe the background, with information based on questionnaire surveys and interviews of the students, and then an English reading lesson. All four teachers are Hong Kong Chinese, sharing the same mother-tongue with their students.

Classroom A: a scenario of compatible habitus

Background

This is a form 3 (grade 9) class of thirty-three students, aged from fourteen to fifteen, in a prestigious girls' school. The majority of the students came from families in the expensive residential area in which the school is located. Their parents were professionals, business executives, or university professors, whose education level ranged from secondary, university, to postgraduate. They spoke mostly Cantonese at home, but sometimes also English, for example, when speaking to their Filipino domestic helpers. They read a variety of extra-curricular materials, including both English and Chinese, both serious and non-serious materials; for example, comics, Chinese newspapers, English newspapers, English fashion magazines, English detective stories, science fiction, pop youth magazines, TV news, Reader's Digest (both English and Chinese editions), and Chinese translations of foreign classics (e.g., Gone with the Wind). The students were fluent in their responses to the teacher's questions and could elaborate their answers with the teacher's prompts.

Teacher A's English was the best among the eight teachers who participated in my study. English seemed to be a tool she readily used in her daily life and not just in academic contexts. She spoke to her students about her daughter, her shopping habits, Mother's Day, and her feelings naturally and comfortably in English. She was interested in both Chinese and English literature, and she read for leisure English magazines. Sometimes, she would bring her old magazines from home to the class library and share them with her students.

The reading lesson described below was run smoothly and the teacher engaged students in high-level (e.g., beyond factual) questions about the story they had read. All through the lesson English was consistently used by both teacher and students and the classroom atmosphere was interestingly both relaxed and seriously on-task.

A reading lesson in Classroom A

The teacher began the reading lesson with the following extended introduction:

T: Okay . . . now . . . have you brought back . . . Flowers for Mrs. Harris? . . . Now . . . I'd like to discuss one thing with you . . . for this lesson for this book. Have you ever wondered WHY this book is called Flowers for Mrs. Harris . . . and not a Dior dress for Mrs. Harris? . . . Now the whole book we are talking about HOW Mrs. Harris . . . saved . . . how she worked extra hard to save up the money . . . so that she could go to Paris to buy the dress. And after that . . . aa . . . again she went through a lot of troubles in order to get the dress back . . . and at the end it was ruined. So all along we were talking about a dress . . . and Mrs Harris . . . but why . . . why Flowers for Mrs. Harris? . . . Alright now . . . I want to spend . . . aa . . . the next five to ten minutes or so . . . and try to discuss in groups, okay? aam . . . you can probably find some hints . . . towards the end of this book, in the last chapter.

The students swiftly formed groups and discussed. The teacher walked to a group and started to engage students in thinking deeper about the story by asking them some guiding questions, e.g., "What did Mrs. Harris see in those flowers?" or, "Besides the flowers, how else can she feel that friends are very important?". After spending some time with one group she moved onto another group and did the same.

After about fifteen minutes she addressed the whole class again and asked more questions about the story. The students readily gave her answers and she built on their answers to bring out the themes of the story: friendship, hard work and courage. Then she talked about the class's upcoming examination and encouraged her students to emulate Mrs. Harris, to work hard and not to lose heart when faced with difficulties. Most of the time during the lesson, the students seemed to be attentive to their teacher or on-task.

Classroom B: a scenario of incompatible habitus

Background

This is a form 2 (grade 8) class of forty-two students, twenty boys and twenty-two girls, aged between thirteen to fourteen. The school is located in a government-subsidized public housing estate. The students largely came from families who lived in the nearby public housing estates. Their parents were manual or service workers and their education level ranged from primary to secondary school. They spoke only Cantonese at home. Most of the boys read comics, newspapers, TV news, and pop youth magazines. Most of the girls read TV news, love stories, ghost stories, newspapers, and pop youth magazines. They did not read any English extra-curricular materials.

I informally interviewed a group of boys who were observed to be the most resistant to the teacher in the classroom. They were playful and testing, as if checking out whether I could understand their insider jokes. When I asked them questions such as whether they liked English or their English lessons, they replied in the affirmative, but in an exaggerated and joking way. I sensed that they were trying to give me what they thought I was after, so I said again that I would like to hear what they really thought and that I would not tell anything they said to the school authorities. Then they seemed to be more willing to voice their feelings. They said they found their English lessons boring and they did not know a lot of the things the teacher said as the teacher would only speak in English. I asked why they did not tell the teacher and request her to explain the things they did not understand. They said the teacher would only explain again in English, and they would still not understand. They said they chatted and played in the classroom because the lesson was too boring but they were also afraid of being asked by the teacher to answer questions. They said they felt very "yyu" ("without face") standing up there in the class and being unable to answer the teacher's questions.

They had a very cynical view about school life and about their future. They said they did not like learning English but they knew they could not find a job without English in this society. They also stated that they did not consider they would be able get into university. Teacher B's relationship with some of the boys appeared to be stressful at times. For example, sometimes she had to chide the boys angrily for not paying attention or chatting with their neighbours. The following reading lesson will give the reader a sense of the atmosphere in her classroom.

A reading lesson in Classroom B

The teacher started by saying they were going to read chapter 30 of the storybook, Adventures of Tom Sawyer, in groups of four or five and each group would send a representative to retell the story in 50 to 60 words to the whole class. Each group was to write down a summary on a piece of paper first and the summary should cover the main points in that chapter. As the teacher was saying these instructions, the class was noisy and some students said loudly in Cantonese that they did not know what to do. The teacher repeated her instructions and walked around to help students to form groups and to explain again what they were expected to do. Most of the students were off-task, chatting and joking in Cantonese. A girl at the back was writing the lyrics of a popular Cantonese love song on a piece of paper. There seemed to be a lot of non-teacher-approved activities going on in the classroom and a lot of noise. The teacher seemed exhausted circulating around the classroom trying to get her students to do the task. All through the lesson English was consistently spoken by the teacher while, in contrast, Cantonese was invariably spoken by the students except when they were called upon to do the story-retelling. When they did that, they read mechanically from a series of sentences they wrote on a piece of paper while most other students continued to chat noisily on their own. After a student had finished reading from the paper, the teacher would say "Very nice, their report includes all the points" or "Quite nice, they have covered some of the points" and then immediately called another group's representative to do the retelling. She seemed to be running out of time and had to get all the retellings done within the lesson. This might explain the brevity of her feedback to the students.

Classroom C: a scenario of incompatible habitus

Background

This is a form 2 (grade 8) class of thirty-nine students, nineteen male and twenty female, aged from thirteen to fourteen. The school is located in a town close to an industrial area. The socioeconomic backgrounds of the students and their sociolinguistic and extracurricular literacy habits are like those of their counterparts in Classroom B. Their English fluency, as can be seen from how and what they spoke in the classroom, seemed to be rather limited for their grade level. There were many words in the textbook that they did not understand or did not know how to pronounce.

When I informally interviewed a group of boys after class, they expressed that they found English "boring" and "difficult" but they also said they knew it was very important to learn English well. They found school work generally boring but said they still preferred to go to school because they said they could at least meet and play with friends at school. They said it would be even more boring to stay all day at home. "Boring" was a word these boys used frequently to describe their life and school. The reader can get a sense of the atmosphere in their classroom by looking at the following reading lesson.

A reading lesson in Classroom C

The reading lesson can be divided into three stages. In the pre-reading stage, the teacher asked some pre-reading questions about the topic of the story – Heaven-Queen Festival, using the Initiation-Response-Feedback (IRF) discourse format (Sinclair and Coulthard, 1975; Mehan, 1979; Heap, 1985). Then the teacher wrote ten numbered reading comprehension questions on the blackboard and the class was given fifteen minutes to read silently and find answers from the text to the ten questions by underlining relevant parts in the text. This constitutes the reading stage. The final stage is an answer-checking stage. The teacher elicited answers from the class using the IRF discourse format. The teacher often had to re-ask or elaborate her English questions in Cantonese to get responses from students and then the teacher rephrased the students' Cantonese response in English (L2).

In the following excerpt taken from the answer-checking stage, we find the creativity of the students bursting out in a niche that they capitalize on in an otherwise rather uninteresting IRF discourse. The teacher had been asking factual reading comprehension questions about the Heaven-Queen story that they have just read. She came to question 9 (What happened when she answered her mother?) and first asked the question in English. No response was forthcoming and so she was now elaborating the question in Cantonese in pursuit of a response from her students:

Lesson Excerpt

(To facilitate reading, Cantonese utterances have been translated into English; they are bolded and placed in pointed brackets. See appendix for other notes on transcription.)

870 T: <What happened? . . . Leih-Lohn-Mihng (2) when she answered her mum (1) her mum called her name, and when she answered her mum, what happened>?

872 Leih: <Her old-man fell off to the (ground)>. { chuckling towards the end of his sentence }=

872.5 Ss:	=Haha! haha! haha! hahahaha! {other Ss laughing hilariously}
872.8 T:	<What?! (2) louder>! {against a background of Ss' laughter}
873.2 Chan:	<Her old-man fell off to the street>! {chuckling } =
873.5 S1:	=Hihihihik!!= { laughing }
873.8 S2:	=<(Is there) a street>?
874 T:	<Is there a street>? {T in an amused tone; some students laugh}
874.5 L:	<fell into // the sea>=
874.8 //T:	=<WHERE did he fall into>? {quite amusingly}
875 L:	<Sea that is>.
875.2 T:	<Yes . . . fell into the sea>.
875.5 S1:	<fell off to the street>.
875.8 S2:	<Her old-man fell off to the street>.
876 T:	// Right? (1) Her father dropped into the SEA!==
876 //S3:	Hekhek! {laughing}
876.5 ==T:	Right? (2) <In that manner died> . . . SHH! (1) <okay> . . . <finally> . . . SHH! number ten . . .

The need to base one's answer (or to "find the answer") in the text has been a recurrent concern of the teacher voiced in her recurrent prompts and follow-up questions such as "Where can you find it?", "Does the book really say so?", "Look at paragraph —, line —" found in other parts of the lesson transcript. However, there are times when a bookish answer is boring to the students. The factual nature of the set of questions has left little room for imagination for these lively thirteen-year-olds. In the above lesson excerpt we see how a student has exploited the response slot to do something playful, to illegitimately put forward a contribution that will turn the whole story into a comic-strip type of story, which they enjoy reading outside school. In their most favourite comic strips, the characters usually do funny, impossible things and amusement and enjoyment come from the superimposing of impossible and unpredictable fantasy with the familiar, predictable, and boring mundane world. It seems that the boy who provides this funny answer (turns [872], [873.2]) is a skillful story-teller with a ready audience, and this is reflected in the hilarious laughter of his fellow students.

Classroom D: a scenario of transforming habitus

Background

This is a form 1 (grade 7) remedial English class of thirty students, twenty boys, ten girls, aged between twelve to thirteen. The students came from families who lived in the nearby public housing estates. The socioeconomic backgrounds of the students and their sociolinguistic and extra-curricular literacy habits are like those of their counterparts in Classrooms B and C.

The classroom atmosphere was very lively. Most students were attentive to the teacher and focused on their lesson tasks most of the time. They seemed to enjoy their English lessons and were both eager and often able to answer the teacher's questions.

When I asked the students in informal interviews after class whether they liked English and their English lessons, they said yes, and they especially liked their English teacher. They said that they liked to hear her tell stories from their English reader book, and that she could also explain things clearly to them. They liked the way she explained some grammatical points. For example, when explaining the difference between "little" and "few", the teacher helped them to remember the difference by saying "little" has more letters than "few" and so is uncountable and "few" has not so many letters and so is "countable". The students said they found this mnemonic tip very helpful to them. They also sounded positive about their studies and their future. They said that they thought they could learn English well because they could see themselves doing better and better in their English dictations, exercises and tests. The teacher had kept a personal progress chart for the students so that they knew how they were doing over time, and the teacher would give prizes for the best-performing students. They felt that they could succeed in their studies and would have a good chance of furthering their studies (e.g., entering university) in the future.

Teacher D used Cantonese to explain vocabulary, give directions, make the English story texts come alive, explain grammatical points, and interact with students most of the time. She was the teacher who used the most Cantonese among the eight teachers in my study. She believed that since the students were still Form 1 students and were not up to a level for using English all the time, using Cantonese could help them become more interested in the lessons and understand the lessons better. She also found that her students had made good progress over the academic year, for instance, as reflected in their increased motivation to learn English, and their improved scores in school tests and examinations.

Teacher D was the form teacher of this class. She spent most of her recess, lunch, and after-school hours talking to individual students who had various problems, for example, forgetting to bring books to school, noisy in other teachers' lessons, scoring poorly in dictations or tests. I got a sense that the good relationships she had with her students (as could be reflected in their eager responses to her questions, and their co-operative responses to her directives) might have something to do with the amount of individual attention she gave to each student in her class. Every day, she had her lunch with a student together. In this way, she maintained both a classroom and a personal relationship with her students. However, that also seemed to make her school days fully packed and busy from early morning till late into the afternoon. She seemed to be an energetic teacher who did not mind doing extra work and spending extra time with her students. The reader can get a sense of the atmosphere in her classroom by looking at the following lesson excerpt.

A reading lesson in Classroom D

The lesson excerpt below is taken from the beginning of the reading lesson. The teacher announces that she is going to ask them questions about the part of the English storybook that they have read in a previous lesson:

469   T: <Okay, let me ask you about the story, and see if you can still remember it! Last time we told the story to page forty, that is the last- the lesson before the last lesson, and then in the last lesson we told the story from page forty to forty-two! Now let me see if you can still remember the story . . . Sinbad was sailing in a boat, remember? Those jewelries, then he had given away half of the jewelries to . . . and he had bought a boat, and he had bought . . . recruited many sailors, after that, he also bought four boats, one sailing towards the East, one towards the South, one towards the West, and one towards the North. Sinbad himself took a boat, sailing back to where? . . . sailing back to where>? {A girl raises her hand; T turns to her and says} Yes,

478 Girl 1 {stands up and speaks}: <Brazil>!
478.5 T: <Go back to Brazil>?! No:::,

478.8	Some Ss {speaking in their seats}: Baa-Gaak-Daaht!
479 T:	No, not <Brazil>! (many students raise their hands now and T points to a boy}
479.5	Boy 1 {stands up and speaks}: <Baghdad>!
479.8 T:	<Baghdad>, how to spell . . . <Baghdad>? English <that is>, in English . . . <Baghdad>. {Girl 1 raises her hand again; T turns to her and gestures her to speak} Yes,
481.5	Girl 1 {stands up and speaks}: b-a-g-h . . . -d-a-d { T writes it on the blackboard as the girl spells it }
483 T:	Yes! <How to read this word>?
483.8	Some Ss {speaking up in their seats}: <Baghdad>! <Baghdad>!
484 T:	No, Baghdad, Baghdad, Baghdad <that is. Okay, as they were thinking of going back home, alas! on the way back, they ran into a GROUP OF> . . .
487	Ss {speaking up in their seats }: <monkeys! monkeys! monkeys!>
488 T:	Monkeys! Yes! {T writes the word "monkey" on the blackboard} <That group of monkey-men, that group . . . monkey-men that is, monkey-men that is, they took them to an island>, what is the na::me of this island? Can you spell the word? { Another girl raises her hand } Yes,
492	Girl 2 {stands up and speaks}: Z-u-g . . .
492.5 T:	Z-u-g . . .
492.8	Girl 2 {standing up}: (d)
493 T:	No, b, b for boy. { T writes the word "Zugb" on the board } <How to read it? A very ugly place.>
494.3	Some Ss {speaking in their seats }: Zugb!
494.5 T:	Z::ugb::
495	Ss {repeating in their seats }: ZUGB!!
495.5 T:	<Alas>! Zugb!! Au ugly place for the ugly men. <An ugly place for those ugly men to live in. Those monkeys brought them there for what>?
498	Boy {speaking in his seat}: <(Dump him there)>! { Another boy raises his hand}
498.3 T:	Yes,
498.5	Boy 2: <(Giant ? ?)>
498.8 T:	<Right! How to say giant in English>?
499	Another boy {speaking in his seat}: <Giant>!
499.5 T:	<Giant in English is . . . Leuhng-Mahn-Yih>!
500 L	{stands up and speaks}: Giant.
500.5 T:	Giant! Very good! Yes! { T writes the word "giant" on board }

In the excerpt above, the teacher dramatizes, with intonations and gestures, the part of the story about Sinbad sailing in a boat. The teacher then asks the students where Sinbad is sailing back to (last three lines in turn [469]).

The teacher gives negative feedback to a student's answer in turn [478.5]. Some other students immediately speak out their answers from their seats (turn [478.8]). The teacher signals to a boy to speak. The boy stands up from his seat and gives his answer (turn [479.5]: Baa-Gaak-Daaht). We see that in this way, the teacher maintains the practice of having a "student-bids-and-teacher-accepts" pre-sequence to a student response.

This time the student's answer is correct (turn [479.5]: Baa-Gaak-Daaht). The teacher repeats it and immediately initiates another question in the feedback-cum-initiation slot (turn [479.8]). This question is interesting. It seems to belong to a different type of question from the first question she asks (see last line in turn [469]: <B>Sinbad . . . sailing back to where?>). Instead of following the storyline and asking about what happens to Sinbad next, the second question requires the students to give the spelling of the English version of the name of the place, "Baa-Gaak-Daaht", which has been offered by a student as a response and acknowledged and repeated by the teacher (turns [479.5], [479.8]). It seems to be a question that requires the students to focus on the linguistic aspects of the story. They have read the English text (pp. 40–42 of their storybook), and the English text is now laid out on their desks before them. The question requires them to shift their focus from the content of the story *for a while* to concentrate on the language in which this content is couched. It seems that the place name in Cantonese ("Baa-Gaak-Daaht") cannot be accepted by the teacher as an acceptable *final* answer. The teacher's follow-up question on the elicited answer would have the effect of getting the students to reformulate the answer into an ultimately acceptable format – "in English" (the words the teacher uses in her follow-up initiation; see line 2 in turn [479.8]).

We see in turns [481.5] and [483] that the teacher ultimately gets the L2 formulation of the answer – "Baghdad", and she writes it on the blackboard. Only L2 answers are written on the blackboard. It seems that the teacher's act of writing the student's response on the blackboard has the effect of conferring a final-answer status on the response of the student (Heyman, 1983).

Unlike Teacher C, who often does her initiations in an L2 (Question) – L1 (Annotation of Question) sequence, Teacher D often starts with L1 to initiate a question about the story. Teacher D seems to be using a couplet of IRF formats to do consecutively two different kinds of things. The first IRF format is always used to engage the students in co-telling the story (e.g., turns [469]–[479.8]). The focus is on the content of the story and the questions asked in the initiation slots follow naturally from the storyline. The second IRF format (e.g., turns [479.8]–[483]) is used to get the students to reformulate in English their Cantonese answer that has been acknowledged in the first IRF format. The second IRF format may be repeated to get the students to focus on the linguistic aspects of the final L2 answer. For example, the second IRF format is repeated in turns [483], [483.8], [484] to get the students to say "Baghdad" in English.

With the paired use of the story-focus-IRF format immediately followed by the language-focus-IRF format, the teacher can get the students to reformulate their earlier L1 responses into the language that they are supposed to be learning in the lesson: English. This special use of the IRF formats in Teacher D's classroom stands in contrast with the use of the IRF format in Teacher C's class. For instance, Teacher C always starts with L2 texts or questions in the initiation slot of the IRF format. She then uses the L2–L1 Annotation format in the same initiation slot to annotate the L2 text or question. Students usually respond in L1. Then the teacher herself reformulates the students' L1 response into L2 and confers on it the final-answer status. This kind of discourse practice has the effect of allowing the students to get away with L1 responses only. The students are not required to do any reformulation of their L1 responses into L2. The teacher does it all for them in the feedback slot of the IRF format. The discourse structure of Teacher C in the reading lesson can be represented as follows:

Teacher-Initiation [L2–L1]
Student-Response [L1]
Teacher-Feedback [(L1–)L2]

In contrast, Teacher D uses two different IRF formats in the following cycle in the reading lesson:

(1) Story-Focus-IRF:
Teacher-Initiation [L1]
Student-Response [L1]
Teacher-Feedback [L1]

(2) Language-Focus-IRF:
Teacher-Initiation [L1/L2] (L1/L2 = L1 or L2)
Student-Response [L1/L2]
Teacher-Feedback [L2], or use (2) again until Student-Response is in L2

(3) Start (2) again to focus on another linguistic aspect of the L2 response elicited in (2); or return to (1) to focus on the story again.

This kind of discourse practice allows the teacher to interlock a story focus with a language focus in the reading lesson. There can be enjoyment of the story, via the use of the story-focus IRF, intertwined with a language-learning focus, via the use of the language-focus IRF. We have noted above that the teacher never starts an initiation in L2. She always starts in L1. This stands in sharp contrast with the discourse practices of Teacher C who always starts with L2 texts or questions in her initiations. It appears to me that by always starting in L1, Teacher D always starts from where the student is – from what the student can fully understand and is familiar with. On the other hand, by using the language-focus IRF format immediately after the story-focus IRF format, she can also push the students to move from what they are familiar with (e.g., L1 expressions) to what they need to become more familiar with (e.g., L2 counterparts of the L1 expressions).

5   Doing-English-lessons in the reproduction or transformation of habitus?

You want to know why I don't pay attention in English lessons? You really want to know? Okay, here's the reason: NO INTEREST!! It's so boring and difficult and I can never master it. But the society wants you to learn English! If you're no good in English, you're no good in finding a job!

The above was said by a 14-year-old boy from Classroom B to the author in an informal interview after class (original in Cantonese). In section 2 above we mentioned Bourdieu's notion of habitus referring to language use, skills, and orientations/attitudes/dispositions/schemes of perception that a child is endowed with by virtue of socialization in her/his family and community. The four classroom scenarios outlined in section 4 above can represent situations where there are varying degrees of compatibility between the habitus of the students and what is required of them in the school English lesson. In Classroom A, the middle class students bring with them the right kind of habitus – cultural capital – to the school lesson: they have both the right kind of attitudes/interest and linguistic skills/confidence to participate in high-level discussions on the themes of the story in English with one another and the teacher. Doing-English-lessons in Classroom A reproduces, and reinforces, the students' cultural capital and both their subjective expectations and objective probabilities of succeeding in school and the society. Both teacher and students are not in any dilemmas caused by incompatibility of habitus, and thus the atmosphere of relaxed harmony in her classroom.

In Classroom B, however, we witness a situation of incompatibility between students' habitus and what is required of them in the English lesson. The 14-year-old schoolboy's voice quoted above expresses vividly what Bourdieu would call a working class child's *subjective expectations of objective probabilities*:

> social class, understood as a system of objective determinations, must be brought into relation not with the individual or with the "class" as a *population*, . . . but with the class habitus, the system of dispositions (partially) common to all products of the same structures. Though it is impossible for *all* members of the same class (or even two of them) to have had the same experiences, in the same order, it is certain that each member of the same class is more likely than any member of another class to have been confronted with the situations most frequent for the members of that class. The objective structures which science apprehends in the form of statistical regularities (e.g. employment rates, income curves, probabilities of access to secondary education, frequency of holidays, etc.) inculcate, through the direct or indirect but always convergent experiences which give a social environment its *physiognomy*, <u>with its "closed doors", "dead ends", and limited "prospects"</u>, . . . in short, the sense of reality or realities which is perhaps the best-concealed principle of their efficacy. (Bourdieu, 1977, pp. 85–86; underlining added)

In Classroom B, we witness students who seem to find themselves confronted with a language in which they have neither interest nor competence/confidence, and yet a language they *recognize*, though angrily, as a key to success in their society. Their conclusion for themselves seems to be that they can never master the language and that they are excluded from any chances of social success. Their behaviour in the classroom seems to stem from their contradictory feelings about both their *self-recognition* of inability to change, and angry protests of, their fate: they engage in classroom practices oppositional to the curriculum and the teacher, fully *expecting* themselves to be never able to master the "difficult", foreign language anyway (e.g., by ignoring the lesson task or the teacher altogether and engaging in peer talk in their mother tongue most of the time). Their resistance seems to resemble that of marginalized ethnic minorities in North American inner city schools (e.g., Solomon, 1992).

We also witness a teacher in dilemma in Classroom B. The dilemma is one of having to teach English in English only, as this is her school's policy and, in general, a methodological prescription dominant in ELT (English language teacher) education in Hong Kong, and at the same time having to get her limited-English-proficiency and apparently uncooperative students to understand her instructions and explanations as well as to complete the lesson task within the time limit of the lesson. We witness a teacher running around the classroom to get her large class of 42 students on-task. She was exhausted and frustrated, and apparently failing to get connected in any meaningful way to her students despite her painful efforts.

Let us turn to Classroom C, where we witness a slightly different picture. The lesson is perceived as equally "boring", a word used by the students describing their lesson and their view of English to the researcher in an informal after-class interview. However, the teacher seems to be (partially) successful in getting her students to collaborate in extracting information from the story text to answer pre-given reading comprehension questions, the kind of questions typically found in school tests and examinations in Hong Kong. She seems to be imparting examination skills albeit in ways that students might find unengaging. The mother tongue is a tool she uses to get her limited-English-proficiency students to collaborate in this text-information extraction process. She seems to be connected to her students at some level, e.g., sharing their joke (she smiles and appears to be amused by the student's fun answer), though she also seems to be eager to socialize students into the text-information extraction mindset. In this respect there is some incompatibility between the students' habitus and what the teacher requires of them in the reading lesson. Using the mother tongue (L1) as a bridging tool, the teacher seems to be partly inducing and partly coercing her students into a specific school mode of orientations to text, albeit with varying degrees of success across her students.

It seems that as a result of the teacher's efforts, the students may become better versed in examination skills although their basic habitus orientation towards English – finding it boring and irrelevant to their daily life – remains unchanged. The teacher's use of L1 seems to reflect her discursive strategy to deal with her dilemma: how to get her students to collaborate in a task perceived as unengaging by her students.

Now let us turn to Classroom D. The students come from a similarly disadvantaged socioeconomic background as their counterparts in Classrooms B and C. Like their counterparts, their habitus does not equip them with the right kind of attitudes and interest, as well as skills and confidence in learning English. However, we witness some sign of their habitus being transformed through the creative discursive agency and efforts of their teacher. For instance, she uses L1 in a strategic way to intertwine an interesting story focus and a language-learning focus in the reading lesson. She helps her students to experience a sense of achievement and confidence in learning English (e.g., by charting their progress so that they can see their own improvement; by giving them mnemonic strategies regarding vocabulary usage). She also spends most of her school spare time with her students to establish a personal relationship with each of them. With all these extra personal creative efforts, she succeeds in helping her students to develop interest, skills as well as confidence in learning a language that is otherwise perceived as "difficult", "boring" and basically irrelevant in the daily lives of these students coming from a Cantonese-dominant working class habitus.

Searching for the appropriate methodology for different kinds of students coming from different cultural and social backgrounds with different habituses becomes an important task and possibility for TESOL practitioners working with students from backgrounds that do not give them the right kind of cultural capital. It seems that TESOL practitioners will benefit more from their own reflective action-research in developing their own appropriate methodology for their students rather than from merely following ELT prescriptions (Holliday, 1994). For instance, while the prescription of using only the target language in teaching the target language is widely held, it becomes clear from observing the above four classrooms that it is not whether L1 or L2 is used that matters, but rather, *how* L1 or L2 can be used to connect with students and to help them transform their attitudes/dispositions/skills/self-image – their habitus or social worlds. For instance, unlike the self-defeating-sounding students in Classroom B (see quotation of a boy's voice above), students in Classroom D are not pessimistic about their life chances: "I want to further my studies.", "I feel confident about learning English." – these are what the students in Classroom C told the researcher. Their school results confirm their newly-found confidence and expectations. The question then is not one of whether to use L1 or not but one of searching for appropriate creative discursive practices with one's own students. In this respect, we confirm Collins' (1993) observation that individual creative, discursive agency can make transformation of one's social world possible despite the larger constraining, reproducing social structures outlined by Bourdieu (1977).

6 Interrogating symbolic violence

Although we can see a glimpse of hope in creative, discursive agency in transforming our habitus and life chances, we cannot neglect the need for the continual interrogation of power and fields of valuation in the larger society (Pennycook, 1994; Luke, 1996). For instance, students in Classroom D might have found a bit of the cultural capital that they need for school and social success through their teacher's and their own extra creative efforts, but they are still in a race the rules of which are laid down by the privileged classes, who are already way ahead of them in the race (e.g., Classroom A students). These rules are, however, often taken for granted and perceived as legitimate by all parties: teachers, students, curriculum designers, and parents – a case of symbolic violence exercised on them (see section 2 above). It seems that TESOL practitioners need to continue to encourage the interrogation, together with their students, of the role of English in their society and in their life chances – to develop a critical social theory of practice (Luke, 1996). As Pennycook points out,

> In some senses, then, the English language classroom, along with other sites of cultural production and political opposition, could become a key site for the renewal of both local and global forms of knowledge. (Pennycook, 1994, p. 326)

Understanding existing practices and the sociocultural and institutional situatedness of classroom practices is a first step towards exploring the possibility of alternative creative, discursive practices that might hold promise of contributing to the transformation of the students' habitus. More of these stories await another opportunity to be told. It is my hope that through telling these lived stories of classroom participants, TESOL practitioners and researchers can gain some insights into how our role as teachers of English in the world can be reassessed, reconceived, and ultimately, repractised.

Appendix: notes on transcription

1   The numeral preceding each turn is the transcribing machine counter no.; a speaking turn is referred to as: turn [counter no.]
2   Simultaneous utterances: The point at which another utterance joins an ongoing one is indicated by the insertion of two slashes in the ongoing turn. The second speaker and her/his utterance(s) are placed below the ongoing turn and are preceded by two slashes. The latching of a second speaking turn to a preceding one is indicated by a single equal sign, "=".
3   Contextual information: Significant contextual information is given in curly brackets: e.g., { Ss laugh }
4   Transcriptionist doubt: Unintelligible items or items in doubt are indicated by question marks in parentheses or the words in doubt in parentheses.

References

Bourdieu, P. (1973) 'Cultural reproduction and social reproduction', in Brown, R. (ed.) *Knowledge, education and cultural change*. London: Tavistock.
Bourdieu, P. (1977) *Outline of a theory of practice* (translated by Richard Nice). Cambridge: Cambridge University Press.

—— (1984) *Distinction: A social critique of the judgement of taste*. London: Routledge and Kegan Paul.

—— (1991) *Language and symbolic power*. Cambridge, Mass.: Harvard University Press.

Bourdieu, P., and Passeron, J.-C. (1977) *Reproduction in education, society and culture*. London: Sage.

Collins, (1993) 'Determination and contradiction: An appreciation and critique of the work of Pierre Bourdieu on language and education', in Calhoun, C., LiPuma, E., and Postone, M. (eds) *Bourdieu: Critical perspectives*, pp. 116–138. Cambridge: Polity Press.

Delpit, L. D. (1988) 'The silenced dialogue: Power and pedagogy in educating other people's children'. *Harvard Educational Review, 58*(3), 280–298.

Heap, J. L. (1985) 'Discourse in the production of classroom knowledge: Reading lessons'. *Curriculum Inquiry*, 15(3), 245–279.

Heyman, R. D. (1983) 'Clarifying meaning through classroom talk. *Curriculum Inquiry*, 13(1), 23–42'.

Holliday, A. (1994) *Appropriated methodology and social context*. Cambridge: Cambridge University Press.

Jenkins, R. (1992) *Pierre Bourdieu*. London: Routledge.

Lin, A. M. Y. (1996) 'Bilingualism or linguistic segregation? Symbolic domination, resistance, and code-switching in Hong Kong schools'. *Linguistics and Education, 8*(l), 49–84.

—— (1997) Hong Kong children's rights to a culturally compatible English education. *Hong Kong Journal of Applied Linguistics, 2*(2), 23–48.

Luke, A. (1996) 'Genres of power? Literacy education and the production of capital', in Hasan, R., and Williams, G. (eds) *Literacy in society*, pp. 308–338. London: Longman.

Martyn-Jones, M., and Heller, M. (1996) 'Education in multilingual settings: Discourse, identities and power'. *Linguistics and Education*, 8(1), 3–16.

Mehan, H. (1979) *Learning lessons: Social organization in the classroom*. Cambridge, Mass.: Harvard University Press.

Pennycook, A. (1994) *The cultural politics of English as an international language*. London: Longman.

Sinclair, J. M., and Coulthard, R.M. (1975) *Towards an analysis of discourse: The English used by teachers and pupils*. London: Oxford University Press.

Sing Tao Jih Pao, May 21, 1998. English important for job promotion: blow to mother-tongue education [in Chinese].

Solomon, R. P. (1992) *Black resistance in high school*. New York: State University of New York Press.

Chapter 18

Assia Slimani

EVALUATION OF CLASSROOM INTERACTION

U NTIL RELATIVELY RECENTLY, THE TRADITION in the field of language teaching and learning has been to expect a better understanding of the teaching/learning phenomenon by making a broad comparison between the learning outcomes and the teacher's plan. The focus was set on the extreme poles of the situation under investigation: those of methods and outcomes. What happened during the implementation of the method was largely ignored when it came to the evaluation of the learning outcomes. This approach is illustrated by the large-scale projects conducted by Scherer and Wertheimer (1964) and Smith (1970), who focused on outcomes and paid relatively little attention to process.

This chapter proposes to analyse and evaluate what is claimed to be learned from classroom interaction. The method, which will be described later, allows a detailed study of the classroom interactive processes in attempting to uncover and evaluate the quality of interaction which leads to learners' claims of uptake. (Uptake is defined as what learners claim to have learned from a particular lesson.)

Importance of the study of classroom interaction

Allwright (1984a) suggests that a high proportion of apparent mismatches between teaching and learning could be explained if instruction is perceived as being the product of both teachers' and learners' contributions. Learning outcomes are not necessarily the reflection of the teacher's plan since, in the process of accomplishing instructional objectives, interactive work takes place among the participants and leads to the creation of a whole range of learning opportunities, many of which are perhaps unexpected.

The observation of language classes typically shows that the discourse is not something prepared beforehand by the teacher and simply implemented with the students. Instead, it is jointly constructed by contributions from both parties so that learners are not just passively fed from the instructor's plan. They can have preoccupations or goals on their personal agendas that they attempt to clarify during interactive work. Teachers know from experience that a lesson does not often take the direction it was planned to take, or, if it does, it might nevertheless include or exclude aspects that neither the teacher nor the learners have anticipated. Problems, queries, perhaps various unexpected teacher's and learner's comments, influenced by the teacher's as well as the learners' psychological and emotional dispositions, arise in the course of the 'planned' lesson and create the learning opportunities from which learners presumably grasp whatever gets learned. Hence, considered from this point of view, lessons are 'co-productions' and 'socially constructed events' brought to existence through the 'co-operative enterprise' (Corder 1977:2) of both parties. The learners' role in the creation of the co-production is not to be underestimated in comparison with the role played by the instructor. No matter how powerful the latter's influence, 'no teacher teaches without consent' (Corder 1977:66).

The perspective of viewing discourse as a co-production adds a new dimension which ties the teacher, in his/her attempts to make instruction relevant and comprehensible, with the learners, in their attempts to understand instruction and manage their own learning. If the classroom negotiation process is disregarded then what learners get might be different from what the instructor or the researcher had intended (see also Allwright 1984b, 1984c for a fuller discussion of these ideas). In fact, teachers' exclamations of surprise, such as, 'But I taught them that last week!', are only too common in staff rooms. They bear witness to the fact that much more than the investigation of the teacher's plan is needed to provide fuller explanations of the learners' reactions.

Seen from this point of view, it appears quite misleading to predict which linguistic items will be 'uptaken' by learners even before the lesson has taken place. As argued by Allwright (1984a), each lesson is a different lesson for each individual learner as different things are likely to be drawn by different learners from the same event.

Some researchers (Lightbown, 1983; Ellis 1984; Ellis and Rathbone 1987) make prior assumptions about what learners might see as optimal in the input. Hence, choosing to examine the teaching effect on the learners' accuracy of use of the -s morphemes (Lightbown 1983), of WH-questions (Ellis 1984), and German word order and verb endings (Ellis and Rathbone 1987) might provide the investigators with the advantage of having a rich description of the developmental stages of such features in first and second language development. However, by predicting the subjects' learning outcomes, such investigators might be missing out on what has actually attracted the learners' attention in discourse.

Therefore, Allwright (1984a) suggested the study of the notion of 'uptake', that is, the investigation of what individual learners claim to have learned from the interactive classroom events which have just preceded. What follows is a discussion of uptake, and of its contribution to a better understanding and evaluation of what gets claimed to be learned during classroom interaction.

Uptake

Learning a language is defined by some proponents of communicative curricula 'as learning how to communicate as a member of a socio-cultural group' (Breen and Candlin 1980:91). Hence, it is amply acknowledged that learning a language is not merely a matter of recalling beads of items but rather of coming to grips with the ideational, interpersonal and textual knowledge which is realised through effective communication in the target language. Therefore, one might argue that attempting to measure learning at the end of a lesson implies a narrow definition of what language learning involves. In this chapter, it is considered to be the realisation of communicative competence as well as performance in relevant situations.

However, since we are concerned with relating learning outcomes to their immediate and potentially determining environment, it appears rather difficult to think of ways of getting at learning evidence through testing and elicitation procedures as traditionally understood. The interactive process lends itself to the creation of an infinite set of learning opportunities which are not pre-established by the teacher's plan. In such circumstances, it appears to be practically impossible to undertake the complicated task of designing a test to assess the effects of interaction as it occurs, especially since the test has to be administered at the end of the lesson. However, the major problem encountered when attempting to research the issue of the direct impact of interaction on the subjects' claims is that of finding a way to identify and collect the learners' performance data or 'uptake'. Once identified, uptake needs to be related to the classroom environment which might subsequently explain its emergence. To do this, uptake has to be captured some time after the interactive event took place, but before too much could happen to the informants that would obscure the direct impact of the event on the learners' claims.

The problem is not restricted to formal test-based evaluation procedures. SLA elicitation techniques would also fail to meet the objectives of getting unmediated learner data. Elicitation procedures, similar to those used by Lightbown (1983), provide the informants with an obligatory context of use; this enables the researcher to evaluate, under experimental conditions, the informants' accuracy when using the features which are being investigated. By their nature, these procedures assume that one is looking for particular features which are predicted from the teacher's plan. However, what is needed is a way of identifying what learners have got from their experience of being in a particular class session.

The solution eventually adopted to the problem of 'uptake' identification must seem somewhat naive at first sight: simply asking the informants to tell the researcher what they believed they had learned in the lesson they had just attended. It was felt that the advantages of the procedure outweighed its obvious shortcomings.

The great advantage of this approach is that it offers an operational way of getting at what learners perceive they have learned. It makes it possible to relate learning claims to the immediate environment from which they emerged in order to see if it is possible to establish a relationship. The idea of requiring learners to tell us what they thought they had learned would supply the researcher with manageable amounts of data, directly referable to the classroom data. For instance, if some learners claimed that they had learned the difference between 'list' and 'least', the investigator could trace the words back in the transcripts and study the opportunities where 'list' and 'least' arose and scrutinise also the circumstances which might have made those items particularly outstanding to the point of prompting learners to claim them as learned.

It should be acknowledged at this stage that I am dealing here with the learners' perceptions of what they believed they have uptaken rather than with 'facts'. However, in the absence of a satisfactory means of getting at learning in such a way as to relate it to its potentially determining environment, a qualitative approach based on the study of uptake seems to be an interesting phenomenon to guide investigation into a possible relationship between interaction and learning outcomes.

Prior to moving to the description of the method, it is relevant to provide brief information about the participants in the study. They were thirteen Algerian male first year university students at l'Institut National d'Electricité et d'Electronique (INELEC). They were aged between eighteen and twenty. They all spoke Arabic as their mother tongue and French as a second or foreign language. They were on a six-month intensive language programme (24 hours per week) to prepare them to undertake their engineering studies in English. To benefit from their language training, the students were put in small groups (in this case thirteen) according to the results of a placement test. Their exposure to English outside their classes was limited to their classroom work and occasionally to listening to folk music. Their instructor was a trained Algerian male teacher.

Method

Uptake

The procedure developed to collect the learners' claims about uptake was to distribute a questionnaire or 'Uptake Recall Chart' at the end of every observed lesson, asking informants to relate, in terms of grammar, words and expressions, pronunciation and spelling, and in as much detail as possible what points they recalled in the events that had just preceded (see Appendix 1 in this chapter for the original layout of the Uptake Recall Chart). After approximately three hours (before too much had happened to them, but after enough had happened to counter immediate recency and primacy effects), each learner was presented with his own uptake recall chart accompanied this time with an 'Uptake Identification Probe' (see Appendix 2 in this chapter for the Uptake Identification Probe). This is another questionnaire asking the participants to annotate their uptake recall charts by clearly dissociating the items they believed they had actually learned in that particular lesson from those they had already seen with other teachers or the same teacher on previous occasions. In this way, I gave the data the strongest possible chance of being relatable to specific interactions in the lesson by asking learners to commit themselves to the things they believed they had encountered and learned for the first time from the preceding events. The three-hour delay allowed the participants to add, if possible, to their first list of items, but above all, it was estimated that the delay allowed time for the learners to absorb what they thought they had learned from today's lesson.

Both instruments, the Uptake Recall Charts and the Uptake Identification Probes, were presented in French, a language with which the researcher and all the learners were familiar.

Learning opportunities

Once uptaken items have been identified, it is necessary to locate them in the relevant interactive events of the lesson in which they occurred. Learners were observed two hours a week during the first six weeks of the term. To carry out the classroom observation procedure a high quality audio-recording of class sessions was crucial to allow the tracing of uptake in the learning opportunities which arose in the lessons. The latter needed to have a good number of instances of interactive work which could be closely studied in an attempt to understand what made learners claim uptake in those particular instances. A monologue where the teacher would be holding the floor during the entire lesson would not have suited the needs of the study. However, a relative lack of interaction seems to be a characteristic of lectures rather than language classes where a fair amount of interactive work generally takes place.

It was felt that the amount of interaction occurring during lessons depended also on the learners' ability level and the subject studied. To produce the right conditions for the project, it was assumed that the teaching of grammar to low intermediate or advanced beginners would offer the most suitable atmosphere. A weak as opposed to a strong group of students might tend to seek more learning opportunities and pay extra attention to what goes on in the classroom in order to improve their language command. It is noted that the subjects of this study were particularly motivated to master the second language. They were expected to take their technical subjects in English at the end of an intensive language programme which served as the setting for this data collection.

Grammar lessons were chosen because discrete points are frequently dealt with in such lessons and it is relatively easy to find out what has become of items in the learners' uptake list. Moreover, it was assumed that it was simpler for the learner to pick up discrete points, such as one might expect to occur during grammar lessons, remember them, and afterwards list them on the charts which would be distributed at the end of the recording.

To investigate the learning opportunities fully, I exhaustively collected all classroom textual materials including all visual and audio aids. I also took notes of what went on the blackboard to help account later for the claims of uptaken items.

Interview

To provide the study with corroborative data, it was felt necessary to interview the subjects twice over the six-week period: once in the middle and once at the end of the data gathering. The idea was to give the researcher a further chance to probe the informants about the possible reasons which made them claim the particular items they reported on their uptake charts. The interview was also believed to allow learners to express other ideas they felt were missing from their uptake charts. As the number of learners was rather small, all thirteen could be interviewed in about one hour, the same day, after the third lesson recording. The subjects were individually asked to answer the researcher's queries while the other learners were outside the room, waiting for their turn to be interviewed.

The interview, conducted in French or in Arabic according to the learners' wishes, was an adaptive structured interview where respondents were free to give details on the five issues which were followed up with all learners during the interview session. The issues could be summarised as follows:

1   Clarifications (if necessary) of self-reported data on the charts distributed at the end of every observed lesson.
2   Rationale for claiming those specific items on today's uptake chart or, if possible, on the uptake charts distributed at the end of the two previous observed lessons.
3   Possibilities for the learners to extend their perceptions of those items.
4   Reactions to the benefits or otherwise of completing the charts at the end of every taped grammar lesson.
5   Feelings about the researcher's presence and the tape-recorder in the back of the classroom during the lesson.

The second question, about the reasons for claiming certain items instead of others, was found to be most problematic to the respondents as some remained evasive while others produced overgeneralised statements as to what made them claim those items. They were unable to tell the researcher the reasons which made any particular item outstanding in their minds. The fact that many of them reacted as if the question was irrelevant or irrational discouraged the researcher from interviewing a second time as this question was the focus of the interview.

The respondents produced responses that were insufficiently precise to be interpreted in relation to what might account for their claims. Because I was observing the same group for the period of six weeks I could have trained the informants by asking perhaps more detailed and specific questions about what most attracted their attention in classroom discourse. However, as I had never even conducted an interview before, I was afraid to put words in the learners' mouths. Moreover, being miles away from any professional consultant, I did not dare meddle with the procedure and run the risk of undermining the data gathering. The interview had to be given within the six observational weeks as the learners' responses had to relate to these precisely observed events.

Method effect

I am aware of the fact that the methodological procedure used to collect the data can strongly raise the subjects' consciousness of the learning process and might, by the same token, pollute the data. This would have been the case if the class observation had lasted over a long period of time. I was however, only thinking of observing two hours a week during six weeks of the informants' timetable, which amounted to twenty-four (24) hours of intensive English lessons per week. It seemed rather unlikely that the methodological procedure would have any major effect on the subjects' behaviour.

However, to confirm this supposition, the results of the Michigan Test were used. This test was already being used, at the beginning of the programme, as a placement test to determine the learners' ability levels. This procedure produced four groups, one of which was the group under study. The other three were, for the purpose of the project, considered as control groups. All four groups were following the same programme, though at their own pace. Without telling the learners in advance, the same test was again administered to the experimental group, as well as to the three control groups, after the six observational periods. The pre- and post-test results were inspected to see whether the study groups' progress had been significantly influenced by the effects of the design.

Table 18.1 summarises the results of the pre- and post-Michigan Tests results (T1 and T2 on the table). The table shows the average score obtained by the participants in the study to be slightly higher (74.76) than the one achieved by group 2 (72.66). In comparison, the average score of group 2 does not overtake that of group 1, and neither does group 4 over group 3. It seems rather unreasonable however to attribute this slight improvement wholly to the procedure itself as it was applied on only two hours of instruction out of 24 hours a week. The merit I can see the procedure objectively deriving from this slight increase is that it did not hinder the group in its activities. My presence and the tape-recorder in the back of the room did not seem to have negatively affected the group.

The total percentage increase for each group is a representation, within the whole programme, of the students' language training development in the first six weeks. It appears to happen in an expected way: the lower groups show more progress than group 1 (20.65%) and 2 (37.53%). This increase in language development is quite comprehensible since knowing much less at the outset of the programme, groups 3 (67.88%) and 4 (103.12%) have more room for improvement. The total percentage increase therefore does not display any convincing sign in favour of an interfering methodological design. The learners in group 3, in spite of my demands on them at the end of each of the observed sessions, do not achieve in any markedly different manner than what would be expected from them if one thought that the procedure could have influenced the quantity of their learning.

In summary, two types of data were gathered for the investigation of the issue: learners' specific claims collected through uptake charts and detailed accounts of the learning opportunities obtained through systematic observation of audio-recorded, naturally occurring classroom data. These were supplemented with field notes taken by the author. The interview which was intended to provide corroborative data did not produce responses that were sufficiently precise to be interpreted in relation to what might account for their claims. In the end, the bulk of what might help us find out about the learners' selective attention mechanism would have to arise from a consideration of classroom transcripts in relation to uptake charts as the learners themselves did not seem to be aware of what directed their attention while attending instruction.

Both the teacher and the learners under study were informed in general terms of the goals of the research. Both parties were told that the project was seeking a relationship

Table 18.1 Average scores and percentage increase for each group

Group 1			Group 2			Group 3*			Group 4		
SS	T1	T2	SS	T1	T2	SS	T1	T2	SS	T1	T2
1	80	88	1	63	70	1	60	85	1	49	73
2	75	83	2	57	73	2	50	72	2	36	81
3	74	84	3	54	79	3	48	68	3	35	63
4	67	83	4	53	78	4	47	83	4	34	71
5	62	76	5	53	68	5	45	82	5	32	78
6	61	78	6	48	75	6	44	74	6	30	37
7	60	75	7	52	63	7	43	66	7	29	63
8	60	64	8	52	76	8	42	84	8	11	54
9	58	75	9	51	70	9	41	77			
10	58	75	10	51	68	10	41	71			
11	57	78	11	50	78	11	41	68			
			11	50	74	12	39	72			
			12	50	74	12	39	72			
						13	38	70			

Average Scores For Each Group											
T1		T2	T1		T2	T1		T2	T1		T2
64.72		78.09	52.82		72.66	44.53		74.76	32		65

Percentage of Increase For Each Group			
Group 1	Group 2	Group 3	Group 4
20.65%	37.53%	67.88%	103.12%

*group under study

between what the informants report as 'uptake' and the interactive process in which the class participates. However, I did not go into any further detail with them, not wanting the teacher to give undue emphasis to linguistic items in order for learners to remember as many as possible. It was hoped that the usual teaching and learning situation would not be influenced by alerting the participants' attention to the researcher's focus of interest.

In fact, when filling out the 'uptake charts' at the end of the first observational lesson, it was noticed that some learners tried to peep at their peers' charts to enable them to report more items than they actually could. At this point it was emphasised to the subjects that they should look upon the author as an outsider, a researcher rather than as a teacher, and that whatever reports and comments they made would be entirely confidential. Their reports were not to be shown to the instructor, nor would they have any bearing on their grades.

As it was planned to observe the same teacher with the same group for two hours a week for six weeks, the procedure became routine and my presence was accepted with ease by the learners. The instructor also appeared much more relaxed after the first hour of observation. Prior to deciding which teacher was to be part of the project, I felt some resistance and avoidance on the part of the staff members who alluded to the fact that 'really, not much is going on in our classes right now'. The procedure discussed in this chapter was part of a doctoral project and this made the teachers particularly apprehensive at having their lessons 'dissected' and looked at through 'magnifying' lenses for research purposes. However, I persisted in spite of their anxiety as their refusal could mean the end of my plans. Therefore, I remain indebted to the 'chosen' teacher who, knowing that he could not openly refuse me without losing face, gracefully adjusted to my persistent presence in the back of his classes.

The rest of the chapter will describe some of the tentative findings (see Slimani 1987 for a fuller report) which might help us understand the relationship between the classroom interactive processes and uptake, and their consequences for evaluation studies. Two interesting characteristics of uptake emerged in the investigation of the learners' uptake charts. The first characteristic is that most of the learners' claims were topicalised during instruction. The second is that learners' uptake is strongly idiosyncratic. Both aspects will be discussed in detail below.

Importance of topicalisation on uptake

A thorough study of the informants' Uptake Charts and Uptake Identification Probes showed that a total of 126 items were claimed to have been learned. These items were verbs, nouns, adjectives, adverbs, connectors, auxiliaries, models and some set phrases. Almost all (112 items or 89 per cent) of what the respondents claimed to have seen and learned for the first time in those six observed lessons, had, in one way or another, been focused upon during instruction. 112 out of 126 were given some sort of prominence by being the topic of conversation while the remaining fourteen items or 11 per cent happened as part of classroom interaction with no particular emphasis brought upon them. The following excerpts illustrate the various means used to focus upon or topicalise those items claimed to have been learned: 'least', 'list', 'like', 'look after', 'look like', 'match', 'in order to'.

1   T: *What's the difference between least and list?*
         [pointing at both items written on the board].
2   T: The mother looks after her son at home. *Can you use another word or expression instead of look after?*
    L1: Don't worry.
    L2: Not worried but uh the same uh.
    L3: Uh, take care.
3   T: OK. When I say uh this car is like that one, *what does 'like' mean?*
    L4: Similar.
    L5: Almost the same.
    T: OK. Now, John's new car looks almost the same. *What is 'looks'?*
    L6: To see . . .
    T: To see, uhuh. So, *can you replace 'to look' here by 'to see' and say 'John's new car sees almost the same?*
4   T: Let's see the instructions given here and see if they match. To match, *that's a new word, I think [writes it on board]. To match. [A long explanation with attempts to find synonyms follows.]*
5   T: *OK, in order to.* What does that mean?

In the above cases the uptaken items have themselves, however briefly, become the ostensible topic of the conversation rather than being simply a part of classroom discourse. The episodes dealing with these particular features are also seen to be terminated by some feedback from the teacher which might be expected to be interpreted by learners as indicating that an item is worth paying attention to.

The difference between the fourteen (11 per cent) and 112 (89 per cent) items claimed to have been learned during the sessions under study is that the latter had, to a greater or lesser extent, been the specific topic of instruction by having their meaning, their spelling, their pronunciation and sometimes two or all three aspects treated by the teacher and/or by the learners. In the case where learners provide their peers with guidance in one or other of the aspects, the teacher is seen to intervene by approving the provision of information.

It must be emphasised however that this does not necessarily mean that the claimed items were intended to be taught prior to the lessons. Many of them, as the following examples show, arose incidentally in the course of events and became topics in discourse terms.

6:    L: . . . Bob/bought/five books and George did too.
      T: Bob? What did he do? [Teacher interrupts]
      L: Five books
      T: What did he do?
      L: /bought/
     LL: Bought [correct pronunciation]
      T: Bought. Which verb is that?
      L: To buy.
      T: To buy, bought bought
7   T: . . . OK. Did you like it?
      L: Yes, yes, I like it.
      T: Yes, I?
      L: Yes, I liked it.
      T: Yes, I liked it or I did.

It appears, then, that within the limits of the analysis so far of the uptaken items, instruction has exercised a rather positive impact on the subjects since 112 out of the 126 items claimed to have been learned for the first time during those observed lessons have become, however momentarily, teaching points. However, a close examination of the data suggests that the above statement alone is far from establishing the instructor's supremacy as a learning facilitator. A further investigation was necessary to find out the proportion of the topicalised items that are claimed as new acquisitions in relation to those which have apparently been the subject of similar intentions and treatment but which failed to lead to any claims on the part of the subjects.

To evaluate the proportion of what has been claimed to be learned from what has been pedagogically focused upon in some way during those six instructional sessions, the sum total of the topicalised items was counted independently of whether they had been claimed as new or otherwise on the learners' uptake charts. The results are summarised in Table 18.2 where column 1 indicates the total number of items topicalised in each lesson. Column 2 presents the total number of items which are both focused upon and also claimed by at least one learner to have been learned. Column 3 introduces those which have not led to any positive assertion on the part of the subjects despite the attention paid to them, and column 4 displays the total number of items which have been claimed to be partly or completely familiar already and therefore 'ineligible' for learning claims in the context of

Table 18.2 Effect of topicalisation

	1	2	3	4
LESSONS	Total No of topicalised items	Topicalised and claimed	Topicalised but not claimed	Topicalised but known
1	40	17	16	07
2	56	21	23	12
3	31	16	12	03
4	60	31	15	14
5	37	11	19	07
6	32	16	07	09
TOTAL	256	112	92	52
%	100%	43.75%	35.93%	20.31%

this study. The data of the last column were derived from the answers to questions b, c, and d on Uptake Identification Probes which were distributed to help learners dissociate the items they believed they had learned during the observed lessons from those they had already encountered in different circumstances. The observed lessons in which these items occurred again could not fully justify their 'uptaking' as they have already happened in situations which might have facilitated their learning.

Table 18.2 shows that out of 256 topicalised cases providing learning opportunities for the class, 92 failed to attract the learners' attention and 52 were claimed to be somewhat known as they had already encountered them in earlier events unrelated to this study. In other words, 43.75 per cent focused episodes have 'reached the target', while 35.93 per cent went completely unnoticed and 20.31 per cent were already to some extent familiar to the subjects.

The above figures provide us with a picture of the 'syllabus as reality' as opposed to the 'syllabus as plan'. The former represents what actually happens in the midst of interactive work done by the participants. The on-going interaction leads to the creation of a whole range of learning opportunities, some of which are the results of the teacher's plan; others arise as a by-product of the plan, but some others arise independently of any intentions, perhaps as a by-product of classroom interaction.

No precise comparison can be made with the 'syllabus as plan' which is defined as a syllabus which attempts to predict what is likely to be learned from a planned learning event. I was not, despite my request, provided with very many details about the teacher's objectives. I was given the title of the structure to be taught and the series of exercises in the textbook to practise the grammatical features to be introduced to the group.

Hence, the detailed study of the classroom discourse has revealed that about 44 per cent only of what has been pedagogically topicalised was claimed by the learners. Even though the teacher's objectives were geared toward the teaching of some particular structural features, most of the 44 per cent were lexical items claimed to be seen and learned for the first time in those observed events. Nevertheless it would be misleading to conclude that the lessons were not successful because learners did not claim many of the structural objectives the teacher had on his plan. Although it might be suggested that the shortage of grammatical claims is due to the possibility that it is much easier to report lexis because this does not require the use of metalanguage, in fact, a close perusal of the learners' uptake charts demonstrates that the informants were perfectly capable of reporting what went on during the course of the lessons in terms of grammar. By and large, learners succeeded in accounting for the teacher's structural intentions by reporting the title if not writing the main points of the sessions. Some even illustrated the teacher's focus of instruction by providing examples of sentences to show their comprehension or at least familiarity with what was taught. This suggests that the informants did not lack the means of expressing the structural objectives.

It is believed that one of the reasons why learners did not report as many structural features as lexical ones is that several of these features were already familiar to the class. In fact, it is not surprising that most of the structural features emphasised during instruction were not reported as newly learned because most of them, if not all of them, were part of the syllabus in high school. For instance, only one informant claimed to have seen and learned the passive and active voices for the first time during the observed events. In fact, these affirmations are confirmed by the 20 per cent of topicalised episodes in the lesson which were claimed to be part of the learners' prior knowledge. One could add that after a few hours of teaching, second language instruction becomes very much remedial as structural features are presented and represented for a review.

It looks as if the learners' claims are somewhat different from what the teacher has planned for them. His intentions might have helped learners to rehearse already encountered (if not mastered) structural features. However, in the process of carrying out the plan, the interactive work has lent itself to the creation of a whole range of perhaps unexpected and beneficial events (at least, to some learners if not to all). The learners' claims (44 per cent on Table 18.2) remain a combination of the teacher's objectives but also their by-product as well as the by-product of the classroom interaction. For these reasons, therefore, attempts to evaluate the learning outcomes against the teacher's plan can be misleading if one does not take into account the mediating interactive processes which characterise classroom interaction.

In view of the data expressed in the table, therefore, the teacher's influence over the subjects' learning did not reveal itself to be as strong as suggested earlier since approximately 56 per cent of what has been focused upon did not apparently bear any immediate fruit: 20 per cent were claimed to be already familiar and 36 per cent were not, in any way, mentioned by the learners.

It should be pointed out that about 77.45 per cent of the topicalisation was effected by the teacher. This is not particularly surprising in view of the fact that the discourse was unidirectionally controlled by the teacher, who did 45 per cent of the talking. What appears to be strikingly interesting though is that a further analysis of the effect of the teacher's versus the learners' scarce opportunities (22.54 per cent) for topicalisation showed that the latter offered much higher chances for items to be uptaken. Learners benefited much more from their peers' rare instances of topicalisation than from the teacher's.

A close scrutiny of the theme of topicalisation reveals that topics initiated by learners attracted more claims from the learners than the ones initiated by the teacher. The analysis shows that out of 46 items initiated by the learners, 34 (73.9 per cent) were claimed, whereas only 78 (49.4 per cent) out of 158 were claimed when topicalised by the instructor. Thus, the chances for claims are much higher when items are triggered by classmates. A further emphasis on the profitability of the learners' initiation is that it attracts more reporters than when topics are brought up by the teacher.

By limiting to himself the initiative of topicalising most items for instruction, the teacher does not give the learners much opportunity to distinguish between items which are important and those which are not. To this particular teacher everything was relevant. It is therefore possible that the reason why the participants of this study were not affected by the teacher's efforts is that in his attempts to focus their attention on everything, no specific aspect appeared as particularly prominent in his discourse. Having little opportunity to raise topics for instruction, learners might have made some features outstanding to their peers if only for the reason that, coming from learners, topicalisation appeared as a memorable event rather than the routine procedure of the teacher (see Slimani 1989 for further details).

Finally, in this discussion it is worth mentioning that the majority of the unnoticed or 'lost' items (36 per cent) are instances of error treatment provided most often by the teacher. Their analysis has allowed the identification of a limited number of features which differentiate their treatment from that allocated to the topicalised and claimed items (112, or 44 per cent). As the illustrations below show, it appears that absence of metalanguage in the teacher's talk and straight provision, most often by the teacher, of the correct form of the item under focus, without further involvement from the teacher or the learners, characterise the strategies used to deal with these items (see examples 8, 9, 10 below). Cueing by the teacher is another common corrective strategy sometimes followed by the immediate provision of the expected forms by the speaker himself, if he swiftly manages to spot the error (example 11), by his peers (example 12) but less often by the instructor.

8   L: . . . and uh sometimes uh on Wednesday.
       T: And sometimes on Wednesdays. Why on Wednesdays?

9   L: . . . I looking for my pen.
      T: You are looking for your pen.

10   L1: . . . [Reading from the book] Bob drink a glass.
     L2: Drinks [Interrupts the speaker].
     L2: Bob drinks a glass of milk every day and George does too.

11   L: Pencils have been sharp
      T: Sharp?
      L: Sharpened
      T: Sharpened, yes.

12   L: . . . The simplest method is by swimming on one side. The rescuer pulls the victim by the /hair/
     LS: Hair, hair [correct pronunciation]
      T: Yes, hair, by the hair. All right . . .

Nearly a third of the lost items consists of corrections of tenses and -s morphemes. Informants can, however, be assumed to be already familiar with these features as they have been the explicit content of instruction in other lessons or in high school. Despite previous exposure to explicit explanation of the rules and recurrent repetitions of the correct forms of these features, the subjects of this study persisted in misusing them when using the target language. It is possible that the informants are not ready to learn these structures as part of their interlanguage system and consequently their continued treatment remains pointless, at least, at this stage of their training. It is widely accepted that features such as the use of articles by Arab speakers and some of the -s morphemes, for many English as a second language speakers, remain unmastered in oral production till an extremely advanced stage of their training even if these features are explicitly known to the trainees. This situation makes us question the necessity or otherwise of attempting to keep on correcting features which have been persistently dealt with but still remain largely ignored by some learners during verbal interaction (see Slimani 1987 for further quantitative and qualitative analysis of error treatment in this setting).

Learners' idiosyncracies

The second characteristic which emerged from the investigation of the learners' claims is that uptake is highly idiosyncratic. The feature is particularly revealing for evaluation which generally assumes the effect of instruction is somehow uniform for most members of the class. Such evaluation takes as its starting point the teacher's plan which is expected to control what learners would see as optimal in the teaching. Even though the teaching in this particular setting was not differentiated in any obvious way, i.e., in the sense that different learners were given different tasks, it appears that typically only very few learners at any one time happened to take the information in. Table 18.3 illustrates the extreme individuality with which learners react to instruction. It presents the total number (N) of items or linguistic features (126) reported to have been learned during the observed sessions as well as the percentage of claims associated with them and the number of reporters that each case has attracted.

Table 18.3 Percentage of claims made by reporters on each linguistic feature

N of items (126)	% of claims	N of reporters
47	37.30%	15
20	15.87	2
27	21.42	3
	Total 74.59%	
7	5.55	4
5	3.96	5
10	7.93	6
3	2.38	7
3	2.38	8
	Total 22.20%	
1	0.79	9
2	1.58	10
1	0.79	11
	Total 3.16%	

The results point to the fact that as many as 74.59 per cent of the total number of claims are reported by no more than three learners at a time, and no fewer than 37.30 per cent of the total are reported by only one person at any one time. A negligible percentage (3.16 per cent) of claims is simultaneously made by nine, ten or eleven subjects. These figures express the high level of 'individuality' and 'autonomy' with which some subjects might face instruction. The figures are particularly striking as the teaching style was not individualised in any sense. It was unidirectionally addressed to the class as a whole. One, therefore, might expect the same items or linguistic features to be claimed by many learners. What happened however is that individual learners reacted individually despite the centrality of the teaching style.

Further evidence that learners show autonomy when undergoing instructions is also clearly illustrated in the 11 per cent or fourteen uptaken items that were mentioned earlier under the heading of the importance of topicalisation. While 112 linguistic features claimed to be learned were the focus of instruction, fourteen happened as a part of the classroom discourse without any specific attention drawn to them. Despite a teaching situation where the classroom discourse is highly controlled by the teacher and does not involve any group work activity, learners have shown considerable individual reaction by claiming items which did not receive any kind of attention in terms of topicalisation, as defined earlier. The above proportion might have been even higher if the teacher had allowed more room for learners to express themselves.

While some of the 11 per cent of the claims were traced back as part of the discourse to deal with classroom routines, some were not found at all in the transcripts. To explain their presence on the learners' uptake charts, one can only assume that what went on during the lessons possibly reinforced some previous learning and brought those particular words back to the learners' minds. The word 'slippers', for instance, remained a complete mystery as I did not even recall the teacher having dealt, however remotely, with a situation which might have led to such a claim on the part of the learner. Moreover, the examination of the learners' charts revealed also the presence of a few examples of appropriate generalisation. For instance, when the words 'thick', 'thickness', and 'thin' were explained, one of the most able learners reported having learned the word 'thinness' even though the latter was not uttered in class. The word 'narrow' was also claimed to have been learned by the same learner in relation to 'thick' and 'thin'.

It is interesting to notice here this learner's tendency to generalise so successfully from a lesson event that he can believe the generalisation was taught. In this respect, it has been suggested that one of the good language learner's attributes is to be able to organise the discrete and disparate information they receive about the target language into coherent and ordered patterns (Rubin 1975; Stern 1975).

Conclusion

The problem of making sense of instruction seems to lie in the difficulty of finding appropriate research techniques capable of evaluating learning outcomes in relation to input. In this paper, input is seen as a co-production by the participants in an instructional setting and therefore renders the task of using traditional testing measures rather difficult. We attempted to find a way of relating the learners' claims to their immediate interactive environment.

The technique used proved to be a useful means of shedding light on what is claimed to be learned from the on-going interactive work which takes place in the classroom. By asking learners to reflect on their perceptions of what they have uptaken, one could see, by examining the interactive work, some of the factors which characterise the emergence of these particular uptaken features.

Most of the learners' claims were topicalised. In this sense, White's (1987) recommendations seem to broadly match the present teacher's behaviour in this particular context. She suggests that

> We should not be afraid occasionally to provide input which is explicitly geared toward
> . . . the form of grammatical teaching, of correction, *or other forms of emphasis on
> particular structures* [my emphasis]; at worst, it will be ignored and at best, it may trigger
> change in the acquisition system. (White 1987: 108)

Bringing particular linguistic features to the class's attention appears to be a rather valuable characteristic of uptake as most of the uptaken items were focused upon during instruction. The fact that most of the 'lost' items were error correction does not necessarily contradict the effect of topicalisation. Learners may not be ready to internalise particular structural features despite their persistent explanation and correction. Correction is often seen, in this study, to be provided in an erratic and confusing manner. The study revealed that while some uptaken features were products of the teacher's plan, others were by-products of the plan or perhaps of the classroom interaction.

These uptaken items, which represent 44 per cent of the participants' interactive efforts, are revealed to be highly idiosyncratic. The detailed analysis of the interactive processes has shown that different features of the same event have been uptaken by different learners. Very few items were claimed by all or even most learners. Moreover, while many of the claims could be traced in the transcripts as having received some kind of emphasis on the part of the participants, mostly of the teacher, others merely occurred as part of the classroom interaction or did not feature at all in the text, suggesting that learners reacted with some autonomy to what went on during the interactive event.

Viewing input as co-produced by the participants has highlighted idiosyncrasy and topicalisation as particularly relevant to evaluation studies which generally tend to assess learning outcomes on the basis of the teacher's objectives: these objectives are subsequently assumed to be learned by most learners in the class. A test based on the teacher's objectives would have taken into consideration the features which the teacher planned to treat. Such a test would, by its nature, ignore the very many other features which incidentally arose during the actual classroom interaction, some of which learners claimed to have benefited from.

Because of the finding that what actually gets topicalised during the classroom interactive work is different from the teacher's plan, and because uptake is strongly idiosyncratic, it is therefore not helpful to use the teacher's plan as a measuring rod for what has been uptaken from the lesson. In fact, a consideration of the actual classroom interactive work which characterises second language instruction and a study of learner idiosyncrasy might help us gain a better understanding of the complexities of second language teaching and learning. This understanding might subsequently inform the improvement of evaluations of what actually gets learned from language programmes.

References

Allwright, R.L. (ed.) (1975a) 'Working papers: language teaching classroom research'. Department of Language and Linguistics, University of Essex, England.

Allwright, R.L. (1975b) 'Problems in the study of the teacher's treatment of learner error', in Burt and Dulay: 96–109.

—— (1983) 'The nature and function of the syllabus in language teaching and learning'. Unpublished mimeograph. Department of Linguistics and Modern English Language, Lancaster University.

—— (1984a) 'Why don't learners learn what teachers teach? The interaction hypothesis', in

D. M. Singleton and D. G. Little (eds) *Language learning in formal and informal contexts*, pp. 3–18. Dublin: IRAAL.

—— (1984b) 'The importance of interaction in classroom language learning'. *Applied Linguistics*, 52: 156–71.

—— (1984c) 'The analysis of discourse in interlanguage studies: the pedagogical evidence', in Davies, Criper and Howatt.

—— (1988) 'Autonomy and individualisation in whole-class instruction', in A. Brookes and P. Grundy (eds) *Individualization and autonomy in language learning*, pp. 35–44. ELT Documents 131. London: Modern English Publications, British Council.

Breen, M.P. and Candlin, C.N. (1980) 'The essentials of a communicative curriculum in language teaching', *Applied Linguistics* 1(2): 89–112.

Burt, M. and Dulay, H.C. (1975) *On TESOL '75. New directions in second language, learning, teaching and bilingual education*. Washington, D.C.: TESOL.

Corder, S.P. (1977) 'Teaching and learning English as a second language: Trends in research and practice', in H.D. Brown, C.A. Yorio, and R.H. Crymes (eds) *On TESOL '77. Teaching and learning English as a second language: trends in research and practice*. Washington, D.C.: TESOL.

Davies, A., Criper, C. and Howatt, A.P.R. (eds) (1984) *Interlanguage*. Edinburgh: Edinburgh University Press.

Ellis, R. (1984) 'Can syntax be taught?: a study of the effects of formal instruction on the acquisition of WH questions by children'. *Applied Linguistics* 5(2): 138–55.

Ellis, R. and Rathbone, M. (1987) 'The acquisition of German in a classroom context'. Unpublished report. Ealing College of Higher Education.

Fanselow, J. (1977) 'The treatment of learner error in oral work'. *Foreign Language Annals* 10: 583–93.

Krashen, S.D. (1980) 'The theoretical and practical relevance of simple codes in second language acquisition', in R. Scarcella and S.D. Krashen (eds) *Research in second language acqusition*, pp. 7–18. Rowley, Mass.: Newbury House.

—— (1981) *Second language acquisition and second language learning*. Oxford: Pergamon Press.

—— (1982) *Principles and practice in second language acquisition*. New York: Pergamon.

Lightbown, P.M. (1983) 'Exploratory relationships between developmental and instructional sequences in L2 acquisition', in H.W. Seliger and M.H. Long (eds) *Classroom oriented research in second language acquisition*, pp. 217–45. Rowley, Mass.: Newbury House.

MacFarlane, J.M. (1975) 'Some types of psychological discussion that help to establish the teacher's treatment of error as a fruitful variable for investigation', in Allwright (1975a) pp. 4–63.

Morray, M. (1976) 'INELEC: Teamwork in an EST program', in *British Council Team teaching in ESP*. ELT Document 106. ETIC Publications.

Rubin, J. (1975) 'What the "good language learner" can teach us'. *TESOL Quarterly* 9(1): 41–51.

Scherer, A. and Wertheimer, M. (1964) *A psycholinguistic experiment in foreign language teaching*. New York: McGraw Hill.

Slimani, A. (1987) 'The teaching-learning relationships: Learning opportunities and learning outcomes. An Algerian case study'. Unpublished doctoral dissertation, Lancaster University, England.

—— (1989) The role of topicalisation in classroom language learning. *System* 17: 223–34.

Smith, P.D. (1970) *A comparison of the cognitive and audiolingual approaches to foreign language instruction: The Pennyslvania Foreign Language Project*. Philadelphia, Penn.: The Center for Curriculum Development.

Spada, N.M. (1987) 'Relationships between instructional differences and learning outcomes: a process-product study of communicative language teaching'. *Applied Linguistics* 8(2): 137–61.

Stern, H.H. (1975) 'What can we learn from the good language learner?' *Canadian Modern Language Review* 31: 304–18; also in K. Croft (ed.) (1980) *Readings on English as a second language: for teachers and teacher trainees* (2nd edition). Cambridge, Mass.: Winthrop.

White, L. (1987) 'Against comprehensible input: the input hypothesis and the development of second language competence'. *Applied Linguistics* 8(2): 95–110.

APPENDIX 1: UPTAKE RECALL CHART

DATE: _____

NAME: _____

QUESTION: WHAT POINTS HAVE COME UP IN TODAY'S LESSON?

Please answer FULLY and in DETAIL. Try to remember EVERYTHING.

1. GRAMMAR: _____
_____
_____
_____
_____
_____
_____

2. WORDS AND PHRASES: _____
_____
_____
_____

3. SPELLING: _____
_____
_____

4. PRONUNCIATION: _____
_____
_____

5. PUNCTUATION: _____
_____
_____
_____
_____
_____

6. WAYS OF USING THE LANGUAGE: _____
_____
_____

7. SUGGESTIONS ABOUT MORE EFFECTIVE INSTRUCTION: _____
_____
_____

8. OTHER(S) . . . (Please specify): _____
_____
_____
_____
_____

Thank you for your cooperation

APPENDIX 2: UPTAKE IDENTIFICATION PROBE

READ CAREFULLY THE FOLLOWING QUESTIONS, MARK YOUR ANSWERS
AS INDICATED ON THE 'UPTAKE RECALL CHART'.

1. Of all the things you wrote on your 'Uptake Recall Chart', which do you think
    you learned today?

    (a) Did you learn anything that was really new to you? If yes, circle it.

    (b) Did you learn anything that was not really completely new, that you knew
         partly already? If yes, underline it.

    (c) Was there anything that you did not learn at all because you knew it already?
         If yes, mark it with a zigzag line.

2. Of all the things you wrote, which do you think the teacher most wanted you to
    learn? Mark them with a T.

Thank you for your cooperation.

Chapter 19

Michael P. Breen

NAVIGATING THE DISCOURSE: ON WHAT IS LEARNED IN THE LANGUAGE CLASSROOM

Introduction

A **CENTRAL CONCERN FOR LANGUAGE** teachers is what learners can learn from language lessons. Allwright, in a somewhat startling paper some years ago, deduced that, regardless of what a teacher taught in a lesson, the learners will inevitably learn different things from the same lesson (Allwright 1984). He explained this unpredictable trend with reference to the overt spoken interaction that takes place between teachers and learners and the covert interaction that takes place between the learner and the various sources of input during a lesson, including the text of the lesson and other written texts available to the learners. Such interaction, he argued, mediates between what the teachers teach as "input" and what learners actually "uptake" from the lesson. In other words, the interactive process of teaching and learning in the particular context of the classroom ensures variation in learning outcomes.

In this chapter, I wish to explore this phenomenon further by focusing upon the discourse of language lessons as revealed by current research. I want to suggest that one of the crucial things which learners learn in the classroom is how to navigate the opportunities and constraints provided by classroom discourse. A central argument will be that relative success or failure in classroom language learning can be at least partly explained with reference to how learners choose or are obliged to undertake such navigation. Of course, the particular features of the classroom context which I describe can not provide a fully adequate explanation of variation in language teaching. The influences of the context of learning are only one set of variables in the broader picture. However, I wish to assert that an account of such influences can enrich Second Language Acquisition research and theory and usefully inform the practical concerns of language pedagogy.

Explaining Second Language Acquisition

Any adequate theory of Second Language Acquisition (SLA) has to account for three key factors and, crucially, their interrelationship. These are: (1) what the learner brings or contributes to the process, from innate predispositions, through the activation of certain psychological processes such as attention or memory, and through affective involvement in the process, to strategic behaviour which may render the process more manageable and unthreatening; (2) the nature of the actual language learning process; and (3) the outcomes from the process in terms of linguistic or, more broadly, communicative competence in the target language.

In exploring this relationship, SLA research to date has primarily focused upon the interaction between what learners contribute, particularly their innate template for language or their cognitive processes, and the language data made available to them. In a recent review of SLA research, I argued that the research appears to favour particular paradigms of learning and, thereby, constructs the learner in particular ways (Breen, 1996). Summarising very briefly, SLA research tells us a great deal about the learner as being interpretative, accommodating, and strategic. That is, the interpretation of meaningful input and the effort to express meaning appear to be the catalysts for language learning. The accommodation by the learner of language data is typified by the learner's creative construction of interlanguages which represent gradual approximations to the target language. And both learning strategies and communicative strategies are adopted by learners in order to make their interpretative and accommodating work much more manageable. These three constructs of the learner which we can deduce from the research contribute significantly to an explanation of how language is learned.

However, this explanation will remain partial if much of SLA research persists in decontextualising learner contributions, the learning process, and learning outcomes from the location in which these three factors are realised. Mainstream SLA research, in focusing upon the relationship between the learner and language data, is conducted and reported on in ways that appear to overlook the social reality in which the research is actually conducted. Dyadic encounters between caretakers and young learners or between native speaker researchers and non-native speaking informants, experimental situations using elicitation techniques, quasi-experimental negotiation tasks undertaken by non-native speakers, or observed interactions during lessons are never socially neutral activities. To reduce the data from such events to a psycholinguistic objectivity of inputs and outputs is to dislocate them from their intersubjective nature. The evidence we obtain from any learning event, even in a quasi-experimental setting, is significantly shaped by the social situation and the social relations within that event.

If we used Ellis's recent very comprehensive review of SLA research (Ellis, 1994) as an indicator of the major focus of SLA researchers to the present time, we find that more than two thirds of the chapters in his account refer to work which assumes that the interaction between the learner's mental resources and features of linguistic input will provide a sufficiently adequate explanation for language learning. Ellis fairly reflects current SLA research in devoting just over a quarter of his review to more recent studies which locate the interaction between learner and language in the context of interpersonal or social situations. His account reveals that context has been defined or framed in particular ways by SLA research. It is addressed in a fragmentary way as a diversity of "social factors" – from identification by the learner with the target language group to the possible effects of different types of language programs – or as the specific features of classroom interaction, or as the possible impact of formal instruction. Ellis himself concludes that "the relationship between social factors and L2 achievement is an indirect rather than a direct one" (1994: 239). In referring to classroom interaction studies, he concludes that they have "contributed little to our understanding of how interaction affects acquisition" (1994: 607). And he deduces that formal instruction can, at most, be credited with "facilitating natural language development" in terms of increased accuracy and accelerated progress (1994: 659).

The apparent assumption in these deductions is that "L2 achievement", "acquisition" or "natural language development" can somehow occur almost regardless of contextual variables. In this chapter, however, I want to suggest that, if we look more closely at the classroom as context, such a focus will reveal that the interaction between learner and data and the differential outcomes from this interaction will be significantly moulded and circumscribed by that context. If we discovered and could implement in the classroom all those ideal conditions which we may deduce from current SLA research as optimal for language learning, learners will still differentially achieve. They will continue to learn mostly different things, at different rates, and to different levels of proficiency. Clearly a part of this variation in outcomes will be due to diversity in the contributions of the learners to the process. But variation will also have to be explained with reference to the particular context in which the learning occurred so that input, process, and outcomes are seen as functions of how the learners variously defined that context and acted in it. If we are concerned with trying to increase the likelihood of success in language learning in the classroom, then we need to take a socially situated perspective on the interaction between learner and data. In order to justify such a claim, I will begin by offering my interpretation of the context of learning.

Second Language Acquisition in context

There is little doubt that the history of SLA not only grew out of the roots put down by studies of first language acquisition and has, over the last twenty years or so, sent up its own shoots and branches in the shadow of this area of research. Building on the influences of sociolinguistics, discourse analysis and the work of Vygotsky (1986), there is a significant body of first language acquisition research which explicitly recognises the interpersonal context of learning as the crucible of the whole process of language development (Donaldson 1978, Bruner 1981, Lock 1980, Schiefelbusch and Pickar 1984, Wells 1981 and 1985, Foster 1990, *inter alia*). Evelyn Hatch brought this kind of perspective into SLA research in revealing how learners extend their grammatical repertoires on the basis of the "scaffolding" provided for them by proficient speakers during conversations (Hatch 1978 and 1992, Hatch *et al.* 1990). Her work has had an indirect influence upon those in SLA research who claim a "social interactionist" perspective in seeing speech modifications during communication between learners or learners and their teachers as central to the acquisition process (Long 1981, 1985 and 1996, Lightbown 1985, Pica *et al.* 1986 and 1987).

Only very recently have a number of SLA researchers returned to Vygotsky's complex ideas which insist on learning as embedded within, and inseparable from social activity. These researchers propose an extension of investigations into SLA to include a "sociocultural" perspective (Lantolf 1994, Lantolf and Appel 1994). Such a perspective is fairly represented by Leont'ev who, like Vygotsky, saw learning as an *interpsychological* undertaking between those in society who have mastered knowledge or capability and those who are discovering such knowledge or developing such capabilities. Leont'ev identified learning as directly equivalent to other social activities in the wider world such as work, or family life, or participation in various everyday situations and institutional settings. For Leont'ev, when we read a text, listen to music, or paint a picture, even when not in the presence of others, we are participating in a process that is socially constructed:

> if we removed human activity from the system of social relationships and social life, it would not exist and would have no structure. With all its varied forms, the human

individual's activity is a system in the system of social relations. It does not exist without these relations. The specific form in which it exists is determined by the forms and means of material and mental social interaction.

(Leont'ev 1981: 47)

Leont'ev is suggesting that an activity like learning a language is a mental process inevitably interwoven in our social identity and our social relationships. But he goes further than this. He is also asserting that the object or content on which we focus in our learning is, by its nature, a social and cultural construct. And linguists such as Halliday support such a claim in revealing that social structure and system may be seen to permeate the whole texture of a language (Halliday 1978). This perspective implies that the interpretative, accommodating, and strategic work of learners as revealed by mainstream SLA research is not merely an act of cognition but that it is simultaneously social action.

If we learn a language in the company of others in a classroom, then the nature of this social action is not merely a superficial frame for our work on language data. Social relationships in the classroom orchestrate what is made available for learning, how learning is done, and what we achieve. These relationships and the purposeful social action of teaching and learning are directly realised through the discourse in which we participate during lessons. The data made available to learners are socially filtered through the particular discourse of the classroom and, thereby, rendered distinctive from what we might describe as naturally occurring language data in a different context. Furthermore, because the data made available to learners in a classroom are a collective product with which teacher and learners interact actively as both creators and interpreters, because what learners actually learn from the classroom is socially rather than individually constructed, any explanation of how language is learned must locate the process *within* the discourse of language lessons.

This implies that language learners need not only be interpretative, accommodating, and strategic as SLA research suggests, but also active practitioners within the discourse of the learning context in which they find themselves. If the context happens to be a classroom, it will provide very particular opportunities for and specific constraints upon language learning. These opportunities and constraints can be identified in the discourse of language lessons and a crucial variable which can contribute to our understanding of the relative success or failure of learners is how they themselves are obliged to navigate within it.

We can express this central issue in terms of a question: Does a learner's success in learning language in a classroom depend upon the learner's successful navigation of the opportunities and constraints inherent in discourse of lessons? This is a difficult question that needs further elaboration and I will offer this by looking more closely at some of the prevailing features of classroom discourse. I will address the question with reference to a number of findings from SLA research.

Dimensions of discourse

Discourse is a difficult concept because, like SLA research, discourse analysis is a relatively young discipline and there are several conflicting and overlapping definitions deriving from a range of theoretical and analytical positions (van Dijk 1985, Macdonnell 1986). Early work in discourse analysis sought to uncover pattern and system at a higher level of organisation than the sentence and to analyse the properties of dialogue such as speech acts, turn taking, topicalisation, and so on. Descriptive discourse analysis was also undertaken in relation to what were seen as distinctive discourses such as media discourse, medical discourse, or legal discourse. More recently, the ideas of social theorists such as Foucault (1972 and 1984) and Bourdieu (1991) have led to an extension of such work to refer to how human knowledge and capabilities and everyday social practices are themselves constructed and sustained through discourse.

In relating social theory directly to earlier and more conventional approaches to discourse analysis with a view to developing a critical approach to analysis, Fairclough (1989 and 1992) has provided a framework of discourse which is made up of three related levels or components. For him, any instance of discourse can be seen as being simultaneously a piece of text, an instance of discursive practice, and an instance of social practice. Applying this framework to the language classroom, the *text* of lessons is all the available language or communicative data, be they spoken, written, or in other visual media from pictures and diagrams to facial expressions. The *discursive practices* are how texts are produced and interpreted and how different types of texts are combined. Clearly, teachers and learners in the classroom produce, interpret, and combine texts. The teaching materials, in whatever medium, are also produced and combined by people not present in the classroom and teacher and learners interpret such materials in ways that serve their immediate purposes. Finally, *social practice* refers to the organisational and institutional circumstances that generate and delimit both the specific text and discursive practices of lessons. Social practices include not only those broader cultural and situational factors which locate classrooms as having a particular function and identity but also those seemingly trivial but nevertheless important practices such as how the furniture is organised in the room or how long a lesson should last. More crucially, perhaps, both teacher and learners are actually positioned and constructed *as teachers* and *as learners* by the social practices of classrooms. The daily routines and procedures which teachers and learners jointly establish in order to work together in a relatively harmonious way, which I have described elsewhere as expressing the underlying culture of the language class (Breen 1985), are also highly significant social practices that are part of the discourse of lessons.

To summarise, therefore, the social practice or the particular culture of the classroom shapes the discursive practices of teacher and learners and these discursive practices generate the text of classroom interaction. However, the process is also reflexive in the sense that the text of lessons may express or limit certain discursive practices and these, in turn, may facilitate or constrain alternative social practices. It is time to step inside the classroom and explore the possible impact upon language learning of the text of lessons, the discursive practices of teachers and learners, and their social practices through some of the evidence provided to us by classroom research.

The text of language lessons

Applying this three-dimensional view of discourse to the findings of SLA research which has focused particularly upon classroom language learning, we find that the text of language lessons, like lessons in other subjects, appears to have a consistent pattern in which teachers initiate, learners respond, and teachers follow up their responses by repetition, reformulation or evaluation (Sinclair and Coulthard 1975). McTear (1975) identified a variation in this dominant pattern which appeared to be specific to language lessons where a teacher's reformulation is often repeated verbatim by a learner or the whole class because they interpret it as a model to be overtly imitated. And this appears to be a discursive practice which teachers sometimes deliberately encourage. Van Lier (1988, see also Chapter 5 of this book) points out that a good proportion of the teachers' utterances in a language lesson are not directed at particular individuals but serve as a kind of communal monologue directed by the teacher at the whole class wherein learner contributions are woven by the teacher into his or her own text.

Chaudron's (1988) review of research on teacher talk in the language class further reveals that a good proportion of teacher input made available to learners has very specific characteristics. Teachers appear to have two-thirds more practice in the target language than all the learners put together. They also modify their speech in ways similar to the characteristics of caretaker speech to young children or native speaker speech to non-native speakers. Interestingly, such teacher modification appears more emphatic when addressing learners whom they regard as having lower proficiency (Dahl 1981, Griffiths 1991, Hamayan and Tucker 1980, Henzel 1979, Kliefgen 1985, Ellis 1985, Wong-Filmore 1982). In other words, the degree of modification in a teacher's direct interaction with an individual learner may signal to that learner the teacher's judgement of his or her capabilities.

A crucial feature of the text of lessons is teacher feedback on learner utterances. Because of the fast flow of lessons, teachers are understandably inconsistent in their reactions to learner errors with the result that different learners may either fail to distinguish a teacher's correction from other kinds of teacher utterance or assume that almost all teacher responses to what they say are some form of judgement or correction (Allwright and Bailey 1991, Edmondson 1985, Nystrom 1983, Van Lier 1988). Underlining Van Lier's observations about the teacher's discursive control of the text of lessons, research reveals that a remarkably high proportion of teacher utterances are interrogatives (Johnston 1990, Long and Sato 1983). And a very high proportion of these are closed display questions in which learners are required to provide information which the teacher already knows rather than open referential questions which genuinely seek information from the learners (Long and Sato op. cit.).

Although acknowledging the centrality of the teacher in the orchestration of classroom discourse, Van Lier (1988) suggests that the text of language lessons constantly shifts due to its being generated by four types of interaction: teacher instructions, teacher's highly structured elicitations of student responses, and procedurally structured learner activities such as small group or dyadic tasks, all of which are occasionally punctuated by small talk or student asides. Van Lier suggests that these different types of talk reflect different degrees of teacher control over topics or activities. From this we may also deduce that each of the four types of interaction will facilitate or delimit particular discursive practices on the part of learners.

There appear to be features of the text of language lessons that may be distinctive as compared with other types of lessons. We might describe this as the inter-textual nature of language input in classroom talk. Allwright (1980) analyses classroom talk into three types: 'samples' or instances of the target language, 'guidance' where communication occurs about the target language, and 'management' wherein procedural talk facilitates the optimal occurrence of samples and guidance. It seems, therefore, that the data made available to the learner in the classroom is an on-going amalgam of three dominant and inter-weaving discursive practices: communication through the target language, metacommunication about the target language, and communication about the teaching–learning process, its procedures and classroom routines. And, as participants in the discourse, learners have to navigate through its inter-textuality identifying the textual cues which signal a transition from one kind of talk to another. It is very likely that different learners will be more or less skilled in such navigation.

We might conclude from these general patterns in the contributions of teachers to the interactive text of language lessons that learners are not actually required to do much overt or explicit discursive work while devoting their discursive energies to keeping track of the teacher's text and being alert to the moments when they have to contribute to it and to the teacher's reactions to their contributions.

Learners' discursive practices in the classroom

So far, on the basis of language classroom research, I have suggested that the discourse of lessons is significantly shaped by the teacher, that learners are positioned in particular ways by this, that the discourse manifests a shifting inter-textuality, and that learners are obliged to undertake pragmatic navigation within this inter-textuality if they are to find their way through it in order to make sense of it. For a fuller picture, however, we need to focus upon variations in the overt participation of learners in the discourse which may be seen as further contributory factors in their differential achievement in learning.

There are few studies of learner input in the classroom apart from the body of work on controversial modifications during group or dyad work on tasks, some of which having been undertaken in classroom settings. Perhaps this is not surprising when, if we examine the research on learner participation and, by implication, their contributions to the text of lessons as discursive practitioners, we find that learners are most often positioned by the discourse in a responsive role (Politzer *et al.* 1981). Generally, it seems that, through their control of the discursive practices of lessons, through their use of questions, explanations, procedural instructions, and, crucially, their evaluation of much of the language produced by learners immediately after it is uttered, teachers construct learners as primarily responsive and seemingly fairly passive participants in the discourse. In offering an explanation for the failure of French immersion students to fully attain native-speaker like levels in their own speech despite years of exposure to content-based and comprehensible language input resulting in very high levels of receptive understanding, Swain (1985) suggests that this failure may be partially due to the relative lack of opportunities for them to participate overtly in classroom discourse through their own speech production.

However, even responsive discursive practices appear to lead to variation in learning. In investigating whether greater learner participation had an effect upon learning, Strong (1983 and 1984) discovered that a high response rate among certain learners correlated with their achievement in tests based upon the grammar, pronunciation and vocabulary of classroom speech. Seliger (1977) suggested that those learners which he identified as "high input generators" performed better on an aural comprehension task than did less participating learners. In their classic study of the good language learner, Naiman *et al.* (1978) found that learners who raised their hands more and more often responded to teacher elicitations did better on tests than other learners.

Studies by Larsen-Freeman (1976a and 1976b), Hamayan and Tucker (1980), Lightbown (1983), and Long (1980), all suggest that the frequency of occurrence of certain linguistic forms in classroom text is likely to correlate with the accurate production of these forms by learners. More significantly, studies by Lightbown (1980 and 1991), Snow and Hoefnagel-Hohle (1982), and White *et al.* (1991) not only confirm this but also show high retention rates of question forms. Given the regular occurrence of questions in the text of lessons, this may not be surprising. Learners are obliged to be alert to questions in case they are directed to them individually. These studies also found that, not only questions, but other kinds of utterances directed specifically at individual learners correlated with higher gain scores in tests taken by those individuals. It appears that, while it may not be surprising that frequent occurrence of certain features in the text of lessons render them more accessible, types of teacher utterances which place what we may describe as *discursive pressure* upon learners, such as questioning or nominated terms, demand overt discursive work on the part of learners that may, in turn, influence their learning outcomes.

The recent research on the kinds of classroom tasks which most facilitate interaction among learners confirms the significance of discursive pressure. A task that entails an information gap between interlocutors, that is unfamiliar to them, that engages learners in social exchanges about shared goals and problems, that is undertaken by learners of different levels of proficiency, and that demands a single, closed solution for successful completion is found to encourage learners to have longer turns, produce more complex language, and devote more time to explicit negotiation for meaning than any other kinds of task (Berwick 1990, Long 1989 and 1996. Plough and Gass, 1993). Furthermore, Tanaka (1991) and Yamazaki (1991) have suggested that learner work on modifying linguistic data through their *own* interaction provides for greater gains in learning than providing them with either unmodified or premodified input. In addition, Lightbown's studies of corrective feedback (Lightbown 1991) and Swain's exploration of the functions of learner output (Swain 1985 and 1995) confirm that feedback is most likely to have an impact on the learner's interlanguage if it occurs at times when the learner is working hard to convey a particular message. In sum, the struggle to negotiate for meaning through overt discursive work renders relatively complex text comprehensible and, consistent with a major assumption in SLA research, thereby facilitates learning.

However, different learners will navigate through the discourse of lessons in different ways depending upon their own definitions of the situation, their previous experiences of classrooms, and their particular understanding of the dynamic social practices or culture of the classroom group (Breen *op. cit.*). Learners will therefore place different values and significance upon their role as a participant in the class. Overt discursive pressure upon particular learners or even spontaneous participation do not alone account for differences in what learners learn from a lesson. Day's (1984) replication of Seliger's study of "high input generators" (Seliger *op. cit.*) and Ely's (1986) investigation of learner initiated utterances found no relationship between overt learner participation and later test attainment. In tracing learners' immediate "uptake" from lessons of previously unknown vocabulary, Slimani (1989 and 1992; Chapter 18 of this book) confirmed Allwright's hypothesis that different learners will learn different things even from the same lesson (Allwright *op. cit.*). Slimani made the interesting discovery that low-participating and even non-participating learners often recalled as much from lessons as did high-participating learners. And, significantly, learners recalled more items from lessons if they were topicalised or introduced into the text of the lesson by *learners* rather than those topicalised by the teacher. Slimani deduced that low-participating learners were directly benefiting from their high-participating colleagues. Allwright interpreted these findings as suggesting that the more proficient learners in a class who appeared to be those more willing to participate were taking on the burden of discursive work but without seemingly gaining from it. In other words, proficiency in the language may enable greater participation rather than participation leading to gains in proficiency. Slimani's study also cast doubt on the claims of mainstream SLA researchers that conversational modifications lead to greater comprehensibility and, thereby, increased likelihood of acquisition. In fact she found no relationship between the number of conversational adjustments occurring in the text of lessons around specific linguistic items and the "uptake" of these items by learners.

A recent replication of Slimani's study by Dobinson (1996) largely confirmed these findings and suggested that differences between learners in what they recalled from lessons were due to a whole range of factors and that some of the previously unknown vocabulary which they not only recalled but also retained over a longer period were never overtly negotiated about in the text of the lesson. Only 27% of retained vocabulary items had been overtly topicalised in the lesson, whilst 56% of retained vocabulary could be traced to the individual learner's personal work upon items occurring in the spoken or written texts of the lesson which triggered efforts to seek items in a dictionary, to make associations with what they knew already, to write the word down to find out its meaning later, and so on. In essence, a key characteristic of items which individual learners learned from the lessons was the relative incomprehensibility of that item to an individual learner and this resulted in covert individual work towards understanding and, thereby, remembering it. In fact, Dobinson discovered that there was a converse relationship between the amount of overt negotiation about new vocabulary items and their retention by learners. The more an item was focused upon in the text of the lesson, the less likely it was to be retained. She concluded that there must be an optimal degree of overt negotiation which facilitates learning. In focusing upon learner participation, Dobinson also discovered that learners who did not participate at all recalled equal or greater numbers of previously unknown words from the lessons as did higher participating learners.

From Slimani's and Dobinson's research it appears that we can deduce that individual learners appear to be capable of navigating the discourse in ways that reflect their individual purposes and agendas. In certain circumstances, discursive pressure to respond or to negotiate with the teacher or other learners facilitates acquisition only for some learners. However, as with all deductions from classroom language learning research, these findings have to be seen in the light of the context from which the data were obtained. Slimani and Dobinson located their studies in classrooms that were conventionally teacher-fronted with strong teacher control over the text of the lessons. It appears, therefore, that there may be a difference in learning outcomes based upon overt negotiation for meaning in this kind of classroom context as compared with dyads or small groups of learners negotiating for meaning without the intervention of the teacher. This discovery, of course, would support the argument that context makes a difference. Overt participation in classroom discourse appears to serve other purposes in addition to the purpose of learning. In these circumstances, some learners will deliberately avoid discursive pressure so that they can devote their attention to their own learning agendas. And the Slimani and Dobinson studies confirm that it is likely that learners will differentially gain from such practices.

Social practices in the classroom

Learners selectively work through the discourse of the classroom not only as discursive practitioners within the immediate lesson but also on the basis of how they judge which social practices are appropriate in the particular classroom group. Their selective participation and the judgements on which they base it are derived from their definition of the particular teaching-learning situation and from their experience with other realms of discourse beyond the classroom. Learners therefore navigate the discourse in two constantly inter-weaving ways; for learning purposes and for social purposes. Differential outcomes from lessons may reflect the fact that learners will differ in their abilities to balance these two priorities and, crucially, in their relative allocation of attention to them.

Classroom discourse is, for the learner, a voyage of discovery in the close company of others with a teacher who leads the expedition or, at least, carries the map. On the one hand, learners navigate classroom discourse in order to discover here and now *what counts* as valid interpretation, what counts as knowledge worth accommodating, and what counts as appropriate strategic behaviour for learning be it overt or covert. On the other hand, they navigate the discourse anticipating that the social practices within the classroom will construct knowledge and the role identities of, and relationships between teacher and learners in very specific ways. They are therefore obliged to work in order to maximise the learning and social benefits they may gain from the discourse while minimising its potential psychological and social costs. Their selective work therefore reflects their understanding of, and contributions to, the emerging culture of the particular classroom group and their own location within it. In an earlier paper, I suggested that this culture is not only asymmetrical in terms of who controls the discourse, or normative in terms of the teacher's judgements of correctness or appropriacy, but that learners *jointly conspire* with teachers in creating and maintaining a manageable working harmony through the particular routines and procedures of the surface text of lessons (Breen *op. cit.*). From SLA research, we know that different types of classroom-based activities and tasks will permit different outcomes for different learners (Larsen-Freeman 1976a, Tarone 1988, Schmidt 1980, Bahns and Wode 1980, Hyltenstam 1984, Lightbown 1991). But we also know that different types of classrooms in terms of their overt routines and procedures or, more broadly, their social practices will generate different learning outcomes as well (Wong-Filmore 1982, Enright 1984, Spada 1987, Allen *et al.* 1990).

Allwright (1989) has suggested that data from classroom interaction often reveal teacher and learners having to solve a recurring discoursal dilemma. The dilemma confronting both teacher and learners is that of maintaining social harmony or avoiding what he calls "social problems" whilst, at the same time, preserving what he regards as "pedagogic possibilities" or genuine opportunities for learning. For Allwright, such social problems include unexpected topics that arise as side issues but become an extended focus of the interaction, or dominating or highly reluctant learners, or procedural confusions that appear to detract from the teacher's plans or lesson management. Allwright suggests that the resolution of "social trouble" is an inevitable part of classroom discourse and that, paradoxically, "good pedagogy" based upon approaches to language teaching which encourage overt learner participation necessarily risks creating social problems. However, the culture of most classrooms is often built upon and preserved by a shared and unspoken assumption that cooperation to maintain relative harmony on the surface of lessons between competing agendas is ultimately easier for both teacher and learners. The costs of social trouble are constantly in balance with the benefits of fairly predictable and stable routines and procedures and the teacher and most learners work hard in order to resolve or avoid such troubles. At different times, it is very likely that some learners will perceive some social troubles as learning opportunities just as they may interpret what the teacher regards as a pedagogic possibility as socially threatening. However, the very salience of social trouble in the discourse will alert learners' attention to it while possibly involving teacher and learners in exactly the kind of resolution work that may be directly beneficial to language learning.

However, learners also navigate through classroom discourse in ways that will enable them to avoid individual trouble for themselves, in particular avoiding to appear foolish in public. The interesting studies of Beebe and Zuengler (Beebe 1977, Beebe and Zuengler 1983) and of Young (1988 and 1991) reveal that the learners will actually vary the style of their production depending upon whom they are addressing and, in particular their perception of the relative status and linguistic competence of their interlocutors. Of direct relevance to the classroom, Takahashi's research suggests that learners will be more hesitant and briefer in their utterances when addressing someone whom they perceive as highly competent in the target language such as their teacher (Takahashi 1989). And Rampton (1987) reveals that learners, while actually capable of more complex language, may revert to earlier features of their interlanguage precisely in order to signal that they *are* learners. Learners may undertake a kind of impression management in their discursive practices which publicly expresses their own construction of themselves as learners and their construction of whom they interact with. Therefore, variations in how learners participate in the text of lessons will also be a reflection of their self assessment and their assessment of both the teacher's language and the teacher's likely reactions to their own production. It seems that some learners' perceptions of the established social relationships in some classrooms may actually encourage them to underachieve.

What learners learn from the discourse of lessons

The foregoing review of classroom language learning research has illustrated some of the ways in which the interaction between the learner and the target language data is situated within social action. In order to summarise what we know of the discursive practices of learners in the language classroom, we can see that learners are obliged to participate overtly and covertly in the discourse of lessons in the following ways:

- Adopt a responsive role in relation to the teacher's management of the discourse through his/her control over the text of lessons.
- Be alert to and adapt to the varying inter-textuality of lessons.
- Act individually in response to discursive pressure within teacher-learner interaction and within tasks and activities during lessons.
- Covertly exploit others' participation in classroom discourse as opportunities to serve own purposes and learning agenda.
- Navigate the discourse of the classroom – its specific text, discursive requirements, and particular social practices – with direct reference to personal costs and benefits.
- Define the situation on the basis of past experience and present understanding of the emerging culture of the classroom group and act in ways that are seen as appropriate to that culture.
- Participate with the teacher and other learners in the ongoing construction of lessons and the maintenance of fairly predictable classroom routines and procedures.
- Manage the presentation of self through the discourse according to one's own definition of both self identity and the demands of the situation.

In general, therefore, a learner who is a successful discursive practitioner in the classroom appears to be someone who avoids risks to self identity in the group and contributes in ways that seem appropriate to the group culture whilst exploiting discoursal opportunities for their own learning. The question I raised at the beginning of this chapter was: Does a learner's success in language learning in the classroom depend upon the learner's successful navigation of the opportunities and constraints inherent in the discourse of lessons? Clearly learners will differ in their responses to the kinds of demands that are placed upon them by such discourse and they will differ in terms of their own priorities and capabilities as discursive practitioners in the specific context of a classroom. I have suggested that learners in classrooms will differentially interpret, accommodate, and adopt strategies largely on the basis of what classroom discourse provides as text, what practices it requires of teacher and learners, and how it constructs both the knowledge to be learned and the unfolding teaching-learning process through social practice. Learners' cognitions are framed within the prevailing discourse through which they learn and there is good evidence that learners navigate that discourse in different ways. It is inevitable that different learners will differentially achieve in such circumstances. In fact, the variables to which I have referred in reviewing second language classroom research are an important explanation for such differentiation.

Implications for classroom pedagogy

We might deduce from the evidence that there is only a very tenuous relationship between successful participation by learners in the discourse of lessons and their actual progress in learning the language. At least it seems that overt participation in lessons has little impact on actual learning whilst overt negotiation for meaning in small group and dyadic tasks is seen by SLA researchers as pivotal for learning. But a crucial issue is that overt participation seems to be relatively rare for individual learners in the kinds of lessons from which most data for second language classroom research are obtained. Navigating the discourse in many language classrooms, whilst resulting in different learning outcomes for most learners, is not a difficult thing for most of them to do. Since their early years at school, language learners have gradually discovered what is expected of them as discursive practitioners in a classroom. In many cases, they have had years of practice at interpreting the texts of lessons, learning and adopting appropriate discursive practices, and understanding and contributing to the social practices of classrooms. As we have seen, the data from second language classroom research primarily reveals that teachers orchestrate the discourse while learners play their parts as a kind of counterpoint to their individual learning agendas. The discourse may momentarily harmonise with these agendas while at other times, there is discordance between the discourse and genuine learning. To be provocative, we might conclude that some learners' highly attentive efforts to avoid trouble by successfully navigating the prevailing discourse of language lessons might actually distract their attention from actually learning something.

There is a growing body of evidence which suggests that the discourse of the language classroom is distinctive. And it is distinctive in many ways from the discourse in which we participate in other contexts (Riley 1977, Gremmo *et al*. 1978, Edmondson 1985, Kramsch 1985, Glahn and Holman 1985, Kasper 1986, Ellis 1992). If, for most learners perhaps, language learning is embedded in the discourse of the classroom, if they learn how to *become* members of a new language community through the discursive practices which they adopt or are obliged to adopt in the classroom, how will these practices prepare them for participation in discourse beyond the classroom? In other words, how are learners to transcend what they have learned in managing classroom discourse in order to participate as speakers of the new language in other realms of discourse?

A paradoxical but central issue for language pedagogy is how it may facilitate the gradual *disembedding* of language learning from what appears to be the prevailing discourse of lessons. In raising this issue I am not intending to imply that all the features of such discourse inhibit the learner's capacity to participate in other kinds of discourse. However, I believe it does imply that we need to consider how we might identify and mobilise the discursive work of learners which actually benefits learning while also identifying and reducing those mutable constraints within the current discursive and social practices of language classrooms which may inhibit it.

If a learner is positioned in a largely responsive role within the discourse, the research suggests that the learner has to fall back upon covert and unguided ways of making sense because the opportunities for overt negotiation which entail the added benefits of individual output and directly formative feedback are significantly curtailed (Slimani; Dobinson; Swain *op. cit.*). If the discourse of a language lesson constraints the kinds of participation which SLA research identifies as genuine negotiation for meaning, in what ways can we vary the text, discursive practices and social practices of the classroom so that genuine negotiation for meaning becomes more possible? If there is a joint conspiracy between a teacher and learners that predictable and trouble free discourse is preferable to having to work harder within it, in what ways might we more overtly mobilise learner efforts to make sense of the unpredictable and to participate directly in resolving both learning and social confusions? The individual effort to confront and reduce complexity in text through discursive negotiation with and about that text is the catalyst for understanding and, thereby, an opportunity for further learning (Long 1996).

All these considerations directly imply that we should be facilitating the kind of discourse in a language class which is more challenging to its participants than it often is. Such a discourse will positively support the kind of risk-taking among learners that can contribute to deeper and more resilient levels of learning. This means focusing upon the potential inherent in those discursive practices which learners are *currently* obliged to adopt. Given that teachers have the major responsibility in managing the discourse of lessons, how can we manage it in ways that may maximise such opportunities? Recalling the discursive practices of learners that I summarised earlier, alternative ways of managing the discourse may include the following:

- Expecting learners to adopt an active and creative role in constructing the text of lessons so that at least two-thirds of it is generated by learners rather than the teacher.
- Building on the learners' alertness and adaptability to the inter-textuality of lessons and familiarity with inter-textuality in the first language by encouraging the understanding and creation of inventive and diverse combinations of written and spoken texts in the new language.
- Positively encouraging learner risk-taking so that discursive pressure is seen by learners as genuine opportunities for creative use of emerging knowledge and skills rather than requiring responses which may be judged in personally threatening ways.
- Enabling learners to make overt and to develop their own on-going learning agendas so that these may be personally reflected upon and refined and also acted upon in a collective way.
- Enabling learners to recognise that the inevitable and on-going costs in learning through a more challenging discourse of lessons are outweighed by both immediate and long term benefits.
- Exploring with learners ways in which the emerging culture of the classroom group can be adapted and constructed in an on-going way in order to facilitate their own learning as a participant in that group.
- Accepting that lessons are jointly constructed by teacher and learners together, seek ways of engaging learner responsibility for them so that routines and procedures are chosen and adapted on the basis of overt teacher–learner and learner–teacher negotiation about such things.
- Appreciating the social risk of doing all these things, facilitate cooperative and supportive ways of working as a classroom group that respects the identity, difficulties, and relative autonomy of the individual including those of the teacher.

Each of these ways of working is, of course, related to one another and, therefore, complementary. The effort to implement one makes it more possible to implement any of the others. Of course, learners in such a context will be confronted by the challenge of having to navigate a discourse that may be different from the kind of classroom discourse with which they are more at ease. However, if we accept the implications of current SLA research, it is possible that a more positive relationship between success in navigating such discourse and success in language learning will emerge.

References

Allen, P., Swain, M., Harley, B., and Cummins, J. (1990) 'Aspects of classroom treatment: toward a more comprehensive view of second language education', in *The development of second language proficiency*, B. Harley *et al.* (eds). Cambridge: Cambridge University Press.

Allwright, R. (1980) 'Turns, topics and tasks: patterns of participation in language teaching and learning', in *Discourse analysis in second language research*, D. Larsen-Freeman (ed.). Rowley Mass: Newbury House.

—— (1984) 'Why don't learners learn what teachers teach? The interaction hypothesis', in *Language learning in formal and informal contexts*, D. Singleton and D. Little (eds). Dublin: IRAL.

—— (1989) *Interaction in the language classroom: social problems and pedagogic possibilities*. Paper presented at Les États Generaux des Langues, Paris, April 1989.

Allwright, R. and Bailey, K. (1991) *Focus on the language classroom: an introduction to classroom research for language teachers*. Cambridge: Cambridge University Press.

Bahns, J. and Wode, H. (1980) 'Form and function in L2 acquisition', in *Second language development: trends and issues*, S. Felix (ed.). Tübingen: Gunter Narr.

Beebe, L. (1977) 'The influence of the listener on code-switching'. *Language Learning* 27, 331–9.

Beebe, L. and Zuengler, J. (1983) 'Accommodation theory: an explanation for style shifting in second language dialects', in *Sociolinguistics and second language acquisition*, N. Wolfson and E. Judd (eds). Rowley Mass: Newbury House.

Berwick, R. (1990) *Task variation and repair in English as a foreign language*. Kobe University of Commerce: Institute of Economic Research.

Bourdieu, P. (1991) *Language and symbolic power*. Cambridge: Polity Press.

Breen, M.P. (1985) 'The social context for language learning: a neglected situation?' *Studies in second language acquisition* 7. 135–58.

—— (1996) 'Constructions of the teacher in SLA research', in *Georgetown University Round Table on Languages and Linguistics 1996*, J.E. Alatis, C.A. Straehle, M. Ronkin, and B. Gellenberger (eds). Washington D.C.: Georgetown University Press.

Bruner, J. (1981) 'The pragmatics of acquisition', in *The child's construction of language*, W. Deutsch (ed.). New York: Academic Press.

Chaudron, C. (1988) *Second language classrooms: research on teaching and learning*. Cambridge: Cambridge University Press.

Dahl, D. (1981) 'The role of experience in speech modifications for second language learners'. *Minnesota Papers in Linguistics and Philosophy of Language* 7. 78–93.

Day, R. (1984) 'Student participation in the ESL classroom, or some imperfections in practice'. *Language Learning* 34. 69–102.

Dobinson, T. (1996) *The recall and retention of new vocabulary from second language classrooms*. Unpublished M.A. dissertation, Edith Cowan University, Western Australia.

Donaldson, M. (1978) *Children's minds*. London: Fontana.

Edmondson, W. (1985) 'Discourse worlds in the classroom and in foreign language learning'. *Studies in Second Language Acquisition* 7. 159–68.

Ellis, R. (1985) 'Teacher-pupil interaction in second language development'. *Input in second language acquisition*, S. Gass and C. Madden (eds). Rowley Mass.: Newbury House.

—— (1992) 'Learning to communicate in the classroom'. *Studies in Second Language Acquisition* 14. 1–23.

—— (1994) *The study of second language acquisition*. Oxford: Oxford University Press.

Enright, D. (1984) 'The organisation of interaction in elementary classrooms', in *On TESOL '83: the question of control*, J. Handscombe *et al.* (eds). Washington D.C.: TESOL.

Ely, C. (1986) 'An analysis of discomfort, risktaking, sociability and motivation in the L2 classroom'. *Language Learning* 36. 1–25.

Fairclough, N. (1989) *Language and power*. London: Longman.

—— (1992) *Discourse and social change*. Cambridge: Polity Press.

Foster, S. (1990) *The communicative competence of young children*. London: Longman.

Foucault, M. (1972) *The archeology of knowledge*. London: Tavistock Publications.

—— (1984) 'The order of discourse', in *Language and politics*, M. Shapiro (ed). Oxford: Basil Blackwell.

Glahn, E. and Holman, A. (eds) (1985) 'Anglica et Americana 22'. *Learner discourse*. Copenhagen: University of Copenhagen.

Gremmo, M., Holec, H., and Riley, P. (1978) Mélanges Pedagogiques. *Taking the initiative: some pedagogical applications of discourse analysis*. University of Nancy: CRAPEL.

Griffiths, R. (1991) 'Pausological research in an L2 context: a rationale and review of selected studies'. *Applied Linguistics* 12. 276–94.

Halliday, M.A.K. (1978) *Language as social semiotic*. London: Edward Arnold.

Hamayan, E. and Tucker, R. (1980) 'Language input in the bilingual classroom and its relations to second language achievement'. *TESOL Quarterly* 14. 453–68.

Hatch, E. (1978) 'Discourse analysis and second language acquisition', in *Second language acquisition*, E. Hatch (ed.). Rowley Mass: Newbury house.

—— (1992) *Discourse and language education*. Cambridge: Cambridge University Press.

Hatch, E., Shirai, Y., and Fantuzzi, C. (1990) 'The need for an integrated theory: connecting modules'. *TESOL Quarterly* 24. 697–716.

Henzel, V. (1979) 'Foreigner talk in the classroom'. *International Review of Applied Linguistics* 17. 159–65.

Hyltenstam, K. (1984) 'The use of typological markedness conditions as predictors in second language acquisition: the case of pronominal copies in relative clauses', in *Second language: a crosslinguistic perspective*, R. Anderson (ed.). Rowley Mass: Newbury House.

Hyltenstam, K. and Pienemann, M. (eds) (1985) *Modelling and assessing second language acquisition*. Clevedon: Multilingual Matters.

Johnston, S. (1990) *Teacher questions in the academic language-content classroom*. Unpublished paper. Tokyo: Temple University Japan.

Johnston, M. and Pienemann, M. (1986) *Second language acquisition: a classroom perspective*. New South Wales Migrant Education Service.

Kasper, G. (ed.) (1986) *Learning, teaching and communication in the foreign language classroom*. Aarhus: Aarhus University Press.

Kliefgen, J. (1985) 'Skilled variation in a kindergarten teacher's use of foreigner talk'. *Input in second language acquisition*, S. Gass and C. Madden (eds). Rowley Mass.: Newbury House.

Kramsch, C. (1985) 'Classroom interaction and discourse options'. *Studies in Second Language Acquisition* 7. 169–83.

Lantolf, J. (1994) 'Sociocultural theory and second language learning: an introduction to the special issue'. *Modern Language Journal* 78. 418–420.

Lantolf, J. and Appel, G. (1994) (eds) *Vygotskyan approaches to second language research*. Norwood, NJ: Ablex Publishing Corporation.

Larsen-Freeman, D. (1976a) 'Teacher speech as input to the ESL learner'. *University of California Working Papers in TESL* 10. 45–49.

—— (1976b) 'An exploration of the morpheme acquisition order of second language learners'. *Language Learning* 26. 125–134.

—— (1983) 'The importance of input in second language acquisition', in *Pidginization and creolization and language acquisition*, R. Anderson (ed.). Rowley, Mass: Newbury House.

Leont'ev, A.N. (1981) 'The problem of activity in psychology', in *Vygotsky and the social formation of mind*, J. Wertsch (ed.). Cambridge, Mass.: Harvard University Press.

Lightbown, P. (1980) 'The acquisition and use of questions by French L2 learners of English', in *Second language development: trends and issues*, S. Felix (ed.). Tübingen: Gunter Narr.

—— (1983) 'Exploring relationships between developmental and instructional sequences in L2 acquisition', in *Classroom oriented research in second language acquisition*, H. Seliger and M. Long (eds). Rowley Mass: Newbury House.

—— (1985) *Can language acquisition be altered by instruction?*, Hyltenstam and Pienemann (eds).

—— (1991) 'What have we here? Some observations on the effect of instruction on L2 learning', in *Foreign/second language Pedagogy Research*, R. Phillipson *et al.* (eds). Clevedon: Multilingual Matters.

—— (1992) 'Getting quality input in the second/foreign language classroom', in *Text and context: cross-disciplinary perspectives on language study*, C. Kramsch and S. McConnel-Ginet (eds). Lexington Mass: D.C. Heath and Co.

Lock, A. (1980) *The guided reinvention of language*. New York: Academic Press.

Long, M. (1980) *Input, interaction and second language acquisition*. Unpublished Ph.D. dissertation. University of California at Los Angeles.

—— (1981) 'Input, interaction and second language acquisition'. *Native language and foreign language acquisition*, H. Winitz (ed). Annals of the New York Academy of Sciences, 379.

—— (1985) 'A role for instruction in second language acquisition: task-based language teaching'. *Modelling and assessing second language acquisition*, K. Hyltenstam and M. Pienemann (eds). Clevedon: Mulitlingual Matters.

—— (1989) 'Task, group, and task-group interactions'. *University of Hawai'i Working Papers in ESL* 8. 251–86.

—— (1996) 'The role of the linguistic environment in second language acquisition', in *Handbook of second language acquisition*, W. Ritchie and T. Bhatia (eds). New York: Academic Press.

Long, M. and Sato, C. (1983) 'Classroom foreigner talk discourse: forms and functions of teachers' questions', in *Classroom oriented research in second language acquisition*, H. Seliger and M. Long (eds). Rowley Mass: Newbury house.

Macdonnel, D. (1986) *Theories of discourse*. Oxford: Basil Blackwell.

McTear, M. (1975) 'Structure and categories of foreign language teaching sequences', in *Working Papers: Language Teaching Classroom Research*, R. Allwright (ed.). University of Essex, Department of Language and Linguistics.

Naiman, N., Fröhlich, M., Stern, H., and Todesco. A. (1978) *The good language learner. Research in Education Series* 7. Toronto: The Ontario Institute for Studies in Education.

Nystrom, N. (1983) 'Teacher-student interaction in bilingual classrooms: four approaches to error feedback', in *Classroom oriented research in second language acquisition*, H. Seliger and M. Long (eds). Rowley Mass: Newbury House.

Pica, T. (1983) 'Adult acquisition of English as a second language under different conditions of exposure'. *Language Learning* 33. 465–97.

Pica, T., Doughty, C., and Young, D. (1986) 'Making input comprehensible: do interactional modifications help? *International Review of Applied Linguistics* 72. 1–25.

Pica, T., Young, R., and Doughty, C. (1987) 'The impact of interaction on comprehension'. *TESOL Quarterly* 21. 737–58.

Plough, I. and Gass, S. (1993) 'Interlocutor and task familiarity: effects on interactional structure', in *Tasks and language learning: integrating theory and practice*, G. Crookes and S. Gass (eds). Clevedon: Multilingual Matters.

Politzer, R., Ramirez, A., and Lewis, S. (1981) 'Teaching standard English in the third grade: classroom functions of language'. *Language Learning* 31. 171–93.

Rampton, B. (1987) 'Stylistic variability and not speaking "normal" English: some post-Labovian approaches and their implications for the study of interlanguage', in *Second language acquisition in context*, R. Ellis (ed.). London: Prentice Hall International.

Riley, P. (1977) *Discourse networks in classroom interaction: some problems in communicative language teaching*. Mélanges Pedagogiques. University of Nancy: CRAPEL.

Schiefelbusch, R. and Pickar, J. (eds) (1984) *The acquisition of communicative competence*. Baltimore MD.: University Park Press.

Schmidt, M. (1980) 'Coordinate structures and language universals in interlanguage'. *Language Learning* 30. 397–416.

Seliger, H. (1977) 'Does practice make perfect? A study of interaction patterns and L2 competence'. *Language Learning* 27. 263–78.

Sinclair, J. and Coulthard, M. (1975) *Towards an analysis of discourse*. Oxford: Oxford University Press.

Slimani, A. (1989) 'The role of topicalisation in classroom language learning'. *System* 17. 223–34.

—— (1992) 'Evaluation of classroom interaction', in *Evaluating second language acquisition*, J. Alderson and A. Beretta (eds). Cambridge: Cambridge University Press.

Snow, C. and Hoefnagel-Höhle, M. (1982) 'School age second language learners' access to simplified linguistic input'. *Language Learning* 32. 411–30.

Spada, N. (1987) 'Relationships between instructional differences and learning outcomes: a process-product study of communicative language teaching'. *Applied Linguistics* 8. 181–99.

Strong, M. (1983) 'Social styles and second language acquisition of spanish-speaking kindergarteners'. *TESOL Quarterly* 17. 241–58.

Strong, M. (1984) 'Integrative motivation: cause or result of successful language acquisition'. *Language Learning* 34. 1–14.

Swain, M. (1985) 'Communicative competence: some roles of comprehensible input and comprehensible output in its development', in *Input in second language acquisition*, S. Gass and C. Madden (eds). Rowley Mass: Newbury House.

Swain, M. (1995) 'Three functions of output in second language learning', in *For H.G. Widdowson: principles and practice in the study of language*, G. Cook and B. Seidlhofer (eds). Oxford: Oxford University Press.

Takahashi, T. (1989) 'The influence of listener on L2 speech', in *Variation in second language acquisition, vol II: Psycholinguistic issues*, S. Gass., C. Madden, D. Preston, and L. Selinker (eds). Clevedon: Multilingual Matters.

Tanaka, N. (1991) 'Politeness: some problems for Japanese learners of English'. *JALT Journal* 9. 81–102.

Tarone, E. (1988) *Variation in interlanguage*. London: Edward Arnold.

Van Dijk, T. (1985) *Handbook of discourse analysis, Vols 1–4*. London: Academic Press.

Van Lier, L. (1988) *The classroom and the language learner*. London: Longman.

Vygotsky, L. (1986) *Thought and language* (new edition, A. Kozulin (ed)). Cambridge, Mass: MIT Press.

Wells, G. (1981) *Learning through interaction: the study of language development. Language at home and school: 1*. Cambridge: Cambridge University Press.

—— 1985. *Language development in the preschool years. Language at home and school: 2*. Cambridge: Cambridge University Press.

Chapter 20

Joan Swann

RECORDING AND TRANSCRIBING TALK IN EDUCATIONAL SETTINGS

Introduction

THIS CHAPTER PROVIDES GUIDANCE FOR those who wish to carry out an investigation into aspects of spoken language. It is designed mainly for use in educational settings, and will probably be particularly appropriate for teachers and other educationists engaged on small-scale research projects. Many of the techniques and principles it discusses, however, apply equally well to investigations of spoken language in non-educational contexts.

I shall discuss factors to take into account when making audio and video recordings of spoken language, then look at different ways of making a written transcript from these recordings. The article does not provide detailed guidance on analysis, but I shall refer to other chapters in this volume that serve as examples of different ways of analysing talk.

Preliminaries: deciding what information you need and how to collect this

I am assuming that, as a reader of this chapter, you will already have in mind a clear purpose for recording and analysing spoken language – that you will have identified certain issues to focus on, perhaps specified, in a formal project, as a set of research questions. These questions will affect the setting in which you carry out your research, the people and events you decide to observe and record, the stance you adopt towards others involved in your research, the particular types of recording you make and how you transcribe and analyse these.

Selecting a sample of people and events

Since you cannot, and will not wish to record everything that is going on you will need to select people and events to focus on. If your interest is in aspects of classroom talk, you may wish to focus on talk between the teacher (yourself or a colleague) and pupils, or between different pupils, or both. You may be interested in whole-class discussion or small-group talk. You may wish to compare contributions from a small number of pupils in different contexts, or to monitor one child closely in a range of activities.

You will also need to think about the representativeness of the types of talk you wish to examine. For instance, how are you selecting the types of activity that you wish to record and analyse? Do these cover the full range of activities normally encountered? Or are you contrasting contexts you think are distinctive in some way?

If you are carrying out a small-scale investigation focusing on talk in one or two contexts, there are two important points to bear in mind about the samples of talk you eventually come up with:

- Your observations may provide great insights into peoples' conversational strategies, the way they manage certain activities or their understanding of certain concepts – but you cannot make broad generalizations on the basis of a small number of observations. For instance, observations of peoples' behaviour in one set of contexts do not provide evidence of how they 'generally' behave.
- A related point is that there are problems in making inferences about people's abilities or understanding on the basis of what they happen to do when you are recording them. For instance, just because students do not produce certain types of talk does not mean they cannot. On the other hand, students may develop coping strategies that make it appear they understand more than they do.

Adopting a researcher stance

A distinction is commonly made in research between *participant* and *non-participant* observation. A participant observer is someone who takes part in the event she or he is observing; a non-participant observer does not take part. There are practical difficulties with this distinction: for instance, by virtue of being in a classroom (or meeting, etc.), or by setting up recording equipment, you are to some extent a participant – and you are likely to have an effect on people's language behaviour. The linguist Labov identified what he termed 'the observer's paradox' (Labov, 1970) – that the mere act of observing people's language behaviour (or, for that matter, other aspects of their behaviour) is inclined to change that behaviour. Different effects are likely to be produced by different observers (it may matter whether an observer is female or male, or perceived as relatively senior or junior). Many linguistic researchers (such as Labov himself) have attempted, in various ways, to minimise the intrusion of their observations in order to obtain more 'authentic' data. Others have argued that such detachment is not a reasonable research goal:

> We inevitably bring our biographies and our subjectivities to every stage of the research process, and this influences the questions we ask and the ways in which we try to find answers. Our view is that the subjectivity of the observer should not be seen as a regrettable disturbance but as one element in the human interactions that comprise our object of study. Similarly, research subjects themselves are active and reflexive beings who have insights into their situations and experiences. They cannot be observed as if they were asteroids, inanimate lumps of matter: they have to be interacted with. (Cameron, Frazer, Harvey, Rampton and Richardson, 1992, p. 5)

For educationists researching in their own institutions, or institutions with which they have a close association, it will probably be impossible to act as a completely detached observer. It will be impossible, for instance, to maintain a strict separation between your role as an observer and your usual role as a teacher or a colleague. When interpreting the talk you collect you will need to take account of the effect your own presence, and the way you carried out the observations, may have had on your data.

It is also important to consider, more generally, the relationship you have, or that you enter into, with those who participate in your research and allow you to observe their language behaviour. I have used the term *researcher stance* to refer to this more general relationship – the way a researcher behaves towards the people and events she or he is observing. Cameron, Frazer, Harvey, Rampton and Richardson (1992) distinguish between three kinds of relationship, or researcher stance:

- 'ethical research', in which a researcher bears in mind the interests of research participants – e.g. minimising any inconvenience caused, protecting privacy – but still carries out research *on* participants: in this case, it is the researcher who sets the agenda, not other research participants;
- 'advocacy', in which researchers carry out research *on and for* participants – e.g. regarding themselves as accountable to participants and being willing to use their expert knowledge on participants' behalf (when required by participants to do so);
- 'empowering research', in which researchers carry out research *on, for and with* other participants – e.g. being completely open about the aims and methods of the research, recognising the importance of participants' own agendas, empowering participants by giving them direct access to expert knowledge.

The kind of researcher stance you feel able to adopt will affect the overall conduct of your research – what you research, the specific methods you adopt, how you interpret your results, the forms in which you disseminate research findings. Points to consider include:

- *What kind of talk is it reasonable to record?* Only 'public' talk or also casual, or 'private' conversation?
- *Do you always need permission to record talk?* Researchers would usually gain permission to make recordings (perhaps from parents in the case of young children), whereas talk may be recorded by teachers as a part of 'normal' teaching activity that does not require permission. But what if the teacher is also a researcher, or if s/he wishes to make use of 'routine' recordings for research purposes?
- *How open should you be about the purposes of your recordings?* Bound up with this question is the notion of the observer's paradox: it is likely that the more you tell people about your research the more their behaviour will be affected. Some researchers compromise: they are rather vague about the precise purposes of their research, though they may say more after completing their recording. 'Empowering' research would require greater openness and consultation. You may also feel that, if you are observing as a colleague or a teacher, it is important to retain an atmosphere of trust between yourself and those you work with.
- *To what extent should you discuss your recordings with research participants?* This has to do partly with the researcher stance you adopt. Discussing recordings with others also lets you check your interpretations against theirs, and may give you a different understanding of your data.
- *How should you identify those you have recorded?* In writing reports, researchers often give pseudonyms to institutions in which they have carried out research, or people whose words they quote. If you have worked more collaboratively with participants, however, they may wish to be identified by name. If you do wish to maintain confidentiality it

may be hard to do this where you are observing in your own institution – the identity of those you refer to may be apparent to other colleagues. One solution is to discuss with colleagues or students how much confidentiality they feel is necessary and how this may be maintained.

- *In what ways should you consult those you have recorded about the dissemination and further use of your work?* People may give permission to be recorded for a certain purpose, but what if your purposes change? E.g. you may wish to disseminate your work to a wider audience, or to use a video obtained for your research in a professional development session with local teachers.

For those interested in the relationships between researchers and 'the researched', Cameron *et al.* (1992) is a useful source. Professional organisations also provide research guidelines – see for instance the British Association for Applied Linguistics (1994) *Recommendations on Good Practice in Applied Linguistics*.

The sections that follow provide practical guidance on making audio and video recordings, making fieldnotes to supplement these recordings, and transcribing talk for detailed analysis.

Making audio and video recordings

When planning to record talk in classrooms or other educational settings, it is important to allow adequate time for this. Unless recording equipment is routinely used, you will need to allow time to collect, set up and check equipment. You will also need to pilot your data collection methods to ensure that it is possible to record clearly the kinds of data you are interested in. When you have made your recordings you will need time to play and replay these to become familiar with your data and to make transcriptions.

An initial decision concerns whether to make *audio* or *video* recordings. Videos are particularly useful for those with an interest in non-verbal behaviour; they are also useful for showing how certain activities are carried out, or certain equipment used. On the other hand, video cameras are likely to be more intrusive then audio recorders, and you may also find it harder to obtain a clear recording of speech.

I have set out below some practical points to bear in mind when making a choice between audio and video recordings.

After you have made recordings, it is useful to make a separate note of the date, time and context of each sequence, and then summarize the content (use the cassette player counter to make an index of your tape and help you locate extracts again).

Audio or video recordings?

Audio-recordings

- An audio-cassette recorder can be intrusive – though this is less likely to be the case in classrooms where pupils are used to being recorded, or recording themselves. Intrusiveness is more of a problem if cassette recorders are used in contexts where talk is not normally recorded, and where there is not the opportunity for recording to become routine (e.g. staff or other meetings).

- Intrusiveness can be lessened by keeping the technology simple and unobtrusive, for example by using a small, battery-operated cassette recorder with a built-in microphone. This also avoids the danger of trailing wires, and the problem of finding appropriate sockets.
- It is also better to use a fairly simple cassette recorder if pupils are recording themselves. In this case, go for a machine with a small number of controls, and check that young pupils can operate the buttons easily.
- There is a trade-off between lack of intrusiveness/ease of use and quality of recording: more sophisticated machines, used with separate microphones, will produce a better quality recording. This is a consideration if you intend to use the recordings with others, for example in a professional development session.
- A single cassette recorder is not suitable for recording whole-class discussion, unless you focus on the teacher's talk. The recorder will pick up loud voices, or voices that are near to it, and probably lose the rest behind background noise (scraping chairs and so on). Even when recording a small group, background noise is a problem. It is worth checking this by piloting your recording arrangements: speakers may need to be located in a quieter area outside the classroom.
- With audio-recordings you lose important nonverbal and contextual information. Unless you are familiar with the speakers you may also find it difficult to distinguish between different voices. Wherever possible, supplement audio-recordings with field-notes or a diary providing contextual information.

Video-recordings

- Video cameras are more intrusive than audio-cassette recorders. In contexts such as classrooms, intrusiveness can be lessened by leaving the recorder around for a while (switched off).
- A video camera is highly selective – it cannot pick up everything that is going on in a large room such as a classroom. If you move it around the classroom you will get an impression of what is going on, but will not pick up much data you can actually use for analysis. A video camera may be used to focus on the teacher's behaviour. When used to record pupils, it is best to select a small group, carrying out an activity in which they don't need to move around too much.
- As with audio-recordings, it is best to have the group in a quiet area where their work will not be disrupted by onlookers.
- The recording will be more useable if you check that the camera has all that you want in view and then leave it running. If you move the camera around you may lose important information, and you may introduce bias (by focusing selectively on certain pupils or actions).
- Video cameras with built-in microphones don't always produce good sound recordings. You will need to check this. A common problem is that you may need to locate a camera a long way from the group you are observing both to obtain a suitable angle of view, and to keep the apparatus unobtrusive. If it is important that you hear precisely what each person says, you may need to make a separate audio-recording or use an external microphone plugged into the video camera.

Making field-notes

Field-notes allow you to jot down, in a systematic way, your observations on activities and events. They provide useful contextual support for audio and video recordings, and may also be an important source of information in their own right. For instance, if your focus is on students in a particular lesson, you may wish to make notes on a (related) discussion between teachers; on other lessons you are unable to record; or on the lesson you are focusing on, to supplement your audio/video recordings. You may also wish to make notes on the audio/video recordings themselves, as a prelude to (and a context for) transcription.

If you are taking notes of a discussion or lesson on the spot, you will find that the talk flows very rapidly. This is likely to be the case particularly in informal talk, such as talk between students in a group. More formal talk is often easier to observe on the spot. In whole-class discussion led by a teacher, or in formal meetings, usually only one person talks at a time, and participants may wait to talk until nominated by the teacher or chair. The teacher or chair may rephrase or summarize what others speakers have said. The slightly more ordered nature of such talk gives an observer more breathing space to take notes.

It is usual to date notes and to provide brief contextual information. The format adopted is highly variable – depending on particular research interests and personal preferences. Figure 20.1 shows extracts from field-notes made by my Open University colleague Janet Maybin while watching an assembly in a school in the south-east of England. Janet Maybin's observations form part of a larger study of 10–12 year old children's collaborative language practices in school. In this extract, she was interested in identifying the values laid down in school assemblies. She wanted to see whether, and how, these might resurface later in children's talk in other contexts.

Janet Maybin was not taking an active part in the assembly, so she could jot down observations and brief comments at the time. She also audio-recorded the assembly for later analysis (she occasionally jots down counter numbers in her field-notes). After school, she wrote up her field-notes, separating observations (what actually happened) from a commentary (her questions, reflections, interpretations, ideas for things to follow up later).

Separating 'observation' from 'commentary' is useful in that it encourages the observer to think carefully about what they have observed, and to try out different interpretations. Bear in mind, however, that no observation is entirely free from interpretation: what you focus on and how you describe events will already depend on an implicit interpretive framework.

Making a transcript

In order to analyse spoken language at any level of detail, you will need to make a written transcript. Transcription is, however, very time-consuming. Edwards and Westgate (1994) suggest that every hour's recording may require 15 hours for transcription. I find that I can make a rough transcript more quickly than this, but a detailed transcript may take far longer, particularly if a lot of nonverbal or contextual information is included.

In small-scale research, transcripts may be used selectively. For instance, you could transcribe (timed) extracts – say 10 minutes from a longer interaction. You could use field-notes to identify certain extracts for transcription; or you could make a rough transcript of an interaction to identify general points of interest, then more detailed transcripts of relevant extracts.

Tape Counter	Notes	Comments / questions
134	3 children take it in turn to read out poems about animals which they have written. Seated classes quiet and attentive.	I can't hear any of this – neither I suspect can most other children in the assembly. What is being communicated here?
	1 child asks teachers to come and sit on two rows of chairs placed diagonally at the front. Teachers go up to the chairs, acting as if reluctant (sounds of 'oh no').	I immediately realise teachers are being asked to pretend to be pupils, and the child will be their teacher. Air of puzzled anticipation among seated children. Maybe they aren't familiar with this kind of 'role-reversal' sketch?
142	Teachers mess about, pretending to punch each other, pull hair, tip chairs etc. Child 'teacher' stands in front looking embarrassed. Seated children laugh and make occasional comments.	Seated children don't seem at ease with this situation and don't quite know how to react. Who exactly is in authority, now? Teachers' acting out of pupil unruliness is exaggerated – to make it unreal?
	The child at the front is pretending to try and restore order to his 'class'.	The child 'teacher' in acting out his role is managing to remain respectful to his teacher 'pupils', so he's really acting two roles simultaneously (pupil and teacher)?
	The seated children watching now start to freely imitate the antics of the teachers at the front, and several scuffles break out as the noise level rises.	It's difficult for the watching children to cope with these two conflicting systems – teacher = fonts of authority v. teacher = naughty pupils. They seem very confused.
	Mr. Brown quickly steps out of the role of naughty pupil, and gives the watching children a threatening look as he says 'sh'.	Watching children seem almost relieved that traditional power relations are restored. They settle down very quickly.
150	Some children echo this 'sh', and the hall quickly becomes quiet. The teachers at the front stop messing about, and their pupil 'teacher' reads them rewritten versions of Jack and the Beanstalk, Goldilocks, and The 3 Little Pigs. Some whispering among seated children during the story.	The stories read by the 'teacher' to his 'class' are suitable for a younger agegroup than any classes in this school. Another way of making the event as 'unreal'?

Figure 20.1 Field-notes of an assembly in a school in south-east England

While transcripts allow a relatively detailed examination of spoken language, they only provide a partial record: they cannot faithfully reproduce every aspect of talk. Transcribers will tend to pay attention to different aspects depending upon their interests, which means that a transcript is already an interpretation of the event it seeks to record. Elinor Ochs, in a now classic account of 'Transcription as theory', suggests that 'transcription is a selective process reflecting theoretical goals and definitions' (1979, p. 44). This point is illustrated by the sample layouts and transcription conventions discussed below.

Transcription conventions

Many published transcripts, such as those cited elsewhere in this volume, use conventions of written language such as punctuation in representing speech. But because written down speech is not the same as writing it can be quite hard to punctuate.

If you do wish to punctuate a transcript bear in mind that in so doing you are giving the speech a particular interpretation. Compare the following two methods of punctuating a teacher's question(s):

Now, think very carefully. What would happen if we cut one of those hollow balls in half? What would we find inside?

Now, think very carefully what would happen if we cut one of those hollow balls in half. What would we find inside?

Use of punctuation represents a trade-off between legibility and accessibility of the transcript and what might be a premature and impressionistic analysis of the data. It is probably best at least initially to use as little conventional punctuation as possible. Several sets of transcription conventions are available to indicate features of spoken language. Some of these are highly detailed, allowing transcribers to record intakes of breath, increased volume, stress, syllable lengthening etc. (see, for instance, Sacks, Schegloff and Jefferson, 1974; Ochs, 1979). Such conventions are designed to produce accurate transcriptions, but there is a danger that they will lend a misleading sense of scientific objectivity to the exercise. Rather than being 'objectively identified' such features of speech are likely to correspond to the transcriber's initial interpretations of their data.

Bearing in mind this caveat, Figure 20.2 illustrates a simple set of conventions for transcribing spoken language.

Further transcription conventions may be added if need be. Alternatively, as in Figure 20.2, you can leave a wide margin to comment on features such as loudness, whispering, or other noises that add to the meaning of the talk (as with other aspects of transcription these will necessarily be selective).

In Figure 20.2 I have used an extract from field-notes to contextualise the transcript. In the transcript itself, I have followed the frequently-used convention of referring to the speakers simply as teacher and students. An alternative is to give speakers pseudonyms (see the discussion of confidentiality under 'Adopting a researcher stance' above). The sequence in Figure 20.2 comes from an English lesson carried out with seven-year-old students in a school in Moscow, in Russia. The students are being encouraged to rehearse certain vocabulary and structures. The teacher addresses each student directly to ensure they contribute and uses features such as humour ('I'm like a tiger') to further encourage the students. In this extract Student 2 seems unsure of how to respond to the teacher's question (as indicated by his hesitation). In an attempt to help, the teacher offers him suggestions for

Teacher begins by telling class the lesson is to be about toy animals. She arranges some stuffed toy animals on her desk, then asks the class 'Have you got any toy animals at home?' Students are selected individually to respond. Teacher first asks a girl, and makes her repeat carefully 'I have got many toy animals at home.' Then turns to a boy, S1.

Transcription			Notes
1	T:	You [student's name] have you got	
2		many toy animals at home	
3	S1:	Yes I have { (.) I have a got	
4	T:	{ mmh	
5	S1:	many toy animals at home	
6	T:	That's good that's right what toy	
7		animals have you got at home (.)	
8		what name for animals (.)	
9		[student's name] what toy animals	low voice
10		have you got at home (.) I'm like a tiger	
11	Ss:	<laughter>	
12	T:	What yes	
13	S2:	I have { I have got { (.) I	T nods; lowers S2's
14	T:	{ mmh {mmh a (.)	hand and places on
15		or maybe two or { maybe three	desk
16	S2:	{ I have got a many	
17		toy animals	
18	T:	mmh I have got { many toy animals	
19	S2:	{ many toy animals	

Key

T	=	Teacher
S	=	Student (S1 = Student 1, etc)
student's name		underlining indicates any feature you wish to comment on
(.)		brief pause
(1sec)		timed pause
{ maybe		brackets indicate the start of overlapping speech
{ I have got		
<laughter>		transcription of a sound etc that forms part of the utterance

Figure 20.2 Transcription of teacher–student talk

the next word in his sentence (*a, two,* or *three* – presumably toy animals). This may be what leads to the student's error (*a many toy animals*) which is subsequently corrected by the teacher.

Laying out a transcript

The most commonly used layout, which I shall call a 'standard' layout, is set out rather like a dialogue in a play, with speaking turns following one another in sequence. This is the layout adopted in Figure 20.2, and in several chapters in this volume. One of the better known alternatives to this layout is a 'column' layout, in which each speaker is allocated a separate column for their speaking turns.

Figures 20.3 and 20.4 illustrate respectively 'standard' and 'column' layouts applied to the same brief extract of talk. This comes from one of a series of English lessons in a secondary school in Denmark, near Copenhagen (Dam and Lentz, 1998). The class of 15-year-old mixed-ability students were carrying out a project on 'England and the English'. The extract shows a group of students, two girls and two boys, beginning to plan what to do for their homework. The students are seated round a table, the girls opposite the boys.

		Transcription	Notes
1	G1:	What are we going to do at home	addresses group
2		(.) any ideas	directly
3	B1:	Yes (.) I take this (.) I take	refers to book which
4		this <general laughter> yes yes	he holds up
5		I take it mmh and I see and I	
6		see if there's something I can	
7		use (.)	
8	G1?:	We can use	
9	B1:	We can use	
10	B2:	So what (would) we do ( )	question towards
11		read it at home (.) the	girls?
12		questionnaire	
13		{ (.) read it at home	
14	B1	{ ( )	
		[. . .]	
15	G2:	Maybe I can get some materials	
16		for this	
17	G1:	From (mother)	
18	G2:	Yes	
19	B1?:	from where	
20	G2	from my mother (.) from the	
21		travel agency	

Key

As in Figure 20.2 with, in addition:

G, B	=	Girl, Boy
(would)		transcription uncertain: a guess
( )		unclear speech – impossible to transcribe
[. . .]		excision – some data excluded

Figure 20.3 Transcription of small group talk: standard layout

In group talk it's often interesting to look at the role taken by different students. In this case, the group seemed to collaborate fairly well and to be generally supportive of one another. Girl 1 seemed to play an organising or chairing role – e.g. by asking for ideas from the rest of the group; by 'correcting' Boy 1, reminding him that his work is for the group as a whole (line 8 of the standard layout); and by completing Girl 2's turn (line 17 of the standard

	G1	G2	B1	B2	Notes
1	What are we going				addresses group
2	to do at home (.)				directly
3	any ideas				
4			Yes (.) I take		refers to book
5			this (.) I take		which he holds
6			this <general		up
7			laughter> yes yes		
8			I take it mmh and		
9			I see and I see		
10			if there's		
11			something I can		
12			use (.)		
13	We can use (?)				
14			We can use		
15				So what (would)	question
16				we do ( ) read	towards girls?
17				it at home (.)	
18				the questionnaire	
19			( )	(.) read it at	
20				home	
	[. . .]				
21		Maybe I can get			
22		some materials			
23		for this			
24	From (mother)				
25		Yes			
26				from where (?)	
27		from my mother			
28		(.) from the			
29		travel agency			

Key

As in Figure 20.3 with, in addition:
(?) Guess at speaker

Figure 20.4 Transcription of small group talk: column layout

layout). I would be interested in looking further at this group's work to see if Girl 1 maintained this role or if it was also taken on by other students.

The way transcription is laid out may highlight certain features of the talk, for instance:

- The standard layout suggests a connected sequence, in which one turn follows on from the preceding one. This does seem to happen in the extract transcribed in Figures 20.3 and 20.4 but it is not always the case. In young children's speech, for instance, speaking turns may not follow on directly from a preceding turn. I shall also give an example of more informal talk below in which it is harder to distinguish a series of sequential turns.

- Column transcripts allow you to track one speaker's contributions: you can look at the number and types of contribution made by a speaker (e.g. Girl 1's 'organising' contributions), or track the topics they focus on – or whatever else is of interest.

- In a column transcript, it's important to bear in mind which column you allocate to each speaker. Because of factors such as the left-right orientation in European scripts, and associated conventions of page layout, we may give priority to information located on the left hand side. Ochs (1979) points out that, in column transcripts of adult-child talk, the adult is nearly always allocated the left-hand column, suggesting they are the initiator of the conversation. In Figure 20.4 I began with Girl 1, probably because she spoke first, but I also grouped the girls and then the boys together. This may be useful if your interest is, say, in gender issues, but it's important to consider why you are adopting a particular order and not to regard this as, somehow, 'natural'.

Accounts of conversational turn-taking have often assumed that one person talks at a time (e.g. Sacks, Schegloff and Jefferson, 1974). As I suggested above, however, this is not always the case, particularly in young children's talk, or in more informal discussion where there is lots of overlapping talk and where speakers frequently complete one another's turns. In her analysis of informal talk amongst women friends, Jennifer Coates developed a method of transcription in which she used a 'stave' layout (by analogy with musical staves) to represent the joint construction of speaking turns (see, for instance, Coates, 1996). Stave transcription has not been used frequently in educational contexts but may be adopted to illustrate highly collaborative talk in small groups. Figure 20.5 comes from a study made by Julia Davies (2000) of English lessons in three secondary schools in Sheffield, in the north of England. Davies was particularly interested in gender issues – in how girls and boys worked together in single-sex and mixed-sex groups. Figure 20.5 shows a group of four teenage girls reflecting on their earlier experiences of school. Davies found (like Coates) that the girls' talk was particularly collaborative (e.g. it contained overlapping speech, joint construction of turns and several indicators of conversational support).

The layout you choose for a transcript will depend on what you are transcribing and why. Here I have tried to show how different layouts highlight certain aspects of talk and play down others. You will need to try out, and probably adapt, layouts till you find one that suits your purposes – bearing in mind, as ever, that such decisions are already leading you towards a particular interpretation of your data.

Including nonverbal and contextual information

Transcriptions tend to highlight verbal information, though I have indicated above how nonverbal information can be shown in a 'notes' column, or by typographical conventions such as capital letters for emphasis or loudness. In some chapters of this book authors use different conventions. Pauline Gibbons and Angel Lin, for instance (Chapters 16 and 17 respectively) include some nonverbal information within brackets in the dialogue. If you are particularly interested in nonverbal information you may wish to adopt transcription conventions that highlight this in some way. As examples, Figure 20.6 shows how a story-teller uses a number of nonverbal features in her performance of a Nigerian story ('A man amongst men'); and Figure 20.7 shows how a teacher uses gaze to nominate female or male students to respond to her questions.

Representing different language varieties

The transcripts of classroom talk I have illustrated so far come from contexts in which English is being used as a medium of instruction. In many contexts, however, even where English is used as a classroom language, teachers and students may also use another language,

1	Bel	Right/anything else? / everyone {have a think/right/
	Jan	{everyone have a think
	Lou	
	Rosa	

2	Bel	
	Jan	about their important memories /
	Lou	
	Rosa	

3	Bel	I've got one (.) /right I remember (.)
	Jan	
	Lou	
	Rosa	

4	Bel	{<laughs> Jan AGAIN/
	Jan	I've got this important {memory of school was-/I got
	Lou	
	Rosa	

5	Bel	
	Jan	{this effort trophy at middle school (.) /
	Lou	{Jan again/ yeah?/
	Rosa	

6	Bel	
	Jan	and I-/oh and I were-/and I was dead chuffed/I thought it were great/
	Lou	
	Rosa	

7	Bel	
	Jan	an effort trophy?/ it were great weren't it?/
	Lou	I got one of them/ yeah/
	Rosa	

8	Bel	
	Jan	{it were great/
	Lou	{at the fourth year of juniors/
	Rosa	

Key

As above with, in addition:

Yeah/   A slash represents the end of a tone group, or chunk of talk

Yeah?/   A question mark indicates the end of a chunk analysed as a question

AGAIN   Capital letters indicate a word uttered with emphasis

Staves are numbered and separated by horizontal lines; all the talk within a stave is to be read together, sequentially from left to right.

Figure 20.5 Transcription of group talk: stave layout
Source: adapted from Davies (2000): 290

Note: Davies follows Coates in representing, within a stave, only those students who are speaking. Here I have included all students throughout the transcription – which illustrates, for instance, that one student, Rosa, does not speak at all in this sequence. Rosa may have been contributing in other ways – e.g. nonverbally – and she does speak later in the discussion.

Transcript	Notes
1 [Once upon a time] a | long | long | long | long | long time ago there was a | hunter a [very well-known and respected hunter]	spreading gesture to start story; downward gestures used for rhythm;
*every day he would go | out into the | bush he would <u>catch whatever meat he needed</u> for the village, he would <u>carry it on his back he would bring it into the village he would throw it down on the floor</u> the people they would see him *they would start <u>clapping their hands</u> <claps, A. claps>	*facing A, or orienting towards A even when embodying actions
	*hands out to A; A also invited by direct gaze, head movement, general body orientation.

Key	
[Once upon a time]	Square brackets indicate beginning and end of large spreading gesture
| long	Vertical slash indicates downward gesture accompanying a word
*every day	Asterisk indicates something that is commented on in the 'Notes' column
catch whatever meat	Underlined speech indicates that the storyteller also mimes the actions she describes
<claps>	As in transcripts above, indicates sound/action that forms part of the utterance
A	Audience

Figure 20.6 Representation of nonverbal features in an oral narrative

such as the students' first or main language, for certain purposes. In this case, it may be interesting to see when a teacher or student uses each language.

There are many different ways of representing the alternation between different language varieties. In Chapter 17 for instance, Angel Lin indicates 'codeswitching' between Cantonese and English, representing Cantonese in translation and in bold type. Figures 20.8 and 20.9 show how researchers have represented languages in their original form whilst also offering an English translation. Figure 20.8, from research carried out by Antoinette Camilleri in bilingual classrooms in Malta, shows a teacher alternating between English and Maltese, where Maltese is used to amplify or explain (rather than simply translate) an English sentence read from a textbook. In this case, an English translation of the Maltese utterances is given in a separate column. Figure 20.9, from research carried out by G.D. Jayalakshmi in Bihar, in northern India, shows how a teacher uses Sanskrit partly to demonstrate his knowledge and also 'because he believes that his function is to instruct students not only in language but also, more generally, in life' (Jayalakshmi, 1996, p. 145). In this case, an English translation is given in brackets beneath the Sanskrit.

In Figure 20.9, Jayalakshmi represents Sanskrit in Devanagari script. It would also have been possible to represent it in transliteration, in Roman script. It is, however, more difficult to decide how to represent language varieties closely related to English, or different varieties of English, that do not have a conventional orthography. Figure 20.5 represented

Teacher: If you have a pendulum (.) which we established last week was a weight a mass (.) suspended from a string or whatever (.) and watch I'm holding it with my hand so it's at rest at the moment (.) what is it that makes the pendulum swing in a downward direction for instance till it gets to there? [1]?

{ (.) just watch it

Mathew: { gravity

Teacher: What is it Mathew? [2]

Mathew: Gravity

Teacher: { Yes (.) } now we mentioned gravity when we were

Boy: { ( ) }

Teacher: actually doing the experiments but we didn't discuss it too much (.) OK so it's gravity then that pulls it down (.) what causes it to go up again at the other side? [3]

Boy: { Force the force }

Boy: { The string Miss }

Key

~~~~~   means gaze to boys

————   means gaze to girls

{ } overlap

(.) pause

( ) unclear

Figure 20.7 Representation of teacher's gaze towards female and male students
Source: Swann and Graddol (1989/1994): 157–9

Note: The full transcript from which Figure 20.7 is extracted shows that the teacher's gaze is more frequently directed towards the boys at critical points in the interaction, such as when a question is to be answered.

England Australia New Zealand and Argentina are the best producers of wool *dawk l-aktar li għandhom* farms *li jrabbu n-nagħag għas-suf* O.K. England *tgħiduli minn licma post* England *għandhom* Scotland *magħrufin tant għall-wool u gersijict tagħhom* O.K.

they have the largest number of farms and the largest number of sheep for wool O.K. England where in England we really mean Scotland they are very well-known for their woollen products

Figure 20.8 Transcript illustrating alternation between English and Maltese
Source: Camilleri (1994) cited in Mercer (1996): 134, and Chapter 15 of this volume

nonstandard grammar ('it were great') but did not attempt to represent the girls' accent. Some transcribers resort to 'eye dialect' (as in *we wuz jus' goin' 'ome*) to give an indication of pronunciation but there is a danger here of representing certain speakers (working class speakers, children, non-native speakers) as somehow deviant or incompetent.

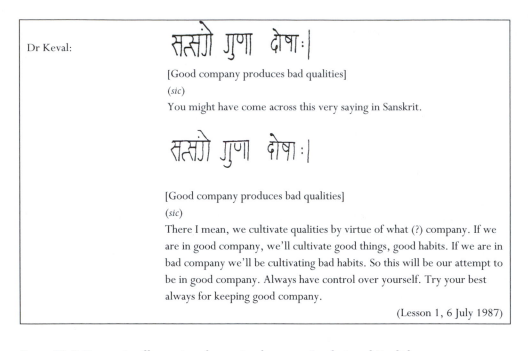

Dr Keval: सत्सो गुणा दोषाः|

[Good company produces bad qualities]

(*sic*)

You might have come across this very saying in Sanskrit.

सत्सो गुणा दोषा:|

[Good company produces bad qualities]

(*sic*)

There I mean, we cultivate qualities by virtue of what (?) company. If we are in good company, we'll cultivate good things, good habits. If we are in bad company we'll be cultivating bad habits. So this will be our attempt to be in good company. Always have control over yourself. Try your best always for keeping good company.

(Lesson 1, 6 July 1987)

Figure 20.9 Transcript illustrating alternation between Sanskrit and English
Source: Jayalakshmi (1996): 145

Note: In this case there is an error in Dr Keval's Sanskrit. Jayalakshmi comments that he may have learnt quotations such as this by rote.

Mark Sebba used a mixed system in his transcription of the speech of young Black speakers in London, who alternate between Creole (derived from Jamaican Creole) and London English. Creole utterances were underlined, London English utterances were not. Underlined utterances were, then, to be 'pronounced as if Creole' (1993, p. 163). Sebba also used some 'eye dialect' features to indicate the pronunciation of specific words or sounds; and certain 'one-off' conventions, such as the use of '%' to represent a glottal stop (the sound used as a variant of /t/ in certain linguistic contexts, and in certain varieties of English – sometimes represented as an apostrophe as in *bu'er* for *butter*). Figure 20.10 illustrates this. One point of interest is that the glottal stop, a feature of London English but not (usually) of Jamaican Creole, is here used within a Creole utterance (*invi%e*, line 4).

Sets of symbols such as the International Phonetic Alphabet (IPA) are used by phoneticians to give a systematic representation of the sounds of English and other languages. Such alphabets are hard for the non-expert to read and are not usually suitable for transcribing long conversational sequences. However if you are interested in learners' pronunciations of English, and you are familiar with the IPA or a similar alphabet, you could use phonetic symbols selectively for certain words, or to represent certain sounds.

Figure 20.11 below illustrates the use of phonetic symbols to represent a young Russian student's pronunciation of the word *bushy* (this is taken from the same lesson as that transcribed in Figure 20.2 above).

```
  1  J:    did you go to Jackie's par%y?
     (1.0)
     C:    who Jackie Lomax
     J:    yeah
     C:    no one never invi%e me
  5  J:    I heard that she had a really nice par%y an' Cheryl said there was a lo% of boys there (0.6)
           you know and they (were) playin' pass the parcel an' that
     C:    is it?
     J:    yeah
 10  C:    she invite you?
     J:    no
     C:    she never invite me neither an Leonie 'ave one as well never invite never tell
           me not'in' (0.4) me no business too!
```

Figure 20.10 Transcription of a conversation using Creole and London English
Source: Sebba (1993): 19–20

Transcription	Notes
1 S: Its tail is short and [bɪʃi]	pronounced to rhyme with *fishy*
2 T: Bushy ([bʊʃi])	more conventional pronunciation
3 S: Bushy ([bʊʃi])	more conventional pronunciation

Figure 20.11 Representation of pronunciation using phonetic symbols

Towards an analysis: quantitative and qualitative approaches

Discussions of research methodology often make a distinction between quantitative and qualitative approaches to research. Broadly, quantitative approaches allow you to identify and count the distribution of certain linguistic features, or certain types of utterance. You can then draw a numerical comparison between, for instance, the types of talk produced in different contexts or by different students, or groups of students. Some forms of quantification can be carried out 'on the spot'. For instance, while observing a lesson you could count the number of times each student responded to a teacher's question. More complex patterns can be identified from scrutiny of audio or video recordings, or from a transcript. G.D. Jayalakshmi, for instance, whose research in Indian classrooms I referred to above, noticed that students participated less in 'traditional' teacher-directed lessons (drawing on textbooks) than in lessons based on videos which she had introduced. To check her impressions, she analysed recordings of a random sample of lessons, counting up the number of times a student initiated talk; and what types of talk this involved (whether the student was seeking clarification, asking about the meaning of a word, making a single word contribution, or making a longer contribution to discussion). She displayed her results in a table (cited as Table 20.1 below). Table 20.1 shows that, in the contexts analysed, students initiated more talk in video than traditional lessons, and they also made a large number of longer contributions.

Table 20.1 Number and type of student-initiated moves in two types of lesson

Type of class	Number of student-initiated moves	Clarification seeking	Meaning of words	Single word contributions	Longer contributions
Traditional	11	3	2	5	0
Video Led	38	2	3	0	33

Source: Jayalakshmi (1993): 287

Chapter 18 in this volume provides a more formal and detailed example of quantification. Assia Slimani was interested in the relationship between students' claims about what linguistic features they had learnt, and the direct teaching of such features. Table 18.2 (p. 296) illustrates this, showing the number of linguistic features that had been explicitly dealt with in lessons (identified from audio recordings), and the proportion of these that were recalled by students, those that were not recalled, and those that were said to have been learned on a previous occasion.

By contrast, a qualitative approach tends to be used if the questions that are asked of a piece of data are more open-ended: if you wanted to know, for instance, what happened during a meeting; how students worked together in certain learning situations; how relationships were established and maintained; or how students achieved an understanding of certain concepts. Most of the chapters in this volume that look at classroom language adopt a qualitative approach to the analysis of talk. In Chapter 15, for instance, Neil Mercer discusses how teachers use language to guide students' learning. While Mercer identifies certain teaching techniques, these are not systematically coded and quantified. Mercer is more concerned with analysing the function of the techniques teachers use than with counting the frequency with which techniques are used, and illustrates this by quoting extracts from transcripts. In Chapter 16 Pauline Gibbons examines children's progression from 'everyday' language to the use of scientific discourse, focusing on the experiences of one student. The language used at different points in a series of lessons is illustrated by transcripts along with a close linguistic commentary. Angel Lin, in Chapter 17, also uses extracts from transcripts of classroom talk to illustrate the extent to which different students' 'habitus' is compatible with what is required of them in school English lessons.

There have been several debates within educational research about the relative merits of quantitative and qualitative approaches. Features of each approach, and some advantages and disadvantages that have traditionally been associated with them, are summarised in the box opposite.

While some researchers argue for an integration of quantitative and qualitative approaches, it has also been suggested that they embody fundamentally different views of the meaning of spoken language (coding language into discrete categories, for instance, suggests that meanings are relatively fixed and unambiguous, whereas qualitative approaches often emphasise ambiguity in language and argue that utterances need to be interpreted in context). For an overview of this debate see, for instance, Edwards and Westgate (1994).

Wegerif and Mercer (1997) suggest that it is possible to progress beyond this apparent divide by drawing on corpus, or computer-based forms of analysis. Corpus-based analyses allow researchers to process huge amounts of spoken or written language and establish quantitative patterns of language use. They have frequently been used to identify meanings of words and phrases and to aid the compilation of dictionary entries. They may also be used

Quantitative and qualitative approaches to the analysis of spoken language

A quantitative approach allows you to represent your data in terms of numbers. You can make a numerical comparison between talk produced by different people or during different events.

When representing data that has been analysed using quantitative methods it is usual to display this in a table. Alternative forms of representation such as histograms or bar charts may be used to point up comparisons between people or events.

Data may be analysed using prespecified categories of talk. Alternatively, as in Jayalakshmi's research, categories may emerge from close scrutiny of data, e.g. from playing, and replaying, an audio or video recording, or working slowly through a transcript. Such categories are not 'naturally' present in the data, but will depend upon your own research interests.

Representing talk in terms of numbers has the disadvantage that it is necessarily a reductive exercise: talk is reduced to a set of categories; it is abstracted from its original context; it is unambiguously pigeon-holed, masking the rather fluid, uncertain and negotiated meanings that are evident when talk is examined in context.

Talk may be recorded and analysed in a more open-ended way. Researchers adopting a qualitative approach to recording can note down and explore any interesting aspects of their data. What count as interesting aspects will depend upon the questions the researcher is concerned to investigate, but sometimes points emerge that are quite unexpected.

Aspects of the data may only begin to make sense when mulled over and compared with other information, or perhaps discussed with speakers. Sometimes interpretations may change, or you may want to allow for a number of different interpretations.

When presenting and discussing data that has been recorded and analysed using a qualitative approach, researchers frequently quote selectively from field-notes or transcripts to support points they wish to make. Transcripts may be supported by a detailed commentary, as in Chapters 18 and 19.

Such ways of analysing and presenting data allow the researcher to preserve important contextual information that affects the meanings of utterances, and also to preserve the ambiguity and fluidity of these meanings. The approach is selective in that two researchers may (legitimately) notice different things about a stretch of talk or provide different interpretations of utterances. There is also a danger of unintended bias, in that researchers may notice features of talk that support a point they wish to make and ignore counter-evidence.

to identify stylistic differences between different (literary) authors or different types of text. Wegerif and Mercer illustrate how corpus-based methods may be used with smaller amounts of data, and in combination with a qualitative exploration of language.

Wegerif and Mercer drew on this combination of methods as part of an ongoing study of exploratory talk in the classroom. They found that primary school children performed better on a standardised test of reasoning after they had been 'coached' in the use of exploratory talk. They also looked at transcript evidence of the quality of children's talk during problem solving activities carried out before and after the coaching intervention. Extracts from transcripts are used to show that, after the intervention children spent more time discussing problems, considered alternative solutions and eventually reached

Focal Group 1 pre-intervention task use of ''cos' or 'because'

Elaine: It isn't *'cos* look that's a square

Graham: No *'cos* look watch there all down there and they are all at the side and they are all up there

Elaine: Wait wait wait its that one *'cos* look it's them two and them two ( ) and them two

John: *'Cos* look that goes out like that –

Elaine: *'Cos* look that goes in

John: *'Cos* look that goes too far out

Graham: Look *'cos* that's got 4

Elaine: No . . . not that one not that one *because* it's got a little bit like that it's that one look – it goes in and then it goes out

John: No it's isn't *because* it's there

Elaine: No *because* it will come along like that

Elaine: Could be that one *because* look stops at the bottom and look

Elaine: It isn't it isn't *because* look

(12)

Focal Group 1 post-intervention task use of ''cos' or 'because'

Graham: Number 6 *'cos* 6 stops in there *'cos* look if you

Elaine: It can't be there *'cos* look if you done that

Elaine: It is look if that goes like that and then it has another one *'cos* those two make

Elaine: He doesn't say what they are *'cos* he might be wrong

Graham: Yeh *'cos* look

Elaine: *'Cos* it would go round

John: It is *'cos* it goes away *'cos* look that one goes like that

Elaine: No it can't be *'cos* look . . . with the square with the triangle you take away the triangle so you're left with the square so if you do just this and then again take that away it's going to end up, like that isn't it?

Graham: Actually *'cos* that's got a square and a circle round it

John: Yeh *'cos* it goes like that and then it takes that one away and does that

Elaine: No *'cos* look

Elaine: Probably one in the circle *'cos* there are only two circles

Graham: *'Cos* if they are lines and then they are going like that it is because they are wonky isn't it

Graham: No actually it ain't *'cos* then

Elaine: Yeh it's number 8 *because* those ones – those two came that those two make that

John: No *because* 1, 2, 3 1, 2, 3

John: No *because* that goes that way and that goes that way

Graham: No *because* it's that one

(21)

Figure 20.12 Incidence of *'cos* and *because* in primary school children's talk

agreement on the correct answer. Wegerif and Mercer point out, however, that such evidence may not be seen as convincing because it consists only of one or two brief extracts from transcripts.

As a way of complementing their initial qualitative approach, Wegerif and Mercer used a computerised concordancing program. This identifies all instances of a word or expression used in a particular set of data, and displays these in their immediate linguistic context. In Figure 20.12 above, for instance, the words 'cos and because are displayed in each speaking turn in which they occurred in one group's interaction before and after the intervention. Wegerif and Mercer suggest that 'cos and because are used differently in the pre- and post-intervention interaction: in the post-intervention interactions they are more frequently used to link reasons to claims. Wegerif and Mercer carried out similar analyses of other terms that might be seen as indicative of reasoning (e.g. if and so used to link a reason to an assertion).

This form of analysis provides quantifiable data (i.e. it is possible to calculate the frequency with which 'cos and because are used in different contexts). It is also possible to see each instance of 'cos and because in a limited linguistic context, which provides further information about their use in each case (as in Figure 20.12). And it is possible, for any one instance, to display further linguistic context (any number of preceding and following speaking turns) to allow a qualitative exploration of the data.

If this form of analysis interests you, it is possible to purchase concordancing software (or, in some cases, to download this from the Internet).[1] You will need, however, to be prepared to spend time exploring the software to see how it can be made to work most effectively for your own purposes. For further discussion and examples of corpus-based analysis see, for instance, Stubbs (1996).

Conclusion

In this chapter I have discussed various techniques you can use to record and transcribe spoken language. There is no 'ideal' way to do this, and I have tried to indicate the strengths and weaknesses of different approaches so that you can select the most appropriate method, or combination of methods, for your own purposes. It is beyond the scope of this chapter to consider, at any level of detail, ways of analysing spoken language, though I have suggested some initial considerations to bear in mind. Other chapters in this volume include examples of research on spoken language, and illustrations of different forms of analysis: these may provide ideas for your own research.

Acknowledgement

I am grateful to Rupert Wegerif for suggestions on computer-based methods of analysing spoken language.

Note

1   See, for instance, the examples of software listed at http://info.ox.ac.uk/ctitext/
resguide/resources/index.html#tat It is often possible to obtain demo versions of text
analysis tools – see, for instance, 'Wordsmith', available from http://wwwl.oup.
co.uk/cite/oup/elt/software/wsmith/

References

British Association for Applied Linguistics (BAAL) (1994) *Recommendations on Good Practice in Applied Linguistics*. BAAL.

Cameron, D., Fraser, E., Harvey, P., Rampton, M.B.H. and Richardson, K. (1992) *Researching Language: Issues of Power and Method*. London: Routledge.

Camilleri, A. (1994) 'Talking bilingually, writing monolingually'. Paper presented at the Sociolinguistics Symposium, University of Lancaster, March.

Coates, J. (1996) *Women Talk*. Oxford: Blackwell Publishers.

Dam, L. and Lentz, J. (1998) *It's up to yourself if you want to learn: autonomous language learning at intermediate level* (Video and print). Copenhagen: Danmarks Laererhøgskole.

Davies, J.A. (2000) *Expressions of Gender: An Enquiry into the way Gender Impacts on the Discourse Styles of Pupils involved in Small Group Talk during a GCSE English lesson, with particular reference to the under-achievement of boys*. Unpublished PhD Thesis. Sheffield: University of Sheffield.

Edwards, A.D. and Westgate, D.P.G. (1994) *Investigating Classroom Talk*. London: Falmer Press (2nd edn).

Jayalakshmi, G.D. (1993) 'Video in the English curriculum of an Indian secondary school'. Unpublished PhD thesis. Milton Keynes: The Open University.

—— (1996) 'One cup of newspaper and one cup of tea', in N. Mercer and J. Swann (eds) *Learning English: Development and Diversity*. London, The Open University/Routledge.

Labov, W. (1970) 'The study of language in its social context', in W. Labov (1972) *Sociolinguistic Patterns*. Oxford: Basil Blackwell.

Mercer, N.M. (with contributions from Douglas Barnes) (1996) 'English as a classroom language', in N. Mercer and J. Swann (eds) *Learning English: Development and Diversity*. London: The Open University/Routledge.

Ochs, E. (1979) 'Transcription as theory', in E. Ochs and B.B. Schieffelin (eds) *Developmental Pragmatics*. London: Academic Press.

Sacks, H., Schegloff, E. and Jefferson, G. (1974) 'A simplest systematics for the organization of turn-taking for conversation. *Language* 50 (4), pp. 696–735.

Sebba, M. (1993) *London Jamaican: Language Systems in Interaction*. London: Longman.

Stubbs, M. (1996) *Text and Corpus Analysis: Computer-assisted Studies of Language and Culture*. Oxford: Blackwell.

Swann, J. and Graddol, D. (1994) 'Gender Inequalities in Classroom Talk', in D. Graddol., J. Maybin and B. Stierer (eds) *Researching Language and Literacy in Social Context*. Clevedon: Multilingual Matters/The Open University.

Wegerif, R. and Mercer, N. (1997) 'Using computer-based text analysis to integrate qualitative and quantitative methods in research on collaborative learning', *Language and Education*, Vol. 11, No. 4, pp. 271–86.

Index